Balancing Family-Centered
Services and Child Well-Being

Balancing Family-Centered Services and Child Well-Being

Exploring Issues in Policy,
Practice, Theory, and Research

ELAINE WALTON
PATRICIA SANDAU-BECKLER
MARC MANNES

Editors

COLUMBIA UNIVERSITY PRESS   NEW YORK

Columbia University Press
Publishers Since 1893
New York,   Chichester, West Sussex

Library of Congress Cataloging-in-Publication Data

Balancing family-centered services and child well-being :
exploring issues in policy, practice, theory, and research / Elaine
Walton, Patricia Sandau-Beckler, Marc Mannes, editors.
      p.   cm.
   Includes bibliographical references.
ISBN 978-0-231-11283-3 (pbk. : alok. paper)

     1. Family social work—United States.   2. Family
services—United States.   3. Child welfare—United
States.   I. Walton, Elaine.   II. Sandau-Beckler, Patricia.
III. Mannes, Marc.

HV699 .B35 2001
362.7'0973—dc21

                                                00-065603

Printed in the United States of America

CONTENTS

Introduction

During the past twenty-five years the emphasis on reintroducing the concept of "family" into child welfare services has had a profound impact. It has reformed and shaped the design and delivery of interventions by public social service agencies and nonprofit organizations. We now have programs such as family-based services, family-centered services, family preservation services, family support services, and intensive family preservation services. The larger structure, within which this mix of programs is implemented, is no longer viewed as just being child focused, and instead is now often defined as the child and family services system. The interjection of family has also altered the way in which curriculum content is written and instruction is provided in social work education programs. Curricula increasingly include courses that do not separate children's issues from family issues. Finally, an increasing interest in the family context has changed the nature of research and scholarship by focusing on vulnerable families and young people at risk of or actually experiencing endangerment or maltreatment, as well as the system charged with the responsibility for meeting their needs. Greater numbers of academics have chosen to pursue lines of inquiry around the intersection of family and children, and professional preparation programs have established centers and institutes to study the topic and serve the needs of the field. Largely as a result of the availability of federal funds over the last two decades, a body of empirical evidence has emerged to make the case that in most instances the best way to protect children is to strengthen children's families.

All these changes have sparked controversy and dissent. There has been interest, excitement, and promotion on the part of believers in and advocates of the importance and value of the reforms consistent with a family-oriented perspective. On the other hand there has been considerable concern, scorn, and even repudiation put forward by those opposed to the changes in the way in which business is conducted. This volume is not intended to provide a full airing of the differences of opinion or provide a forum for multiple conflicting perspectives on family-oriented efforts, although that is certainly a useful and important topic.

We know all too well that an effective response to the needs of a single child or group of children in danger of or actually experiencing abuse or neglect in the context of family cannot be made at the expense of those children. In the title we have chosen the term *family-centered services* to represent all the various programs constituting family-focused work. But the title cannot end there because it only reflects half the story. The inclusion of *well-being* in the title reflects our understanding that family-centered services need to be conceived and operated in ways that support positive growth and development for children and adolescents. The chapters in this book remind us and reinforce the fact that focusing on the family does not automatically or necessarily compromise the health and wellness of the young. Collectively the chapters provide rich testimony that practitioners and service systems can, and do, engage in family-centered work that fosters the well-being of young people across the first two decades of life.

This group of essays pulls together the knowledge, wisdom, insights, and opinions of academics and professionals who have been deeply involved with the conceptualization and application of critical aspects of family-centered work. One of the more beneficial developments associated with the rise in family-centered activity has been the degree to which faculty have been involved in real-world efforts—interacting and learning with those who ply their trade in the living rooms and kitchens and on the back porches of family homes. Still another positive event has been the extensive collaboration and exchange among professors and agency staff around family-centered activities. We have felt compelled to make sure these perspectives are available to the reader and sought to include articles from individuals who have worked across traditional boundaries. The experiences and expertise of educators/researchers/practitioners possessing national and international recognition for their accomplishments in the family-centered services arena have been marshaled for this publication. Contributors include individuals and groups who have played major roles in the formulation of policy, programs, treatment approaches, and the provision of technical assistance at the local, regional, and national levels. Chapters are also authored by those who have orchestrated the design and execution of research on and evaluation of family-centered services at both the community and larger levels. Finally, there are manuscripts from social work educators who are teaching core and advanced family-centered content and conducting applied research.

Several chapters are included to help frame family-centered services and address the family-centered reform movement. The initial chapter, written by Peter J. Pecora, Kellie Reed-Ashcraft, and Raymond S. Kirk, places the family-centered movement in historical perspective, defines the program elements making up family-centered services, and considers program implementation and evaluation issues. Two chapters at the end of the book are included to consider the future. The chapter by Marc Mannes describes the family-centered services movement's loss of momentum and offers suggestions on how it can once again stimulate a reform agenda. In the last chapter, Kristine Nelson speculates on the future of the movement in light of child and family system forces evident at the transition from the twentieth to the twenty-first century.

Many of the chapters included in this collection illuminate core aspects of family-centered services. Elaine Walton identifies and explains the eclectic mix of theories that are typically applied to the design and operation of family-centered programs. John Ronnau discusses the unique set of values and ethics that guides worker practice with family members. Pat Sandau-Beckler examines core practice issues including forging positive working relationships, conducting appropriate assessments, and designing relevant case plans. Elizabeth Tracy describes and analyzes the range of "hard" and "soft" interventions commonly used within family-centered programs. Gary Anderson assesses the critical importance and application of kinship care to family-centered services. Ramona Denby focuses on the vexing "targeting" issue that family preservation continues to wrestle with. A slew of authors, representing the true spirit of worker and family partnerships, offer ideas and suggestions on how to make improvements in the delivery of services. Rowena Fong provides us with ideas and techniques for working with families as partners in culturally competent ways. Finally, Marianne Berry, Marian Bussey, and Scottye J. Cash deal with the challenges of evaluation in the ever-changing environment in which family-centered programs are implemented.

A number of chapters are also included to describe successful existing and potentially valuable approaches to family-centered services. Colleen A. Halliday-Boykins and Scott W. Henggeler offer a thorough presentation of multisystemic therapy. Lisa Merkel-Holguin and Kimberly Ribich examine the origins and application of family group conferencing. Marc Mannes explores the relevance and promise of the developmental assets framework to support the developmental well-being of children and adolescents.

This book offers a perspective on family-centered services at the beginning of the twenty-first century. By shedding light on how family-centered services have evolved, providing the rationale and basis for using the approach, describing the ways in which services are implemented, highlighting dilemmas the field currently faces, and presenting prospects for its future, the book's editors and contributors hope readers will come to a deeper understanding and richer appreciation of how family-centered services and child and adolescent well-being come together on a daily basis to make life better for many parents and young people.

Contributors

Gary R. Anderson is director of the School of Social Work at Michigan State University and former director of the National Resource Center for Permanency Planning at Hunter College in New York City. He is also editor of the journal *Child Welfare*. He received a Ph.D. in social work from the University of Chicago.

Marianne Berry is an associate professor of social welfare and director of the Office for Child Welfare Research and Development at the University of Kansas. She has authored numerous publications focused on services to children and families. She received a Ph.D. from the School of Social Welfare, University of California at Berkeley.

Marian Bussey is a research analyst for the Children's Division of the American Humane Association. She has coauthored several articles on outcomes for children served by Child Protective Services. She received a Ph.D. in social work from the University of Texas at Arlington.

Scottye J. Cash is an assistant professor of social work at Florida State University. Her research has focused on the evaluation of family preservation services and risk and safety assessment in child welfare. She received a Ph.D. in social work from the University of Texas at Arlington.

Ramona W. Denby is an assistant professor in the School of Social Work at the University of Nevada at Las Vegas. She has authored numerous publications on cultural specificity and child welfare services. She received a Ph.D. in social work from The Ohio State University.

Rowena Fong is an associate professor in the School of Social Work at the University of Hawaii Manoa campus. A member of the board of directors of the National Association for Family-Based Services, her research focus is culturally competent social work practice and child welfare. She received an Ed.D. from Harvard University.

Colleen A. Halliday-Boykins is an assistant professor in the Department of Psychiatry and Behavioral Sciences and Family Services Research Center at the Medical University of South Carolina. Her research interests focus on understanding and effectively treating youth problem behavior in the ecological context. She received a Ph.D. in clinical psychology from the University of California at Los Angeles.

Scott W. Henggeler is professor of psychiatry and behavioral sciences and director of the Family Services Research Center at the Medical University of South Carolina. He has published extensively, with a focus on antisocial behavior in adolescents, and he is on editorial boards of eight journals. He received a Ph.D. in clinical psychology from the University of Virginia.

Jill Kinney is cofounder of the nationally recognized Homebuilders program. Currently, she is executive director of Home Safe, a nonprofit child welfare agency with services including consulting, training, and materials development, in Tacoma, Washington. Her current focus is the development of professional and natural helper partnerships. She is a licensed psychologist and received a Ph.D. from Stanford University.

Raymond S. Kirk is an associate professor at the Jordan Institute for Families at the University of North Carolina at Chapel Hill. His research activities have focused on program evaluation and client-centered outcome evaluation in child welfare and other youth and family programs. He received a Ph.D. in clinical psychology from the University of Vermont.

Marc Mannes is director of research and evaluation for Search Institute, Minneapolis, Minnesota, and previous director of the National Resource Center for Family Centered Practice. Formerly, he was a program specialist for the Children's Bureau and a member of the social work faculty at New Mexico State University. He has authored numerous publications on family-centered services and system reform. He received a Ph.D. in human service studies from Cornell University.

Lisa Merkel-Holguin is manager of the National Center on Family Group Decision Making at the Children's Division of the American Humane Association. As such, she has authored numerous publications, organized national events, and provided training and technical assistance. She is a former program manager for the Child Welfare League of America. She received a master of social work degree from the University of Illinois at Urbana-Champaign.

Kristine E. Nelson is a professor in the Graduate School of Social Work at Portland State University. Previously, she was director of research at the National Resource Center on Family-Based Services. Her publications and research have focused on family preservation services and child neglect. She received a D.S.W. from the University of California at Berkeley.

Peter J. Pecora has a joint appointment as manager of research services for the Casey Family Programs and as professor in the School of Social Work at the University of Washington, Seattle. His publications focus on child welfare program design, administration, and research. He received a Ph.D. in social work from the University of Washington.

Kellie Reed-Ashcraft is an assistant professor in the Social Work Program at Appalachian State University in Boone, North Carolina. Her research has focused on state mental health and child welfare service delivery with an emphasis on family preservation services evaluation. She received a Ph.D. in social work from the University of North Carolina at Chapel Hill.

Kimberly Ribich is a policy assistant with the Children's Division of the American Humane Association. Her primary affiliation is with the National Center on Family Group Decision Making. Previously, she was project director for the Special Needs Adoption Network, Inc., in Milwaukee, Wisconsin. She received a master's degree in applied communication from the University of Denver.

John P. Ronnau is dean of Graduate Studies and Sponsored Programs at the University of Texas, Brownsville. Previously, he served as associate dean in the School of Social Work at the University of Utah and as graduate program director in the Department of Social Work at New Mexico State University. He received a Ph.D. in social welfare from the University of Kansas.

Patricia Sandau-Beckler is an associate professor in the School of Social Work at New Mexico State University. She has served as president of the National Association for Family-Based Services, and her research and training activities have focused on family-centered practice with substance-affected families. She will soon be awarded a Ph.D. in social work from Case Western Reserve University.

Kathy Strand is program director for Home Safe, a nonprofit child welfare agency with services including consulting, training, and materials development, in Tacoma, Washington. Her current focus is the development of professional and natural helper partnerships. She received a master of social work degree from the University of Washington.

Elizabeth M. Tracy is an associate professor of Social Work at the Mandel School of Applied Social Sciences, Case Western Reserve University. Her research and publishing interests focus on social work models that support families and make use of and strengthen natural helping networks. She received a Ph.D. in social work from the University of Washington.

Elaine Walton is an associate professor and director of the School of Social Work at Brigham Young University. She is a member of the board of directors of the National Association for Family-Based Services, and her research interests focus on evaluating family-strengthening programs in the child welfare system. She received her Ph.D. in social work from The University of Utah.

Balancing Family-Centered
Services and Child Well-Being

1

Family-Centered Services

A Typology, Brief History, and Overview of Current
Program Implementation and Evaluation Challenges

PETER J. PECORA
KELLIE REED-ASHCRAFT
RAYMOND S. KIRK

Reform of the policies and systems that provide services to families and children is underway throughout the nation.[1] Public agencies, not-for-profit agencies, for-profit companies, and grassroots organizations are developing new service approaches, integrating services across traditionally separate domains, and collaborating with new partners to demonstrate the potential of reform and to better serve families. While the terminology differs by area—in education the watchword is "restructuring," in health care it is "managed care," in mental health "systems of care," and in social services "family-centered" or "family-based services"—the underlying themes of these reform efforts are remarkably similar: meeting changing family needs, maximizing limited resources, and increasing program effectiveness.

Various forms of family-centered services (FCS), such as family support services, wraparound services, family-based services (FBS), and intensive family preservation services (IFPS), represent some of the fastest growing program areas in child welfare, mental health, and juvenile justice. These services are designed to strengthen family functioning in order to achieve a number of outcomes. For some families the desired outcome is prevention of child maltreatment, for others it is a reduction in parent-adolescent conflict, and for some families the goal is to improve some aspect of a child's behavior. In still other cases the goal is to improve the family situation to a point where child placement can be prevented or the child can be returned from substitute care (e.g., family foster care, residential treatment). This chapter proposes a typology of these innovative service models, provides a history of the development of these programs, and discusses current challenges, with a focus on the more intensive family-based programs.

A PROGRAM TYPOLOGY OF FAMILY-CENTERED SERVICES

Diverse Program Models

Various terms are used to describe different program models in the area of family-centered services. Within the broad framework of family-centered, or family-based, services, there is wide variation across the nation in the kind of interventions, duration of services, size of caseloads, and components of service that characterize such programs. Perhaps this variation is inherent in all service innovations, but it is one of the reasons research findings on family-centered service programs have been confusing. Despite a growing body of literature, it is not clear what these services are, how much service is provided, and who benefits from them. As a result of the enormous variation in the service characteristics of the new programs, the programs themselves are often described using more specific terms, such as "family preservation," "family support," "home-based," and "placement prevention services."

Family-Centered Services Program Models

In all family-centered services the family is not seen as deficient but as having many strengths and resources (Kagan, Powell, Weissbourd, & Zigler, 1987). One term, *family support*, has been used to encompass a broad range of family-strengthening programs. Although family-based and family preservation services have both been cited as family support programs, these programs (family based and family preservation) are distinct from primary prevention and child development–oriented family support programs such as prenatal care, home visiting, early childhood education, parent education, home-school-community linkage, child care, and other family-focused services that tend to provide one type of service (e.g., education, housing, financial assistance, or counseling), work with clients exclusively in an office or classroom, provide treatment over a long period of time (one year or more), or plan and monitor client services delivered by other agencies.[2] (See figure 1.1.)

The Child Welfare League of America further clarifies family-centered services by means of a three-part typology of programs including (a) family

FIGURE 1.1. A Sample Array of Family-Centered Services

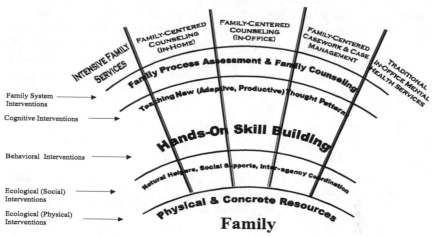

Source: From "The Challenge and Potential of Family Preservation Services in the Public Child Welfare System" by A. L. Sallee and J. C. Lloyd, 1991, *Protecting Children, 10* (3), p. 5. Copyright 1991 by American Humane Association. Reprinted with permission.

resource, support, and education services; (b) family-centered services; and (c) intensive family-centered services.

Family Resource, Support, and Education Services

These community-based services assist and support adults in their role as parents. Services are available to all families with children and do not impose criteria for participation that might separate or stigmatize certain parents (Child Welfare League of America, 1989). We will refer to these as "family support services." Examples are the school- or community-based family resource centers being implemented in states such as Connecticut, Maryland, Kentucky, Minnesota, and Missouri (Farrow, 1991).[3]

Family-Centered Services (i.e., Family-Based Services)

These services encompass a range of activities, such as case management, counseling/therapy, education, skill building, advocacy, and provision of concrete services (such as housing, food, and clothing) for families with problems that threaten their stability. As mentioned earlier, the philosophy of these programs differs from the more traditional child welfare services in the role of parents, use of concrete and clinical services, and other areas (Child Welfare League of America, 1989).

The more common term is *family-based services*, although in some states programs are referred to as *family preservation services*. Most of these programs are currently found in child welfare agencies, although a number have been initiated by mental health centers. FBS programs have recently been started in a number of new service arenas, including juvenile justice, developmental disability, adoption, and foster care reunification programs. An example of an FBS program with a broad public health and family-centered focus is Hawaii's Healthy Start program, which provides a comprehensive array of health care, counseling, and concrete services to families judged to be at moderate to high risk of child maltreatment (Breakey & Pratt, 1991).

Although program designs and specific interventions differ, most of the programs fitting the broader name of family-based services share some or all of the following characteristics:

- ☐ A primary worker or case manager establishes and maintains a supportive, empowering relationship with the family.
- ☐ A wide variety of helping options are used (e.g., concrete forms of supportive services such as food and transportation may be provided along with clinical services).
- ☐ Caseloads of two to twelve families are maintained.
- ☐ One or more associates serve as team members or provide backup for the primary worker.
- ☐ Workers (or their backup) are available twenty-four hours a day for crisis calls or emergencies.
- ☐ The home is the primary service setting, and maximum utilization is made of natural helping resources, including the family, the extended family, the neighborhood, and the community.
- ☐ The parents remain in charge of and responsible for their family as the primary caregivers, nurturers, and educators.
- ☐ Services are time limited, usually one to four months.[4] (Bryce & Lloyd, 1981)

Intensive Family-Centered Crisis Services
These services are designed for families "in crisis," at a time when removal of a child is perceived as imminent or the return of a child from out-of-home care is being considered. Yet the reality is that this service model is also being applied to chronic family situations, involving child neglect or abuse, which do not involve crises. These programs often share the same philosophical orientation and characteristics as family-centered services but are delivered with more intensity (including shorter time frame and smaller caseloads), so they are often referred to as intensive family preservation services, or IFPS, programs. Caseloads generally vary between two and six families per worker. Families are typically seen between six and ten hours per week, and the time period of intervention is generally between four and twelve weeks.

The emphasis of these services is to provide intensive counseling, education, skills training, and supportive services to families, with the goal of protecting the child, strengthening and preserving the family, and preventing the unnecessary placement of children (Whittaker, Kinney, Tracy, & Booth, 1990). In some cases, however, the primary case goal is to reunite children with their families (Child Welfare League of America, 1989). We will refer to these programs as IFPS—intensive family preservation services—and they include programs such as Homebuilders in Washington, Intensive Family Services in Maryland, and certain types of Families First programs in various states. Although such programs may share core features, there exists much diversity in treatment models.

Intensive family-centered crisis services have been described as "family-based services," "home-based services," "services to children in their own homes," and "family preservation services."

Target Populations for Family-Centered Services

The target population for family-centered services varies greatly. For example, both FBS and IFPS programs are generally targeted to families in serious trouble, including families no longer able to cope with problems that threaten family stability, families in which a decision has been made by an authorized public social service agency to place a child outside the home, and families whose children are in temporary out-of-home care. Although some programs may emphasize a "crisis orientation," many families who are served by these agencies are not in crisis and have for some time been trying to cope with an abusive or neglectful family member, child mental illness, juvenile delinquency, or other problem. Thus these services may be appropriate for families seen by the child welfare, juvenile justice, or mental health systems, as well as for adoptive or foster families facing potential disruption.[5]

The distinction between the various program categories is not definitive, but the CWLA taxonomy helps to clarify some distinguishing features of the three types of programs and to suggest some of the program design features highlighted by practitioners and administrators in the field. Throughout the remainder of this chapter, when reviewing the general literature on family support, family-based, or family preservation services we will use the term *family-centered services* (FCS) (and occasionally FBS). When referring specifically to programs that deliver both concrete and clinical services primarily in the home on an intensive basis, we will use the term *intensive family-preservation services* (IFPS).

A number of other program advocates are promoting the use of the term *intensive family preservation services* to designate programs that deliver both clinical and concrete services in the home setting and provide a more intensive service than do other programs (e.g., provision of a minimum of five hours of client contact per week with a service duration of about sixty days or less) (Edna McConnell Clark Foundation, 1985; Whittaker et al., 1990). The IFBS programs listed in this chapter meet the criteria commonly listed for intensive family-based crisis services, including being home based and intensive—lasting one to four months.

HISTORY OF FAMILY-CENTERED SERVICES

Overview

Recent home-based forms of family-centered services are most directly attributable to concerns that in the United States, traditional child welfare services were not meeting the needs of children and their families. More specifically, the field of child welfare was criticized during the 1960s and 1970s in the following areas:

- Children who could have remained at home were placed in substitute care, with disproportionate rates of placement occurring among ethnic minority families.
- Children in substitute care lacked clearly specified case plans.
- "Foster care drift" occurred in some situations, resulting in long-term placements, multiple placements, and no sense of permanence for many children.
- Parental involvement and visitation were discouraged by some workers.
- Termination procedures and adoption practices constrained the use of adoption as a bona fide case goal.
- Categorical federal funding policies encouraged foster care maintenance services (i.e., placement) and did not adequately fund preventive or restorative services.
- Most state agencies did not have adequate management information systems in place; consequently, program administrators did not know how many children were currently placed in substitute care, their average length of placement, or other essential planning information. (e.g., Gruber, 1973; Jones, 1985; Knitzer, Allen, & McGowan, 1978)

Crises in the Child Welfare System

Exposés of the quality of child welfare services, and of foster care in particular, were written and widely publicized by both child welfare experts and investigative reporters (e.g., Fanshel & Shinn, 1978; Gruber, 1973; Knitzer et al., 1978; Maas & Engler, 1959; Mnookin, 1973; Wooden, 1976). In addition, the growing incidence and costs of foster care, concern about the harmful effects of substitute care, the belief that some placements could be prevented, and the trend toward deinstitutionalization all prompted the development of a variety of foster care preventive programs (Emlen, Lahti, Downs, McKay, & Downs, 1978; Magazino, 1983; Jones, 1985). Further, in child welfare it was thought that some children were placed in foster care, juvenile justice facilities, or residential treatment centers who could have remained at home or in less restrictive settings. Children in the substitute care settings usually lacked clearly specified case plans. This resulted in foster care drift, with unnecessarily long-term placements, multiple placements, and a sense of impermanence for many children (Gruber, 1973; Maas & Engler, 1959).

When children were in foster care or other substitute arrangements, parental involvement and visitation were not encouraged (Fanshel & Shinn, 1978). In addition, substitute care arrangements, termination procedures, and adoption practices constrained the use of adoption as a realistic case goal. Furthermore, federal funding policies encouraged foster care maintenance services (i.e., placement) and did not adequately fund preventive or restorative services. Finally, most state agencies did not have adequate management information systems in place; consequently, program administrators did not know how many children were currently placed in substitute care, average lengths of placement, or other essential planning information (see Knitzer et al., 1978; National Commission on Children, 1991).

One of the principal assumptions underlying foster care prevention and planning efforts for children at risk of child maltreatment is that in most cases, a child's development and emotional well-being are best ensured through efforts to maintain the child in the home of her or his biological parents or extended family (providing that at least minimal standards of parenting are maintained). Most practitioners and researchers agree with this assumption, while realizing that child placement in some situations may be the more beneficial and necessary option.[6]

Permanency Planning

The shortcomings in the child welfare system led to the desire of many advocates to focus on foster care prevention and on permanent case plans for children in the system, known as "permanency planning." A number of policy and program innovations were instituted by federal, state, and local authorities to address critiques of the child welfare system. Most notable among these were permanency planning and the related program and fiscal reforms promoted by the Adoption Assistance and Child Welfare Act of 1980 (Public Law 96-272). This federal law mandated that a series of reforms be implemented in state child welfare agencies in order for the agencies to qualify for special supplemental Title IV-B federal appropriations under the Social Security Act. PL 96-272 also required that states implement a variety of placement prevention services as part of their strategy in order to ensure that "reasonable efforts" have been made to preserve the family before a child is placed in substitute care (Pine, 1986). This law was recently supplanted by the Adoption and Safe Families Act (PL 105-89).

Permanency planning refers first to efforts to prevent unnecessary child placement and second to efforts to return children in foster care to their biological families or to some other form of permanent placement, such as an adoptive home or long-term foster care family with guardianship. This emphasis took hold in child welfare agencies in the late 1970s and 1980s with the leadership of the Oregon Permanency Planning Project and other training efforts. Permanency planning has been helpful in reducing the numbers of children lingering in family foster care: as of September 30, 1999, 37 percent of the children who left substitute care had been there for five months or less; 50 percent of the children were in placement less than twelve months (Adoption and Foster Care Analysis Reporting System, 2000). There is, however, a remaining concern about the lack of program alternatives for family reunification and foster care reentry (Goerge, 1990; Goerge, Wulczyn, & Harden, 1996).

Criticism of the child welfare service delivery system has been brought to public attention by the numerous class action suits filed by the American Civil Liberties Union and other advocacy groups. In fact, many would argue that the focus on permanency planning, creating service alternatives, and child stability has not been supported through staff training, supervision, or provision of the necessary resources (Fanshel, 1992). Although the child population in substitute care had fallen from 502,000 in 1977 to 276,000 in 1985 (Tatara, 1992, 1993), as of March 31, 1998, 520,000 children were residing in foster homes in the United States (U.S. Department of Health and Human Services, 1999). Some of this increase in placements is no doubt due to increased substance abuse among parents. A number of studies have found that various forms of child maltreatment are associated with abuse of alcohol or other drugs (Murphy et al., 1991). There have been large increases in the number of drug-exposed infants coming into foster care. In addition, increasing rates of teen parenthood, a rise in never-married parents, AIDS, urban poverty, a growing shortage of affordable housing, and significant rates of unemployment among certain groups have all contributed to the rise in child placement rates (e.g., Testa, 1992).

Some experts believe that state child welfare agencies have improved their efforts to reduce the number of unnecessary placements. Although in many states the percentage of children placed in relation to the number of child protective service cases being reported appears to have decreased (Wald, 1988), this may be due to a lack of emergency placement resources. Child advocates, therefore, remain concerned that essential preventive services are not being provided. They maintain that it is possible to identify families with a sufficiently high risk of maltreatment or harm to justify an intensive intervention to prevent further family deterioration or child placement. But such services are not being provided, in part due to ineffectual enforcement of PL 96-272, a general lack of funding for preventive services (Forsythe, 1992), and continuing problems of targeting and screening families most in need of the service. Consequently, many children have been placed outside their homes not once but multiple times in different family, group home, residential treatment, juvenile justice, and psychiatric hospital settings (Fanshel & Shinn, 1978; Rzepnicki, 1987).

The current difficulties evident in the child welfare system and in the development of the current FCS and IFPS programs have a long and varied history in the United States. Following a description of the history of family-based service programs, the authors discuss some of the major program implementation and evaluation issues for such programs.

Early Child Welfare Preventive Service Programs

The first foster care prevention or home-based service programs in America consisted of the "friendly visitors" of the Charity Organization Societies (COS), who in the late 1800s and early 1900s worked with immigrant and low-income families in their own homes to promote self-sufficiency and assimilation into American society (Axinn & Levin, 1982; Bremner, 1970–1971; Chambers, 1963).[7] (Table 1.1 documents some of the major events in the evolution of family-centered services.) Services provided by friendly visitors included access to food or heating supplies, legal assistance, welfare stipends from wealthy patrons, health care, and educational assistance (Waugh, 1997). The friendly visitors operated on the assumption that poverty resulted primarily from the behavioral failures of individuals. By enhancing the "moral adjustment" of such individuals, proponents of the COS believed that poverty and its associated problems could be eradicated (Waugh, 1997).

Although not home based, the settlement house movement of the 1800s and early 1900s also aided families in achieving self-sufficiency (Addams, 1912; Holden, 1970). Settlement houses were often located in cities and served immigrant and other low-income families (Addams, 1912). Services provided through settlement houses included casework, day care, education, recreation, health care, legal assistance, and community action (Holden, 1970).

Focus on the Individual

By the 1920s and 1930s, leaders in the mental health field began focusing on the individual and the deficits inherent in the individual. Sigmund Freud (1948) is perhaps best recognized as a leader in this area of inquiry known as "psychoanalysis." Along with C. G. Jung, Alfred Adler, and others, Freud formed the International Psychoanalytical Association in 1910

TABLE I.I. Significant Events and Projects Related to FBS

Date	Event or Project
1800s	The use of "friendly visitors" becomes a popular approach for addressing the needs of the urban poor in the United States (Bremner, 1970, 1971).
1877	Charity Organization Societies are developed in the United States and Canada to begin to address the societal conditions creating poverty (Bremner, 1970, 1971).
1889	Hull House is established in Chicago in order to help immigrants by addressing neighborhood living conditions, work opportunities, education, social activities, and other services.
1954	Family-Centered Project in St. Paul, Minn., is initiated to work with "multi-problem families" (Horejsi, 1981).
1954	Bowen and his colleagues conduct family therapy sessions with schizophrenic patients and their families at the Meninger Clinic (Bowen, 1985).
1959	Maas and Engler publish a research report criticizing foster care in the United States (Maas & Engler, 1959).
1969	Home-based treatment for emotionally and behaviorally disturbed children is initiated by the Mendota Mental Health Institute, Madison, Wisc. ("Home and Community Treatment Program" Cautley, 1979).
1972	The Lower East Side Family Union case management approach to FBS with multiethnic families in New York City is developed (Beck, 1979; Dun, 1979).
1973	Nashville-Davidson Emergency Services Project and other programs are created to provide a variety of services to prevent long-term foster care placement (Burt & Balyeat, 1974).
1974	The Homebuilders approach to intensive FCS is first implemented in Tacoma, Wash. (Kinney et al., 1977).
1977	PACT (Parents and Children Together) FCS program is developed to address the needs of single-parent minority families in Detroit (Callard & Morin, 1979).
1980	The Adoption Assistance and Child Welfare Act of 1980 is passed (PL 96-272), which requires that "reasonable and persistent efforts" to preserve families be made by child welfare agencies before a child is placed in substitute care (Pine, 1986).
1980	Intensive Family Services is funded by the Children's Services Division, Oregon, involving the location of contract providers of FCS in the offices of local public child welfare agencies (Nelson et al., 1988).
1981	San Diego Center for Children begins FCS program for preventing residential treatment placement and for shortening the length of stay of current inpatient clients.
1981	National Resource Center on Family-Based Services begins operation at the University of Iowa School of Social Work, with funding from the U.S. Children's Bureau.
1987	Homebuilders begins a special IFPS program to serve adoptive families at risk of child placement and disruption (Haapala et al., 1988).

(Table continues)

TABLE I.I. *(continued)*

Date	Event or Project
1987	First National Conference on Family-Based Services is held in Minneapolis, Minn.
1987	Minnesota and other states form their own family-based services associations.

Source. From *Evaluating Family-Based Services*, by P. J. Pecora, M. W. Fraser, K. Nelson, J. McCroskey, & W. Meezan, 1995, New York: Aldine de Gruyter. Copyright 1995 by Walter de Gruyter. Reprinted with permission.

(Freud, 1960). He suggested that a person's mental health and well-being was the result of conscious and unconscious drives that alternate between periods of excitation and relaxation (Freud, 1948). If there are unresolved conflicts between the conscious and unconscious, those conflicts often result in mental difficulties for the individual (Freud, 1960). The apparent influence of this movement on family-based approaches was to distract attention from family interactions, systems, and ecological approaches (however rudimentarily perceived at the time) and to shift focus to individuals.

Reemergence of a Family Focus

Even though interest in the individual psyche continues today, in the late 1940s interest in family-based services reemerged with the work of family therapists and family-based projects. The *Family Unit Report Study*, written in 1948 by Buell (1952), identified a small number of families with multiple needs who received services from the majority of human service agencies in St. Paul, Minnesota. The report resulted in the development of the St. Paul Family-Centered Project. Staff workers visited identified families in their homes to offer services, conduct assessments, and coordinate additional services (Geismar & Ayres, 1959). Target families had children under 18 who were at risk of delinquency, neglect, severe health problems, or severe economic hardship (Overton & Tinker, 1957).

At the same time, a number of family therapists were developing their theories of family therapy through work with different groups of families. In 1954, Bowen (1985) and his colleagues initiated a research/therapy project with schizophrenic patients and their families. The project initially provided individual psychotherapy to the schizophrenic patients and their mothers. By the second year, fathers and other family members were also included in the treatment process. According to Bowen, the inclusion of additional family members required a conceptual change from thinking of schizophrenia as an individual process to thinking of it as a family-based process. In addition, the child and family members were no longer provided individual therapy but were treated as a family unit through family therapy sessions.

Another group, Minuchin, Montalvo, Guerney, Rosman, and Schumer (1967), focused their work on disadvantaged families in New York City who had more than one child considered to be delinquent. The therapists/researchers were interested in identifying both the variables evident in these families and the most successful treatment techniques. The most successful treatment techniques involved family group problem solving, subgroup interactions (e.g., parental subsystem and sibling subsystem), and interdisciplinary team meetings (e.g., therapists and the identified child's caseworker).

Other family therapists also contributed their expertise. Like Minuchin, Satir (1983) focused on the full participation of all family members in therapy sessions. She suggested that families attempt to maintain homeostasis in their familial relationships, and when one family member attempts to upset the family's balance, he or she is often "blamed" by other family members for all the difficulties experienced by the family. In the 1950s Jay Haley and his colleagues also conducted work with people who were diagnosed as schizophrenic and their families. Haley (1963) suggested that when one individual in a family is diagnosed as the member with a "problem" or "mental illness," that person not only serves as the scapegoat for the family but also functions within the family by experiencing the psychopathology for the entire family. Therefore, changes in the individual, including changes initiated by therapy, will cause changes in the entire family system.

In addition to the development of family-based therapy, several family-based programs were developed in the 1950s and 1960s to treat "multiproblem families" in order to improve family functioning and reduce welfare dependency (Brown, 1968; Geismar & Ayers, 1958; Geismar & Krisberg, 1966; Levine, 1964; Overton, 1953). Characteristic of these programs were high worker caseloads and client contact that was limited to once a week or once a month for a one-to-two-year period (Hutchinson & Nelson, 1985).

Connections Between Foster Care Prevention and Family-Based Services

During the late 1960s and mid-1970s, new program models for preventing foster care placement began to emerge, many of which used the cognitive-behavioral or family therapy treatment techniques that were being developed during that time. Some of these intensive home-based service programs are still in operation. For example, in 1969 the Home and Community Treatment Team was established at the Mendota Mental Health Institute in Madison, Wisconsin. Still operating today, this program works with families with 3-to-10-year-old children who have emotional and behavioral problems. Both in-home (four hours per week) and in-office (two hours per week) services are provided for an average of fifteen months (Cautley, 1979; Kaplan, 1986).

During the early 1970s, a number of child welfare agencies also were successful in preventing child placement through intensive counseling (Hirsch, Gailey, & Schmerl, 1976) or through the use of a variety of "emergency services," such as crisis counselors, homemakers, emergency shelters or foster homes, and emergency caretakers (Burt & Balyeat, 1974; National Center for Comprehensive Emergency Services to Children, 1978). These programs recognized the importance of crisis intervention and time-limited supportive services for families as means for preventing long-term foster care placement. At the same time, a multidisciplinary family-centered approach to preventing child maltreatment and placement was developed in Philadelphia (the SCAN program, or Supportive Child Adult Network). Still operating today, this program works primarily with black, single-parent families and renders services for a minimum of two to four hours each week over nine-to-fifteen-month periods (Tatara, Morgan, & Portner, 1986).

A more time-limited and intensive home-based service, the Homebuilders program, was developed in the mid-1970s at Catholic Community Services in Tacoma, Washington. In the 1970s and still today, Homebuilder therapists receive referrals from the state child welfare agency for those cases where previous counseling or other services have been provided but the children are in "imminent danger of placement" outside the home. In practice, this imminent risk criterion has been interpreted to mean that the children will be placed within one week or less unless a more intensive service is offered.[8] The Homebuilders model is characterized by low worker caseloads, high intensity, short time frames, provision of both clinical and concrete services (i.e., provision of an average of thirty-eight client contact hours in thirty days), and use of a variety of clinical and concrete services (e.g., Kinney, Madsen, Fleming, & Haapala, 1977; Haapala & Kinney, 1979, 1988). In a number of quasi-experimental studies, the Homebuilders program has been shown to reduce the need for foster care placements for certain kinds of families (e.g., Fraser, Pecora, & Haapala, 1991; Kinney et al., 1977; Haapala & Kinney, 1979, 1988).

Other less intensive family-based programs have been effective in treating families where child neglect is the major problem. The PACT program, begun in the 1970s in Wayne County (Detroit), has been successful in working with low-income and ethnic minority families and represents a successful partnership between a university-based program and a state department of social services (Cabral & Callard, 1982; Callard & Morin, 1979; Van Meter, 1986). Another less intensive approach used individual caseworkers as the primary service providers (the New York State Preventive Services Demonstration Project). One of the most well-researched FCS programs, it began in 1974 and involved special units set up in two county departments of child welfare in New York City (Jones, Neuman, & Shyne, 1976). These units delivered a variety of services that produced continuing beneficial effects for children and families some five years after services were provided (Jones, 1985).

Another famous FCS program is the Bowen Center (Sullivan, Spasser, & Penner, 1977), which used a variety of services, such as emergency shelter care, homemaker assistance, preschool day care, and laundry facilities at the center to reach out to parents and strengthen families. Initially, five-person teams were used with a dual focus on helping clients meet both concrete and psychosocial service needs. More recently, the program model shifted to one that is more home based, with caseworkers seeing families individually for an average of 8.1 months, providing clinical, educational, and concrete services designed to promote healthy child development (Giblin & Callard, 1980; Kaplan, 1986). This program, also successful in working with low-income and ethnic minority families, represents a successful partnership between a university-based program and a state department of social services (Cabral & Callard, 1982; Van Meter, 1986).

Finally, the state of Oregon followed its implementation of permanency planning with FBS programs. The first four IFPS projects were implemented in 1980, based on a proposal approved by the 1979 state legislature to divert money from the foster care budget to IFPS. Although the original proposal was to train Children's Services Division (CSD) staff to provide family treatment, the legislature required the program to contract with private family therapy providers. Each of the four pilot projects was located in a different sociocultural area selected for its relatively high number of children in placement. Based on the success of the pilot project, the program was expanded in late 1981 and 1982 to sixteen projects. During this expansion, qualified private providers were not available in five of the locations; at these sites, new CSD employees were hired to provide IFPS. Project standards and regulations are the same for the "in-house" (state-operated) projects as they are for the contracted programs.

Small caseloads (about eight families per worker) and a time-limited service period of ninety days characterize the more intensive units. The program operates from a treatment model based on principles of family systems theory. The behavior of one family member is seen as necessarily affecting the behavior of other family members; the presentation of a "problem child" is viewed as an indication of a problem family, with the child having been consciously or unconsciously selected by the rest of the family as the symptom bearer. Family treatment is directed toward healing relationships between parents as well as between children and their parents and is broken down into three phases: assessment, treatment, and termination. About a third of the work done with families is accomplished through cotherapy, and much of the counseling is provided using office-based sessions (Nelson et al., 1988).

Recent Developments

Currently in many states, only a small percentage of the children reported to child protective services are ever placed in some form of substitute care. For example, in six major states about four in one thousand children ages 0 to 4 will enter foster care and about two in one thousand children ages 5 to 17 will enter foster care (Wulczyn, Harden, & Goerge, 1997). Some researchers argue that although there are few "unnecessary" placements, a proportion of those families experiencing the removal of their children could have been provided with FBS at an earlier time. Criticism of the child welfare service delivery system has continued with the recent increase in foster care placements (after a decrease in the rate of child placement in the early 1980s). A foundation report charged that "children are separated from their families by default. Too few alternatives are available to help [families] stay together safely" (Edna McConnell Clark Foundation, 1985, p. 2). In fact, many children have been placed outside their homes not once but multiple times, using different family, group home, or institutional settings (Fanshel & Shinn, 1978; Rzepnicki, 1987).

Another reform has had a major impact on the evolution of FCS and IFPS services: the Adoption Assistance and Child Welfare Act of 1980 (PL 96-272). As noted earlier, federal law mandated that a series of reforms be implemented in child welfare agencies in each state that wanted to qualify for special supplemental federal appropriations. PL 96-272 also required that every state implement a variety of placement prevention services as part of its strategy to ensure that "reasonable efforts" have been made to preserve the family before a child is placed in substitute care. In response to this mandate, the states have continued placement prevention efforts such as homemaker, emergency day care, parent aide, and crisis nursery services. These services have been supplemented recently also by FCS and IFPS programs, which are designed to help families to remain together safely.

Another response to the rising number of child placements has been decisions made in the courts. Some juvenile court judges are ordering local departments of social services to provide housing assistance or FBS under the "reasonable efforts" mandate of PL 96-272 (Judge Richard Fitzgerald, personal communication, 1991). The program reforms promoted by PL 96-272, increasing placement rates, and a search for "revenue-neutral" (i.e., programs that do not increase budget costs) service innovations have all combined to produce an environment that supports the development of FBS programs. Although these programs have different names and program characteristics,[9] they provide a viable alternative to out-of-home placement for some children and help to improve family functioning in specific areas.

Current Status of FBS Programs

A large variety of FBS programs have recently been developed by both private and public child welfare agencies (some of which use more of an office-based approach to service delivery). The National Resource Center on Family-Based Services published in 1988 an annotated bibliography of 333 programs in more than twenty-five states, a huge increase from the 20 programs listed in 1982 (National Resource Center on Family-Based Services, 1988). Although there has not been a recent cataloguing of such programs, we expect that they have continued to grow since the passage of the federal Omnibus Budget Reconciliation Act in 1993. Yet a recent analysis of where the funds were being spent under this legislation revealed that most of the spending was targeted to family support services rather than to FBS or IFPS.

FCS and IFPS programs are serving clients from child welfare, mental health, developmental disabilities, juvenile corrections, and other major service areas. A variety of staffing, treatment models, and approaches to evaluation are being used,[10] including those related to supporting families whose children are returning from foster care or residential treatment or are in danger of experiencing adoption disruption.

The field has therefore experienced a shift from a few small-scale and isolated demonstration projects to the use of FBS programs on a statewide basis in a number of states, including Florida, Illinois, Maryland, Michigan, Minnesota, and Tennessee (e.g., Grohoski, 1990; Holliday & Cronin, 1990; Nelson & Landsman, 1992; Tracy, Haapala, Kinney, & Pecora, 1991). The implementation of these programs represents a commitment on the part of state and local governments to operationalize the principle stated earlier that society should be willing to invest as many resources in preserving families as might be spent for substitute family care (Lloyd, Bryce, & Schultze, 1980). Thus these services were developed to provide alternatives to out-of-home placement by improving family functioning as well as by linking families to sustaining services and sources of support (Bryce, 1979).

As discussed earlier in this chapter, these programs have many different names and characteristics, but some of them appear to have the potential to provide a viable alternative to out-of-home placement, either reducing the number of children who are placed in substitute care or decreasing their time in care.[11] While initial program results are positive to mixed, it is important to note that FBS programs will not replace the need for other types of child welfare services. Some families will always need one or more of the other more restrictive services in the child welfare continuum of service, such as family foster care, day treatment, or residential treatment.

According to Farrow (1991), Nelson (1991), Whittaker (1991), and others, FBS, like some of the new family support programs, represents a significant departure from the more traditional categorical services that embrace a child-rescue philosophy, place treatment within a narrowly "person-centered" perspective, and give little attention to addressing the family's needs in a holistic manner. According to Whittaker (1991), these new ideas represent alternative conceptualizations of human services toward the following goals:

1. *Establishing a service continuum*—from preclusive prevention to secure treatment—with expanded capacity for individualized case planning through *flexible* funding and service eligibility.

2. *Promoting competence and meeting basic developmental needs of children and families in "normalized" settings*, by teaching practical life skills and by providing environmental supports as opposed to uncovering and treating underlying pathology. Evidence for this trend is apparent in the explosion of educational or life-skills approaches (Danish, D'Angell, & Hauer, 1980); the move away from presumptive labeling and toward more developmentally focused, competence-oriented assessment; and the move in many fields toward "normalization" of both the location and focus of treatment (Wolfensberger, 1972).

3. *Considering services as family supportive and family strengthening, not as "child saving."* The rapid expansion of crisis-oriented family support services (Whittaker & Tracy, 1989), the family support movement (Zigler & Black, 1989), and the renewed emphasis on family involvement in child placement services (Jenson & Whittaker, 1987) all offer partial evidence of the strength of this idea.

4. *Reestablishing a person-in-environment perspective in theory, empirical research, and clinical practice as a foundation for intervention design.* Bronfenbrenner's (1979) ecology of human development, the empirical work of Garbarino, Schellenbach, Sebes, and Associates (1986) on the environmental correlates of child maltreatment, and the rapid growth of preventive-remedial intervention designed to enhance social support (Gottlieb, 1988; Biegel, Farkas, Abell, Goodin, & Friedman, 1988) indicate a return to traditional social work paradigms (Whittaker & Tracy, 1989; Brieland, 1987).

PROGRAM LIMITATIONS AND POLICY PITFALLS

Although family-centered and family-based services represent a significant step in the evolution of social services and initial program results showed promise (although not uniformly so), it is important to note that FCS programs cannot replace other types of child and family services or substitute for broader societal and service system reforms (Halpern, 1990). While a number of case situations can be addressed by FCS programs alone, some families will always need one or more other child welfare services, such as day treatment, family foster care, or residential treatment or adoption; and most will need other preventive or supportive services, such as income support, child care, parent education, substance abuse treatment, or job training. (See figure 1.2.)

Studies of FCS and other programs have repeatedly shown that many families need assistance with housing, food, medical care, employment, and basic financial support. Most families served by public systems either live in communities with few resources to help parents or support healthy child development or fail to access those systems without extrafamilial assistance or intervention. In addition, many families experience other problems, such as ineffective communication among family members, poor self-esteem, serious mental illness, lack of social support, and pro-

FIGURE 1.2. An Array of Child and Family Supports

Source: From *Evaluating Family-Based Services* (p. xxii), by P. J. Pecora, M. W. Fraser, K. Nelson, J. McCroskey, & W. Meezan, 1995, New York: Aldine de Gruyter. Copyright 1995 by Walter de Gruyter. Reprinted with permission.

nounced deficits in parenting or basic social skills. Many of these problems derive from larger societal problems or significant psychological or social impairment (Polansky, Ammons, & Weathersby, 1983; Polansky, Gaudin, & Kilpatrick, 1992). As with other social service interventions such as home visiting (Weiss, 1993), there is a danger that FCS and IFPS will be oversold as a cure-all for families because of those services' emphasis on family strengthening and early reports of cost-effectiveness.

Therein lies one of the major dangers of this movement—public assistance, housing, health care, and other more preventive family support services essential to child and family well-being might be cut in order to fund the more intensive or residual forms of FCS. While significant foster care and residential treatment program savings may be realized for some children, FCS programs are just one of an array of services that must be available to support families throughout the life cycle. Without a broader network of family supports available in the larger society and local community, families may not be able to maintain the gains made during FCS, and children may be vulnerable to continued abuse or neglect. Furthermore, some families need services on a long-term basis and are not well served by a short period of intensive work (Maluccio, 1991). Other families need high-quality foster care to help them through a difficult period or until an older child reaches adulthood (Fanshel, Finch, & Grundy, 1990).

It is incumbent on evaluators and program staff to locate FCS and IFPS programs within the larger network of services and to emphasize to policymakers that both the short- and long-term success of such programs depends on the family's ability to access a range of community services and other societal supports. More immediately, an evaluator must consider how the availability of these community services will affect the success of the program. While some families may need only FCS, for many families, maintenance of gains made in FCS is affected significantly by the availability of continuing FCS or other services in the community.

Policy and Program Questions

As the number of FCS and IFPS programs has grown and claims of effectiveness have increased, agency administrators and policymakers have begun to ask a variety of questions:

- □ What specific services are we funding?
- □ What types of children and families benefit most from these services?
- □ How effective are these services in relation to improving child/family functioning and preventing foster care placement?
- □ Can the use of FCS and FBS save child welfare service or other funds?
- □ Can these "savings" be redirected toward other services in the continuum?

Responding to these questions has been difficult, in part because of the challenges associated with implementing rigorous evaluation designs, accurately targeting the population of clients most likely to be placed without substantial service investment, and distinguishing among dissimilar programs using the same categorical title or description. For example, as described previously, the service characteristics of these programs vary tremendously, and the programs themselves are sometimes described using different terms such as "family support," "home-based," "family-centered," "family preservation," or "placement prevention" services.

Empirical Data of Success

As mentioned, the program evaluation results from experimental and quasi-experimental studies, while promising, do not show dramatic differences between control and treatment groups and are far from conclusive (e.g., Fraser, Nelson, & Rivard, 1997). In addition, a number of administrative and evaluation problems have confounded studies. Problems in administration include referral, staff training, and community resources. Evaluation problems include the use of nonexperimental designs, premature use of experimental designs during program implementation (when the treatment model, and therefore the independent variable, is evolving), randomization problems in experimental designs, small samples, poor case targeting, differences in the treatment (independent variable) across sites, underuse of qualitative study designs, inappropriate assessment measures, and poorly administered assessment measures.

Recent meta-analyses of laboratory and clinic-based studies of psychotherapy also have found a lack of dramatic differences between control and experimental groups (Weisz, Weiss, & Donenberg, 1992). Across many different fields, evaluation studies appear to suggest that we cannot expect single services to produce dramatic changes in complex social problems. Most literature reviews report only a fraction of the research data generated by this selected group of major studies. The full reports must be read in order to understand the particular objectives, findings, and limitations of each study, since intake criteria, treatment model, program maturity, services, and other critical program components differ.

SELECTED PROGRAM IMPLEMENTATION CHALLENGES IN FAMILY-CENTERED SERVICES

Theory Building

Theory building is an area that promises to be challenging in the development of FBS. Despite the work of a number of program developers and researchers (e.g., Barth, 1990; Bryce & Lloyd, 1981; Jones, 1985; Kinney,

Haapala, & Booth, 1991), documentation of theories to guide FBS remains to be fully accomplished. And yet, ideally, high-quality evaluations use theory as a way of guiding the choice of dependent and independent variables, as well as the research design and measures. Perhaps this is where various qualitative approaches can make significant contributions (Wells & Freer, 1994).

Case Targeting

Targeting services to cases at imminent risk of placement, if placement prevention is the purpose of the program, remains a serious challenge. Many of the largest FBS and IFBS studies with placement prevention objectives were unable to target services to children truly at risk of imminent placement, as evidenced by the fact that few children were placed within thirty days of referral to these studies. In addition, it may be important to evaluate the use of FBS and IFBS with "nonimminent risk" and other types of families to determine if other populations exist for which FBS and IFBS are effective.

Serious efforts are needed in programs with the target imminent risk population to refine placement criteria, implement interdepartmental screening committees, involve juvenile court personnel, better manage the politics of implementation, and address staff concerns about child safety in order to improve case targeting and screening. Otherwise, for imminent risk cases we will continue to find only small differences in placement rates between treatment and comparison groups.

Program Implementation

Another serious issue inadequately addressed by many FBS initiatives is the need to achieve program consistency and rigor with respect to model specification, staff selection, staff training, program funding, quality control, staff turnover, and *planned* program refinement in contrast to model "drift" (Pecora, Fraser, & Haapala 1991). For example, during the third year of implementation, when control groups were being formed, a major California FCS evaluation encountered staff turnover and decreased state administrative support. Other recent statewide evaluation studies have also faced considerable methodological and implementation challenges.[12]

One of the most comprehensive studies thus far, conducted in Illinois, found no significant differences in child placement rates between the experimental and comparison sites. But this was a likely finding, given that only 7 percent of the comparison group cases were placed within thirty days and 16 percent at six months (Schuerman, Rzepnicki, Littell, & Chak, 1993, p. 104). Despite some innovative approaches to random assignment and careful measurement strategies, a number of complications arose with respect to the following: (a) considerable variation among sites and variations in outcomes due to characteristics of cases and the services provided to them; (b) substantial differences in the risks of subsequent maltreatment, placement, and case closing among the experimental sites; (c) substantial variation across sites regarding the independent variable, which was IFBS treatment (i.e., the "dose" of the intervention varied in terms of amounts, types, and duration of services provided to Family First and regular services cases); and (d) substantial differences in patterns of case openings and closings across all sites (Schuerman et al., 1993).

As illustrated by the Illinois, California, Iowa, New Jersey, Utah, Washington, and other evaluations of FCS and IFPS, the program implementation process, worker training, variation in services, and other implementation factors are critical in interpreting study findings and in developing effective research designs. One of the immediate challenges for FBS is to better address the fundamentals of program implementation that will lead to more accurate evaluation studies. Some of these fundamentals, identified below, need even greater attention.

□ *Be careful and rigorous about how to specify the treatment model.* For example, what are the theory base, intervention methods, caseload size, intensity, and approach to the provision of concrete services? Unfortunately, program developers do not take the time to consider what it will really take to make a meaningful difference for the consumer. In research this issue is somewhat analogous to calculating effect sizes and power.

Dosage does matter. In the field of medicine, no one gives a person half the prescription needed. Thus the issue for child welfare is specifying what it will take to make a difference in the lives of the families. Therefore, the child welfare field needs to have the data required to say to legislators, for example, that for high-risk families in which neglect of young children is the issue, an average of twelve months of fairly intensive efforts is needed, which are likely to be followed by either termination of parental rights or some less intensive community services with occasional booster sessions to help the at-risk children safely reach adulthood.

Similarly, with wraparound neighborhood services, some youth will be able to be maintained in their families. This will save some funds that will need to be reinvested in the neighborhood in the way of housing, employment, and health care supports so the cycle can be broken. If this amount can't be invested, then do not expect the work to be clinically effective or cost-effective, or to have enduring qualities.

□ *Adequately staff the service.* Selection criteria, training, performance standards, and the use of paraprofessional staff are all important issues to address. Staff turnover is very expensive and programs need to use cost data to support better pay, benefits, equipment, and working conditions.

☐ *Provide supervision and clinical consultation to staff in order to minimize treatment model drift.*

☐ *Establish an organizational and community climate supportive of continuing program innovation and ongoing quality assurance.* We have to constantly innovate in order to best meet consumer needs and to customize our intervention models for the community. In child welfare we do not sufficiently involve our consumers in program planning and refinement, and yet they have much to offer us if we are willing to listen.

☐ *Collect cost-benefit data.* In times of continuing funding scarcity, we need to be able to tie key outcomes to service costs. And if a service will be insufficient in power or intensity to have a major effect, then maybe we should not use that service.

☐ *Identify "realizable" proximal and distal outcomes.* Researchers should help inform FBS program planners regarding the development of "reasonable" proximal outcomes and time frames (e.g., differences in family functioning, family safety, foster care placement, school reports, and school attendance records). For example, foster care placement may be a reasonable outcome to achieve within three months of receiving FBS. However, after a two-year period, other factors could affect whether the child is placed in foster care. Yet since the FBS program's proximal outcome was prevention of foster care placement, the program gets "blamed" for the placement. Thus the outcome is not "achievable." Similarly, distal outcomes, such as child abuse and delinquency reports within the community, are at times tied to FBS programs and are considered "achievable," even though researchers and others recognize that other factors outside the FBS program may have an impact on these outcomes. In these instances, researchers must help inform FBS program planners regarding distal outcomes that can realistically be affected by FBS programs.

The foregoing represent some of the major challenges that FCS and IFPS administrators and evaluators need to overcome. To date, the field lacks conclusive evidence that FBS programs prevent child placement and information about which types of FBS programs are most effective with different client subpopulations, including those involved in physical abuse, neglect, parent-child conflict, or other problems. We also need a better understanding of effectiveness with different age groups of children and of program components that contribute to success with different families (e.g., in-home services, active listening, client goal setting, concrete services). Studies are beginning to look at subpopulations and to estimate the value of different intervention components (e.g., Bath, Richey, & Haapala, 1992). These are all-important evaluation goals, along with the fundamental need for FCS and IFPS programs to assess effectiveness, refine interventions, and be accountable to funding agencies. These are just a few of the program implementation challenges that remain to be fully addressed.

Problems in any one of these areas can complicate or compromise aspects of the evaluation effort, as discussed in the chapters that follow.[13]

□ □ □

Family-centered services represent an enduring and valuable approach to working with families at a time when "orphanages" and quick termination of parental rights are being touted as easy solutions to complex problems. Evaluation data from well-constructed research studies can help guide service reform efforts. We hope the following chapters provide you with a clear perspective about the benefits and challenges of family-centered services, as well as some guidelines for refining and improving those services and programs.

NOTES

1. This chapter is adapted from the following sources:

   Fraser, M. W., Pecora, P. J., & Haapala, D. A. (1991). *Families in crisis: The impact of intensive family preservation services* (pp. 17–47). Hawthorne, NY: Aldine de Gruyter. Copyright 1991 by Walter de Gruyter. Adapted with permission.

   Pecora, P. J., Fraser, M. W., Nelson, K., McCroskey, J., & Meezan, W. (1995). *Evaluating family-based services.* New York: Aldine de Gruyter. Copyright 1995 by Walter de Gruyter. Adapted with permission.

   Pecora, P. J., Whittaker, J. K., Maluccio, A. N., & Barth, R. P. (with R. Plotnick). (2000). *The child welfare challenge.* Hawthorne, NY: Walter de Gruyter. Copyright 2000 by Walter de Gruyter. Adapted with permission.

   Reed, K. B., & Kirk, R. S. (1998). Intensive family preservation services: A short history but a long past. *Family Preservation Journal, 3* (1), 41–58. Copyright 1998 by Eddie Bowers Publishing, Inc. Adapted with permission.

2. For examples of family support programs, see Jones (1985, pp. 27–34), Weissbourd and Kagan (1989), Yale Bush Center in Child Development and Social Policy and Family Resource Coalition (1983), and Zigler and Black (1989).

3. For examples of these types of family support programs, see Jones (1985, pp. 27–34), Weissbourd and Kagan (1989), Yale Bush Center in Child Development and Social Policy and Family Resource Coalition (1983), and Zigler and Black (1989).

4. For more information regarding the treatment philosophy and practice principles of FBS and IFPS, see Cole and Duva (1990); Dunst, Trivette, and Deal (1988); Haapala and Kinney (1979); Kinney, Haapala, and Gast (1981, 1990); Lloyd and Bryce (1983); and Pecora, Delewski, Booth, Haapala, and Kinney (1985).

5. See Haapala, McDade, and Johnston (1988); Hodges, Guterman, Blythe, and Bronson (1989); Maluccio (1991); and Whittaker and Maluccio (1988).

6. The current FCS and IFPS casework philosophies differ from the belief of many Charity Organization Society (COS) workers. COS workers tended

to believe that social problems were the result of character flaws, and that such flaws differentiate the worthy from the unworthy poor. In contrast, most modern FPS programs share much of their philosophy with the Settlement House movement—another early program that was more focused on community organization and was not necessarily home based. Settlement House organizers established houses in poor or immigrant-filled neighborhoods by "socially concerned middle-class and upper-class university students and others, who . . . shared their lives with the poor—a kind of Peace Corps of the time" (Wood & Geismar, 1989, p. 47). Settlement Houses were begun about the same time as the Charity Organization Societies, but their philosophical approaches were significantly different (Leiby, 1978).

7. See, for example, Barth (1991), Bryce and Lloyd (1981), Hinckley and Ellis (1985), Kagan and Schlosberg (1989), Kammerman and Kahn (1989), Kaplan (1986), Maybanks and Bryce (1979), and Nelson, Emlen, Landsman, and Hutchinson (1988).

8. However, there is considerable variation across program sites in the operationalization of the concept of imminent risk. This variation is thought to have contributed to the equivocal findings of much of the experimental research on the effectiveness of IFPS (e.g., Fraser, Nelson, & Rivard, 1997; Feldman, 1991; Rossi, 1992a).

9. See Bath, Richey, and Haapala (1992); Feldman (1991); Fraser et al. (1991); Lewis (1991); Haapala (1983); and Nelson et al. (1988).

10. For critical reviews of selected evaluation studies of family-based services or the research as a whole, see Bath and Haapala (in press), Frankel (1988), Fraser et al. (1997), Jones (1985), Magura (1981), Rossi (1992a, 1992b), Stein (1985), and Wells and Biegel (1991). For an incisive discussion of similar challenges with home-visiting program research see Olds and Kitzman (1993).

11. See Lewis (1991), Haapala (1983), and Nelson et al. (1988).

12. See Gershenson (1993) and Schuerman, Rzepnicki, and Littell (1991); for an incisive discussion of similar challenges with home-visiting program research see Olds and Kitzman (1993).

13. The need for continuing research on FCS and IFPS continues to be documented even in the most current literature. A variety of research approaches have been suggested, and there is increasing specificity of research questions being suggested in literature reviews (Fraser et al., 1997; Reed & Kirk, 1998, Holosko & Holosko, 1999).

REFERENCES

Addams, J. (1912). *Twenty years at Hull House with autobiographical notes.* New York: Macmillan.

Adoption and Foster Care Analysis and Reporting System [Online database]. (2000, October). Available: http://www.acf.dhhs.gov/programs/cb/stats/tables/tarreport/rpt10004/ar1000.htm

Axinn, J., & Levin, H. (1982). *Social welfare—A history of the American response to need* (2nd ed.). New York: Harper and Row.

Barth, R. P. (1990). On their own: The experiences of youth after foster care. *Child and Adolescent Social Work, 7*, 419–46.

Barth, R. P. (1991). An experimental evaluation of in-home child abuse prevention services. *Child Abuse and Neglect, 15*, 363–75.

Bath, H. I., & Haapala, D. A. (1994). Family preservation services: What does the outcome research really tell us? *Social Service Review, 68* (3), 386–404.

Bath, H. I., Richey, C. A., & Haapala, D. A. (1992). Child age and outcome correlates in intensive family preservation services. *Children and Youth Services Review, 14* (5), 389–406.

Biegel, D. E., Farkas, K. J., Abell, N., Goodin, J., & Friedman, B. (1988). *Social support networks and bibliography, 1983–1987.* New York: Greenwood.

Bowen, M. (1985). *Family therapy in clinical practice.* Northvale, NJ: Jason Aronson.

Breakey, G., & Pratt, B. (1991). Healthy growth for Hawaii's "healthy start": Toward a systematic statewide approach to the prevention of child abuse and neglect. *Zero to Three, 9* (4), 16–22.

Bremner, R. (Ed.). (1970–1971). *Children and youth in America* (Vol. 1, 1600–1865; Vol. 2, 1865–1965). Cambridge: Harvard University Press.

Brieland, D. (1987). History and evolution of social work practice. In *Encyclopedia of Social Work* (18th ed., Vol. 1) (pp. 739–54). Silver Spring, MD: National Association of Social Workers.

Bronfenbrenner, U. (1979). *The ecology of human development.* Cambridge: Harvard University Press.

Brown, G. (Ed.). (1968). *The multi-problem dilemma.* Metuchen, NJ: Scarecrow Press.

Bryce, M. (1979). Home-based care: Development and rationale. In S. Maybanks & M. Bryce (Eds.), *Home-based services for children and families: Policy, practice, and research.* Springfield, IL: Charles C Thomas.

Bryce, M., & Lloyd, J. C. (Eds.). (1981). *Treating families in the home: An alternative to placement.* Springfield, IL: Charles C Thomas.

Buell, B. (1952). *Community planning for human services.* New York: Columbia University Press.

Burt, M. R., & Balyeat, R. (1974). A new system for improving the care of neglected and abused children. *Child Welfare, 53* (3), 167–97.

Cabral, R. J., & Callard, E. D. (1982). A home-based program to serve high-risk families. *Journal of Home Economics, 74* (3), 14–19.

Callard, E. D., & Morin, P. (1979). *Parents and children together: An alternative to foster care.* Detroit, MI: Wayne State University, Department of Family and Consumer Studies.

Cautley, P. W. (1979). *The Home and Community Treatment process: Helping families change.* Madison, WI: Mendota Mental Health Institute, Home and Community Treatment.

Chambers, C. A. (1963). *Seedtime of reform: American social service and social action, 1918–1933.* Minneapolis: University of Minnesota Press.

Child Welfare League of America. (1989). *Standards for services to strengthen and preserve families with children.* Washington, DC: Author.

Cole, E., & Duva, J. (1990). *Family preservation: An orientation for administrators and practitioners.* Washington, DC: Child Welfare League of America.

Danish, S. J., D'Angell, A. R., & Hauer, A. L. (1980). *Helping skills* (2nd ed.). New York: Human Sciences Press.

Dunst, C. J., Trivette, C. M., & Deal, A. G. (1988). *Enabling and empowering families: Principles and guidelines for practice.* Cambridge, MA: Brookline Books.

Edna McConnell Clark Foundation. (1985). *Keeping families together: The case for family preservation.* New York: Author.

Emlen, A., Lahti, J., Downs, G., McKay, A., & Downs, S. (1978). *Overcoming barriers to planning for children in foster care* (DHEW Publication No. [OHDS] 78-30138). Washington, DC: U.S. Department of Health and Human Services, U.S. Children's Bureau.

Fanshel, D. (1992). Foster care as a two-tiered system. *Children and Youth Services Review, 14,* 49–60.

Fanshel, D., Finch, S. J., & Grundy, J. F. (1990). *Foster children in a life course perspective.* New York: Columbia University Press.

Fanshel, D., & Shinn, E. (1978). *Children in foster care: A longitudinal investigation.* New York: Columbia University Press.

Farrow, F. (1991). Services to families: The view from the states. *Families in Society: The Journal of Contemporary Human Services, 72* (5), 268–75.

Feldman, L. H. (1991). Evaluating the impact of intensive family preservation services in New Jersey. In K. Wells & D. A. Biegel (Eds.), *Family preservation services: Research and evaluation* (pp. 47–71). Newbury Park, CA: Sage.

Forsythe, P. W. (1992). Homebuilders and family preservation. *Children and Youth Services Review, 14,* 37–47.

Frankel, H. (1988). Family-centered, home-based services in child protection: A review of the research. *Social Service Review, 62* (1), 137–57.

Fraser, M. W., Nelson K. E., & Rivard, J. C. (1997). Effectiveness of family preservation services. *Social Work Research, 21* (3), 138–53.

Fraser, M. W., Pecora, P. J., & Haapala, D. A. (1991). *Families in crisis: The impact of intensive family preservation services.* Hawthorne, NY: Aldine de Gruyter.

Freud, S. (1948). *Beyond the pleasure principle.* London: Hogarth.

Freud, S. (1960). *The ego and the id.* New York: Norton.

Garbarino, J., Schellenbach, C. J., Sebes, J., & Associates. (1986). *Troubled youth, troubled families: Understanding families at risk for adolescent maltreatment.* New York: Aldine de Gruyter.

Geismar, L., & Ayers, B. (1958). *Families in trouble.* St. Paul, MN: Family-Centered Project, Greater St. Paul Community Chest and Councils.

Geismar, L., & Ayres, B. (1959). *Patterns of change in problem families: A study of the social functioning and movement of 150 families served by the Family-Centered Project.* St. Paul, MN: Greater St. Paul Community Chest and Councils.

Geismar, L., & Krisberg, J. (1966). The family life improvement project: An experiment in preventive intervention. *Social Casework, 47* (6), 563–70.

Gershenson, C. P. (1993). The child well-being conundrum. *Readings: A Journal of Reviews and Commentary in Mental Health, 8* (2), 8–11.

Giblin, P. T., & Callard, E. D. (1980). Issues in evaluation of action research: A social service model. *Social Work Research and Abstracts, 16* (4), 3–12.

Goerge, R. M. (1990). The reunification process in substitute care. *Social Service Review, 64,* 422–57.

Goerge, R. M., Wulczyn, F., & Harden, A. (1996). New comparative insights into states and their foster children. *Public Welfare, 54,* 12–25, 54.

Gottlieb, B. (1988). *Marshaling social support.* Beverly Hills, CA: Sage.

Grohoski, L. (1990). *Family-based services in Minnesota: A statewide view and case study.* Unpublished manuscript, Minnesota Department of Human Services, Research and Planning Unit, Community Social Services, St. Paul.

Gruber, A. R. (1973). *Foster home care in Massachusetts: A study of children— Their biological and foster parents.* Boston: Governor's Commission on Adoption and Foster Care.

Haapala, D. A. (1983). *Perceived helpfulness, attributed critical incident responsibility, and a discrimination of home-based family therapy treatment outcomes: Homebuilders model* (Grant #90-CW-626 OHDS). Report prepared for the Department of Health and Human Services, Administration for Children, Youth, and Families. Federal Way, WA: Behavioral Sciences Institute.

Haapala, D. A., & Kinney, J. M. (1979). Homebuilder's approach to the training of in-home therapists. In S. Maybanks & M. Bryce (Eds.), *Home-based services for children and families* (pp. 248–59). Springfield, IL: Charles C Thomas.

Haapala, D. A., & Kinney, J. M. (1988). Avoiding the out-of-home placement of high-risk status offenders through the use of intensive home-based family preservation services. *Criminal Justice and Behavior, 15* (3), 334–48.

Haapala, D. A., McDade, K., & Johnston, B. (1988). *Preventing the dissolution of special needs adoption families through the use of intensive home-based family preservation services: The Homebuilders Model* (Clinical Services Final Report from the Homebuilders Adoption Services Continuum Project). Federal Way, WA: Behavioral Sciences Institute.

Haley, J. (1963). *Stategies of psychotherapy.* New York: Grune and Stratton.

Halpern, E. S. (1990). *Auditing naturalistic inquiries: The development and application of a model.* Unpublished doctoral dissertation, Indiana University.

Hinckley, E. C., & Ellis, W. F. (1985). An effective alternative to residential placement: Home-based services. *Journal of Clinical Child Psychology, 14* (3), 209–13.

Hirsch, J. S., Gailey, J., & Schmerl, E. (1976). A child welfare agency's program of service to children in their own homes. *Child Welfare, 55* (3), 193–204.

Hodges, V. G., Guterman, N. B., Blythe, B. J., & Bronson, D. E. (1989). Intensive aftercare services for children. *Social Casework, 70* (7), 397–404.

Holden, A. C. (1970). *The settlement idea: A vision of social justice.* New York: Macmillan.

Holliday, M., & Cronin, R. (1990). Families first: A significant step toward family preservation. *Families in Society, 71,* 303–6.

Holosko, M. J., & Holosko, D. A. (1999). What have we learned from articles published in the *Family Preservation Journal? Family Preservation Journal, 4* (1), 1–12.

Horejsi, C. R. (1981). The St. Paul family-centered project revisited: Exploring an old gold mine. In M. Bryce & J. C. Lloyd (Eds.), *Treating families in the home* (pp. 12–23). Springfield, IL: Charles C Thomas.

Hutchinson, J. R., & Nelson, K. E. (1985). How public agencies can provide family-centered services. *Social Casework, 66* (6), 367–71.

Jenson, J. M., & Whittaker, J. K. (1987). Parental involvement in children's residential treatment: From preplacement to aftercare. *Children and Youth Services Review, 9,* 81–100.

Jones, M. A. (1985). A second chance for families five years later: Follow-up of a program to prevent foster care. New York: Child Welfare League of America.

Jones, M. A., Neuman, R., & Shyne, A. W. (1976). *A second chance for families: Evaluation of a program to reduce foster care.* New York: Child Welfare League of America.

Kagan, R., & Schlosberg, S. (1989). *Families in perpetual crisis.* New York: Norton.

Kagan, S., Powell, D., Weissbourd, B., & Zigler, E. (Eds.). (1987). *America's family support programs: Perspectives and prospects.* New Haven: Yale University Press.

Kamerman, S., & Kahn, A. (1989). *Social services for children, youth, and families in the United States.* New York: Columbia University School of Social Work (Annie E. Casey Foundation).

Kaplan, L. (1986). *Working with multiproblem families.* Lexington, MA: Lexington Books, D. C. Heath.

Kinney, J. M., Haapala, D., & Booth, C. (1991). *Keeping families together: The Homebuilders model.* Hawthorne, NY: Aldine de Gruyter.

Kinney, J. M., Haapala, D., & Gast, J. E. (1981). Assessment of families in crisis. In M. Bryce & J. C. Lloyd (Eds.), *Treating families in the home: An alternative to placement* (pp. 50–67). Federal Way, WA: Behavioral Sciences Institute.

Kinney, J. M., Madsen, B., Fleming, T., & Haapala, D. A. (1977). Homebuilders: Keeping families together. *Journal of Consulting and Clinical Psychology, 45* (4), 667–73.

Knitzer, J., Allen, M. L., & McGowan, B. (1978). *Children without homes: An examination of public responsibility to children in out-of-home care.* Washington, DC: Children's Defense Fund.

Leiby, J. (1978). *A history of social welfare and social work in the United States.* New York: Columbia University Press.

Levine, R. A. (1964). Treatment in the home. *Social Work, 9* (1), 19–28.

Lewis, R. E. (1991). What are the characteristics of intensive family preservation services? In M. W. Fraser, P. J. Pecora, & D. A. Haapala (Eds.), *Families in crisis: The impact of intensive family preservation services* (pp. 93–108). New York: Aldine de Gruyter.

Lloyd, J. C., & Bryce, M. E. (1983). *Placement prevention and family unification: A practitioner's handbook for the home-based family-centered program.* Iowa City, IA: University of Iowa, School of Social Work, National Resource Center on Family-Based Services.

Lloyd, J. C., Bryce, M. E., & Schultze, L. (1980). *Placement prevention and family reunification: A practitioner's handbook for the home-based family-centered program.* Iowa City, IA: University of Iowa, School of Social Work, National Resource Center on Family-Based Services.

Lloyd, J. C., & Sallee, A. (1994). The challenge and potential of family preservation services. *Protecting Children 10* (3), 5.

Maas, H., & Engler, R. (1959). *Children in need of parents.* New York: Columbia University Press.

Magazino, C. J. (1983). Services to children and families at risk of separation. In B. G. McGowan & W. Meezan (Eds.), *Child welfare: Current dilemmas, future directions* (pp. 211–54). Itasca, IL: F. E. Peacock.

Magura, S. (1981). Are services to prevent foster care effective? *Children and Youth Services Review, 3* (3), 193–212.

Maluccio, A. N. (1991). The optimism of policy choices in child welfare. *American Journal of Orthopsychiatry, 61* (4), 606–9.

Maybanks, S., & Bryce, M. (Eds.). (1979). *Home-based services for children and families: Policy, practice, and research.* Springfield, IL: Charles C Thomas.

Minuchin, S., Montalvo, R., Guerney, B. G., Rosman, B. L., & Schumer, F. (1967). *Families of the slums.* New York: Basic Books.

Mnookin, R. H. (1973). Foster care: In whose best interest? *Harvard Educational Review, 43* (4), 599–638.

Murphy, J. M., Jellinek, M., Quinn, D., Smith, G., Poitrast, F. G., & Goshko, M. (1991). Substance abuse and serious child mistreatment: Prevalence, risk, and outcome in a court sample. *Child Abuse and Neglect, 15* (3) 197–211.

National Center for Comprehensive Emergency Services to Children. (1978). *Comprehensive emergency services: Training guide* (2nd ed.) (OHDS Publication No. [01 and D5] 77–30120). Washington, DC: U.S. Department of Health and Human Services, Office of Human Development Services.

National Commission on Children. (1991). *Beyond rhetoric: A new American agenda for children and families.* Washington, DC: Author.

National Resource Center on Family-Based Services. (1988). *Annotated directory of selected family-based programs.* Iowa City: University of Iowa–Oakdale Campus, School of Social Work.

Nelson, K. (1991). Populations and outcomes in five family preservation programs. In K. Wells & D. E. Beigel (Eds.), *Family preservation services: Research and evaluation.* Newbury Park, CA: Sage.

Nelson, K., Emlen, A., Landsman, M. J., & Hutchinson, J. (1988). *Family-based services: Factors contributing to success and failure in family-based child welfare services. Final report* (OHDS Grant #90-CW-0732). Iowa City: University of Iowa, School of Social work, National Resource Center on Family-Based Services.

Nelson, K., & Landsman, M. J. (1992). *Alternative models of family preservation: Family-based services in context.* Springfield, IL: Charles C Thomas.

Olds, D. L., & Kitzman, H. (1993). Review of research on home visiting for pregnant women and parents of young children. *The Future of Children—Home Visiting, 3* (3) 53–92.

Overton, A. (1953). Serving families who don't want help. *Social Casework, 34,* 304–9.

Overton, A., & Tinker, K. H. (1957). *Casework notebook.* St. Paul, MN: Family-Centered Project, Greater St. Paul Community Chest and Councils.

Pecora, P. J., Delewski, C. H., Booth, C., Haapala, D. A., & Kinney, J. M. (1985). Home-based family-centered services: The impact of training on worker attitudes. *Child Welfare, 64* (5), 529–40.

Pecora, P. J., Fraser, M. W., & Haapala, D. H. (1991). Intensive, home-based family preservation services: Client outcomes and issues for program design. In K. Wells & D. E. Biegel (Eds.), *Family preservation services: Research and evaluation.* Newbury Park, CA: Sage.

Pecora, P. J., Fraser, M. W., Nelson, K., McCroskey, J., & Meezan, W. (1995). *Evaluating Family-Based Services.* New York: Aldine De Gruyter.

Pecora, P. J., Whittaker, J. K., Maluccio, A. N., & Barth, R. P. (with R. Plotnick) (2000). *The child welfare challenge* (2nd ed.). Hawthorne, NY: Aldine de Gruyter.

Pine, B. A. (1986). Child welfare reform and the political process. *Social Service Review, 60* (3), 339–59.

Polansky, N. A., Ammons, P. W., & Weathersby, B. L. (1983). Is there an American standard of child care? *Social Work, 28,* 341–46.

Polansky, N. A., Gaudin, J. M. Jr., & Kilpatrick, A. C. (1992). Family radicals. *Children and Youth Services Review, 14,* 19–26

Reed, K. B., & Kirk, R. S. (1998). Intensive family preservation services: A long short history but a long past. *Family Preservation Journal, 3* (1), 41–58.

Rossi, P. H. (1992a). Assessing family preservation programs. *Children and Youth Services Review, 14* (1, 2), 77–97.

Rossi, P. H. (1992b). Strategies for evaluation. *Children and Youth Services Review, 14* (1, 2), 167–91.

Rzepnicki, T. L. (1987). Recidivism of foster children returned to their own homes: A review and new directions for research. *Social Service Review, 61* (1), 56–70.

Satir, V. (1983). *Conjoint family therapy.* Palo Alto, CA: Science and Behavior Books.

Schuerman, J. R., Rzepnicki, T. L., & Littell, J. H. (1991). From Chicago to Little Egypt: Lessons from an evaluation of a family preservation program. In K. Wells & D. E. Biegel (Eds.), *Family preservation services: Research and evaluation.* Newbury Park, CA: Sage.

Schuerman, J. R., Rzepnicki, T. L., Littell, J. H., & Chak, A. (1993). *Evaluation of the Illinois Family First placement prevention program: Final report.* Chicago, IL: University of Chicago, Chapin Hall Center for Children.

Stein, T. J. (1985). Projects to prevent out-of-home placement. *Children and Youth Services Review, 7* (2, 3), 109–22.

Sullivan, M., Spasser, M., & Penner, G. L. (1977). *Bowen Center project for abused and neglected children: Report of a demonstration in protective services*. Washington, DC: U.S. Department of Health, Education, and Welfare.

Tatara, T. (1992). *National child substitute care flow data for FY91 and current trends in the state child substitute care populations* (VCIS Research Notes No. 7). Washington, DC: Voluntary Cooperative Information System, American Public Welfare Association.

Tatara, T. (1993). *U.S. child substitute care flow data for FY '92 and current trends in the state child substitute care populations* (VCIS Research Notes No. 9). Washington, DC: American Public Welfare Association.

Tatara, T., Morgan, H., & Portner, H. (1986). SCAN: Providing preventive services in an urban setting. *Children Today, 15* (6), 17–22.

Testa, M. F. (1992). Conditions of risk for substitute care. *Children and Youth Services Review, 14,* 27–36.

Tracy, E. M., Haapala, D. A., Kinney, J. M., & Pecora, P. J. (Eds.). (1991). *Intensive family preservation services: An instructional sourcebook*. Cleveland, OH: Case Western Reserve University, Mandel School of Applied Social Sciences.

U.S. Department of Health and Human Services, Administration for Children and Families, Administration on Children, Youth, and Families, Children's Bureau. (1999). *The AFCARS Report: Current estimates as of January 1999*. Washington, DC: U.S. Government Printing Office.

Van Meter, M. J. S. (1986). An alternative to foster care for victims of child abuse/neglect: A university-based program. *Child Abuse and Neglect, 10* (1), 79–84.

Wald, M. S. (1988). Family preservation: Are we moving too fast? *Public Welfare, 46* (3), 33–38, 46.

Waugh, J. (1997). *Unsentimental reformer: The life of Josephine Shaw Lowell*. Cambridge: Harvard University.

Weissbourd, B., & Kagan, S. L. (1989). Family support programs: Catalysts for change. *American Journal of Orthopsychiatry, 59,* 20–31.

Weiss, H. B. (1993). Home visits: Necessary but not sufficient. *The Future of Children—Home Visiting, 3* (3), 113–28.

Weisz, J. R., Weiss, H. B., & Donenberg, G. R. (1992). The lab versus the clinic: Effects of child and adolescent psychotherapy. *American Psychologist, 47* (12), 1578–85.

Wells, K., & Biegel, D. E. (1991). *Family preservation services: Research and evaluation*. Newbury Park, CA: Sage.

Wells, K., & Freer, R. (1994). Reading between the lines: The case for qualitative research in intensive family preservation services. *Children and Youth Review, 16* (5), 323–78.

Whittaker, J. K. (1991). The leadership challenge in family-based services: Policy, practice, and research. *Families in Society: The Journal of Contemporary Human Services, 72* (5), 294–300.

Whittaker, J. K., Kinney, J., Tracy, E. M., & Booth, C. (Eds.). (1990). *Reaching high-risk families: Intensive family preservation in human services*. New York: Aldine de Gruyter.

Whittaker, J. K., & Maluccio, A. N. (1988). Understanding families in trouble in foster and residential care. In F. Cox, C. Chilman, & E. Nunnally (Eds.), *Families in Trouble: Vol. 5. Variant family forms.* Newbury Park, CA: Sage.

Whittaker, J. K., & Tracy, E. M. (1989). *Social treatment: An introduction to interpersonal helping in social work practice* (2nd ed.). New York: Aldine de Gruyter.

Wolfensberger, W. (1972). *Normalization.* New York: National Institute on Mental Retardation.

Wood, K. M., & Geismar, L. L. (1989). *Families at risk: Treating the multi-problem family.* New York: Spring Street.

Wooden, K. (1976). *Weeping in the playtime of others.* New York: McGraw-Hill.

Wulcyn, F. H., Harden, A., & Goerge, R. M. (1997). *Foster care dynamics, 1983–1984: An update from the multistate foster care data archive.* Chicago, IL: University of Chicago, Chapin Hall Center for Children.

Yale Bush Center in Child Development and Social Policy and Family Resource Coalition. (1983). *Programs to strengthen families: A resource guide.* Chicago, IL: Family Resource Coalition.

Zigler, E., & Black, K. (1989). America's family support movement: Strengths and limitations. *American Journal of Orthopsychiatry, 59,* 6–20.

2 Values and Ethics for Family-Centered Practice

JOHN P. RONNAU

Ironically, family-centered, home-based services are viewed by some as less rigorous than the more "clinical" and traditional approaches (e.g., office-bound contacts). This perception is both inaccurate and fraught with perils for both practitioners and the families they serve. The reality is that family-centered, home-based services are extremely demanding and challenging. They require that workers constantly be on their toes regarding theory, knowledge, and skills for helping families. Among the most challenging issues confronting family-centered workers are boundaries, confidentiality, and safety. Although empowering, mandates to assess and use the family's strengths, build partnerships, and establish an atmosphere of mutuality also add to the complexity of those challenges. A clear understanding and consistent application of values and ethics provide guidance and safeguards for the responsible delivery of home-based services. This chapter will clarify the values and ethics underlying this important mode of practice and consider some of the major implications for their use.

THEORETICAL FOUNDATION

A great deal is said these days about the importance of values. Leading business consultants espouse the importance of being clear about and ad-

hering to the values a company holds (Covey, 1990). Our day-to-day behaviors are determined by what we value—a certain area of the city we
live in; a type of house, clothes, or car; time with our family; safe neighborhoods; friends. For many of us, our values are implicit, operational but
unstated in our daily lives. One can argue the need, or even the desirability,
to be conscious of our values as private citizens, but as paid providers of
human services we have an obligation to be clear about the values that
drive behaviors, agencies, and profession.

According to the *American Heritage Dictionary* (1976), a value is "a
principle, standard, or quality considered worthwhile or desirable." Others
think of values as "a conception of what is preferred" (Chambers, 1986,
p. 20) and "strongly held beliefs about how the world should be, how people
should normally behave, and about preferred conditions of life" (Hepworth
& Larsen, 1993, p. 8). Values are an important topic not only to the human
services but also to people in business (Arria, 1999), religion (Sterba, 1999),
and science (Goodwin 1995; Kassirer, 1998).

Since its inception, social work has been known as a values-based profession (Loewenberg & Dolgoff, 1996). According to the National Association of Social Workers' *Code of Ethics*, "The mission of the social work
profession is rooted in a set of core values. These core values, embraced by
social workers throughout the profession's history, are the foundation of
social work's unique purpose and perspective: service, social justice, dignity and worth of the person, importance of human relationships, integrity,
competence" (NASW, 1996, p. 1). Values and professional ethics are integral to social work practice (Loewenberg & Dolgoff, 1996). Although closely
related, values and ethics are not synonymous: "The difference between
them is that values are concerned with what is *good* and *desirable*, while
ethics deal with what is *right* and *correct*" (Loewenberg & Dolgoff, 1996,
p. 21). To understand and practice family-centered services it is important
to be aware of the values that guide them.

THE IMPACT OF VALUES IN PRACTICE

It's all about values! Ultimately, society's values determine the support
extended to vulnerable populations. A community's values determine how
the homeless, the poor, or persons with disabilities will be accepted and
which opportunities will be extended to them. In America, children under
16 comprise 40 percent of the poor, and estimates of the number of homeless range from 300,000 to more than 3 million (Zastrow & Kirst-Ashman,
1997). On a personal level, the values each of us holds lead us to such
fundamental decisions as what we do for work, with whom we build relationships, and how we spend our free time.

Values are similarly powerful guides for human service workers: "All professions have value preferences that give purpose, meaning, and direction to people who practice them" (Hepworth & Larsen, 1993, p. 8); "values and assumptions mold and shape the delivery of services as thoughts mold actions" (Cole & Duva, 1990, p. 5). Of course, all human service professionals are charged with adhering to agency policies and upholding the laws of the land. But just how those policies and laws are implemented is powerfully affected by what we value. Laws that ensure civil rights, for example, have been on the books in this country for some time but are still enforced selectively and to varying degrees, depending on the region and political climate (Hatchett, 1992). But even though values are subjective and are applied with greater or lesser fervor, they still have a powerful impact on behavior: "Professional values provide a framework for practice" (Zlotnik, 1997, p. 21); "values guide and direct practice" (Compton & Galaway, 1984, p. 9).

EVOLUTION OF VALUES IN FAMILY-CENTERED SERVICES

The important issue of conceptual clarity for family-centered services, dealt with in depth elsewhere in this volume, is not the focus of this chapter. The terms *home-based, family preservation,* and *family-centered services* have been used interchangeably (Cole & Duva, 1990; Nelson & Landsman, 1992). Critics of these approaches point out that there is no single agreed-upon definition of family preservation (Bernard, 1992; Hartman, 1993; Lindsey, 1994). Family preservation has been described as an approach, a model, and a service (Lindsey, 1994; Nelson, 1997). Various authors have argued for each term (Kinney, Haapala, & Booth, 1991; Lloyd & Sallee, 1994; Nelson & Landsman, 1992), and a case can be made for each. Of course, this lack of conceptual uniformity remains a major challenge for evaluators of family-centered programs (Wells & Biegel, 1991). The family-centered intervention being implemented in one site may have several key characteristics that vary from those in another (Nelson, 1990).

Family-centered service is not a professional discipline in and of itself. Family-centered practitioners represent a variety of professions, including social work, counseling, psychology, and education. While there are similarities, the values to which each of these various professional groups subscribe are different. It may be more accurate to think of family-centered services as a rallying point, a common cause around which practitioners from these various groups gather. Perhaps it is the case with all human service endeavors that the values that actually guide the workers' day-to-day actions come from a combination of personal, professional, community, and societal factors. The cluster of values that predominates at any one time may vary with each person. While program designers and evaluators have articulated the philosophy or values believed to underlie particular approaches and models, the reality is that no one definitive set of values guides all family-centered services. This chapter reviews the literature pertaining to prominent family-centered services, models, and approaches in order to determine which statements of philosophy or values consistently appear. It is assumed that those that surfaced with some consistency underlie family-centered services.

HISTORICAL BACKDROP

Family-centered services have seen a phenomenal resurgence in the last decade. While in important ways this approach to working with families is revolutionary and unique, it also has deep historical roots (Nelson & Landsman, 1992; Kaplan & Girard, 1994). In many respects, family preservation takes the best of the old ways, makes some important additions, and repackages it for the needs of today's families.

> The family preservation movement grew out of a number of forerunners: the settlement house movement, research and treatment projects in the 1950s focusing on multiproblem families, Head Start programs, and family systems theory. Family-based services, united by a common philosophy, began in private agencies and were later adapted by public agencies. Federal and state legislation has played a role, too, as have national and state clearinghouses on family-based services. (Kaplan & Girard, 1994, p. 1)

Early and Hawkins (1994) provide a succinct overview of U.S. family policy, which has brought us to the current emphasis on family-centered services:

> Past U.S. policy toward families has aimed at the problem of child maltreatment, seeking to balance the parents' right to privacy and the state's obligation to protect vulnerable children from harm. The policy has evolved from child rescue to child protection, and recently, to family preservation. (p. 310)

The emergence of family-centered services is a significant departure from an attitude toward families in need that has predominated in the past: "What is revolutionary about the family-based services movement is its rejection of a world view which blames families for their failures in child rearing and sees foster care or institutional placement as the best way to save children" (Nelson & Landsman, 1992, p. 3). The motivation and undercurrents for the shift in attitude toward families in distress is an interesting study in itself. This shift is tied in part to the parents' rights and consumers' rights movements. The shift has been significant to "one which sees that families are worth saving, as well as children. Indeed, we have begun to recognize that the best and often the only way to save children is through their families" (Nelson & Landsman, 1992, p. 3). A striking element in the view of families in need is a shift away from a primarily deficit-blaming model to a willingness and even emphasis on assessing and using strengths: "The new model of child welfare differs from the old paradigm in valuing families' strengths and respecting their needs and views, even in the face of serious child maltreatment" (Nelson & Landsman, 1992, p. 3).

Both an indicator of the shift in attitude toward families and a major propelling force in its own right is the Omnibus Budget Reconciliation Act of 1993: "Although many systems have for years reached out to families as well as children, the new legislation encourages a shift in focus at all levels of the system" (Winterfeld, 1994, p. 2). In addition, "the language and intent of the new federal act suggests more broadly applying the values and principles of intensive family preservation, thereby designing an array of services which incorporates the competencies and values of family preservation as appropriate to all families' needs" (Lloyd & Sallee, 1994, p. 3). According to language in the act, the purpose of the legislation is "to promote family strengths and stability, enhance parental functioning, and protect children through funding a capped entitlement to states to provide family support and family preservation services, which the law defines broadly" (Program Instruction, 1994, p. 2). Each state was charged with developing its own specific plan for implementing the act, with a stipulation that the plan be organized around guiding principles or values that are generally accepted in family preservation programs (Early & Hawkins, 1994).

VALUES THAT DIRECT FAMILY-CENTERED SERVICES

While family-centered programs hold many values in common, these programs vary greatly in other characteristics such as auspices, theoretical orientation, target population, caseload size, and duration of services (Landsman & Nelson, 1992). The following paragraph clarifies the important distinction between services (approaches) that are truly "family centered" and those that are simply delivered in the home. There is a keen philosophical difference.

> Family preservation is not just another categorical service; it is a philosophy that is systematically important to all service delivery systems. Adapting a family-based approach requires a profound systemwide philosophical reorientation that begins by reevaluating our philosophy and values concerning families. (Kaplan & Girard, 1994, p. 11)

Cole and Duva further emphasize the distinction:

> They are not just any services, but a distinctive form of family assistance with characteristics that vary dramatically from those ordinarily available now and in the past. At their core is a deeply embedded set of values about families and the nature of help to them. These beliefs shape and sustain the programs. The synergism of values and characteristics results in a powerful and effective service. (Cole & Duva, 1990, pp. 1–2)

It would be difficult to overstate the role values play in the development and delivery of family-centered services: "The most fundamental aspect of family preservation practice is its value base which represents beliefs and ideas about families and how practitioners work with families to optimize functioning" (University of Washington, 1994, p. 1).

Homebuilders, a prominent model of intensive family preservation services, adheres to the following beliefs and values about providing services to families: (a) it is best for children to grow up with their natural families; (b) it is difficult to determine in advance which types of families are "hopeless," and which will benefit from intervention; (c) it is the practitioner's job to instill hope; (d) clients should be considered and treated as colleagues; (e) family members are doing the best they can; and (f) practitioners can do harm as well as good (Kinney, Haapala, Booth, & Leavitt, 1990).

According to Nelson and Landsman (1992), "most family-based programs share the following fundamental assumptions:"

> 1) The family has a powerful influence on children and should be maintained and supported whenever possible; 2) children need continuity and stability in their lives, and most children are better off with their own families; 3) separation has detrimental effects on both parents and children; 4) the first and greatest investment should be in replacement services, and society should be willing to spend at least as much on attempting to keep families together as it does on placement; and 5) time-limited intensive and comprehensive services including therapeutic, concrete and supportive services should be provided in accordance with the needs and priorities of each family. (Nelson & Landsman, 1992, p. 5)

By means of a careful study, which included a sample of nationally prominent practitioners, policymakers, and researchers, the Family Preservation Institute identified a set of values that guides the family preservation approach. Interestingly, while there was a lack of consensus among the respondents as to how family preservation should be defined, there was considerable agreement on the values that guide the approach:

1) The definition of "family" is varied and each family should be approached as a unique system; 2) people of all ages can best develop, with few exceptions, by remaining with their family or relying on them as an important resource; 3) families have the potential to change, and most troubled families want to do so; 4) the dignity and right to privacy of all family members should be respected; 5) the family members themselves are crucial partners in the helping process; 6) the family's ethnic, cultural, religious background, values and communities are important resources to be used in the helping process; and 7) policies at the program, community, state, and national levels should be formulated to strengthen, empower and support families. (Family Preservation Institute, 1996)

Based on his review, Maluccio (1990) has stated that the following values and beliefs guide all family preservation services: (a) focusing on the family as the unit of help or attention; (b) respecting each family's and family member's strengths, potential, natural strivings toward growth, and capacity for change; (c) emphasizing staff members' roles in teaching or helping family members to develop coping and mastery skills, rather than "treating them"; (d) shifting from an illness or deficit orientation to a health/growth orientation in understanding and working with the family; (e) instilling hope and enhancing motivation in family members; (f) regarding clients as colleagues or partners in the helping process; (g) empowering families to "do" for themselves; (h) valuing cultural diversity; and (i) supporting staff members in their efforts to help families (p. 114).

According to Leverington and Bryce (1991), "Home-based family-centered services refer to a way of thinking, which shapes the treatment programs" (p. 52). Among the key program "characteristics" are these: "the family is the focus of service, the family's home is the primary service base, the family therapist maintains a family systems and ecological perspective, and client assessment and services are keyed to needs of the family in its environment, rather than services available in the agency" (p. 52).

Marckworth (1991) contends that "family preservation has a distinctive value base—beliefs and ideas about families and about how practitioners can work with families to help them function as well as possible" (p. 29). The three most important values noted by the author are these: (a) clients are our colleagues, (b) it is our job to instill hope, and (c) people are doing the best they can. Friedman (1991) refers to "key ecological attitudes" that must be adhered to "if family preservation practice is to flourish and become a guiding perspective in human services" (p. 32). These key attitudes are appreciating that families are impacted by large formal and informal social systems, local and national economic and political forces, ethnicity, race, gender, and class, and that how workers are treated by their agencies affects how they, in turn, treat client families.

The preceding lists are a sample of what some of the prominent authors in the field believe family-centered service values to be, but there is no universally agreed-upon list of values (variously referred to as values, principles, and characteristics) that guides family-centered services. Yet certain commonalties show up again and again in the literature. Seven such commonalities, or values, are briefly described below.

Family Plays an Essential Role in Child Development

The value of family in the long-term health and well-being of children is expressed by numerous other proponents of family-centered services (Bryce, 1981; Cole & Duva, 1990; Larsh, Pine, & Maluccio, 1995; Lloyd & Sallee, 1994; Mannes, 1993; Nelson & Landsman, 1992; University of Washington, 1994; Wells & Tracy, 1996; Whittaker & Tracy, 1990; Winterfield, 1994). In a seminal text on family-centered services edited by Bryce and Lloyd (1981), Marvin Bryce articulated one of the movement's underlying values: "The emotional scars perpetrated by the prolonged separation of children from family are deeper and more permanent than those that may develop without placement" (p. 6). Likewise, "families are worth saving, as well as children," and "the best and often the only way to save children is through their families" (Nelson & Landsman, 1992, p. 3). Thus, "supporting families is seen as the best way of promoting children's healthy development" (Administration for Children and Families [ACF], 1994, p. 11), and "the inherent integrity of the family as the primary care systems must be at the core of any kind of social policy development, and there must be built-in safeguards against harm to that system" (Hoffman, 1979, p. 11).

The Family Is Part of a System

The whole family systems perspective acknowledges that neither individual members nor the family itself lives in isolation. Attention must be given throughout assessment and intervention to how family members affect each other and to the total environment in which the family lives (ACF, 1994; Cole & Duva, 1990; Lloyd & Sallee, 1994; Nelson & Landsman, 1992; Whittaker & Tracy, 1990).

Clients Are Colleagues

Conventional approaches to working with families subscribe to a more hierarchical arrangement. The worker is considered the expert, who diagnoses and treats the problem. The family and its members are the patients, who are expected to submit to "examination" and take the "medicine" prescribed to them. In the family preservation or the family-centered approach, the family is the center of the process. The full involvement and cooperation of its members are integral to success of the helping process. Family members are treated as partners during assessment, goal setting, and intervention (ACF, 1994; Bryce, 1981; Kaplan & Girard, 1994; Lloyd & Sallee, 1994; Nelson & Landsman, 1992; University of Washington, 1994).

Strengths Are to Be Emphasized

What has been referred to as a "strengths perspective" (Saleebey, 1992) has gained prominence as a centerpiece of family-centered services. The strengths perspective is akin to the empowerment process, which "seek[s] to reduce the distance between professionals and families by allowing families to choose whether to participate in services, by meeting them on their own ground, and by treating them with respect and courtesy" (Nelson, 1997, p. 108). Workers who use a strengths perspective conscientiously look for positive attributes and abilities in the family, including past successes, talents, skills, relationships (with friends, family, and neighbors), cultural beliefs or ties, and spirituality, any of which may become resources to help meet the family's needs (ACF, 1994; Bryce, 1981; Lloyd & Sallee, 1994; Whittaker & Tracy, 1990).

Home Is the Primary Service Setting

Cole and Duva (1990) state that "family preservation services are premised on a philosophy about the locus of service radically different from tradition: it should be delivered where the family lives" (p. 3). A hallmark of family-centered services has been the place where the bulk of services are delivered. Traditional models require family members to meet workers in their offices on a regular basis. Family-centered workers are expected to conduct business regularly on the family's turf (ACF, 1994; Bryce, 1981; Nelson & Landsman, 1992; Whittaker & Tracy, 1990).

The Family's Needs Determine Services

Programs provide services based on the family members' needs, instead of referring a family member to a service—a parent education class for example—simply because it is available. This value also recognizes that a family may need a range of services as its situation changes over time. Its need for intense crisis-oriented services, for example, may recur over time but with less frequency and intensity as its knowledge and resources increase commensurately (ACF, 1994; Bryce, 1981; Lloyd & Sallee, 1994; Nelson & Landsman, 1992; Whittaker & Tracy, 1990).

The Family and Workers Operate in the Community

This value logically flows from those values requiring the use of a systems perspective and an array of services. Because families do not live in isolation but instead are affected by the environment in which they live, it is important that the worker operate within that context. Resources and barriers in the total community should be assessed and used on the family's behalf (ACF, 1994; Bryce, 1981; Kaplan & Girard, 1994; Whittaker & Tracy, 1990).

It is a good news–bad news scenario. The good news is that family-centered services, or family preservation, is a potentially powerful philosophy that can have a very positive impact on families. In addition, "the most fundamental aspect of family preservation is its value base which represents beliefs and ideas about families and how practitioners work with families to optimize functioning" (University of Washington, 1994, p. 1). But investing in a values-driven approach, one that relies on "vague principles that take on specific meaning—and generate controversy—only as policies and programs flesh them out" (Nelson, 1997, p. 102), is fraught with perils. Values are at best meaningful guides to practice, and at worst they are meaningless. They are subject to interpretation, lacking objective, measurable outcome criteria. How do we know if values are being applied? Is it realistic to expect workers to implement them?

The concept of client-centered management (Rapp & Poertner, 1992) is in keeping with a family-centered approach. Among the four principles of client-centered management put forth by Rapp and Poertner is "creating and maintaining the focus." The authors state, "the organization that performs is the one that has clearly defined its mission, purpose, and performance and commits all its knowledge, resources, and talents to getting it done" (Rapp & Poertner, 1992, p. 19). Values can and should serve as the "mission" for family-centered services and as a framework for practice. The program's policies, characteristics, expectations for workers, and the way families and workers are treated should be consistent with the family-centered values. Of course, fundamental to family-centered values is responsible program design. Being emotionally committed to a program may not be enough to make it successful; indeed, there is much more to creating high-quality and effective programs (Perters & Waterman, 1982; Rino, Poertner, & Rapp, 1989; Weinbach, 1990). According to Rapp and Poertner (1992), client-centered managers produce performance in client outcomes, productivity, resource acquisition, efficiency, and staff morale. But values can and should serve as a centerpiece for family-centered programs, the standards against which programs and behaviors of administrators and workers are measured.

Practitioners of family-centered services stick with this very demanding and challenging work because they are committed: "A not insignificant finding in evaluating family preservation programs is the high morale, enthusiasm, commitment, and conviction on the part of workers, supervisors, and administrators in the programs" (Hartman, 1993, p. 511). While financial compensation is obviously essential, it is probably not the primary motivator that keeps people in this line of work. They do it because they believe in it! The philosophy of the programs fits with their values regarding the importance of families and the ways they should be treated.

The impact on job satisfaction of the fit between employee and program values is an important topic (Rapp & Poertner, 1992) and one well worth thinking about in the context of family-centered programs. Specht and Courtney (1994) call for a renewal of social work's mission "to build a meaning, a purpose, and a sense of obligation for the community" (p. 27). Reamer (1992) states the issue succinctly: "What matters is motive." He urges social work to reclaim its focus on the public good and recognize that its work should "once again resemble a calling," since people enter this field because they care deeply about "matters of social justice—those who are disadvantaged and oppressed, and those who are at risk" (Reamer, 1992, p. 28). If people get in and stay with this line of work because they believe in it (it "fits" for them), then it behooves us to be clear about the values that guide our programs and keep them center stage. It would make sense to monitor and adjust the programs continually so that maximum fit is ensured between programs and worker values. If we do so, the programs, workers, and the families served will all be winners.

The values that are the focus of this chapter are not carved in stone. Each program should determine which values will guide it. That determination should be an ongoing and dynamic process. Value statements written, distributed, and then tossed in a file cabinet never again to see the light of day are a waste of time. They should be reviewed continuously for their fit and suitability to the clients' needs and the program purpose. They should be referred to frequently to the point of posting them in each meeting room and administrator's office. As agency supervisors discuss and consider changes, they should ask, *Are these actions consistent with our values? How much can be compromised and still be true to our values? What barriers has the agency placed in the way of workers fulfilling our values (e.g., unrealistic workloads, too much paperwork, too many meetings)?* As workers meet to discuss the progress of their families, solve problems, and share resources, the values should be looked to (literally) as guides for their practice. *Are we involving the parents as partners in the helping process? Are we focusing on the most important outcomes? Are we maximizing our time with clients, or spending too much of it in meetings with other workers?*

Values by their very nature are ideals. They are standards to be strived for. The reality that some ideals, such as family-centered values, can never be fully realized in all cases is not an excuse for not using them as guides for practice. Nor should failure to always reach the ideal be cause to berate workers. When a plan falls short or a goal is not realized with a family, it is an opportunity to reexamine the system. *For what reasons did we fall short of this value in this situation? Why are we having such difficulty identifying strengths for this family? Why are we not able to establish a collaborative working relationship with the mental health center?* Such questions as these, which reflect family-centered values, can help keep a program focused on values as guides for practice.

Applications, implications, and program characteristics for the seven family-centered services values are presented in the following sections. The impact of each value is discussed in terms of its applications. What would it mean to put the value into practice? Program designers and practitioners of family-centered programs should be realistic and consider the implications of each value. Practical guidelines are presented for what a program that implements the values may look and feel like. The guidelines can be thought of in terms of a checklist of program characteristics.

FAMILY PLAYS AN ESSENTIAL ROLE IN CHILD DEVELOPMENT

Application

Practitioners of family-centered services should begin their work with an understanding and appreciation of the value of "family" to a child. They should realize that those family members are the only family of origin the child will ever have. Whereas in the past there was often a knee-jerk response to remove a child from a troubled family, the system and the workers within it should be very cautious about severing those ties. Other less traumatic and harmful options should be explored first. Then and only then should a child be placed outside his or her family. If removal is necessary it should be done in the least damaging manner, one that maintains the integrity of the family to the greatest extent possible. For example, is a safe and healthy relative placement available? Proximity to family members is important so that visits can be facilitated and feasible.

Implications

The most scathing criticism of family-centered or family preservation services is that children are placed at risk in order to keep a family intact. "Obviously, children should not be taken from their family if it is possible to keep them safe at home. The problem is that the child welfare field has not developed a proven technology which can assure the adequate safety of endangered children" (Lindsey, 1994, p. 279). It is a mistake (and a disservice) to idealize the family, a social structure in which both wonderful and horrific things can happen and that can be used as a vehicle for oppression (Bernard, 1992). No family is perfect, and family-centered services by their very nature deal with the most troubled families. In some cases, children or other members who have been harmed or are at risk must be removed from danger. Family preservation is grossly misrepresented when viewed as an all-or-nothing safety-versus-status-quo proposition (Warsh, Pine, & Maluccio, 1995). According to Lloyd and Sallee (1994), "we believe increased risk to children and families occur when either protection or preservation is emphasized to the exclusion of the other" (p. 3). Child welfare is an immensely challenging and complicated field. We must continue efforts to improve assessment procedures, especially in the area of risk. Protecting children and other vulnerable members has been and always will be the first priority of family-centered services.

Program Characteristics

□ Administrators and workers will be well versed on the importance of family to child development (literature, ongoing inservice training).

□ A "bias" will be introduced and reinforced that families are worth the effort, that most parents want to do what's right most of the time.

□ Family members are included on the program's "board of directors" and are consulted regarding program design and monitoring issues.

THE FAMILY IS PART OF A SYSTEM

Applications

The application of systems frameworks in family-centered services has far-reaching implications, one of the most obvious being that it would be inappropriate and poor practice to work with only one member of the family. "Families are systems. Any particular family is composed of a number of individuals, the elements making up the system. Each individual has a unique relationship with the other individuals in the family" (Zastrow & Kirst-Ashman, 1997, p. 151). No person, especially a child, lives in isolation, unaffected by the surrounding people and systems. Families become involved in family-centered services because they have needs or problems. The people and systems that are involved to help the family should depend upon their impact (are they a resource or barrier?) and the needs of the client system. In order to assist a child at risk, for example, the child's parents, siblings, grandparents, other extended family, neighbors, friends, church members, and other people involved with the family may be included in the helping process. Invariably, especially when the needs are great, multiple systems (health, schools, juvenile justice, mental health) will be enlisted to meet the family's needs. Each of these systems (within the larger community system) may operate under different policies and values. Systems concepts like homeostasis, boundaries, subsystems, and equifinality (Zastrow & Kirst-Ashman, 1997) can help workers make sense of complicated situations and arrive at useful interventions. A major benefit of a systems perspective is an assessment process that takes into account the environment in which the family lives. Sometimes the family is not the problem. Perhaps an unreasonable landlord, substandard housing, threat of violence, or a reluctant school system may be barriers to the family's ability to meet its needs. If so, change efforts should be focused on the environment, not only on the family.

Implications

A downside of the systems perspective is that it's messy. If everything is a part of everything else and each is affected by the other, where do you focus your efforts? The number of people involved on behalf of a family can quickly become unwieldy.

Use of a systems perspective raises concerns for confidentiality. As more and more agencies are involved, more and more people have access to very private information about the family. A worst-case scenario (which happens all too often) is that members are required to repeat their intimate stories over and over as they apply for additional services.

Program Characteristics

- ☐ Practitioners will be recruited from disciplines that subscribe to a systems framework or provide in-service training.
- ☐ Workers will be knowledgeable and skilled in coordination of services.

CLIENTS ARE COLLEAGUES

Applications

The family members receiving services are neither abstract numbers nor patients. They are not passive onlookers. They are full partners in the helping process, with all the rights, privileges, and responsibilities thereof. The worker is obligated to reach out to the family members, involve them, solicit their opinions, and respect their wishes. Workers must be willing and able to give up the "expert" role and share power with their clients. They must be willing to invest the time and energy needed to train and equip family members to be fully involved in the helping process. Workers must also not be put off by less-than-enthusiastic initial responses, since many family members are not accustomed to being involved and may lack the skills for becoming so. Furthermore, too many parents are used to being blamed and criticized by professionals. It will take time to build trust.

Implications

Treating clients as colleagues makes a difficult and time-consuming process even more trying. Asking for opinions and allowing clients a voice in deciding goals and priorities can result in false starts and wrong directions. The best case is that these beginnings become learning opportunities, but they are still a use of precious time.

Program Characteristics

- ☐ Workers should be hired who have a predisposition to respect clients, a willingness to involve them, and the patience to do so.
- ☐ Workers must be able to relinquish the expert role and share power with their clients.
- ☐ Supervisors must treat workers as colleagues, respecting them as sensitive, knowledgeable, skilled, and valued members of the team.

STRENGTHS ARE TO BE EMPHASIZED

Applications

In the past, more traditional approaches to practice have made use of a deficit model. A great deal of the worker's energy was put into finding problems, naming what the client did wrong, and then trying to fix those problems. This approach tended toward a blaming posture or deficit model. The strength perspective is a very different way of looking at the world. The worker spends as much or more energy assessing strengths in the family as he or she does finding problems. Strengths are defined in an encompassing manner to include talents, skills, hobbies, fulfilling responsibilities as a parent, dreams, and aspirations. They also include relationships with friends, neighbors, and extended family. Workers using a strength perspective are especially careful to learn about the family's past successes—for example, if any family members have graduated from school, completed a training course, or served in the military. A key strength to be explored is the family's culture, including art, music, religious affiliations, spiritual beliefs, rituals, and ethnic identity. All these strengths may become resources to help meet the family's needs.

Implications

Many of the families involved in the child welfare system are experiencing multiple problems across multiple generations, such as substance abuse, physical abuse, and neglect (Lindsay, 1994; McDonald, 1994). Some researchers go so far as to use the disparaging term "family fragments" to refer to "the mother-child groupings that are forever moving in and out of combination with boyfriends, aunts, cousins, and grandmothers" (McDonald, 1994, p. 50). Workers may have a difficult time even engaging these families in the process, let alone seeing their strengths. Practicing from a strength perspective is not as easy as it sounds. It requires skill, practice, and perseverance. The challenge is further complicated because for many family members the concept of strengths is very foreign. They are not accustomed to thinking about what they do right; they are used to being criticized and blamed. Workers conducting a strengths assessment may be met with doubt, disbelief, or even hostility.

Program Characteristics

- Assessment tools emphasize looking for strengths.
- Administrators and supervisors use a strengths approach with workers.
- Client loads are manageable so that workers are not overwhelmed.
- Group supervision or team meetings provide a supportive and resource-sharing environment for workers.
- Expectations for program outcomes are reasonable and are clearly communicated.

HOME IS THE PRIMARY SERVICE SETTING

Applications

The family-centered approach does not preclude meeting with family members in the office, but work should be conducted where it will be most effective and useful for the family, and in most cases that will be in the family's home. There are many advantages to conducting the work within the family's context (community, neighborhood, home). Assessments are more thorough and accurate. The worker can see parents interact with their children in the real-life setting. Family members are usually more comfortable and at ease in their home; thus the helping relationship may be established more quickly and work speeded up. The worker is also sending subtle but important messages to clients by his or her willingness to meet on the family's turf. He or she expresses a willingness to share power, spend the time and energy to reach out, and experience the real world in which the family lives.

Implications

Professional boundaries and ethical issues mushroom in number, complexity, and severity: it is more difficult to establish and clarify roles; parents who may be needy and vulnerable may more easily misinterpret kindness as romantic affection; and the family's right to privacy is in even greater jeopardy when workers enter the home (Levenstein, 1981). In addition, issues of confidentiality multiply because the worker will see and hear much more about the family's life when in the home, and safety issues arise for the worker both in the home and on the way there.

Program Characteristics

- □ Client loads are manageable to allow for home visits.
- □ Adequate training and consultation allow workers to manage boundary issues.
- □ Safety plans for workers must be developed, implemented, and reviewed.

THE FAMILY'S NEEDS DETERMINE SERVICES

Applications

One of the major shortcomings of the traditional approach to working with families is that services are categorical. In order for a family to get the help it needs, a different door must be entered for each service. Typically, the keys for entering each door are different. Eligibility criteria and agency policies may be very dissimilar from program to program. Consequently, the family must go here, there, and everywhere. Equally troubling is the one-size-fits-all notion of the more traditional family services. For example, in such approaches every family is enrolled in parenting classes and therapy, whether the family needs them or not, simply because that is what's available.

The concept of an "array of services" is used in family-centered services because the family's needs may be varied and complex (Lloyd & Sallee, 1994). The package of services provided to the family should be designed to fit its needs. This package must be flexible, since the family's needs will change over time. Because the service needs of family members will cut across many different systems, coordination and collaboration are essential. If the services a family needs don't exist, they should be created. Informal, naturally occurring services should be used first and whenever possible. Again, if they do not exist, they should be created.

Implications

The reality is that most communities lack needed services. There may be deficits in many areas, or existing services may be financially out of reach. Creating and making use of informal services is very time consuming. Service coordination becomes a mammoth task. There is a danger of overburdening the family with involvement in multiple services. Turf issues between agencies may create barriers and additional problems for workers and families.

Program Characteristics

- ☐ Workers are knowledgeable and skilled in coordination of services.
- ☐ Workers are highly skilled in assessment.
- ☐ Agency is committed to collaboration with other agencies on behalf of the families served.
- ☐ Use of group supervision and teamwork encourages resource sharing.

THE FAMILY AND WORKERS OPERATE IN THE COMMUNITY

Applications

Families live in neighborhoods. Neighborhoods exist within communities. It is at best inefficient and at worst irresponsible to work with the family in isolation from its community. While the community may at times present barriers, more often it is a source of potential resources. Volunteers, neighbors, service groups, and churches are but a few of the resources that may be mobilized to meet a family's needs. The family lives in the community, so solutions to its problems must be not only user-friendly but also community-friendly if they are to be effective and long lasting.

Implications

The community is a big place. Workers often have their hands full just meeting with the family, let alone trying to coordinate multiple services. Trying to operate across the community may be overwhelming. Collaboration is great in theory but a challenge to implement, especially in times of shrinking resources and the managed care environment.

Program Characteristics

- ☐ Workers are knowledgeable and skilled in coordination of services.
- ☐ Agency is committed to collaboration with other agencies on behalf of the families served.

Family-centered practice is a different way of working with families. It keeps the family the center of focus, attention, and activity during all phases of the helping process. Implementing a family-centered model requires adherance to a set of values. These values have far-reaching implications for the way families are treated. Family-centered programs should be diligent in their assessment of the extent to which these key values are incorporated during design, implementation, and evaluation. Implementing family-centered values is a real challenge, but one with substantial payoffs for the families being served and the workers who practice them.

REFERENCES

Administration for Children and Families. (1994). *Program Instruction* (DHHS Publication No. ACYF-PI-94-01). Washington, DC: U.S. Government Printing Office.

Arria, D. (1999, May 24). Ethics and entrepreneurs: Amid high-tech complexity, business values—as well as the public perception of the entrepreneurial role in society—need to undergo a radical change. *Time International, 153* (120), 70–71.

Bernard, L. D. (1992). The dark side of family preservation. *Affilia, 7* (2), 156–59.

Bryce, M. (1981). Home-based family-centered care: Problems and perspectives. In M. Bryce & J. C. Lloyd (Eds.), *Treating families in the home* (pp. 5–11). Springfield, IL: Charles C Thomas.

Chambers, D. E. (1986). *Social policy and social programs.* New York: Macmillan.

Cole, E., & Duva, J. (1990). *Family preservation: An orientation for administrators and practitioners.* Washington, DC: Child Welfare League of America.

Compton, B., & Galaway, B. (1984). *Social work processes.* Chicago: Dorsey Press.

Covey, S. R. (1990). *The seven habits of highly effective people: Restoring the character ethic.* New York: Fireside.

Early, B. P., & Hawkins, M. J. (1994). Opportunity and risks in emerging family policy: An analysis of family preservation legislation. *Children and Youth Services Review, 16* (5, 6), 309–18.

Family Preservation Institute. (1996). *Framework for family preservation.* New Mexico State University, Department of Social Work, Family Preservation Institute.

Friedman, R. S. (1991). Key ecological attitudes and skills. In A. L. Sallee & J. C. Lloyd (Eds.), *Family preservation: Papers from the Institute for Social Work Educators* (pp. 32–36). Riverdale, IL: National Association for Family-Based Services.

Goodwin, J. S. (1995). Culture and medicine: The influence of puritanism on American medical practice. *Perspectives in biology and medicine, 38* (4), 567–77.

Hartman, A. (1993). Family preservation under attack. *Social Work, 38* (5), pp. 509–12.

Hatchett, D. (1992). The future of civil rights in the 21st century. *The Crisis, 99* (1), 10–14.

Hepworth, D. H., & Larsen, J. A. (1993). *Direct social work practice.* Pacific Grove, CA: Brooks/Cole.

Hoffman, G. (1979). Turning ourselves around: A challenge to the professional community on behalf of children and families. In S. Maybanks & M. Bryce (Eds.), *Home-based services for children and families* (pp. 5–12). Springfield, IL: Charles C Thomas.

Kaplan, L., & Girard, J. L. (1994). *Strengthening high-risk families.* New York: Lexington Books.

Kassirer, J. P. (1998). Managing care: Should we adopt a new ethic? [Editorial]. *New England Journal of Medicine, 339* (6), 397–99.

Kinney, J., Haapala, D., & Booth, C. (1991). *Keeping families together.* New York: Aldine de Gruyter.

Kinney, J., Haapala, D., Booth, C., & Leavitt, S. (1990). The Homebuilders Model. In J. K. Whittaker, J. Kinney, E. M. Tracy, & C. Booth (Eds.), *Reaching high-risk families* (pp. 31–64). New York: Walter de Gruyter.

Larsh, R., Pine, B. A., & Maluccio, A. N. (1995). The meaning of family preservation: Shared mission, diverse methods. *Families in Society, 76* (10), 625–27.

Levenstein, P. (1981). Ethical considerations in home-based programs. In M. Bryce & J. C. Lloyd (Eds.), *Treating families in the home* (pp. 222–36). Springfield, IL: Charles C Thomas.

Leverington, J. J., & Bryce, M. (1991). Barriers to the provision of home-based family-centered services in mental health centers. In D. Haapala, V. O. Pina, & C. Sudia (Eds.), *Empowering families: Papers from the Fourth Annual Conference on Family-Based Services* (pp. 51–61). Riverdale, IL: National Association of Family-Based Services.

Lindsey, D. (1994). Family preservation and child protection: Striking a balance. *Children and Youth Services, 16* (5, 6), 279–94.

Lloyd, J. C., & Sallee, A. L. (1994). The challenge and potential of family preservation services in the public child welfare system. *Protecting children, 10* (3), 3–6. Englewood, CO: American Humane Association.

Loewenberg, F. M., & Dolgoff, R. (1996). *Ethical decisions for social work practice.* Itasca, IL: F. E. Peacock.

Maluccio, A. (1990). Family preservation services and the social work practice sequence. In J. K. Whittaker, J. Kinney, E. M. Tracy, & C. Booth (Eds.), *Reaching high-risk families* (pp. 113–26). New York: Walter de Gruyter.

Mannes, M. (1993). Family preservation: A professional reform movement. *Journal of Sociology and Social Welfare, 20* (3), 5–24.

Marckworth, P. (1991). Practice skills and knowledge: View from the field. In A. L. Sallee & J. C. Lloyd (Eds.), *Family preservation: Papers from the Institute for Social Work Educators* (pp. 29–31). Riverdale, IL: National Association for Family-Based Services.

McDonald, H. (1994, Spring). The ideology of "family preservation." *The Public Interest, 115,* 45–60.

National Association of Social Workers. (1996). *NASW Code of Ethics.* Washington, DC: Author.

Nelson, K. E. (1990). Program environment and organization. In. Y. T. Yuan & M. Rivest (Eds.), *Preserving families.* Newbury Park, CA: Sage.

Nelson, K. E. (1997). Family preservation—what is it? *Children and Youth Services Review, 19* (1, 2), 101–18.

Nelson, K. E., & Landsman, M. J. (1992). *Alternative models of family preservation: Family-based services in context.* Springfield, IL: Charles C Thomas.

Peters, T. J., & Waterman, R. H. (1982). *In search of excellence.* New York: Harper and Row.

Rapp, C. A., & Poertner, J. (1992). *Social administration: A client-centered approach.* New York: Longman.

Reamer, F. G. (1992). Social work and the public good: Calling or career? In P. N. Reid & P. R. Popple (Eds.), *The moral purposes of social work* (pp. 11–33). Chicago: Nelson-Hall.

Rino, J. P., Poertner, J., & Rapp, C. (Eds.). (1989). *Managing for service effectiveness in social welfare organizations.* New York: Haworth Press.

Saleebey, D. (1992). *The strengths perspective in social work practice.* New York: Longman.

Specht, H., & Courtney, M. (1994). *Unfaithful angels.* New York: Free Press.

Sterba, J. P. (1999). Reconciling public reason and religious values. *Social theory and practice, 25* (1), 1.

University of Washington. (1994). Family preservation values, skills, and knowledge. University of Washington, School of Social Work, Seattle.

Warsh, R., Pine, B. A., & Maluccio, A. N. (1995). The meaning of family preservation: Shared mission, diverse methods. *Families in Society, 76* (10), 625–27.

Weinbach, R. W. (1990). *The social worker as manager.* New York: Longman.

Wells, K., & Biegel, D. E. (Eds.). (1991). *Family preservation services.* Newbury Park, CA: Sage.

Wells, K., & Tracy, E. (1996). Reorienting intensive family preservation services in relation to public child welfare practice. *Child Welfare, 75* (6), 667–92.

Whittaker, J. K., & Tracy, E. M. (1990). Family preservation services and education for social work practice: Stimulus and response. In J. K. Whittaker, J. Kinney, E. M. Tracy, & C. Booth (Eds.), *Reaching high-risk families* (pp. 1–11). New York: Walter de Gruyter.

Winterfeld, A. (1994). To protect children—focus on families. *Protecting children, 10* (3), 2. Englewood, CO: American Humane Association.

Zastrow, C., & Kirst-Ashman, K. K. (1997). *Understanding human behavior and the social environment.* Chicago: Nelson-Hall.

Zlotnik, J. L. (1997). *Preparing the workforce for family-centered practice: Social work education and public human services partnerships.* Alexandria, VA: Council on Social Work Education.

3

Cultural Competency in Providing Family-Centered Services

Rowena Fong

Diversity in American family life has become complex and challenging. With changing family structure and size, nuclear families have been replaced with blended, same-sex, or multigenerational single parents. In adoption and foster care, many families face dilemmas such as multiple parenting with kinfolk or definitively inaccessible birth parents, as in the case of the People's Republic of China. Okun (1996) reports that "in the past twenty-five years, we have seen the steady increase of varied family type . . . . What is a normal family today?" She observes:

> There has been a significant shift in the nature and composition of families. In the 1950s and 1960s, a family consisted typically of heterosexual parents in a long-term marriage raising their biological children. Since then divorce, remarriage, intermarriage, and different kinds of adoption have become much more prevalent along with openly gay and lesbian relationships, commingling of races, and women's changing roles. (p. 13)

Although variations exist in family composition, size, structure, and norms, the commingling of races continues to challenge practitioners to understand and to be able to work effectively with the diversity between and within ethnic groups. Culturally competent social workers are needed because the census projections continue to predict that families of color in America will make up more than 50 percent of the total population by the year 2050 (McAdoo, 1999). McAdoo also asserts, "Whites of European descent will become a new minority group by then" (p. 207).

Changing demographics affects the social work profession and family-centered practice. Although families of color share common problems, such as single parenting, child abuse, neglect, and divorce, the diversity within a single ethnic group mandates a reexamination of culture and its role in problem solving. The future direction in the twenty-first century for family-centered services needs to shift to using cultural values and strengths as the foundation to formulate assessments and to develop interventions. The differences within groups of ethnic families should be recognized as assets derived from cultural values and norms. A systematic approach of infusing cultural values as the guideposts to assessments and interventions is missing. Cultural values have to play a bigger role in determining services to families of color. The biculturalization of interventions, a process of blending Eastern and Western interventions, ought to replace or at least supplement current family-centered services in order to reflect culturally competent social work practice. Culture needs to be more integrative rather than tangential. Leigh (1998) cites culture as a "problem-solving device and a technical tool that facilitates the helping process and should not be viewed as an impediment to it" (p. 30). Cultural values and norms, the core strengths of ethnic families, have yet to be implemented to maximize the appropriateness and effectiveness of culturally competent family-centered services.

This chapter covers the evolution, history, and definitions of culturally competent social work practice. An assessment framework to help assess the minority family for appropriate family-centered services is presented, using cultural strengths as resources. Culturally competent interventions for family-centered services in the context of biculturalization of interventions are discussed. Suggestions for using cultural values as guideposts for service development conclude the chapter, along with some recommendations for future direction.

HISTORY OF CULTURALLY COMPETENT PRACTICE

Within the last fifteen to twenty years, social work as well as other professional disciplines have been concerned with the cultural appropriateness and effectiveness of services offered to ethnically diverse families. The evolution of cultural competency in social work, as evidenced by the plethora of literature, began developing in the early 1980s. Terms dominating the literature were "culture awareness" (Green, 1982), "ethnic sensitive practice" (Devore & Schlesinger, 1981), and "process-stage approach with people of color" (Lum, 1986). The core of the argument was that social workers needed to be aware of their own cultural values in order to understand the culture and norms of their clients.

Affiliated disciplines such as psychology and multicultural counseling (Dana, 1998; Pope-Davis & Coleman, 1997; Sue, Arrendondo, & McDavis, 1995) were also striving to instill knowledge, values, and skills in trained professionals, but with more of an emphasis on understanding culture through competencies. In the field of mental health, a culturally competent system of care known as the Child and Adolescent Service System Program (CASSP) targeted effective services to minority children who were severely emotionally disturbed (Cross, Bazron, Dennis, & Issacs, 1989).

Cross disciplines, such as family studies and family therapy, factored ethnicity into family-centered assessments and interventions (Ho, 1987; McGoldrick, Giordano, & Pearce, 1982, 1996). Interdisciplinary problem areas, such as substance abuse, also focused on culture, as evidenced by the Center for Substance Abuse Prevention (CSAP), which has recently been promoting a Cultural Competence Monograph Series. The eighth installment of this collaborative series was titled *Responding to Pacific Islanders: Culturally Competent Perspectives for Substance Abuse Prevention* (Mokuau, 1998). Other interdisciplinary efforts in cultural competency are in health, social, and human services, as evidenced by the work of Lecca, Quervalu, Nunes, & Gonzales (1998), *Cultural Competency in Health, Social, and Human Services: Directions for the Twenty-first Century.*

The conceptual and definitional development of cultural competency began with cultural awareness and ethnic-sensitive practice in the 1980s. Professionals working with ethnic minority clients were warned to be sensitive to clients' ethnicity, social class, language, norms, customs, and help-seeking ways (Devore and Schlesinger, 1981). According to Devore and Schlesinger (1981, 1996), the ethnic-sensitive social worker was and is concerned with the interaction of ethnicity and social class that affects life's problems and solutions.

Green (1982, 1999), the author of *Culture Awareness in the Human Services,* asserted that ethnic-competent practice involves a knowledge base, professional preparation, interventions, and comparing and understanding culturally different worlds. The emphasis on a social work process approach with people of color was developed by Lum (1986, 1992, 1996, 2000), who advocated that even within a single ethnic group there was diversity. It soon became evident in practice that people of color within an ethnic group were diversified. However, interventions and assessments did not change to reflect this.

According to Lum and Lu (1997) academic curriculum and professional training moved from the focus on ethnic sensitivity and cultural awareness to multiculturalism and competency. In the 1990s the profession of multicultural counseling shifted cultural diversity to a competency-based practice. This made an impact on social work, whose own adoption of multiculturalism and cultural diversity was shifting. The definition of the term *multicultural* was broadened. Culture could be defined from a sociological perspective as ways of living in a society of many groups of people (Gordon, 1978). An anthropological perspective of culture, according to Ogbu (1999) citing Robert Levine, encompassed customary ways of behaving, assumptions underlying the customary ways of behaving, patterns of social relations, and cultural frame of reference (p. 75).

Definitions and purposes of culture as related to the problems of clients infiltrated the field of social work. Lum (1999) reiterated Pinderhugh's point that culture defines "the problem perspective, the expression of the problem, the treatment provider, and the treatment options" (p. 2). Thus the definition of culture was and is not simplistic. Multiculturalism examined the challenges of professionals who were serving clients with multiple cultures to have the skills to integrate all those cultures.

Because of the differing definitions and purposes of culture, the development and translation of the meaning of cultural competency has changed and continues to change. It has evolved from merely sensitivity to mastering skills and attitudes with the awareness of differences. It acknowledges that ethnicity can intersect with gender, race, sexual orientation, and poverty. Culturally competent practice does address effective micro practice, interacting with the client's ethnicity, gender, and sexual orientation and with the mezzo and macro level systems simultaneously. However, most of the focus thus far has been on what practitioners need to know and not enough on how to obtain this knowledge or on what to do with it once obtained. Cultural competency is based on competencies that are a "set of culturally congruent beliefs, attitudes, and policies which make cross cultural work possible" (Cross, Bazron, Dennis, & Issacs, 1989, p. 13). Needed for the future direction of family-centered, culturally competent practice is a new procedure of habitually and systematically including culture as an integrative part of assessments and intervention planning. Culture needs to be discussed and used more consistently as a strength and resource, not merely as another descriptive attribute tangential to practice. This is important in order to achieve culturally competent family-centered practice.

CULTURALLY COMPETENT SOCIAL WORK AND FAMILY-CENTERED PRACTICE

Culturally competent social work practice has many definitions, but it really focuses on two areas: (a) the social worker and his or her knowledge and (b) the skills and training of the social worker to implement culturally appropriate and effective social work assessments and interventions (Congress, 1994; Lum, 1999). Social workers need to be competent, which means having the knowledge, skills, and training needed to work effectively with the different ethnic groups. There is cultural knowledge involved, but culturally competent social work should be more than just learning about norms, customs, and values of the minority groups while imposing Western interventions and methods on the clients. Lynch and Hanson (1998) take the position that in developing cross-cultural competence it is important that the role of professionals as interventionists include the obligation "to work with families to develop interventions that are culturally competent. It is also our obligation to interpret the new (i.e., mainstream) culture to families and help them find ways to negotiate it effectively" (p. xv). Cultural competence means that the social worker knows how to simultaneously assess the problem situation at the micro, mezzo, and macro levels and offer an intervention that will work in a culturally compatible way for the client system.

Culturally competent social work practice with ethnic clients often does not focus on the individual alone, since family systems dominate the major ethnic groups in America. Families of color have within-group diversity that comprises the traditional ethnic groupings of Asian, Hispanic, Native American, and African American clients. Terminology has changed, as evidenced among a growing number of Native Americans (Weaver, 1998; Yellow Bird, 1999) who advocate the recognition of their families and people as Indigenous Peoples and First Nations Peoples. Asians and Pacific Islanders have distinguished themselves with subgroupings, as evidenced in the 2000 census.

Among the Latino population it is generally acknowledged that the term *Hispanic American* is a census derivation, and other terms, such as Latino, are more self-applied identifiers focusing on mainly Cubans, Puerto Ricans, and persons of Mexican origin with others from Central and South America (Hayes-Bautista, 1999; Zuniga, 1998). The within-group diversity is also important to acknowledge in the African American community, among subgroups from Ethiopia, Ghana, Nigeria, Jamaica, and Trinidad.

This range of the diversity of ethnic families is important for culturally competent social workers to understand. In the Asian and Pacific Islander cultures, the literature distinguishes the Asian (Chinese, Japanese, Filipino, Korean), Southeast Asian (Vietnamese, Hmong, Laotian), and Pacific Islander (Tonga, Samoa, Chamorro) families. In Latino families, which are largely Spanish speaking, the largest groupings are of Mexican, Puerto Rican, Cuban, and Central American origin. There may be recent immigrants from Central America who know no English. Asian families have extended family members, and Pacific Islander families have *hanaied* (adopted) family members. Latino families have *compadrazgo* (coparent) family systems of godparent and godchild. This knowledge base of the roots and composition of the different ethnic families may have been made known to practitioners, but in the twenty-first century, family-centered services need to reflect on how this knowledge is actually used in determining and providing services.

In the twenty-first century, family-centered services will have to shift in order to make assessments and interventions congruent with the cultural values and norms of the multiethnic groups existing in the United States. Family-centered social work practice (Hartman & Laird, 1982) "locates the family in the center of the unit of attention; . . . the family system has an environment and must be seen in that context" (p. 4). However, the environments for ethnically diverse families are often assessed in a disparate manner that disregards the integration of family roles, structure, norms and values, relationships, power and authority, and decision making. Case managers or family therapists conduct individual assessments or family assessments in the context of one-dimensional environments, which often focus statically on the mezzo level of functioning rather than all three levels of micro, mezzo, and macro simultaneously. Lynch and Hanson (1998) assert:

> All interactions and interventions take place in a larger sociopolitical context. This context varies from family to family and is powerfully influenced by one's culture, race, language, and economic status. (p. xv)

Variation from family to family is an important factor in determining family-centered services to ethnic families. Lee (1997) describes five types of Asian American families (pp. 11–13):

- Type 1, Traditional—members are born and raised in Asian countries.
- Type 2, Cultural Conflict—members hold different cultural values; strong traditional beliefs clash with more acculturated and Westernized patterns of behavior.
- Type 3, Bicultural—well-acculturated parents are both bicultural and bilingual, familiar with Eastern and Western cultures.
- Type 4, Americanized—parents and children are born in the United States.
- Type 5, Interracial—parents have entered into interracial marriages.

Although Lee (1997) cites these types of Asian American families, other ethnic groups may also have these differential types of families, so practitioners offering family-centered services need to first assess the type of family before proposing treatment plans. By assessing the family type, interventionists will know which family members to include (and how to include them) as supports and resources in family planning, decision making, and implementation of services.

ASSESSING FAMILY-CENTERED SERVICES FOR ETHNIC FAMILIES

To be culturally competent in family-centered services, social workers need to have a lot of information about the family's cultural systems. Important variables to consider are (a) family cultural norms and values, (b) family cultural structure, (c) family cultural roles, (d) family cultural power and authority figures in the family, (e) family composition, and (f) family decision making. The importance of all this information is that it is used to ascertain family strengths and means of empowerment. For example, in Latino families, the *compadrazgo* (coparent) family system includes godparents and godchildren, with social relationships bound by mutual respect and help. Family-centered services need to include these members as strengths and resources. Lynch and Hanson (1998) talk about the cultural continua and mention seven variables to consider: (a) family constellation, (b) interdependence and individuality, (c) nurturance and independence, (d) time, (e) tradition and technology, (f) rights and responsibilities, and (g) harmony and control. These continua reflect the range of strengths to consider with each family system. Traditions are strengths in families and are not used enough in the developing family-centered services.

To include traditions and cultural values in assessing for services is important, especially in the context of using a culturally competent framework. Fong (1997) proposed a person-in-family-in-community (PFC) framework for assessing immigrant Chinese families for social services related to child welfare issues. Although Fong focuses on the Chinese culture, the same principles can be used with other immigrant populations whose family functioning is predicated by the values and norms of traditional culture. The approach presupposes that the client be viewed in contexts of both family and society simultaneously. The context includes assessing the kind of societal environment from which the immigrant family came and to what kind of societal environment the family is trying to adapt. The simultaneous assessment will highlight differences in environments that need to be reconciled.

The PFC assessment framework for family-centered services is built on several premises:

1. The macro level values and norms of the ethnic culture of the immigrant client affect the client's understanding of social systems and services.

2. The nuclear family is not the unit of attention; the primary client/ family system will encompass both nuclear and extended family members.
3. Individual family members are subsumed under roles and responsibilities dictated by gender, sibling order, and language capacity.
4. Cultural norms at the macro level are to be viewed and treated as strengths at the mezzo and micro levels.

The PFC framework poses assessment questions in the following categories:

1. Society Assessment
   a. What kind of societal background dominates the family?
   b. Is the family from a society with a conservative, moderate, or liberal philosophical stance on politics and family matters?
   c. What kinds of family-centered services are available in its cultural society?
   d. What is the societal stance on family problems and family services?
   e. What cultural values are promoted by the larger ethnic society and how can they be used as strengths?
2. Community Assessment
   a. To what extent do the family members associate with their ethnic community?
   b. What services are available to families in the community?
   c. What protocols need to be followed in order to obtain those services?
   d. What barriers due to community pressure might there be to families trying to obtain family-centered services?
3. Organizations
   a. How do family associations supplement family-centered services?
   b. How do family-centered organizations complement or compete with one another?
   c. What cultural protocols are expected to be followed in these organizations?
4. Family
   a. How does the culture define family?
   b. What are the spoken and unspoken roles of family members?
   c. Who in the family will support family-centered services?
   d. Who in the family will oppose family-centered services?
   e. What resistant factors (perhaps based on cultural norms) are operating to hinder family-centered services?

5. Groups Within the Family
   a. Are there subgroupings within the nuclear or extended family systems?
   b. Who are the leaders of the subgroupings?
   c. How are the subgroupings organized?
   d. Do the subgroupings support or resist family-centered services?
   e. What do the subgroupings stand to gain and lose by participating in family-centered services?
6. Individual
   a. Is there an individual who does not feel a part of the family and is reluctant to participate in family-centered services?
   b. Will individual members be able to join with the family therapist/facilitator when family-centered services are provided?
   c. Will there be barriers for individuals due to gender, roles, status, age?

Culturally competent assessments need to reflect the values and strengths in conjunction with the barriers of the client's culture. Those values are to be used as strengths and converted to resources. The process of converting strengths to resources is outlined in the following four steps.

1. The social worker is to know the values and norms of the culture so that they can be held as a comparison when the problem area is assessed.
2. The social worker is to critically analyze to ascertain if those values are upheld by the family and play any critical role in the family's functioning.
3. The social worker is to use the cultural values as functional strengths, resources, and supports in intervention planning.
4. The intervention must be congruent with the cultural values in order for the values to be used as resources.

Several assessment activities are related to culturally competent family-centered services:

1. Acknowledging the different family types reflecting immigrant or acculturative status
2. Identifying and targeting the cultural values and norms at the macro level that are important to the family
3. Using a person-in-family-in-community framework to assess the kinds of family-centered services necessary and acceptable to the ethnic family

These assessments are to be integrated into the interventions and treatments planned for the families.

PLANNING CULTURALLY COMPETENT
FAMILY-CENTERED SERVICES

Culturally competent interventions for family-centered services should reflect those interventions indigenous to the family's cultural system as well as those interventions derived from Western models. Fong, Boyd, and Browne (1999) write about the biculturalization of interventions, a process of using a Western model combined with a family-centered practice model based on the strengths of the family's culture. This biculturalization of intervention is the process of integrating the values and beliefs of a westernized intervention and an indigenous one in order to modify services to successfully serve minority clients. This is an empowerment approach for social workers working with clients from traditional cultures. The steps in the process are as follows:

1. Identify the important values in the ethnic culture that can be used to reinforce the therapeutic interventions.
2. Choose a Western intervention whose theoretical framework and values are compatible with the ethnic cultural values of the family client system.
3. Analyze an indigenous intervention familiar to the ethnic client system in order to analyze what techniques can be reinforced and integrated into a Western intervention.
4. Develop a framework and approach that integrates the values and techniques of the ethnic culture and both the indigenous and Western interventions.
5. Apply the Western intervention by explaining the techniques and reiterating to the family client system how to support the techniques and reinforce cultural values and support indigenous interventions.

An example of the biculturalization of interventions in the child welfare system is Hawaii's *'ohana* conference model (Livingston, Slaten, & Tochiki, 1997). To reduce out-of-home placements, the Department of Human Services in Hawaii has created a diversion project for public child welfare clients to receive help in planning services in order to avoid the legal system removing the child from the home. The model is based on the Hawaiian cultural family value *'ohana* and involves ten steps (Livingston, Slaten, & Tochiki, 1997):

1. *Welcome.* The family session begins with a formal welcoming and family-directed prayer (*pule*).
2. *Introduction.* The participants introduce themselves and identify their relationship to the family.
3. *Project description.* The history of *'ohana* conferencing is presented to the family members and confidentiality is discussed.

4. *Purpose.* The child protective service worker presents his or her purposes for the conferencing.
5. *Goals for the children.* The family members discuss what they want for the children as decisions are made.
6. *Concerns.* The concerns for the parents and children are discussed. Long-term consequences are mentioned, and the Department of Human Services and the family court timelines are presented.
7. *Resources.* Family resources in the neighborhood, community, and social service agencies are discussed. Limits to the family's decision making are raised.
8. *Family time.* Food and drinks are offered as the decisions are made. No limits are placed on time.
9. *Agreement.* Options and negotiation happen, and foster home licensing is discussed.
10. *Closure.* Hugs and handshakes occur, as well as a closing prayer.

'Ohana conferencing includes professionals and family members, and it follows a Hawaiian style of offering services. In determining and offering culturally competent services, practitioners must factor in several principles. Because of the complexities of families and the wider recognition that family systems are multicultural, it is important to incorporate cultural values as resources and guides to set up treatment plans and implement interventions.

CULTURAL VALUES AS GUIDEPOSTS TO SERVICE DEVELOPMENT

Although cultural values are the mainstay of cultures, ethnic families selectively designate those values that underpin their family functioning. In any culture, a culturally competent practitioner should be trained to take the cultural values as strengths and systematically incorporate them into the practice guidelines for service development. For example, achievement and education are highly regarded in the Chinese culture. In developing services for traditional Chinese families, practitioners should realize that some parents may feel more comfortable supporting interventions that are educational or follow a didactic model. Family support services that emphasize sharing feelings and venting may not be respected or welcomed as the intervention of choice by some of those families because the educational component is perceived as emotional and not cognitive.

In Latino families, Zuniga (1998) writes, parent-child relationships are more highly valued than are marital relationships. In determining family services, one might assume that the marital relationship takes precedence when, indeed, in some Latino families the parent-child relationship may take priority. If parents were determining service plans and prioritized treatment for the child and the social workers thought the marital relationship should have the primary focus, the services might not be as effective or reflect cultural competency.

Petr (1996) discusses the integration of the strengths perspective into family-centered services and defines family-centered practice as

> family-centered service delivery, across disciplines and settings, recognizing the centrality of family in the lives of individuals. It is guided by fully informed choice made by the family and focuses upon the strengths and capabilities of these families. The three core elements of family-centered practice: family as the unit of attention, informed choice, and strengths perspective. (p. 43)

In providing culturally competent practice to families of color, the family as the unit of attention, the definition of family, and the type of family are determined simultaneously in assessments and in intervention planning. In Asian and Pacific Islander families, there are the extended family members and also *hanaied* (adopted) family members. Both need to be considered in the planning and implementing of family-centered services.

In summary, it is important for professionals to be sensitive to and competent in working with the diverse family populations projected for the twenty-first century. The evolution of culturally competent practice reflects society's changes in the last fifteen years. Family types and composition are diversified, challenging family-centered services to identify the significant family members to be included in planning. Cultural values are underutilized and need to play a bigger role to foster family strengths and facilitate resources in treatment planning. Interventions with philosophies and goals contradictory to indigenous and traditional societal and cultural values can no longer be imposed on clients. Indigenous interventions and Western interventions should supplant the method of using interventions that do not blend the two environments of the ethnic client. A biculturalization of interventions needs to become the modus operandi in delivering family-centered services to families of color. Family-centered services provided to these various families must be accessible, available, and accommodating to norms and values of each specific ethnic group, a challenging goal for practitioners entering the twenty-first century.

REFERENCES

Congress, E. (1994). The use of culturagrams to assess and empower culturally diverse families. *Families in Society, 75,* 531–39.

Cross, T., Bazron, B., Dennis, K., & Issacs, M. (1989). *Towards a culturally competent system of care.* Washington, DC: CAASP Technical Assistance Center.

Dana, R. (1998). *Understanding cultural identity in intervention and assessment*. Thousand Oaks, CA: Sage.

Devore, W., & Schlesinger, E. (1996). *Ethnic-sensitive social work practice*. Boston: Allyn and Bacon.

Fong, R. (1997). Child welfare practices with Chinese families: Assessment issues for immigrants from the People's Republic of China. *Journal of Family Social Work, 2* (1), 33–48.

Fong, R., Boyd, C., & Browne, C. (1999). The Gandhi technique: A biculturalization approach for empowering Asian and Pacific Islander families. *Journal of Multicultural Social Work, 7* (1, 2), 95–110.

Gordan, M. (1978). *Human nature, class, and ethnicity*. New York: Oxford University Press.

Green, J. (1999). *Cultural awareness in the human services*. (3rd ed.). Boston: Allyn and Bacon.

Hartman, A., & Laird, J. (1982). *Family-centered social work practice*. New York: Free Press.

Hayes-Bautista, D. (1999). *Changing demographics and the new millenium: Implications for culturally competent social work training*. Paper presented at the Annual Program Meeting of the Council of Social Work Education, San Francisco.

Ho, M. (1987). *Family therapy with ethnic minorities*. Newbury Park, NY: Sage.

Lecca, P., Quervalu, I., Nunes, J., & Gonzales, H. (1998). *Cultural competency in health, social, and human services*. New York: Garland.

Lee, E. (Ed.). (1997). *Working with Asian Americans*. New York: Guilford Press.

Leigh, J. (1998). *Communicating for cultural competence*. Boston: Allyn and Bacon.

Livingston, A., Slaten, D., & Tochiki, L. (1997). *'Ohana conferencing: Final report*. Honolulu, HI: Department of Human Services.

Lum, D. (1999). *Culturally competent practice*. Pacific Grove, CA: Brooks/Cole.

Lum, D. (2000). *Social work practice and people of color*. Belmont, CA: Brooks/Cole.

Lum, D., & Lu, E. (1997). *Developing cultural competency within a culturally-sensitive environment*. Paper presented at the Annual Program Meeting of the Council of Social Work Education, Chicago.

Lynch, E., & Hanson, M. (1998). *Developing cross-cultural competence* (2nd ed.). Baltimore: Paul Brookes.

McGoldrick, M., Giordano, J., & Pearce, J. (Eds.). (1996). *Ethnicity and family therapy*. New York: Guilford Press.

Mokuau, N. (Ed). (1998). *Responding to Pacific Islanders: Culturally competent perspectives for substance abuse prevention* (CSAP Cultural Competence Series No. 8). Washington, DC: U.S. Department of Health and Human Services.

Okun, B. (1996). *Understanding diverse families*. New York: Guilford Press.

Petr, C. (1996). *Social work with children and families*. New York: Oxford University Press.

Pope-Davis, D., & Coleman, H. (Eds.). (1997). *Multicultural counseling competencies: Assessment, education and training, and supervision.* Thousand Oaks, CA: Sage.

Sue, D., Arredondo, P., & McDavis, R. (1995). Multicultural counseling competencies and standards: A call to the profession. App. 3. In J. G. Ponterotto, J. M. Casas, L. A. Suzuki, & C. M. Alexander (Eds.), *Handbook of multicultural counseling* (pp. 624–40). Thousand Oaks, CA: Sage.

Weaver, H. (1998). Indigenous people in a multicultural society: Unique issues for human services. *Social Work, 43* (3), 203–11.

Yellow Bird, M. (1999). What we want to be called: Indigenous peoples' perspectives on racial and ethnic identity labels. *American Indian Quarterly, 23,* 1–22.

Zuniga, M. (1998). Families with Latino roots. In E. Lynch & M. Hanson (Eds.), *Developing cross-cultural competence* (2nd ed., pp. 209–50). Baltimore: Paul Brookes.

4 | A Conceptual Framework for Family-Centered Services

Elaine Walton

The welfare of children is a complex issue. Removing a child from an abusive or neglectful home may be an appropriate short-term solution. However, one must consider the long-term consequences of the disruption in the child's life and the fact that children are likely to feel closely bonded to parents in spite of abuse or neglect. So in addition to the temporary solution of protecting children from a harmful environment, child welfare workers are faced with the responsibility of changing that environment to ensure long-term protection. Parents may need help in learning more effective forms of discipline and ways to organize the family, and there may be serious problems such as unemployment or drugs and alcohol that parents have not been able to solve by themselves. In order to function adequately and provide a nurturing environment, families often need help in a variety of dimensions. Family-centered services in the child welfare arena should be flexible and comprehensive, and should incorporate treatment plans that reflect the unique strengths, resources, and needs of the family. Consequently, a theoretical framework for conceptualizing family-centered services may not look like a single model for intervention but rather the summary of a plethora of social work theories and models.

The framework for treating families in the child welfare system, as conceptualized in this chapter, consists of a variety of theories, models, and perspectives integrated within five major typologies: (a) family systems theory, (b) ecological theory, (c) social work models, (d) strength-based perspective, and (e) empowerment theory. These theories are intended to be integrated as needed in working with populations at risk in the context of a service array, from prevention of child abuse to family support to intensive in-home family support to intensive in-home family services.

FAMILY SYSTEMS THEORY

The idea of focusing on the family rather than on an individual within the family is derived from systems theory. Systems theory, as presented by the biologist Bertalanffy (1968) and applied to social interaction by Anderson and Carter (1984), is a paradigm for organizing and assessing a family's environment. Whether regarded as a metatheory, a framework, or a model, systems theory provides a way to view any dynamic process of events, thus helping us understand people, both individually and collectively, in terms of concepts such as structure, boundary, equilibrium, entropy, interaction, dependence of parts, conflict, and input and output of energy (Rodway, 1986). All parts of any system are interrelated, interconnected, and interdependent—dynamic and in a constant state of flux (Andreae, 1996). Systems theory fits the "person-in-situation" concept identified as the base from which the social work profession has developed (Hepworth, Rooney, & Larsen, 1997).

The concept of family therapy evolved out of a recognition of the family as a system. For example, professionals were perplexed when adolescents who improved in the environment of a hospital reverted to mental illness as soon as they returned home; or when one child in a family became ill as another improved (Rhodes, 1986). Regardless of the type of family (e.g., nuclear, single-parent, blended, extended), the family unit functions as a system. Carlson, Sperry, and Lewis (1991) purported that all family therapy approaches are based on a family systems model of therapy and have the following common tenets:

□ The whole is greater than the sum of its parts.
□ Individual parts of a system can be understood only within the context of the whole system.
□ Traditional models of linear cause and effect are replaced by notions of circular, simultaneous, and reciprocal cause and effect.
□ Change in one part of a social system will affect all other parts of that system.

- □ Systems tend to seek homeostasis, or equilibrium. This balance-seeking function serves to maintain stability and sometimes prevents change.
- □ Feedback mechanisms attempt to bring the family back into balance when a family is out of balance, or equilibrium.
- □ Methods used to restore equilibrium (for example, the identified attempts of a patient to solve problems) can become problems themselves.
- □ Interventions from an interpersonal/family systems perspective must focus on relationships within the entire family system rather than on one individual in the family (that is, on the identified patient). (Walsh & McGraw, 1996)

Intergenerational Family Systems

Families are generally viewed as open systems whose members enter and exit over time and thereby alter the boundaries of the family. Therefore, most families are best understood from an intergenerational perspective of interlocking reciprocal and repetitive relationships (Rhodes, 1986).

Murray Bowen (1976), one of the first advocates for using systems theory in working with families, theorized that individual problems are explained in terms of emotional tension related to fusion or differentiation of self within the family. He further theorized that an understanding of the family system requires exploration into the extended family (Bowen, 1976, 1978). His multigenerational model for family therapy led to the use of the genogram as a tool in family therapy (McGoldrick & Gerson, 1985).

Currently, some child welfare workers address issues of abuse and neglect from a multigenerational perspective, extending Bowen's theory beyond history and insight to a more pragmatic, here-and-now application of the genogram (e.g., Walton & Smith, 1998). In this case, the genogram is a visual diagram that documents a host of information and provides insight into intergenerational patterns of problems (e.g., sexual abuse or drug and alcohol abuse), as well as intergenerational patterns for problem solving and potential resources through extended family members (Walton & Smith, 1998).

Communications Theory

Communications theory, in the context of family therapy, is rooted in the work of Virginia Satir (Zastrow, 1992). She focused her systems-oriented approach on treating families in their communication patterns. She believed that "communication is the greatest single factor affecting a person's health and his relationship to others" (Satir, 1972, p. 58), noting that communication among troubled families tends to be vague and indirect. For example, spouses avoid talking with one another about their needs and desires, or they talk to each other through their children, and children are maneuvered into the stressful position of allying with one parent or the other.

In Satir's view, there is a direct correlation between communication and self-esteem—feelings of worthlessness generate incongruity (e.g., the need to act confident to hide low self-esteem). This incongruity leads to misunderstanding and conflict (Satir, 1972).

Satir's goals for family therapy were to enhance self-esteem and improve communication skills. Those goals were judged to have been accomplished when

- family members can complete transactions and check and ask for feedback;
- family members can correctly interpret hostility;
- family members can see how others see them;
- one member can tell other members how he or she manifests him- or herself;
- one member can tell another what he or she hopes, fears, and expects from him or her;
- family members can disagree;
- family members can make choices;
- family members can learn through practice;
- family members can free themselves from harmful effects of past models; and
- family members can give a clear message—that is, be congruent in their behavior, with a minimum of difference between feelings and communication and with a minimum of hidden messages. (Satir, 1983, p. 176)

To accomplish these goals, Satir used a variety of techniques including humor, touch, and various experiential exercises. For example, she might connect each member of the family physically using a rope, position family members in body postures representative of their communication patterns, or ask family members to act out a scene in the life of the family. She might also create a visual representation of the family (similar to a genogram), which she referred to as a map (Carlson et al., 1991).

Child welfare workers involved in helping families often rely on the work of Satir in teaching families practical ways of communicating more effectively. A particularly popular term is "I messages"—a concept for helping family members own and share their feelings directly.

Structural Theory

Structural family therapy, though systemic in theory, includes the assumption that the history of the family is manifest in the present and is therefore accessible through interventions in the here and now. Hence, environmental factors are given priority over hereditary factors, and there is an emphasis on process over content (Carlson et al., 1991).

Salvador Minuchin, a theorist most closely associated with structural family therapy, was a staunch believer in the family systems perspective. In fact, if an individual was referred for therapy due to certain undesirable symptoms, he assumed that the behavior was generated and maintained by the needs of the family as a whole (Zastrow, 1992). His way of addressing those family needs was through restructuring the major subsystems within the family (i.e., spouse, parental, sibling); hence, the label *structural theory* (Zastrow, 1992). Minuchin (1974, 1987) accomplished that restructuring by joining with the family and using family membership to change the structure.

Minuchin's restructuring techniques fall into three categories: (a) boundary making, (b) unbalancing the current dysfunctional family structure, and (c) complementarity (changing perceptions of hierarchical relationships within the family) (Minuchin & Fishman, 1981). He accomplished the restructuring through a variety of spontaneous techniques ranging from direct education to the use of paradoxical suggestion; he often moved family members and himself around physically during the therapy session to enact appropriate and inappropriate subsystem boundaries (Zastrow, 1992).

An example of restructuring is clear in the case of a family with a young girl suffering from hysterical paralysis. After examining the function of the symptom and the various roles of the family members, Minuchin joined with the family in facilitating a restructuring process. First, the father was assigned to replace the mother as caretaker of the paralyzed daughter. Then a crutch took a symbolic parental role, giving the daughter more independence and allowing the spouse subsystem to develop. At one point, the father was assigned to join with the daughter in replicating her symptom (dragging the paralyzed leg). Eventually, it was clear that the function of the paralysis was to enable the parents to lean on the daughter. This young girl had subconsciously convinced herself that her disability would keep her parents together and prevent them from divorce. Therapy, then, became a process of addressing the issues and feelings directly and allowing the parents to "fire" the daughter from her job as protector of the marriage (Minuchin, 1993).

Strategic Theory

One of the first advocates for strategic family therapy was Jay Haley (Zastrow, 1992), an adherent of the family systems approach; however, rather than searching for intrapsychic causes for behavioral symptoms, he looked instead for interpersonal meanings of symptomatic behavior. For example, he viewed symptoms such as illnesses, alcoholism, or phobias as creative means for exerting control in a relationship (Zastrow, 1992). He was convinced that "the motivation of a person's behavior, and the cause of a problem, was not in the past but in the current sequence in which the person was enmeshed" (Haley, 1997, p. 250). Maintaining that it was impossible to explain everything in therapy, he opposed therapy focused on insight (Haley, 1997). Instead, he believed the most efficient way to change the client was to focus on the troubling symptom.

Strategic family therapy, as explained by Cloé Madanes, includes the following features:

- ☐ The responsibility is on the therapist to plan a strategy for solving the client's problems.
- ☐ The therapist sets clear goals, which always include solving the presenting problem.
- ☐ The emphasis is not on a method to be applied to all cases but on designing a strategy for each specific problem.
- ☐ Since the therapy focuses on the social context of human dilemmas, the therapist's task is to design an intervention in the client's social situation. (Madanes, 1981, p. 19)

Interventions usually take the form of directives in which family members are given a task to do. The intent of these directives is to change the pattern of interpersonal interactions in the family (Madanes, 1981). Directives may take many different forms because they are uniquely designed for each problem. They may be straightforward or paradoxical, simple or complex. Madanes's strategies are often metaphorical, playful, and humorous (Madanes, 1987).

An example of a paradoxical directive is seen in the case of a 10-year-old boy whose fire-setting behaviors disturbed his mother. The mother was instructed to set aside a time every evening for a week when she and her son would set fires and put them out together. When the boy unpredictably started fires, he was in a position of power. When he set fires under direction, his mother had the power, and predictably, he lost interest in setting fires (Madanes, 1981).

Another example of a strategic directive is taken from Madanes's sixteen-step model for treating adolescent sex offenders (Madanes, 1990). One of the steps, a strategy for self-forgiveness, is a directive to the offender that every time he has an inappropriate sexual thought, he should do a good deed for someone—preferably anonymously. Guilt would eventually be replaced by self-esteem generated from the good deeds, and the greater the self-esteem, the smaller the chance for reoffending.

Critics of strategic family therapy most frequently point to the superficial nature of the interventions. However, in following the therapist's directive, the young sex offender not only extinguished his inappropriate sexual behavior but also changed his thinking patterns, enhanced his self-esteem, and discovered new and meaningful relationships because of his good deeds. This is an example of Haley's belief that if the therapist can help a family experience positive change, family members will learn from the results of their actions and transfer the learning to an additional system of change (Zastrow, 1992).

Attachment Theory

Bowlby (1982) theorized that human infants have a biological predisposition to develop an attachment relationship with their primary caregiver, and that early relationship leads to the development of an internal working model of self in relation to others that determines the individual's expectations regarding relationships with other significant figures later in life (Bowlby, 1988). Although the model may be modified with new experiences over time, the original model tends to persist and to operate outside of conscious awareness (Bowlby, 1980). In a landmark study James and Joyce Robertson found that infants separated from their parents responded first with protest (crying and clinging), then despair (not eating or being involved in the immediate environment), and then detachment (not seeming to recognize the mother when visited)—also described as *defensive numbing* (Chornesky & Meek, 1997). Upon reunification with the caregiver, there was no immediate evidence of a meaningful connection, but later on the child would cling intensely and appear anxious about losing the caregiver again (Chornesky & Meek, 1997).

Attachment theory has implications for many aspects of psychological and social behavior, but it is particularly relevant for child welfare families (Chornesky & Meek, 1996). Infants with adolescent mothers, socially isolated mothers, or depressed mothers with unresolved mourning issues may be particularly vulnerable, and children in foster care or adoption processes may be greatly affected by issues of separation and loss (Chornesky & Meek, 1996).

Interventions based on attachment concepts will be directed toward developing, enhancing, and maintaining the attachment relationships between primary caregivers and children. In the child welfare arena this implies that priority efforts will be given to (a) prevent unnecessary out-of-home placement, (b) maintain the emotional bond between the child and the primary caregiver when removal occurs, and (c) expedite adoption when permanent placement is necessary and facilitate appropriate mourning and new attachment bonds (Chornesky & Meek, 1996). Effective family-centered practice in child welfare will include both a profound respect for existing attachments and strategies for promoting and strengthening attachments (Chornesky & Meek, 1996).

ECOLOGICAL THEORY

The "person-in-environment" perspective of social work demands that in an effort to help their clients, workers look beyond the individual, or even the family, to the environment. Ecological theory includes a holistic way of viewing the client's world as well as the possibility for intervention at any point along a continuum from micro to macro.

Holistic Approach

The holistic approach expands the systems perspective to include not only the interaction of the individuals within a system and systems with systems but also the total human being with all the accompanying needs. The all-inclusive categories of functioning are generally referred to as biological, psychological, and social, but the categories "cultural" and "spiritual" might also be included. In other words, clients are complex and multidimensional and must be treated as such. Just as the child cannot be treated effectively in isolation from the family, in a similar manner, it is pointless to address only social or psychological issues without considering biological, cultural, and spiritual issues. Consequently, workers must be prepared to help families address issues of health and nutrition, dental and medical problems, as well as their intrapsychic, interpersonal, and systemic functioning. Workers must also be sensitive to cultural and spiritual values and resources.

Ecological Systems Theory

Just as a child's problems are nested within the family system, a family's problems are nested within a larger environment. This system of systems, or social ecology, is a composite of interdependent social systems organized at family, school, community, and institutional levels (Heying, 1985). Through the perspective of social ecology, theorists endeavor to explain the ways in which the various systems accommodate each other within the context of the larger environment (Bronfenbrenner, 1979).

Ecological systems theory, as explained by Germain and Gitterman (1980) in their "life model," is a framework for viewing people as constantly adapting in an interchange with many different aspects of their environment. The development and change of individuals supported by the environment is called *reciprocal adaption*. When the environment breaks down, however, social problems (e.g., poverty and discrimination) reduce the possibility of reciprocal adaption and increase the need for intervention (Payne, 1991).

Bronfenbrenner (1979), an apologist for ecological systems theory, wove an ecological framework around the concepts of parental role, life stressors, and social supports. He argued that child-rearing practices are a function of the interplay between a person and the environment, and he observed:

> Whether parents can perform effectively in their child-rearing roles with the family depends on role demands, stresses, and supports emanating from other settings. . . . Parents' evaluations of their own capacity to function, as well as their view of their child, are related to such external factors as flexibility of job schedules, adequacy of child care arrangements, the presence of friends and neighbors who can help out in large and small emergencies, the quality of health and social services, and neighborhood safety. The availability of supportive settings is, in turn, a function of their existence and frequency in a given culture or subculture. This frequently can be enhanced by the adoption of public policies and practices that create additional settings and societal roles conducive to family life. (Bronfenbrenner, 1979, p. 7)

Garbarino (1982) further emphasized the need for attention to environmental issues:

> Children who grow up wanting for food, for affection, for caring teachers, for good medical care, and for values consistent with intellectual progress and social competence grow up less well than those children who do not lack these things. Their absence places a child "at risk" for impaired development. (Garbarino, 1982, p. 32)

Families involved in the child welfare system are frequently high-risk families with multiple needs that cut across many social systems and dimensions of family life. These families are often all too familiar with the social service system and may have been alienated by workers or labeled as impossible or hopeless (Kaplan & Girard, 1994).

Ecological systems theory underpins the creation, activation, and coordination of a variety of systems-level support strategies to address multiple needs. Although social workers are often involved at the policy-changing level of social issues that arise from their cases, family-centered intervention is most likely to be a process of developing and enhancing a supportive network (Payne, 1991). Ideally, that supportive network may include both soft and hard services and both formal and informal support.

Soft services include counseling and the teaching of various skills. These are explicated under the section headings "Family Systems Theory" and "Social Work Models." The term *hard services* refers to concrete, or tangible, services. Maslow (1954) theorized an innate hierarchy of human needs, and basic needs must be met prior to addressing higher-order needs, such as human growth and potential. Consistent with Maslow's theory, Kinney, Haapala, and Booth (1991) explained: "People . . . don't need communications skills if they're starving to death . . . . Clients need help with basic needs because they will not be able to concentrate on anything else until those needs are met" (1991, p. 105).

The list of concrete services is inexhaustible because the services are intended to fit the specific and unique needs of the family. The most common needs addressed by the Homebuilders Model, as reported by Kinney et al. (1991), were obtaining (a) food, clothing, furniture, and other household items; (b) transportation; (c) housing; (d) employment; (e) utility benefits or services; (f) medical, dental, or legal services; (g) child care; (h) help with house cleaning; and (i) recreational toys and activities.

Some of the concrete services come from community agencies (e.g., food banks, employment services, homemaking services, and day care services). Some of the soft services are also available through community agencies (e.g., youth services, psychiatric and counseling services, parenting classes). These are all examples of formal services—services in the community and usually available for a fee. Having a wide variety of services available is an important part of addressing families' needs. Perhaps more important, however, is the way in which the services are coordinated and delivered. The ecological systems perspective includes the interaction of the providing systems with each other as well as with the family in need. Consequently, in recent years, emphasis has been placed on "wraparound services"—wrapping multiple services around the family in a coordinated effort as specific and unique needs require, rather than finding ways to fit families into predefined service delivery categories (Golden, 1997).

The network of social support systems is strengthened further by including natural (informal) supports (e.g., friends, neighbors, clergy, or extended family members) (Payne, 1991). Some individuals or systems already have a natural or personal interest in the family and need only some direction or coordination to become part of a larger, formal support system. The growing number of kinship foster care placements in the United States is an excellent example of including informal supports in the coordinated network of social support systems. Barth, Courtney, Berrick, and Albert (1994) pointed out that the 49 percent increase in foster care from 1980 to 1992 is less troubling juxtaposed with the "phenomenal growth" of kinship care—now accounting for approximately 40 percent of foster care placements (p. 259).

Families or clients who have roots in a community generally have established helping networks that respond supportively in times of need, and the task of the worker is to identify those support systems and to include them in a coordinated effort (Hepworth et al., 1997). Additional informal supports may be included in the network through involvement with self-help, mutual aid, or support groups (Galinsky & Schopler, 1995). Support groups are a source of emotional support and information on specific issues of concern (e.g., parenting, caregiving, physical and psychiatric illnesses), but they are also valuable as a mechanism for the helpee to become empowered through being the helper as well (Payne, 1991).

In organizing, coordinating, and maintaining the supportive network in the ecological systems perspective, the worker moves from the role of provider of services to the role of intermediary between people. "The aim is interdependence among the client and others rather than the independence of the client. The worker acts as a consultant rather than as a clinician and is empowering rather than being a simple provider of services" (Payne, 1991, p. 147).

SOCIAL WORK MODELS

The social work models of intervention provide a practical structure for various kinds of problem solving. A few of those models are described below.

Crisis Theory

Crisis theory developed out of a need to understand sufferers of loss who had no pathological diagnosis but who exhibited pathological symptoms (Gilliland & James, 1997). Lindemann (1944) helped professionals recognize that responses associated with grief are normal, temporary, and amenable to alleviation through short-term intervention techniques. Crisis has subsequently been defined as "an acute emotional upset in an individual's usual steady state, accompanied by a perceived breakdown in his or her usual coping abilities" (Ell, 1996), and crisis theory has been applied to any number of traumatic events in addition to grief and loss (Gilliland & James, 1997).

Crisis theory has been expanded and explicated through the perspective of many theories including psychoanalytic, systems, adaptational, interpersonal, and ecological. Moreover, it has been broken down into the categories of developmental, situational, and existential crises (Gilliland & James, 1997). All these perspectives, however, share common elements, described as a sequence of events by Parad and Parad:

1. a specific and identifiable stressful precipitating event;
2. the perception of the event as meaningful and threatening;
3. the disorganization or disequilibrium response resulting from the stressful event; and
4. the coping and interventive tasks involved in resolution, which may be adaptive or maladaptive. (Parad & Parad, 1990, p. 5)

The adaptive/maladaptive nature of the resolution is identified as both a danger and an opportunity. In fact, the word *crisis* in the Chinese language is two characters—one translated as "danger" and the other as "opportunity" (Gilliland & James, 1997). Crisis has the potential to bring out the noblest of human traits, and during the crisis state, individuals are motivated and open to the benefits of therapy. At the same time, however, people are also more vulnerable than usual in the crisis state, and in the absence of appropriate coping tasks or intervention, pathological outcomes and psychological damage may result (Ell, 1996).

Intervention in crisis situations is brief and direct. Roberts identified seven stages in the process:

1. Plan and conduct a thorough assessment (including issues of safety).
2. Establish rapport with client.
3. Identify major problems (including the precipitating event that led client to seek help).
4. Deal with feelings and emotions with active listening.
5. Generate and explore alternatives for problem solution.
6. Develop and formulate an action plan.
7. Follow up. (Roberts, 1996, p. 27)

Families in the child welfare system experience a variety of crises stemming from abuse, neglect, delinquent behavior, or family violence. Intervention from family courts, educators, or social services staff may, in fact, be the precipitating event in a family's crisis state (Kagan & Schlosberg, 1989). Moreover, their ways of bringing resolution are frequently maladaptive. Workers trained in crisis intervention can take advantage of the window of opportunity presented by the crisis to effectively help families not only deal with the crisis but make positive, long-lasting changes in the process.

Brief Solution-Focused Approach

Brief solution-focused therapy has been used frequently in the context of crisis intervention. It is being used increasingly, however, as the treatment of choice for families or clients that need to set goals and make changes (O'Hanlon & Weiner-Davis, 1989). It fits particularly well within the model for providing intensive family-centered services because such services are, by definition, brief and solution-oriented.

The solution-focused approach to therapy is a pragmatic way of solving here-and-now problems, as opposed to facilitating insight and understanding based on revisiting problems from the past. Briefly stated, the therapist's mottos are (a) "If it ain't broke, don't fix it"; (b) "Once you know what works, do more of it"; and (c) "If it doesn't work, don't do it again—do something different" (Berg, 1994). The solution-focused approach evolved from a belief that it is easier to construct solutions than to dissolve problems, and that it is also easier to repeat already successful behavior patterns than it is to try to stop or change existing problematic behavior. For example, getting parents to repeat their successful methods of child rearing is easier than trying to teach them totally new and foreign skills. The presumption is that all clients have strengths that can be enhanced or discovered in order to find solutions, and clients are the best judge of what they need and what will work. Through this approach, clients are empowered to take the lead in finding solutions to their problems, and therapy is a process of jointly setting realistic and meaningful short-term goals and objectives, and then systematically achieving those goals.

A favorite technique for Berg (1994) in her solution-focused approach is "the miracle question." Through it she helps clients envision a future in which the presenting problem is solved. The question goes something like this:

> Suppose one night there is a miracle while you are sleeping and the problem that brought you [in for help] is solved. Since you are sleeping, you don't know that a miracle has happened or that your problem is solved. What do you suppose you will notice different the next morning that will tell you that the problem is solved? (Berg, 1994, p. 97)

The purpose of the miracle question is first to help clients get a vision of a future free of the problem, and second, to help clients discover that those changes envisioned in the miracle scenario are most likely within their power to bring about. For example, if clients notice in their miracle scenario that they are smiling, eat breakfast, get to work on time, ask for what they want, and so on, it does not take long to realize that nothing is stopping them from making at least some of those changes now.

This approach may seem rather superficial when considering the needs of families with long-standing and severe problems. However, such families frequently struggle with dysfunction in dealing with day-to-day life problems, and the here-and-now solutions are likely to be a priority for them.

Task-Centered Theory

Task-centered theory fits well with crisis theory and the brief solution-focused approach. It evolved from Perlman's problem-solving model (Payne, 1991) and is generally attributed to the work of William Reid and Laura Epstein (Zastrow, 1992). It is not linked to any particular theory of human functioning or to any fixed set of intervention methods. Instead, it includes a basic core of value premises, theory, and methods that can be augmented by compatible approaches. Fundamental to the model is a focus on client-acknowledged problems through a brief, collaborative, problem-solving approach with a well-defined sequence of planned activities (Reid,

1996). Further, an underlying assumption in the model is that the primary agent of change is the client, not the social worker. The worker's role is to help the client bring about changes the client wishes and is willing to work for (Reid, 1996).

The worker helps the client select appropriate tasks and plan the implementation of the task, including a rehearsal of the plan in some cases as well as an analysis of obstacles that might stand in the way. The worker then reviews the client's accomplishments, provides corrective feedback, and works with the client on developing new tasks (Reid, 1996). In contrast to psychodynamic approaches, the counseling sessions are not intended to provide the essential ingredients of change but to set in motion and guide subsequent actions through which change will be effected (Reid, 1996).

Reid (1996) emphasized the importance of "contextual change" in the planning process. In other words, there should be an effort to focus problem-solving efforts on the context of the targeted problem as opposed to any stress-relieving action. Also, although workers are encouraged to respect clients' rights to manage their own affairs, they may supplement the client's problem-solving efforts by taking responsibility for accomplishing certain tasks related to the client's social system or environment that may be beyond the ability of the client to solve (Reid, 1996). In providing family-centered services, these tasks are differentiated as "client goals" and "service goals."

In working with families, the model is modified somewhat and borrows from behavioral, structural, strategic, and communications models for family therapy (Reid, 1996). Problems are defined in interactional terms, and tasks are reciprocal or undertaken jointly. A primary role for the worker is to deal with family members' varying perceptions and to achieve consensus with regard to definition and priority of the problems (Payne, 1991). In this process, the worker employs "points of leverage," or interactions designed to help change clients' beliefs so that their perceptions are accurate, their scope of the problem is not limited, and their beliefs are consistent (Payne, 1991).

Cognitive-Behavioral Theory

Behavioral family therapists believe that families are influenced solely by their environments. Because behavioral patterns are learned, dysfunctional behaviors can be unlearned and replaced by more adaptive ones (Carlson et al., 1991). Cognitive-behavioral therapists expand that perspective to include the recognition that thoughts influence behavior, and they develop techniques for confronting irrational thinking as well as modifying behavior (Carlson et al., 1991).

Behavioral interventions involve an assessment wherein problem behaviors are inventoried and desired changes (i.e., goals) identified. The behaviors targeted for change are defined in terms of the ABC (antecedents, behavior, and consequences) paradigm. After developing specific goals and contracts (including new consequences) for change, baseline data are obtained, and the target behavior is monitored on an ongoing basis (Thomlison & Thomlison, 1996). Techniques for altering the target behavior include (a) positive reinforcement—rewarding behavior that is desired, (b) negative reinforcement—removing an aversive consequence following the display of the target behavior, (c) punishment—aversive stimulus after a maladaptive behavior, and (d) extinction—removing all reinforcement when the maladaptive behavior is displayed (Hodges, 1994).

Practitioners working with families often find that family members lack specific skills and have difficulty displaying the desired behaviors. Consequently, shaping and modeling are frequently employed in helping family members change. A "shaping" intervention is a way to teach a new behavior by rewarding small steps or approximations of the desired target behavior so that gradual, incremental changes are made in the direction of the desired goal (Hodges, 1994). Modeling is a way to teach a new behavior by demonstrating it. Learning comes through observation and imitation (Hodges, 1994).

Social learning theory (Bandura, 1973) is an example of behavioral theory that incorporates modeling. It is widely used by workers who provide family-centered services. The worker teaches specific skills (e.g., communication, anger management, problem solving, self-control, conflict resolution, parenting) through direct instruction, modeling, and contingency management (Kinney et al., 1991). It is important for the worker to model the skills informally in all worker-client interaction as well as formally as part of the teaching process; and the learning is further reinforced through role-playing, feedback, and homework assignments. Contracts are made for specific behavior changes with corresponding rewards. Moreover, parents are coached in contracting with their children for specific behavior changes and corresponding rewards (Henggeler, Melton, & Smith, 1992).

Generally, in cognitive-behavior theory, not only does the worker assess the functioning of the family on an ongoing basis, but family members are also taught to assess their relationships to each other and to implement the strategies of change in strengthening their relationships. This is essentially a teacher-and-learner model (Carlson et al., 1991).

Teaching strategies focus on enhancing skills such as communication (e.g., "I messages"), decision making (e.g., identifying areas of power and control), conflict management (e.g., recognizing stages of conflict), contracting (e.g., win-win approach to conflict resolution), and cognitive restructuring (e.g., testing the validity of interpretations through collecting and processing data) (Carlson et al., 1991).

The cognitive-behavioral approach to intervention emphasizes learning, as opposed to psychopathology, in assessing and treating families. In contrast to the labeling that many of these families have endured in the past, through this perspective the family's ability to learn and change is viewed with optimism—a necessary companion to the strength-based perspective.

STRENGTH-BASED PERSPECTIVE

Social work educators commonly acknowledge the importance of building on clients' strengths (e.g., Hepworth et al., 1997; Zastrow, 1992). Nevertheless, social work has developed practice principles around the supposition that clients need help because they have deficits (Saleebey, 1992). In large measure, social work has inherited (or borrowed) from the medical model a philosophy that (a) authorizes the professional to define problems and to determine the plan for intervention and (b) marks the relationship between helper and client by distance and inequity. Caseworkers too frequently look for a diagnostic niche while selectively ignoring information supporting the uniqueness of an individual—operating under the assumption that "naming the poison leads us to the antidote . . . . Such linear thinking ignores the steamy morass of uncertainty and complexity that typify human affairs" (Saleebey, 1992, p. 5).

The strength-based perspective is more than an optimistic view of human potential. According to Dennis Saleebey (1992), a leading apologist, it is a practical and relevant way to utilize the most valuable resources available in the helping process:

> Relevance [in the assessment process] does not simply refer to society's investment in, or concern about, the problem, but to the individual client's investment as well. To what extent are clients consulted about matters relevant to them? What do they want? What do they need? How do they think they can get it? How do they see their situation—its troubles as well as its possibilities? What do they see as resources from within and in the environment? What values do they want to maximize? How have they managed to survive so far? (p. 5)

The primary assumptions of the strength-based perspective are as follows:

- Clients have many strengths.
- Clients are respected as the experts on their own situations.
- Client motivation is based on fostering client strengths.
- The worker's role is one of collaborator with the client.
- Any environment is full of resources.

☐ Awareness of strengths helps in avoiding the "victim mindset." (Saleebey, 1992, pp. 6–7)

The strength-based perspective emphasizes empowerment—not "returning power to the people" but discovering the power within the people. Additional key concepts include (a) membership—recognition that all whom we serve are members of the human race and entitled to the dignity, respect, and responsibility that come with such membership; (b) regeneration and healing from within; (c) synergy—resources intrinsically expanding and renewable; (d) dialogue and collaboration—including empathy, identification with, and inclusion of the other person; and (e) suspension of disbelief—giving up "scientific" skepticism (Saleebey, 1992, pp. 8–12).

Commitment to a strengths perspective requires a commitment not only to a set of values but also to a set of skills. The process of respecting and engaging clients' ways of viewing themselves demands openness, flexibility, and creativity—characteristics not easily acquired by workers who rely on specific labels and models with a cookbook approach to intervention. Workers need specific training that sensitizes them to the process of assessing client strengths.

A number of models and tools have been developed to help professionals assess clients' strengths. One example will be provided here. However, the reader is referred to Chapter 5 by Pat Sandau-Beckler, in which she treats the subject of strength-based assessments comprehensively and provides many examples of tools and models.

DeJong and Miller (1995) developed a model for assessing client strengths by borrowing from the solution-focused approach. The model consists of a series of questions that aid in identifying strengths through eliciting from the client exceptions to the presenting problem (i.e., occasions in the client's life when the problem could have occurred but did not) or exceptions to the problem as conceived in a problem-free future (as envisioned through the miracle question). Some examples of these questions are given below.

You said that when the "miracle" happens, you and your husband would notice yourselves "communicating more about your days and hug each other more." Are there times now or in the past when the two of you were able to do that? (DeJong & Miller, 1995, p. 732)

I'm wondering, are there days when you feel less scared about the future? . . . When was the last time you had a better day? What was different about that day that made it better? Where did that happen? Who was there with you? What might [those people] have noticed you doing differently that would tell them that you were doing better? (DeJong & Miller, 1995, p. 732)

After the client is able to remember or envision the exception (i.e., strength), the client anchors various points of a scale (usually 1 to 10) that measure the presence or absence of the problem. The client is then asked to assign a number on the scale to describe his or her current functioning or feeling; and progress is initiated and monitored as the worker asks not "What would it take to resolve the problem?" but rather "What would it take to get one point higher on the scale?" (DeJong & Miller, 1995). Through this process of small, incremental changes in behavior—all of which are the client's ideas—progress is made, and problems are resolved in a way that identifies and builds on the client's strengths.

EMPOWERMENT THEORY

Empowerment theory is a logical companion to the strength-based approach. However, in addition to personal empowerment through identifying and building on strengths, it uses political empowerment in working with oppressed groups (e.g., the poor, people of color, women, and those who are oppressed by virtue of sexual orientation, physical or mental challenges, youth, or age)—a dual focus on clients' potential and on structural/environmental change (Lee, 1996). This approach also fits within ecological systems theory. As stated by William Schwartz, "personal troubles of milieu and public issues of structure must be stated in terms of the other, and of the interaction between the two" (1974, p. 75).

Judith Lee, a leading apologist, provides a conceptual framework for empowerment theory that includes (a) a historical perspective of oppression and related social policy, (b) an ecological perspective including a stress-coping paradigm, and (c) "ethclass" and feminist perspectives appreciating the ceilings and floors imposed by class and race (Lee, 1996, p. 220).

Empowerment is a process of negotiating or eliminating barriers to problem solving imposed by external society. The dimensions of empowerment, as described by Lee, are (a) development of a more positive and potent sense of self; (b) construction of knowledge and capacity for more critical comprehension of social and political realities of one's environment; and (c) cultivation of resources and strategies, or more functional competence, for attainment of personal and collective social goals, or liberation (1996, p. 224).

Workers using this approach have the responsibility to both help clients overcome negative self-valuations and advocate for clients in removing barriers and in finding supportive resources for clients (Payne, 1991). In order to be effective in this role, workers must understand the concept of learned helplessness, and they must have a high degree of self-awareness in terms of their own biases and stereotypes in working with oppressed groups. Moreover, they should be able to model empowerment themselves

(Lee, 1996). Workers must be prepared to advocate for their clients. However, technically speaking, "the empowerment process resides in the person, not the helper" (Lee, 1996, p. 224). The worker cannot truly empower; rather, clients empower themselves through the help of the worker. Thus it is important to provide opportunities for clients to empower themselves. For example, a client who suffers from discrimination and oppression may participate in a grassroots community group or mutual aid group for the purpose of attaining political empowerment. However, the by-products of that involvement are likely to be personal satisfaction, growth, community or ethnic pride, and heightened self-esteem (Lee, 1996).

A CONCEPTUAL FRAMEWORK: INTEGRATION OF THEORIES

Theories serve to organize clinical information, concepts, and experiences in a way that positions reality within plausible, cause-effect, and goal-means-results parameters (Carlson et al., 1991). In defining those plausible parameters, therapists generally limit their observations, reflections, and interventions to a reasonable and manageable number of variables. In order to keep that set of variables manageable, one can argue for adhering to only one theory of intervention (Haley, 1987). However, therapists increasingly conclude that no single theory or set of interventions can be applied to all cases. "The shortcomings of the various family therapy approaches have prompted the search for more comprehensive and integrative theories of family therapy" (Carlson et al., 1991).

An integration of theories is the combining of theories or parts of theories in constructing a more useful model. The way in which theories are integrated is a reflection of the scope of the conceptual framework as well as the process of categorizing information. Some examples of integrative theory in working with families, as explained by Carlson et al. (1991), are evident in the work of Feldman (1992), Walsh (1991), Nichols (1988), and Will and Wrate (1985).

Feldman (1992) conceptualized therapy as a "multilevel" (i.e., intrapsychic and interpersonal) method of assessment and intervention with corresponding explanations for the change process. Added to the multilevel dimension of therapy is the relevance of both individual and family interventions. Thus he incorporated compatible concepts from four different psychotherapeutic perspectives (i.e., psychodynamic, cognitive, behavioral, and family systems perspectives).

Walsh (1991) proposed a highly structured format for intervention that combines several interpersonal models with an intrapsychic component. In this model, theory is based primarily on an integrative evaluation of the family that is guided by five factors: (a) family structure (based on Minuchin's work), (b) roles, (c) communication and perceptions (a modification of Satir's work), (d) themes related to the problems, and (e) the personality dynamics of significant individuals (based, in part, on Ackerman's work). These five factors are combined with an individual psychotherapy model to account for intrapsychic influences (Carlson et al., 1991).

In Nichols's (1988) approach to marital therapy, eight concepts from systems theory are integrated with three therapeutic interventions derived from object-relations/psychoanalytic theory in order to give a contextual explanation for unconscious fears and mispreconceptions. Added to that combination is social-learning theory—a seemingly inappropriate companion to psychoanalytic theory. However, the combination provides for behavioral problem solving in the context of complex psychodynamic and systemic issues.

The problem-centered psychodynamic family therapy approach (Will & Wrate, 1985) combines the structural model of Minuchin with the problem-centered systemic model of the McMasters group (Carlson et al., 1991) and object relations theory. This combination bridges the family as a system and family members as individual persons in addition to providing a framework for solving multiple problems.

These examples illustrate the limitations of using a single theoretical model in working with families. Workers involved with child welfare families are particularly limited because of multidimensional issues. Moreover, the philosophy and values underpinning these family-centered services demand a conceptual framework and practice guidelines that are broad and flexible enough to address the content and context of intrapsychic, interpersonal, and environmental issues from a holistic perspective that empowers and strengthens the family as well as the individual family members. Because of the need for family-centered services to be as comprehensive as needed and tailored specifically to the unique situation of each family, a number of other theories could appropriately be added to this chapter, such as client-centered theory (Rowe, 1996), existential theory (Krill, 1996), narrative theory (Kelley, 1996), problem-solving theory (Turner & Jaco, 1996), and transpersonal theory (Cowley, 1996). But even these would not make the list complete. The brand of family-centered practice described in this book is good social work practice in all its forms. Particular attention is given to these theories in an integrative context as a reminder that good social work practice with multiproblem families in the child welfare arena cannot effectively be compartmentalized.

REFERENCES

Anderson, R. E., & Carter, I. (1984). *Human behavior in the social environment: A social systems approach* (3rd ed.). New York: Aldine de Gruyter.

Andreae, D. (1996). Systems theory and social work treatment. In F. J. Turner (Ed.), *Social work treatment: Interlocking theoretical approaches* (4th ed., pp. 601–16). New York: Free Press.

Bandura, A. (1973). *Aggression: A social learning analysis.* Englewood Cliffs, NJ: Prentice Hall.

Barth, R. P., Courtney, M., Berrick, J. D., & Albert, V. (1994). *From child abuse to permanency planning: Child welfare services pathways and placements.* New York: Aldine de Gruyter.

Berg, I. K. (1994). *Family based services: A solution-focused approach.* New York: Norton.

Bertalanffy, L. V. (1968). *General system theory.* New York: George Braziller.

Bowen, M. (1976). Theoretical aspects and clinical relevance of the multigenerational model of family therapy. In P. J. Guerin Jr. (Ed.), *Family therapy* (pp. 91–110). New York: Gardner Press.

Bowen, M. (1978). *Family therapy in clinical practice.* New York: Jason Aronson.

Bowlby, J. (1980). *Attachment and loss: Vol. 3. Loss, sadness and depression.* New York: Basic Books.

Bowlby, J. (1982). *Attachment and loss: Vol. 1. Attachment* (2nd ed.) New York: Basic Books.

Bowlby, J. (1988). *A secure base: Parent-child attachment and healthy human development.* New York: Basic Books.

Bronfenbrenner, U. (1979). *The ecology of human development: Experiences by nature and design.* Cambridge: Harvard University Press.

Carlson, J., Sperry, L., & Lewis, J. (1991). *Family therapy: Ensuring treatment efficacy.* Pacific Grove, CA: Brooks/Cole.

Chornesky, A., & Meek, H. W. (1996). The importance of attachment theory for family-based services. In E. Walton, R. E. Davis, & P. Sandau-Beckler (Eds.), *Empowering families: Papers from the Ninth Annual Conference on Family-Based Services.* Riverdale, IL: National Association for Family-Based Services.

Cowley, A. S. (1996). Transpersonal social work. In F. J. Turner (Ed.), *Social work treatment: Interlocking theoretical approaches* (4th ed., pp. 663–98). New York: Free Press.

DeJong, P., & Miller, S. D. (1995). How to interview for client strengths. *Social Work, 40,* 729–36.

Ell, K. (1996). Crisis theory and social work practice. In F. J. Turner (Ed.), *Social work treatment: Interlocking theoretical approaches* (4th ed., pp. 168–90). New York: Free Press.

Feldman, L. (1992). *Integrating individual and family therapy.* New York: Brunner/Mazel.

Galinsky, M. J., & Schopler, J. H. (Eds.). (1995). *Support groups: Current perspectives on theory and practice.* Binghamton, NY: Haworth Press.

Garbarino, J. (1982). *Children and families in the social environment.* Hawthorne, NY: Aldine de Gruyter.

Germain, C., & Gitterman, A. (1980). *The life model of social work practice.* New York: Columbia University Press.

Gilliland, B. E., & James, R. K. (1997). *Crisis intervention strategies* (3rd ed.). New York: Brooks/Cole.

Golden, R. (1997). *Disposable children: America's welfare system.* New York: Wadsworth.

Haley, J. (1987). The disappearance of the individual. *Family Therapy Networker, 11,* 39–40.

Haley, J. (1997). Changes in therapy. In J. K. Zeig (Ed.), *The evolution of psychotherapy: The third conference* (pp. 245–55). New York: Brunner/Mazel.

Henggeler, S. W., Melton, G. B., & Smith, L. A. (1992). Family preservation using multisystemic therapy: An effective alternative to incarcerating serious juvenile offenders. *Journal of Consulting and Clinical Psychology, 60,* 953–61.

Hepworth, D. H., Rooney, R. H., & Larsen, J. A. (1997). *Direct social work practice: Theory and skills* (5th ed.). New York: Brooks/Cole.

Heying, K. R. (1985). Family-based, in-home services for the severely emotionally disturbed child. *Child Welfare, 64,* 519–27.

Hodges, V. G. (1994). Home-based behavioral intervention with children and families. In D. K. Granvold (Ed.), *Cognitive and behavioral treatment: Methods and applications* (pp. 90–106). Pacific Grove, CA: Brooks/Cole.

Kagan, R., & Schlosberg, S. (1989). *Families in perpetual crisis.* New York: Norton.

Kaplan, L., & Girard, J. L. (1994). *Strengthening high-risk families: A handbook for practitioners.* New York: Lexington Books.

Karen, R. (1994). *Becoming attached: Unfolding the mystery of the infant-mother bond and its impact on later life.* New York: Warner Books.

Kelley, P. (1996). Narrative theory and social work treatment. In F. J. Turner (Ed.), *Social work treatment: Interlocking theoretical approaches* (4th ed., pp. 461–79). New York: Free Press.

Kinney, J., Haapala, D., & Booth, C. (1991). *Keeping families together: The Homebuilders Model.* New York: Aldine de Gruyter.

Krill, D. (1996). Existential social work. In F. J. Turner (Ed.), *Social work treatment: Interlocking theoretical approaches* (4th ed., pp. 250–81). New York: Free Press.

Lee, J. A. B. (1996). The empowerment approach to social work practice. In F. J. Turner (Ed.), *Social work treatment: Interlocking theoretical approaches* (4th ed., pp. 218–49). New York: Free Press.

Lindemann, E. (1944). Symptomatology and management of acute grief. *American Journal of Psychiatry, 101,* 141–48.

Madanes, C. (1981). *Strategic family therapy.* San Francisco: Jossey-Bass.

Madanes, C. (1987). Advances in strategic family therapy. In J. K. Zeig (Ed.), *The evolution of psychotherapy* (pp. 47–57). New York: Brunner/Mazel.

Madanes, C. (1990). *Sex, love, and violence.* New York: Norton.

McGoldrick, M., & Gerson, R. (1985). *Genograms in family assessment.* New York: Norton.

Minuchin, S. (1974). *Families and family therapy.* Cambridge: Harvard University Press.

Minuchin, S. (1987). My many voices. In J. K. Zeig (Ed.), *The evolution of psychotherapy* (pp. 5–14). New York: Brunner/Mazel.

Minuchin, S., & Fishman, H. C. (1981). *Family therapy techniques*. Cambridge: Harvard University Press.

Minuchin, S., & Nichols, M. P. (1993). *Family healing: Tales of hope and renewal from family therapy*. New York: Free Press.

Nichols, W. (1988). *Marital therapy: An integrated approach*. New York: Guilford.

O'Hanlon, W. H., & Weiner-Davis, M. (1989). *In search of solutions: A new direction in psychotherapy*. New York: Norton.

Parad, H. J., & Parad, L. G. (1990). Crisis intervention: An introductory overview. In H. J. Parad & L. G. Parad (Eds.), *Crisis intervention: Book 2. The practitioner's sourcebook for brief therapy* (pp. 3–66). Milwaukee: Family Service America.

Payne, M. (1991). *Modern social work theory: A critical introduction*. Chicago: Lyceum Books.

Reid, W. J. (1996). Task-centered social work. In F. J. Turner (Ed.), *Social work treatment: Interlocking theoretical approaches* (4th ed., pp. 617–40). New York: Free Press.

Rhodes, S. L. (1986). Family treatment. In F. J. Turner (Ed.), *Social work treatment: Interlocking theoretical approaches* (3rd ed., pp. 432–52). New York: Free Press.

Roberts, A. R. (1996). *Crisis management and brief treatment: Theory, technique, and applications*. Chicago: Nelson-Hall.

Rodway, M. R. (1986). Systems theory. In F. J. Turner (Ed.), *Social work treatment: Interlocking theoretical approaches* (3rd ed., pp. 514–40). New York: Free Press.

Rowe, W. (1996). Client-centered theory: A person-centered approach. In F. J. Turner (Ed.), *Social work treatment: Interlocking theoretical approaches* (4th ed., pp. 69–93). New York: Free Press.

Saleebey, D. (1992). Introduction: Power in the people. In D. Saleebey (Ed.), *The strengths perspective in social work practice* (pp. 3–17). White Plains, NY: Longman.

Saleebey, D. (Ed.). (1992). *The strengths perspective in social work practice*. White Plains, NY: Longman.

Satir, V. (1972). *Peoplemaking*. Palo Alto, CA: Science and Behavior Books.

Satir, V. (1983). *Conjoint family therapy* (3rd ed.). Palo Alto, CA: Science and Behavior Books.

Schwartz, W. (1974). Private troubles and public issues: One social work job or two? In R. W. Klenk and R. W. Ryan (Eds.), *The practice of social work* (2nd ed., pp. 62–81). Belmont, CA: Wadsworth.

Thomlison, B., & Thomlison, R. (1996). Behavior theory and social work treatment. In F. J. Turner (Ed.), *Social work treatment: Interlocking theoretical approaches* (4th ed., pp. 39–68). New York: Free Press.

Turner, J., & Jaco, R. M. (1996). Problem-solving theory and social work treatment. In F. J. Turner (Ed.), *Social work treatment: Interlocking theoretical approaches* (4th ed., pp. 503–22). New York: Free Press.

Walsh, W. (1991). *Case studies in family therapy: An integrated approach.* Boston: Allyn and Bacon.

Walsh, W. M., & McGraw, J. A. (1996). *Essentials of family therapy: A therapist's guide to eight approaches.* Denver: Love.

Walton, E., & Smith, C. (1998). The genogram: A tool for assessment and intervention in child welfare. *Journal of Family Social Work, 3* (3), 3–20.

Will, D., & Wrate, R. (1985). *Integrated family therapy: A problem-centered psychodynamic approach.* London: Tavistock.

Zastrow, C. (1992). *The practice of social work* (4th ed.). Belmont, CA: Wadsworth.

5 Family-Centered Assessment and Goal Setting

PAT SANDAU-BECKLER

Assessing the family is one of the most critical skills in family-centered practice. It sets the stage for goal setting and guides the change process. Assessment can be considered in two ways. The first is the initial assessment, or snapshot, of a family. Finding out the family's strengths, resources, capabilities, goals, dreams, and aspirations helps build the total framework for the picture. Inventories, assessment tools, interviews, home observations, and referral information are often the basis for the development of a family assessment. The second way to assess families is much like an ongoing video. New information about family interactions, dynamics, problem-solving capacities, cultural beliefs and values, and skills can be added to the family assessment process. Both angles of assessing families can provide important frameworks in assisting families to achieve positive family-centered outcomes. This chapter addresses the issues of comprehensive family assessment—tools and techniques as well as insights into the process. Linking goal-setting activities to the assessment process is also examined.

EXPANDED ROLES OF FAMILY MEMBERS AS EXPERTS
ON THEIR HISTORY AND CHALLENGES

During the last twenty years, a new focus on empowering families has been the major thrust of family-centered practice. Spurred by the Adoption Assistance and Child Welfare Act of 1980, the Omnibus Budget Reconciliation Act of 1993, and most recently the Adoption and Safe Families Act of 1997, new family-centered services have become available. These new strength-focused technologies call for strong family participation, which is increasingly evident in the assessment and goal-setting processes for children's mental health, juvenile justice, and schools in addition to the traditional child welfare settings. New populations and unique ways of applying family-centered practice have been based on long-standing traditional methods of focusing on family participation. The St. Paul Family Centered Project captures the essence of this approach in the following statement:

> We like to think of the casework relationship as a partnership working toward a common purpose, with as much clarity in mutual understanding and collaboration on the objectives as can be obtained. In the early days of social work, we thought up plans that were good for people and often told them just what to do—kindly, but in terms of our ideas of what their objectives should be. For example, we found a much better house for a family and then were disappointed that they did not move or appreciate our help. Later on, we began to appreciate that it does no good to help people off to a start of our choosing. They have to move under their own power and in a direction of their own choice. (Overton, Tinker, & Associates, 1959, p. 21)

Effective workers hold firmly to the family-centered values outlined in detail by Dr. Ronnau in an earlier chapter. These values provide a practice framework that works toward a systems approach in order to support the provision of family-centered services to all families. When workers approach a family, they recognize that it knows its own history and needs. The family's expertise on its culture, beliefs, and challenges is a valuable resource for the worker in assisting it in its change process. Respecting that expertise and placing a high value on developing a truly collaborative partnership increases the likelihood that the relationship between the family and the worker, which studies have determined is often the key to families making a change, will be reinforced (Greenburg & Pinsof, 1986). The Wraparound Services for children's mental health have developed a thirty-eight-point framework for parent-professional partnerships that sets the ground rules for these relationships (Grealish, Piña, & Vandenberg, 1995). The framework calls for parents to believe in themselves as equal partners in the decision-making and planning process. It outlines suggested parental behaviors in the areas of assertiveness and cooperation with professionals and advises families to expect respectful treatment. The thirty-eight points also include guidelines based on family-centered values for interacting with parents. Sharing those guidelines with families prepares both parents and professionals for family-centered practice to be different from past experiences with helping systems. The Philosophy Statement of the Federation of Families for Children's Mental Health (1990) also speaks to families and professionals who dare to hope and dream about the possibilities for assistance in providing effective services for youth.

USE OF SELF IN RELATIONSHIP TO FAMILY-CENTERED PRACTICE PRINCIPLES

After receiving the referral for services, the worker thoroughly reviews the information to determine the process of the family's involvement with the agency and the potential avenues to join and build a relationship with the family and its surrounding systems. When reviewing the referral, workers assess the motivations of the referring agency or person and the potential responses from the family. How the referring party views the family's strengths can be a great asset to the process.

Although some referring parties focus on convincing the worker about concerns, knowledge of the family's strengths is useful in developing a relationship during the first interviews with the family. Knowing strengths of a family before meeting with it is helpful in framing positive interactions. The worker's acknowledgment of the family's strengths also can help it recognize the worker's perception that the family is not the problem (Berg, 1994). If families have previous case records or are being transferred, reviewing for safety issues and the context of past services can be helpful. However, it is important to withhold judgment because relationship development can be hindered by the worker's awareness of others' negative perceptions of the family.

Not all referrals are voluntary, and in the joining process workers should take extra care to have empathy for involuntary referrals. What workers face is no different from their own reactions to being forced to do something against their will. Change is always occurring, and it affects equilibrium. Also, family members use a variety of tactics to demonstrate their reluctance. Therefore, resistance to forced changes should be regarded as a normal response to a perceived threat of loss of freedom. Taking immediate steps to contract or support the restoration of freedoms is helpful, and the skilled worker normalizes resistance by addressing it before moving into the change process. Rooney (1992) lays out a framework for suggested discussions with reluctant families. Reviewing the family's perspective on the reasons for the referral to services and discussing the requirements and mandates of the referral is the first step. Assessing the extent of the external pressure and exploring the costs and benefits of making the changes with the family are the next steps. Exploring free choice within the change process and the options and negotiable items available to the family within the constraints is also helpful. As clients proceed through this process, every effort should be made to support their autonomy and to respect them. The contract should be finalized by reviewing their decision to continue while respecting the process by reinforcing the need for their approval. Specificity in small steps and rewards tied to efforts to make progress are essential to the engagement process. For some, the worker must wait until the relationship is established before change occurs. As a wise family member once stated, "It takes as long as it takes for family members to gain trust and start to make movement." For some, the introduction to the change process and normalizing the experience of change is critical. Not every family member knows what to expect in the family assessment or knows how change occurs.

Even voluntary referrals have elements of coercion for some family members (Rooney, 1992). Finding the areas of freedom within a voluntary but coerced service is a special challenge. Contracting to restore freedoms through choices within the confines of coerced services and forming a partnership to assist family members are critical. The family member for which the family is concerned can then regain control over the behaviors that made the service imperative to other family members. Knowing the referral agency's or individuals' concerns and knowing especially what outcomes they desire are also critical to assessing the family effectively.

MAINTAINING A NONJUDGMENTAL STANCE

Maintaining a nonjudgmental stance with families is essential in order to gain their trust. Barriers can occur when a misunderstanding of meaning or cultural differences are interpreted as being judgmental. Labels frequently are given to family members based on either legitimate criteria for funding, such as those contained in the *DSM-IV-R*, or less legitimate societal judgments. Such labels can be value-laden, blameful, and disruptive to the family members' abilities to be more than their label. Families may belong to groups that have experienced stigma and discrimination and are adept at perceiving judgmental behavior.

Being truly nonjudgmental and separating the behavior from the person takes skill and effort. Reframing, redefining, and relabeling are all parts of that process. The National Resource Center for Family-Centered Practice

(Lloyd, 1984) has developed an exercise to look for the strengths in common labels. Using alternative meanings for common labels such as hostile, submissive, insensitive, controlling, or impulsive gives workers additional resources and capacities to work with the family member. Advocacy groups have long been active in such strength-based relabeling as, for example, the common term for a person with a disability. Viewing the abilities of the person diminishes the discouragement and the blameful and negative consequences of the label that frequently demoralize the person and his or her family and are hard to reverse.

PREPARING FOR FAMILY-CENTERED ASSESSMENT

Prior to meeting with the family, the worker prepares for the assessment in a variety of ways. The first consideration is determining what will be required in order to join with the family.

Planning for Partnerships with Families in the Assessment Process

Preparing to join with the family involves learning what is important to it. The family's culture and cross-cultural issues should be a priority in the worker's awareness when planning for the assessment process. For example, understanding the cultural background of the family may raise questions about immediate language differences or needs. In addition, knowledge of the acculturation of the family and its ideological values with regard to receiving help from outsiders is a key element in building trust and assisting the family to be in charge of the change process.

Preparing for Home-Based Work and Entry to the Neighborhood

In home-based work, safety is always a priority—safety of children, parents, and the worker—and it is less likely to be a problem if it is included as an issue in the planning stage of the assessment. Safety contracts may be the most immediate need for family members. Safety practices for workers, including community safety and an assessment of the history of violence, are equally important for the worker and family members. Steps to create safety for workers in dangerous communities sometimes rely solely on the family. For example, family members' demonstrating their relationship by publicly greeting the worker often assists the neighbors in supporting the worker in the vicinity. Familiarity engenders trust by members of the community toward the worker. The family can participate in helping workers gain safe access to the neighborhood. Meeting the worker at a familiar setting, such as a gas station or store, and going to the home together are examples. Moreover, in homes that have a history of violence, workers can prepare for their own safety by using strategies of home entrance such as sitting close to exits and staying away from windows. Useful also are skills for defusing volatile behavior, such as making good eye contact, practicing reflective listening, avoiding too many questions, modeling calmness, matching and pacing family members' style of communication, remaining neutral, and responding appropriately to silences (Sandau-Beckler, 1999). In some situations it may be necessary to put those involved in an explosive argument in different rooms while remaining in the doorway between the two.

HOME OBSERVATION

Observation in the home gives workers new opportunities not just to talk about family dynamics but to actually see them in action. Observations about living conditions, household management, and the safety of both the home and the community can give context to the family's struggles and patterns of behavior. How family members portray themselves is reflected in the furnishings and the use of space in their home environment. How families organize their interactions can be observed in terms of the places and times in the home for family activities. The home environment becomes a potential learning environment for the family and serves as an excellent source of assessment through observation of daily family life and interactions. It also can provide the opportunity for the teachable moment that comes when the parent or child is in need of a skill in the immediate environment. Immediate use of the skill results in increased motivation.

Safety issues relevant to the care and well-being of family members should be noted (e.g., poor structural condition of the home, sanitation problems, safety hazards, rodent infestation, nonfunctional utilities, or lack of water). Lack of housing stability or imminent eviction can affect the long-term security and safety of the family. Risk behaviors such as drug use and gang or violent activities in the home or neighborhood also are included in the assessment. Home management issues based on observations require that the worker, in order to remain nonjudgmental, explore his or her own standards for organizing the household versus the family's standards. Exploration of the impact on the well-being and safety of family members is the key.

Deciding on the best service setting is important when working with families. Sometimes more neutral community resources are more comfortable for the family and its members. Sometimes families prefer the agency. Sometimes the necessary conversations might be constrained by other family members. Often a neutral atmosphere is requested when large numbers of family and agency members are involved in the meeting (Merkel-Hougin, 1998).

ETHICAL CONSIDERATIONS OF WORKING
IN THE FAMILY'S HOME

Workers need to consider many issues as service provision moves to the home environment (Anderson, 1991), among them how they enter the home, the timing of the visit, and even where to sit. Many such customs are culturally defined and take extensive cultural knowledge in order not to offend the family. Dosser, Shaffer, Shaffer, Clevenger, and Jefferies (1996) have reviewed the value dilemmas experienced by workers. They suggest that a heightened sense of consideration of those dilemmas is critical and that workers should be prepared for such naturally occurring dilemmas when working in the family's home. They also point out that one of the more striking differences from traditional settings is that family-centered services often include the provision of concrete, or "hard," services within the home. Workers often serve families who are experiencing major home maintenance, organization, and environmental issues. In another chapter, Dr. Elizabeth Tracy discusses the extent to which these services play a critical role in family development and functioning. The worker's and the team's roles in the services often are more flexible than in traditional office settings.

Unlike traditional office visits, the handling of disruptions and distractions (e.g., telephone and television) is within the context of the family's choice and negotiations with the worker. Such disruptions often are cited as discussion topics. Another ethical consideration is the confidential nature of providing services in the home. The training curriculum of the National Resource Center for Family-Centered Practice provides discussion tools for how a worker may be identified to visitors or callers to the home. Of course, following the family's lead is always the best idea. Discussing these dilemmas with the family and seeking direction from them on how to handle introductions can be helpful. Workers need to know how to identify themselves when accompanying family members on visits, such as doctor or school, where there are opportunities to model enhanced relationships with other service providers. How to handle offers of gifts, food, or requests to attend meaningful family transition events are also concerns expressed by workers. Such situations are often unique and call for supervisory consideration and review of agency policies. However, cultural significance and meanings to the relationship must be weighed cautiously when making these decisions. Experiences of home-based workers also indicate that animals in the yard or in the home can be a source of concern. Traveling with dog biscuits reduces some of the immediate threat, but long-term plans for handling animals are another source of conversation. Each dilemma must be carefully considered with the family. Creative solutions need to be sought with our main partner, the family, in handling each dilemma (Dosser et al., 1996).

FAMILY-CENTERED ASSESSMENT PROCESS

Engaging the Family in Planning for Assessment

Historically, joining with family members has been an essential concept in family work (Minuchin, 1974). The empowerment practice that family-centered work embraces includes a collaborative strength-based process that emphasizes the partnership between the family and the worker. Families are seen as vital resources for assisting in the change process of individual family members and the family as a whole. The capacities and capabilities of the individual members and of the family as a whole are activated and developed. Instilling hope and interviewing the family for past successes are vital avenues to establishing a collaborative partnership. Seeking the family's competencies and helping the family realize those strengths and abilities are central to the joining process. Workers bring hope to the process of change. Family members may have strained resources and capacities. Borrowing hope from workers can activate new avenues in the family members' confidence in initiating change.

Encouragement and support can create an atmosphere that fosters change. Rogerian skills such as reflective listening, positive regard, acceptance, support, a nonjudgmental attitude, and empathy are pivotal skills for joining with family members. Motivational interviewing, a new comprehensive model, successfully pulls together these skills to enhance engagement and to decrease resistance (Miller & Rollnick, 1991). Commitment to assisting the family in its change process is also essential. The worker's belief in the family's ability to change is something the family can rely on for support, even if it does not have that confidence in itself. Self-efficacy grows as the family realizes that workers stick with it throughout the uneasiness of change.

The joining process emphasizes the uniqueness of each family. Part of that uniqueness is the way in which the family defines itself, and that defining process (i.e., who is in the family) is essential in the joining process. Broad extensions of critical participants often move beyond the nuclear family to extended family, neighbors, friends, and other resource persons who may be central to the change process. New avenues to create and assist in family change, such as family group conferencing, discussed by Ms. Merkel-Holguin in another chapter, demonstrate the usefulness and cultural responsiveness of being flexible and inclusive with families.

Joining activities, such as matching and pacing, are helpful as well. Mirroring back to the family helps in the validation of their experiences and demonstrates respect for their processes and boundaries. As the worker and family develop the relationship that is critical to the change process, the respect and validation from the worker will help the family consider taking risks to make changes. Respect for the family's autonomy, culture, and expert role in understanding its history, needs, and desires are essential to the engagement process.

Assessing Family Uniqueness Through Cultural Background, Beliefs, and Values

When working with families, an important goal is to provide culturally responsive family assessments (Cross, Bazron, Dennis, & Isaacs, 1989). A critical component of the assessment is looking at the cultural strengths of the family. The background and history of the family's culture, including ethnic background, can give context for current family patterns of functioning and assessing the patterns of oppression and discrimination the family may experience. Hodges (1991) points out that responsive workers allow the family to define its membership, which may include extended family or fictive kin. The common cultural beliefs and values, especially about family organization, patterns, and relationships, are critical elements in the assessment process. Responsive workers seek to understand how the values and beliefs of the family provide direction for the family's life. Successful workers reflect on the common values and beliefs they share with the family while also seeking to understand the differences. Seeking to understand the family's ideas about outside assistance or professional help can give a context for the worker-family relationship. Understanding the acculturation levels for various family members may also be helpful in assessing value conflicts or stressors. Culturally responsive workers learn about the minority communities, whether they represent differing classes, family variations, ethnicities, races, or sexual orientations. They also employ partnerships with cultural resources or cultural guides who can assist in interviewing and supporting the change or healing processes occurring in the family (Leigh, 1998). These resources could include indigenous workers, nontraditional healers, traditional healers, medicine men, *curanderas* and *curanderos*, godparents, cultural mediators, spiritual leaders, fictive kin, and any other culturally specific resources. Culturally responsive workers view culture as a strength and modify their skills to better adapt their interview styles and assessment process to meet family needs. They work vigorously to understand the complexities of the family's culture, including assessing their strengths and facilitating family empowerment (Lee, 1996; Orit, Bib, & Mahboubi, 1996).

Two assessment tools have been developed to assist workers in the assessment process. One, called the Cultural Genogram, provides an opportunity for workers to explore and understand more fully their own culture—its migration patterns, history of oppression, intragroup conflicts, and its roles in the daily life of the worker (Hardy & Laszloffy, 1995). Rules, rituals, religion or spirituality, and sources of pride or shame are reflected in the learning opportunity. The cultural identity of the worker and its impact on the work with families is explored. Assumptions and stereotypes are challenged, and emotional triggers are identified in order to refine effective culturally responsive practice.

The second tool, which focuses on the effects of immigration and migration on family functioning and acculturation, is the Culturegram, as developed by Elaine Congress (1994). The Culturegram supplements two traditional family assessment tools discussed later in this chapter, the Eco-map and the genogram. It is designed to help workers visually explore the family's cultural history and patterns of migration. The acculturation process is assessed in terms of the length of time in the community, age at the time of migration, and legal or undocumented status of individual family members. The language spoken at home and in the community and contact with cultural institutions and groups also are explored. Elements such as health beliefs, traditions of celebrations, important holidays, education expectations, and values about family, education, and work are evaluated. Crisis events and the culture's impact on family members are measured as well. This tool is especially effective in hearing the story of the family and the hopes and dreams for its members in the new country. Workers come to understand the diversity of cultural beliefs and practices between different cultural groups and within the same cultural group. The tool assesses the acculturation nuances and gives the worker opportunity to affirm the richness of culturally diverse families, whose cultural strengths and resources can be of assistance in the family change process.

Family Strengths Assessment

Assessing family strengths can help the worker and the family explore the positive aspects of the family's functioning as a unit, the unique strengths and contributions of individual members, and the family's strengths in interacting with other systems outside the family (Cowger, 1994; Ronnau, 1995; Saleebey, 1992). The worker helps the family define and explore its strengths. Often this approach is unfamiliar to families as they focus on a problem-solving model that is characteristically taught in our educational system. Families need help in learning how a definition of strengths, such as family members' talents, abilities, capacities, aspirations, competence, skills, opportunities, resources, and dreams, can potentially assist in meeting goals (Ronnau, 1995). Workers also can interview to observe strengths within the family domains of interaction by looking for positive characteristics in family functioning (De Jong & Miller, 1995). The family's support of its members, their commitment, their appreciation of each other, their identity as family members, their adaptability and flexibility, the family's involvement, and family pride are all examples of family relationship strengths. In the last domain, workers also can assess the family's strengths in its interactions with others by observing the family in the areas of asking others for help, advocating for family members, seeking resources for family members, obtaining needed care, and using resources for the family.

Workers may identify family strengths through a process of observation and modeling (i.e., how to observe and point out strengths). This may be unfamiliar for families, but tools have been designed to assist in the process (Deal & Veeken, 1997; Veeken & Deal, 1999). For example, Strength Cards, pictures of common strengths, can be used to help family members identify their strengths. Strength Cards for Kids also have been developed, with pictures exemplifying the strengths. They can be used as discussion openers in focusing on the children's strengths or the activity surrounding the strength that is portrayed in the picture. Another method is a blank portrait on which other persons list the strengths they see in an individual or family. Interviews focused on the family's culture, personal stories, and lore can also be a profound source of strength identification (Rapp, 1998).

Another avenue is to ask the members of the family's natural and professional support network to identify strengths (Ronnau, 1995). Others may be keenly aware of everyday strengths that can be described to the family and used as resources for change. This method may be unfamiliar also to the providers. The shift to a strength-based approach has been the hallmark difference in family-centered practice in the last thirty years. As one mother put it, "When I went to the conference for my son, they talked about my family's strengths. I looked around to see who they were talking about. Now I know that my family had strengths all the time, but I just hadn't recognized it."

Another way to find strengths is to have the family take notice of the stressors it has overcome in order to recognize its successful coping strategies in managing the struggles of daily living. What family members have learned about themselves and others in overcoming abuse, trauma, oppression, or confusion is also a source of strength (Saleebey, 1992). Hearing the family's narrative story about its members' lives and exploring their growth might provide an opportunity to see things in a new, more empowered strength-based story. As Rapp (1998) points out, we don't know the limits of a person's capacity to grow and change. The family's individual, group, and community aspirations and visions can be a source of strength as well.

Family strengths are used to increase a family's sense of competence and to enhance motivation by increasing the family's self-efficacy and confidence. Likewise, professionals and community members who are partnering in the change efforts can have increased awareness and hope for the family through a comprehensive family strengths assessment. It is an acknowledgment of unlimited resources, potential, and capacity to grow and change. Family strengths can be used to help family members feel better about themselves and to represent family members to other professionals (Ronnau, 1995).

The Family Strengths Inventory, developed by New Mexico Children, Youth and Families for its Family Centered Assessment (Martinez et al., n.d.), is an example of a tool designed to help families identify their strengths and challenges. The instrument is flexible and can be structured around two versions of a twenty-four-item questionnaire or a simple uniquely planned strengths assessment with the family. The unique advantage of this tool is that it was designed with families. The questions are conversation points intended to identify accomplishments of the family in meeting its daily-living needs.

Other tools for assessing strengths include the family life-cycle development (Turnbull, Summers, & Brotherson, 1983) and areas of family functioning addressed in more detail by Elaine Walton in a previous chapter. A strength-based behaviors checklist developed by Helene Elko (Lindblad-Goldberg, Dore, & Stern, 1998) focuses on strength behaviors in the areas of school, developmental/organic growth, emotional health, behavioral health, social relationships, medical care, and family relationships.

Assessing Family Stress and Resiliency

Family resiliency and the strengths, resources, and natural healing processes that are protective in families is another framework for assisting in the assessment of families. The individual, family, and community abilities, resources, and coping strategies can help the worker design effective interventions (McCubbin, Thompson, Thompson, & Fromer, 1998). Rubin Hill's (1949) ADCX framework and recent adaptations including the Double ABCX Model and the FAAR (Family Adjustment and Adaptation Response Model) (McCubbin & Patterson, 1983) assess families' precrisis and postcrisis responses to stressful events.

Recognizing normal developmental and nondevelopmental events and their impact on family functioning is important in determining how families will react and how services designed to assist the family can reduce or counter the impact of family stressors. Hill (1958) assesses five categories of family crisis: (a) accession of new roles, such as marriage or remarriage, parenthood, stepparent additions (foster or adoption), and recovery in health (substance abuse treatment); (b) family dismemberment or loss, including death of a family member, hospitalization, work or employment separation, children leaving home, and new employment; (c) demoralization, including income loss, infidelity, substance abuse, and delinquency; (d) demoralization plus loss or accession of new roles such as illegitimate pregnancy, desertion, runaway, divorce, imprisonment, suicide, or homicide; and (e) changes in status such as shifts in poverty or wealth, moves, and changes in status of women.

The Resiliency Model of Family Stress, Adjustment, and Adaptation assesses areas of social support for family life events, family systems resources, family adaptation styles and coping and problem-solving abilities, cultural coherence, and meaning of the events for the family. Reestablishing family balance and harmony is essential for families when coping with these events (Cross, 1998). Rapid assessment tools used in the assessment process include the Family Inventory of Life Events and Changes, Family Hardiness Index, Social Support Index, Family Coping Inventory, Family-Member Well-Being Index and Family Distress Index, and Family Regenerativity and Adaption–General (McCubbin, Thompson, & McCubbin, 1996). These tools can contribute to the assessment process by facilitating the development of a culturally relevant intervention plan.

Family Challenges

Karl Tomm (1987) developed a method of asking questions that help the family describe its concerns and behaviors while gaining insight into the patterns that have led to the issues it currently faces. Issue definition questions about the family's perceptions of what changes it would like, how those changes would alter the current situation, and what change would look like are useful in helping family members observe and reflect on their interactions. Hypothetical questions help family members examine possibilities for family change.

Family's Capacities and Past Successes in Problem Solving and Solution Finding

When reviewing with the family or family members their current concerns, solution-focused questions can provide direction for the assessment process (Berg, 1994). These questions are designed to help identify the outcomes that family members desire and to explore their past successes in coping with and managing their issues. The following "miracle question" is designed to give the worker direction on how the family or family member describes his or her preferred outcomes: "Suppose when you go to sleep tonight (pause), a miracle happened and the problems that brought you here today are solved (pause). But since you are asleep you can't know this miracle happened until you wake up tomorrow. What will be different tomorrow that will let you know this miracle has happened and the problem is solved?" (Berg, 1994, p. 97). Embedded in the individual's responses are the details of the issues the family is most interested in changing. This gives the worker an idea of the areas of most concern. Many families are unsure what to tell workers and don't know what areas are important to cover. The miracle question helps the worker focus on the areas to be more fully explored in the assessment process. The question also helps orient the family to a process of creatively visualizing its goals. Scaling questions, which consist of asking family members to rate on a scale of 1 to 10 the progress they have made toward meeting their goals, are also useful (Berg, 1994).

This conversation with the family facilitates an assessment of strengths, skills, and achievements. Noting the progress already achieved is helpful in building confidence to make advancements toward the family's miracle.

Coping and managing questions from the brief solution-focused approach support exploration into the family's past abilities and strategies (Berg, 1994). When looking for past successes in problem solving, other questions about exceptional times are useful. What family members are feeling, thinking, and doing when the problem behavior is not occurring also opens up the discussion about what does work to reduce the problem issues. In these exception-finding questions are hidden resources that also help family members identify present and past successful strategies and strengths that can further support behavior change through more active substitution of already successful solutions (De Jong & Miller, 1995). Simple strategies of asking family members to keep track of when things are going well offer them opportunities to become aware of these successes (Berg, 1994).

Solution-focused strategies of change can assist families to set goals as well. By pretending the miracle happened, the family is asked to visualize a day when the problem did not exist and to explore more fully the emotional benefits of potential change. The family visualizes the kinds of changes that would have to occur to make that happen, and that exploration leads to further assessment and goal-setting activities (Berg, 1994).

Assessing the Family's Readiness for Change

Motivation is considered an important element in successful evaluations of the family's readiness for change. It is an interactive process between worker and family members. New models and intervention strategies have been developed to assess and increase the family's readiness for change (Prochaska, DiClemente, & Norcross, 1992). Intervention techniques used to interview families in a manner that decreases resistance, called motivational interviewing, have been gaining momentum in assisting workers to accurately assess and intervene with families, particularly in the substance abuse field, as well as with eleven other health and risk behaviors (Prochaska et al., 1992; Prochaska, 1994).

The Transtheoretical Model of Change describes readiness for change in five discrete stages (Prochaska et al., 1992). In the first stage, precontemplation, an individual either does not recognize that a problem exists or believes that the consequences of the problem are insubstantial and sees no reason to make a change at this time. The second stage, contemplation, is characterized by the person beginning to recognize that there might be a problem and considering a need to change. The individual typically feels ambivalent, and is weighing the pros and cons of making the change. He or she is in a decision-making process but has not yet resolved to make a change. In this stage the decisional balance is beginning to move in favor of change, and the individual may anticipate the change's likelihood to occur for the next six months. Preparation, the next stage, is marked by the person experimenting with change and considering options for change. The treatment options, social supports, and barriers to each option are considered. The person usually considers change to occur in the immediate future, sometime in the next thirty days. The fourth stage is action: individuals take action-oriented steps toward making a change. During this stage they consider the effects of the steps toward change on their life and consider how the change affects their social support network. If the steps are not successful, they modify the plan until it works for them. In this stage the person has typically worked on taking action to change behavior for anywhere from one day to six months. The last stage, maintenance, is the stage in which the person maintains the behavior change for more than six months. Relapse may occur during the stage and is seen as a normal part of obtaining ongoing change. Relapse is considered a temporary repeat of the first three stages, through which skills gained in understanding the contributors to relapses can lead to permanent maintenance (Prochaska et al., 1992).

The progression of these stages is not necessarily a linear process, but is frequently cyclical, with regression to earlier stages. This finding led the authors to describe the progression of the stages as a spiral process (Grimley, Prochaska, Velicer, Blais, & DiClemente, 1994; Prochaska et al., 1992). The significance of using this model in assessment is that certain strategies or processes of change need to be tailored to the stage of readiness of the client (Saunders, Wilkinson, & Towers, 1996). Motivational interviewing, which focuses on strategies such as reflective listening, summarizations, open-ended questions, and affirmation-eliciting self-motivation statements, has been used at the early stages of engagement and reduces barriers for individual family members in their change process (Miller & Rollnick, 1991).

Ten processes to support successful change have been compiled through interviewing people who had successfully accomplished their goals; the processes are matched to the stages just described (Prochaska, DiClemente, & Norcross, 1992; Prochaska, 1994). In the precontemplation stage, consciousness-raising focused on individual family members increased their perceptions of the risk involved in their current behaviors or the consequences of inaction. Engagement skills outlined above involve empathy to empower family members, and in taking ownership of the process they realize that change is ultimately their decision. This decreases the reluctance to move toward change because the pressure comes from other family members rather than a worker. Awareness of the effects of their behaviors on other family members is an effective incentive, and dramatic relief is evident as family members experience the negative emotions associated with their own behavior and take responsibility for that behavior. Called environmental reevaluation, realizing the negative impact on others in the physical and social environment can allow family members to move toward contemplating change. This has been used quite successfully in family interventions with substance-affected family members.

Contemplation processes that are helpful include self-reflection. A client's assessing the discrepancy between where he or she is and what his or her life would be like without the problem behaviors or concerns opens up a visualization process of what the future could be. It is necessary to examine the ambivalence and fully explore the costs and benefits of both staying the same and making changes. While in the preparation stage, the process of self-liberation occurs when people make a firm commitment to change. Exploring options once the commitment occurs and reducing barriers for options help the individual and the family make the change happen.

In the action stage, change is facilitated in part by social liberation, a process of realizing that social norms support the goal and the helping behaviors. Preparation is needed, however, to deal with resistance from those in the family or within the social support network who find the old behaviors familiar and sometimes beneficial. This is especially true if financial benefits accompanied a family member's unhealthy behavior.

The processes most helpful in the maintenance stage include increasing the rewards for positive behavior changes and decreasing rewards for unhealthy behaviors. Counterconditioning can occur through substitution of new behaviors and cognitions for the old ones. Stimulus control of identified cues and triggers that remind the person of the old behavior that could put him or her at risk for further unhealthy behavior also are used. The last process, and probably the most interesting in the maintenance stage, is the need for a helping relationship. Actively seeking support for the change appears critical for movement through these stages.

Motivation is a contributing factor to the success of family-centered practice. Accurately assessing what stage family members are in and helping family members move toward the next stage of change can decrease the time it takes for family issues to be resolved. Increasing the speed and effectiveness of the family change process can have beneficial effects on family well-being. This is particularly true for workers with time constraints, such as those posed by current child welfare policy and managed-care funding.

Assessing Family Dynamics and Structure

Hartman and Laird (1983) examined internal family dynamics, including the structure of the family, rules and decision making, conflict resolution methods, family climate, and family cohesion and adaptability. Roles, including sharing, conflict, flexibility, shifts, coalitions, and role strains, are evaluated. Communication patterns, rules, expression, and communication loop conflicts also are assessed. Power dynamics, including sharing of power, handling confrontation, abuses of power, and expressing critical or angry feelings, are examined. Finally, the nature of intimacy is examined, including expressions of affection and love, sexuality, shared expectations, closeness, values, and the handling of secrets.

The Circumplex Model, developed by David Olson, Joyce Portner, and Yoav Lavee (Olson, 1989; Olson, Portner, & Lavee, 1985), also provides an excellent framework for understanding family dynamics when conducting a family-centered assessment. The model explores family cohesion, adaptability, and communication. It identifies four dimensions of cohesion, which are rated on a continuum, from disengaged to separated to connected to enmeshed. The cohesion dimensions that are assessed using this continuum are demonstrated by objective criteria. Examples are in the areas of emotional bonding; family involvement; marital relationship; parent-child relationship; internal boundaries of time, space, and decision making; and external boundaries of friendship, interests, and activities. Potential problem areas are marked by extremes on the continuum. The adaptability continuum ranges between rigid, structured, flexible, and chaotic, with the extremes representative of potential problematic behaviors. The dimension of leadership includes control, discipline, negotiation, roles, and rules. The family communication dimension rates facilitating skills from low through high with either extreme marking potential problem areas. The dimensions include listeners' skills of empathy and attentive listening, speakers' skills of speaking for self or speaking too much for others, self-disclosure, clarity, continuity, and tracking with respect and regard.

Assessing Family Dynamics Using Rapid Assessment Tools

Several tools are available to provide a rapid measure of family dynamics. These are found in *Measures of Clinical Practice: A Sourcebook* (Fischer and Corcoran, 1994). The Family Adaptability and Cohesion Evaluation Scale (FACES) is a rapid assessment tool measuring the Circumplex Model (Olson, 1989). It consists of a twenty-item inventory completed by both the family and the worker. This has been developed to assess the family in balanced, midrange, and extreme dimensions, using the first two dimensions of cohesion and adaptability. The assessment can assist in goal setting toward midrange responses to the observations made by both the family and the worker. The tool can be used for pretest and posttest changes in the family-functioning areas. Adaptations have been made for culturally diverse groups (Vega et al., 1986).

Another useful tool is the Family Assessment Device (FAD), based on the McMaster Model, which assesses structural, operational, and transactional properties of families (Epstein, Baldwin, & Bishop, 1983). It is a sixty-item questionnaire designed to evaluate family functioning on six dimensions (i.e., problem solving, communication, roles, affective responsiveness, affective involvement, and behavior control) and on a seventh general functioning scale. These two tools, plus others, not only help to give a quick assessment to add to the fuller picture of the family but also serve as important elements to consider when making an observation or as areas to cover in interviews that lead toward a complete assessment of the family's relational dynamics. An exercise using the Circumplex Model for family assessment to help families evaluate their communication has been developed in a curriculum called Understanding Us (Carnes, 1981). It is called a house-building exercise. Family members are given paper, scissors, markers, pens, pencils, and a stapler and are asked to build a paper house together. The only rule is that they cannot talk. Processing the family's dynamics during the exercise, such as how they communicate, where the leadership arises, how they handle conflict, and how they give support can be useful for all the family members, as they have an opportunity to describe their family dynamics.

Assessing Families Using Intergenerational Tools

Intergenerational issues that affect family functioning warrant exploration in order to help families demonstrate new behavior and change established patterns of functioning. Murray Bowen (1978) developed the multigenerational transmission process in the 1960s. Tools were developed and adapted to assist the family to better understand the historical impact of its family of origin on its current family processes (McGoldrick & Gerson, 1985). The genogram assesses family structure, life-cycle events, patterns repeated across generations, life events and family functioning, relational patterns and triangles, and family balance and imbalance. Recently, the genogram was modified to assess intergenerational strengths (Family Learning and Growing, 1999). Another new tool was developed by Wayne Maes and Nicholas Sanfilipo (1999) to look at intergenerational patterns of family resiliency. Focused genograms (DeMaria, Weeks, & Hof, 1999) build on the traditional genogram approach by developing a family map that combines structural family maps (Minuchin, 1974) and Hartman's (1978) Eco-maps in order to assess transactional patterns in special topic areas. Several of these tools are described below.

Strength-Based Genograms

The strength-based genogram is a visual format for recording information about family members and their relationships over three or more generations. Unique qualities and strengths of family members are identified. Significant patterns of strengths, attributes, and talents and the events surrounding their influence on family members are assessed for recurring significance. The picture of the family's relationship emerges as the family tells its story. Adaptations to use the strengths from cultural networks, such as clan, fictional kin, and godparents, are adapted for specific cultural groups.

Resiliency-Based Genograms

PATH (Perspective: Ancestral Tales of Hope), a strength-based tool, was designed as an alternative to the genogram. The tool assesses generational members who function as heros or heroines, resilient members, courageous members, wise members, compassionate members, and special family attributes called the family choice. Once the members are identified, icons are used to represent these qualities. The family members enjoy the creativity of designing the icons, and this enjoyment aids in the symbolic connection between them. How these members have influenced the family, what their lives have taught them, and the strengths needed for the family members are part of the family assessment. Understanding what qualities the family member has from this legacy aids in seeing the strengths in all family members. Those strengths become resources for the individual and the family to use in meeting goals. The connections to these family members are also a source of strength and pride and often lend hope to the families as they face difficult issues. Some family members choose goals around future modeling of this behavior for their family and future generations.

Focused Genograms

Focused genograms (DeMaria et al., 1999) are a special aspect of the assessment process. They provide an opportunity for the family and the worker to explore in detail a focused genogram about a special topic area of family dynamics and influences. Areas covered are culture, gender, emotions, attachments, health, sexuality, love, and marriage. The focused genogram process is guided by in-depth family questions in each of these areas. Family dynamics, patterns, and beliefs are explored. Family art therapy techniques, family sculpting, the Kuethe Felt Figure Technique, and pictures and photographs can be used to explore family feelings about family experiences.

Assessing Family Safety

Child and family safety is of utmost concern when working with families. Several methods of assessing safety issues have been developed to look at risk factors and determine the level of perceived risk to family members. Most safety tools focus on both threats to and support for family members, but they also look at the strengths and resources used to provide protection (Day, Robinson, & Sheikh, 1998). Areas assessed for children include physical abuse, emotional abuse, sexual abuse, emotional neglect, and physical neglect. The protective safety concerns that can lead to imminent risk are situations in which one or more of the parents is out of control, the parents are predominately negative and have unrealistic expectations of the child, the harm already done has been moderate to severe, and there is some belief that the family will flee with the child. There is a problem if one or more of the parents is unable, possibly due to his or her own threat of abuse, to protect the child according to the Illinois Child Endangerment Risk Assessment Protocol (Illinois Department of Children and Family Services, n.d.).

Several risk assessment tools have been developed, including the New Mexico Structured Decision Making Tool (Meyer, 1999), the Washington Risk Assessment (English, Aubin, Fine, & Pecora, 1993), and the Michigan Empirical Predictors Method of Risk Assessment (Baird, Wagner, Caskey, & Neuenfeldt, 1995). The critical areas for assessment of risk factors for abuse and neglect include characteristics of the caretakers, current substance abuse patterns, parenting abilities, history of domestic violence, numbers of past complaints, motivation to improve parenting skills, parents' mental health issues, and financial problems (Day et al., 1998).

More recently, the North Carolina Family Assessment Scale (NCFAS), a strength-based family assessment scale, was developed not only to look at risk indicators but also to assess strength indicators for family functioning where family preservation services have been offered to high-risk families (Kirk, Reed, & Lin, 1995). This tool can be used both for continued measurement of growth and change and as a pretest and posttest for evaluating outcomes that demonstrate the family's improved areas of strength. McCroskey and Meezan (1997) developed the Family Assessment Form, which assesses (a) the family's environment, including the physical environment, financial resources, and social support; (b) the caregiver characteristics, including history, personal characteristics, and child-rearing abilities; and (c) interactions including parent to children, children to parent, and between the parents or primary caregivers. This tool also represents an extensive guide to assessment indicators and can be used by workers for evaluation of their practice with families.

Family safety planning is also an important aspect of assessing family safety. Most workers who work in a high-risk situation are required by mandate or practice wisdom to develop formal safety plans when a risk incident brought the family to the attention of outsiders. The risk can be, however, to any and all family members. Spouse abuse and child abuse are frequently cofactors in families seeking assistance. Folaron (1993) and Hess and Proch (1988) developed a formal safety-planning tool for children that was modified to provide a strength-based approach for the protection of all family members (Sandau-Beckler, 1998). The Family Safety Plan is a tool for identifying, together with the family, a safety goal. The children's warning signs are discussed and identified and are written on the Family Safety Plan. The knowledge the children possess is assessed. The knowledge they need as well as their strengths to identify the warning signs are noted as well. The resources to discuss the warning signs are laid out and can include family, friends, neighbors, teachers, and counselors. A written safety plan for the child is developed that draws on the strengths and supports of the extended family, the worker, and the community to assist the family in meeting its safety goals. A full experiential practice of the plan with the parents' support and assistance occurs.

The same process occurs for the parents. Warning signs are discussed in terms of the high-risk indicators or triggers they observe prior to the abuse, neglect, or relapse. The parents' knowledge, skills, and strength to identify the warning signs are written on the plan. The parents' resources to discuss warning signs are developed and noted on the plan. The safety plan for the parents is outlined, and the use of extended family, the worker, and community resources and strengths to assist them in meeting their goals are identified. The parents experientially practice their safety plan in front of the family. The critical assessment issue is whether the parents give permission for their children to take action and protect themselves. The safety plan is signed by all family members. If parents are unable to support their children in having that protection, the level of risk for the children is increased. The unique aspect of the Family Safety Plan is that the parent is supported and has permission to ask for help in high-risk situations. Many parents are also victims of physical and emotional abuse or have substance abuse issues that make them vulnerable to relapse. They also see the family-centered worker supporting the safety needs of all the family's members, thus reducing the strain sometimes experienced when the only concern is focused on the child.

Assessment for Specialized Challenges

Specific to each family are the special challenges it faces. Areas that need specific attention and have specialized assessments might include substance abuse, mental health for children or adults or both, homicidal and suicidal risk, school functioning, developmental functioning, health functioning, child abuse or neglect or both, sexual abuse, spouse abuse, physical violence toward others, and attachment. What to assess in each of these areas is beyond the scope of this chapter, but awareness of these issues is critical to the assessment process. Workers should seek special tools that have been developed in these areas that can augment their family assessment. The Child Welfare League of America has put together an Assessment Tool Kit that could provide some tools in the areas listed above (Day et al., 1998). However, questions regarding the description of the behaviors, onset and frequency of the behaviors, changes in patterns of behaviors, and their effects on the family are helpful. Adjusting to the concerns related to the issue is also helpful for workers as they assess the effects on the functioning of the family and the systems that surround it (U.S. Marine Corps Family Advocacy Program, 1997). Facilitating communication between the family and the systems becomes part of the assessment process as well as an important source of information and resources for plan development, implementation, and evaluation.

Exploring Resource Systems

Exploring the family's resource systems is another aspect of the assessment process. Friends, family, and coworkers make up the social support network of many families. Both informal supports and concrete services are necessary for family functioning. Exploring the abilities of its social support systems to provide assistance is essential in helping a family meet its goals. Several visual tools can assist both worker and family to identify and describe resources (Hartman, 1978; Tracy & Whittaker, 1990). These tools are designed to help the family assess itself within the context of its social environment. A supportive network is central not only to the goal-setting process but also to the change process.

By assessing this area with family members, workers can gain further understanding of the history and story of the family in its relationships with outside agencies and institutions. While those relationships may be sources of tension and conflict for familes, the initiation, enhancement, maintenance, or reconnection of such resources can support successful plan development and can be sources of goal-setting directions. However, to repair or end relationships with conflicting supports and systems may be necessary for the family to reach its goals. For example, a family member who is in recovery for substance abuse may need to cease contact with other family members or friends who are unwilling to accept or support his or her decision to seek sobriety. Some family members need help in developing a support system. The reduction of isolation is influenced by the ability to use one's social supports. It has been found that perceived levels of support buffer stress and assist families in functioning. Frequently, isolated families, especially where domestic abuse or child abuse has occurred, will have fewer contacts and relationships with others (Thompson, 1995). The shame involved in these issues propels family members to withdraw from their normal social support or discourages them from even initiating a support network.

The first tool is the Eco-map (Hartman, 1978), a construction of the narrative story and history of the family's relationships that helps it identify sources of support, strengths, and tension and drain on family resources. The map is a graphic representation of the family as it exists amid the individuals, groups, organizations, and agencies that the family influences and by which the family is influenced (Sandau-Beckler, 1999). The Eco-map helps the family acquire an awareness of its connections, its resources, the directions of the flow of energy, and the negative factors in its resource systems. Eco-maps can set the stage for work with the family. The family dynamics are observed as family members discuss and share their perceptions of the family's history. The rules for communication and daily life and roles of the family members can be observed in the interactions. It provides an opportunity for the family to organize such information easily in a visual format that depicts the relationships between the family and its resource systems. The process of completing the map with family members is an opportunity for discussing individual perspectives and exploring possibilities regarding support systems. The family can then capitalize on the sources of support and determine where to start strengthening and expanding the network.

The Social Network Map (Tracy & Whittaker, 1990) is another visual tool to aid family members in assessing the people that make up its support system and in conducting an evaluation of the levels of support. The tool identifies areas of concrete support, emotional support, and advice. Comparing these levels of support helps family members clarify when and under what circumstances they may ask friends or family for support and advice. Family members discover how they can successfully use the identified support and how they could explore underutilized resources. The tool also identifies under what conditions or in what areas the family may not seek assistance from others who may be too critical or may not have the knowledge or the resources to assist in specific situations: "The direction of the help, the closeness of feeling to the individuals in their social support network, the frequency of contact and the long-standing nature of the network are examined" (Sandau-Beckler, 1999, p. 8). The results of the experiential activity provided by this tool can help family members set goals for further development and use of resources in addressing their change process.

The Circle of Friends (Families Learning and Growing, 1999) is another visual tool that organizes the family within its social support network, the organizations with which it interacts, and its community resources. The tool assists family members in evaluating their kinship and family membership, friendship network, organizational memberships, informal and formal social services supports, and paid organizational services. Like the others, this tool helps the family create a visual representation of its supportive network and how it is nested in those systems.

Assessment areas outlined by Dunst, Trivette, and Deal (1996) offer a framework for exploring general support and resources available to the family. These include (a) concrete resources such as phone, transportation, and medical care; (b) the family's sense of belonging, participation, and meaningful connections in social or group activities or organizations; and (c) cultural, ethnic, or spiritual resources. In addition, underidentified and underutilized resources and sources of support are explored. The family members' assessment of the meaning of the support and resources, whether a help or a burden, are evaluated with the family, and the concept of reciprocity is discussed. The family also evaluates the services in terms of cultural responsiveness and value conflicts with the neighborhood and community environment. Key factors in the assessment are (a) promoting family skills in order to evaluate the success of the help offered and (b) promoting the family's connections with both formal and informal services while fostering its independence.

Larger Systems Assessment of the Family's Challenges

Evan Imber-Black (1988) has done seminal work in developing the Family and Larger Systems Assessment. Larger systems such as school, workplace, health care system, and caregiving agencies are a part of the family's life but not always a source of support. Assessing the experiences of families and those of their members with outside systems is an important element of the assessment process. Workers seek information about the roles agencies and helpers play in the lives of the family and the extent of their involvement. Interventions may need to be designed that also effect change within and for those agencies. The perspectives of the various agencies should be a part of the assessment (i.e., what they regard as the family's issues and what directions they would support in assisting the family). Differing perspectives between agencies or even workers within agencies can detract from successful assessment and intervention. Sometimes it is helpful to assess what has and has not been tried and what worked and did not work in previous service provision. The relationships between the family and the outside system or systems and how those relationships perpetuate or maintain issues or constrain the family from successfully setting goals or achieving outcomes is also critical to the assessment process. Sometimes systemic constraints such as policy, finances, and systems resources can detour the family from meeting its goals. Workers creatively assess these relationships and intervene in areas that reduce conflict and triangulation and make for better transitions and relationships with families and the larger systems with which they work. Effective assessment can enhance the development of successful relationships, maintain viable relationships, and repair strained or unproductive relationships in moving toward successful intervention outcomes.

CONNECTING FAMILY ASSESSMENT TO
GOAL-SETTING ACTIVITIES

Linking Assessment to Change-Oriented, Family-Centered Outcomes

The assessment process naturally brings forth areas of concern and potential solution-focused goals for the family. Goals should be specific and measurable and should take a collaborative course of action and build on past successes and available resources. Outcome-oriented goals facilitate change and require review and monitoring (Kinney, Strand, Hagerup, & Bruner, 1994). Family members and workers can recognize the change, celebrate the successes, and learn from the setbacks. The elements of a family-centered outcome plan include (a) the family concerns with a focus on identifying solutions, (b) the desired family outcomes, and (c) one or more indicators of progress for each outcome. Also identified for each of the outcomes in the plan are methods of data collection, performance targets, and the family's strengths and resources. Additional information is provided regarding worker activities and resources needed. The strengths and resources of the worker, the natural helpers, and formal helpers are noted, and tasks to facilitate change are outlined. Some plans cannot be effective without changes in formal systems or in the community (Lee, 1996; Gutierrez, 1990; Gutierrez, GlenMaye, & DeLois, 1995).

The family-centered approach requires identifying outcomes that are strength based and culturally responsive. While the desired outcomes spring out of a collaborative decision-making process, they are very uniquely individualized. Goals are specific and realistic as well as creative and flexible. They are written in the language of the family, and they provide accountability to the family and to the agency. Cultural factors, such as language, resources, natural supports, nontraditional healing, and cultural barriers, should be taken into account. Preference with regard to approaches to change and the kinds of interventions that would benefit most may differ markedly depending on the culture. For example, a sweat lodge used by a Native American family or a *Ho'oponopono*, a Hawaiian mediation ritual for parent-child conflict, may be effective interventions but might not fit the traditional concepts of change. Many partners will not be formally trained. As Briar-Lawson (1998) points out, indigenous helpers are often primary service providers.

Family-Centered Goal Setting

In order to be effective, goals must offer safety for the family members. The expectations for change must be clear, and there should be permission given for all family members to proceed (Schroeder & Sandau-Beckler,

1997). The skills to be developed and the resources to accomplish the goals must be specific. Key players in the change process are identified and committed.

Prior to writing treatment plans, families assess their needs and goals. The use of strengths and resources to help them accomplish their plans is critical to achieving successful outcomes. Managing the change process by making specific the small steps to accomplish change is of great value to families. Several strategies assist families in defining and prioritizing goals, assessing strengths and resources to meet their goals, and using methods to measure and evaluate their progress.

Assessing Family Prioritization

Client self-determination is essential to building partnerships with families, and successful assessment may be enhanced by teaching families to prioritize goals. There are tools that can assist in this process. For example, Homebuilders (Kinney, n.d.) developed a set of cards to identify common goals in the areas of relationships, moods, rest and relaxation, sexuality, recreation and exercise, money and bills, agencies and authority, personal growth and fulfillment, parenting, health, health care and dental care, parents, jobs, housework, personal safety, transportation, food, daily routines, schools, alcohol and drugs, child behavior, past trauma, abuse, pets, education, child care, safety, trouble with Child Protective Services (CPS), legal issues, clothes, appearance, pests, and dangerous animals. The client sorts the cards to prioritize his or her needs and develop a plan.

Recognizing the importance of linking goals to important family values, Homebuilders (Kinney, n.d.) also developed Value Cards. Value Card sorting can help family members define and learn more about themselves and their values and recognize discrepancies between their current lives and how they would like their lives to be.

Prioritization of goals includes building family consensus with regard to priorities. The discussion involved in using the tools may help family members become aware of their differing priorities and differing perceptions about goals (Madsen, 1999). Workers often need resolution skills and cultural competence to mediate the process of prioritizing goals—both within the family and between the family and its support systems (Kinney et al., 1994).

Family Plans for Solutions

Following are several unique tools for the tailoring of family plans. The tools are visual, and some involve drawing and pictures in a creative process to assist families in envisioning their change process. Family members often feel empowered when the creative goal-setting process comes from them and is in their own form of communication. As Kinney et al. (1994)

point out, when families have a voice in designing the plan, they are more likely to be committed and adhere to the plan.

Five-Column Approach

Through the Five-Column Approach (St. Luke's Innovative Resources, n.d.-a), family members are asked to identify current challenges and a vision of what their life will look like after they resolve the challenges using brief solution-focused questions. Bear Feeling Cards assist the family in further exploring the emotional impact of the challenges they face. Family members identify their current progress in reaching their goal and identify indicators that will lead to the next step. Strength Cards identify special abilities to help attain their goals. Also identified are current resource systems and social network supports. A description is given of the first step to be taken toward their vision, and brief solution-focused scaling questions are used to document progress and define future steps.

Planning Alternative Tomorrows with Hope (PATH)

Developed by Pearpoint, O'Brien, and Forest (1992), the PATH tool describes a process for short-term goal setting. Family members are asked to define driving forces and strengths. They are asked also to define goals they would like to accomplish in the next six months, which will assist them in becoming the kind of person or family they want to be. This tool documents family members' current behaviors and behaviors required in order to attain their goal. It also identifies new knowledge and skills that will be needed. It assists them in planning and tracking their progress (e.g., the first step for action and what is to be accomplish by the end of one month, three months, and at the time of completion). The tool incorporates drawings and pictures to illustrate indicators of progress. Flexibility in setting time frames to meet the needs of the family or the agency services is stressed.

Families Learning and Growing (FLAG)

Several tools were developed through San Juan County Families Learning and Growing. Three will be described briefly.

Personal Strengths and Goals. The Personal Strengths and Goals tool (FLAG, 1999b) helps people identify their feelings about their successes, the achievements they would like to make, and the timelines to meet their goals. Barriers to making change and strategies for reducing those barriers are also identified.

The Family Plan. The Family Plan (FLAG, 1999c) helps families assess two goals they are willing to work on. It concretely defines the changes that will be made through goal attainment. Action steps are identified along with persons responsible and timelines. It also provides for a review of the goals achieved.

Family Goal Setting. The Family Goal Setting tool (FLAG, 1999a) assists families in identifying what they want for their children, their family strengths, and their personal hopes and dreams. A list is created of community services needed in order to meet the goals, and the family is helped in assessing the steps required to reach its plan.

These tools are practical, build on the family's creativity and family support, and organize the change process. They facilitate productive and motivating discussion, and they can be used easily as visual reminders of the goals or treatment plan—with families retaining a copy of the planning document. They can be used individually or collectively by family members and can be adapted to unique situations as needed. When family members learn of each other's goals, they are often surprised and become a source of support for each other in attaining those goals. Children in particular like the concreteness of these goal-setting activities.

Measuring Family Change

Methods of measuring change must be linked to the goal-setting process and can also be creative. These methods operationalize progress in terms that can be reported and visualized by all involved, but especially by the family. Progress indicator tools were developed by St. Luke's Innovative Resources (n.d.-b) in Bendigo, Australia. They include using graphs, thermometers, scenes of a river, progressive circles, ladders, and scales where progress can be marked or graphed. The review of the change process opens up conversations about what family members see as indicators of further change and how family members will know the process is complete (Madsen, 1999). Goal attainment is accompanied by recognition and celebrations as well as the discovery of unexpected benefits. A method for tracking progress also provides for discussion about the meaning of unachieved goals and exploration of modifying plans. The best plans have a built-in trial solution so that if the plan doesn't work, another plan can be implemented. Commitment, hope, and flexibility are especially important attributes of the worker during the progress-measuring process.

COLLABORATIVE TEAM BUILDING TO SUPPORT FAMILY ASSESSMENT AND GOAL SETTING

Teamwork is vital when developing a unified system to support family-centered assessment and goal setting. The level of collaboration and relationship building that occurs around the family during assessment and goal setting is a key to successful change and often makes the difference in reaching family-centered outcomes. Creativity in putting together the formal and informal resources to support accurate assessment and well-developed plans is much like putting a puzzle together.

Following is a summary of the many simple strategies that can assist in this process:

1. Maintain respect for the family and for other team members as a fundamental principle.
2. Ask families what they need for support and how to include them in teams (Madsen, 1999).
3. Explain the nature of team relationships to the family, clarifying confidentiality and developing mechanisms for communication among team members.
4. Be honest and specific in sharing with the family and team members the results of strength and risk assessments including the basis on which suggestions are made and personal concerns.
5. Don't make decisions without consulting the family.
6. Don't be reluctant to ask for help.
7. Be open in discussing value disagreements and explore common values and purposes.
8. Maintain a commitment to "be with" the family throughout the change process.
9. In order to maintain a strength-based focus, be willing to risk making a mistake.
10. Be an audience for the family's new identity and behaviors in helping them present the new changes to each other (Madsen, 1999).

Collaborative Team Building During Team Conferences

Team conferences are frequently held to conduct joint planning, check progress, coordinate services, obtain commitments, review work, and clear up communication issues. At times differences are mediated, and workers or others may explain their approaches or differences in perceptions of the success of the change process. It is important to put the parents in charge of these discussions and assist them in gaining the skills to take the lead in team conferences. This role may be unfamiliar, and strategies such as modeling or role-playing the procedure for conducting a strength-based conference may be helpful. In addition, families may need help in learning how to ask for strength-based feedback. Team members may find it helpful to start a team conference by asking each to share one strength of the family and the child as well as one hope or dream. Asking family members to report on their goal-attainment progress and assistance needed can empower them to feel confident and provide an opportunity for the team to celebrate their successes with them.

Other strategies for involving the family during team conferences include writing progress notes with the family and summarizing with the family their progress report, for example, a court report or a quarterly report to CPS. This provides an additional forum for discussing varying perceptions of the progress and assistance needed.

Use of Team Consultation and Reflecting Teams

Team consultation and reflecting teams have been used in family-centered practice (Anderson, 1987). The team provides consultation directly to the family by reflecting on the strengths and underscoring the family members' insight into their concerns. The team uses the language of the family to provide these reflections and allows for the family system to seek its own solutions. Team members give tentative impressions and allow the family to decide if they are useful. Opportunities are then given for the family to reflect on the impressions of the outsiders. These teams observe the family both in and out of the room through a one-way mirror but most commonly give their responses directly to the family, allowing for the family to have time with the worker to reflect on what is said by the team. In-home workers can videotape their sessions and ask team consultants to audio- or videotape their reflections to present to the family. This provides validation for the family and reflects back to them the significant statements that support their change process.

□ □ □

This chapter summarizes possible opportunities for obtaining a complete family picture in the process of conducting a family-centered assessment and using the results of that picture for effective family-centered goal setting. It addresses the concept of a comprehensive family assessment through a variety of perspectives and as a product of the family-centered and strength-based philosophy and values. It is hoped that the reader has gained a deeper understanding of those values, knowledge regarding an array of traditional and creative options for support tools, and enhanced skills in fostering relationships and partnerships with families, who are the ultimate source of success.

REFERENCES

Anderson, G. R. (1991). Ethical issues in intensive family preservation service. In E. M. Tracy, D. A. Haapala, J. Kinney, P. J. Pecora (Eds.), *Intensive family preservation services: An instructional sourcebook.* Cleveland: Case Western Reserve University, Mandel School of Applied Social Sciences.

Anderson, T. (1987). The reflecting team: Dialogue and meta-dialogue in clinical work. *Family Process,* 26 (1), 415–28.

Baird, C., Wagner, D., Caskey, R., & Neuenfeldt, D. (1995). *The Michigan Department of Social Services structured decision-making system: An evaluation of its impact on child protection services.* Madison, WI: Children's Research Center.

Berg, I. K. (1994). *Family based services: A solution-focused approach.* New York: Norton.

Bowen, M. (1978). *Family therapy in clinical practice.* New York: Aronson.

Briar-Lawson, K. (1998). Capacity building for integrated family-centered practice. *Social Work, 43,* 539–50.

Carnes, P. J. (1981). *Understanding Us.* Minneapolis: Printing Arts.

Congress, E. P. (1994). The use of culturegrams to assess and empower culturally diverse families. *Families in Society: The Journal of Contemporary Human Services, 75,* 531–40.

Cowger, C. D. (1994). Assessing client strengths: Clinical assessment for client empowerment. *Social Work, 39,* 262–68.

Cross, T. L. (1998). Understanding family resiliency from a relational world view. In H. McCubbin, E. Thompson, A. Thompson, & J. Fromer (Eds.), *Resiliency in Native American and immigrant families* (pp. 143–57). Thousand Oaks, CA: Sage.

Cross, T. L., Bazron, B. J., Dennis, K. W., & Isaacs, M. R. (1989, March). *Toward a culturally competent system of care.* Washington, DC: CASSP Technical Assistant Center, Georgetown University, Child Development Center.

Day, P., Robinson, S., & Sheikh, L. (1998). *Ours to keep: A guide for building a community assessment strategy for child protection.* Washington, DC: Child Welfare League of America.

De Jong, P., & Miller, S. D. (1995). How to interview for client strengths. *Social Work, 40,* 729–38.

Deal, R., & Veeken, J. (1997). *Strength Cards.* Bendigo, Victoria, Australia: St. Luke's Innovative Resources.

DeMaria, R., Weeks, G., & Hof, L. (1999). *Focused genograms.* New York: Hamilton.

Dosser, D. A., Shaffer, R. J., Shaffer, M. M., Clevenger, D., & Jefferies, D. K. (1996, Winter). Toward the development of ethical guidelines for family preservation. *Family Preservation Journal, 1,* 75–83.

Dunst, C. J., Trivette, C. M., & Deal, A. G. (Eds.). (1996). *Supporting and strengthening families: Vol. 1. Methods, strategies, and practices.* Cambridge, MA: Brookline Books.

English, D., Aubin, S., Fine, D., & Pecora, P. (1993). *Improving the accuracy and cultural sensitivity of risk assessment in child abuse and neglect cases.* Seattle, WA: Washington State Department of Social and Health Services, Children, Youth, and Family Services Administration, Office of Children's Administration Research.

Epstein, N. B., Baldwin, L. M., & Bishop, D. S. (1983). The McMaster Family Assessment Device. *Journal of Marital and Family Therapy, 9,* 171–80.

Families Learning and Growing (FLAG). (1999a). *Family Goal Setting.* Farmington, NM: San Juan County FLAG Program.

Families Learning and Growing (FLAG). (1999b). *Personal Strengths and Goals.* Farmington, NM: San Juan County FLAG Program.

Families Learning and Growing (FLAG). (1999c). *The Family Plan.* Farmington, NM: San Juan County FLAG Program.

Federation of Families for Children's Mental Health. (1990, March). *Philosophy Statement.* Washington, DC: Author.

Fischer, J., & Corcoran, K. (1994). *Measures for clinical practice: A sourcebook* (2nd ed.). New York: Free Press.

Folaron, G. (1993). Preparing children for reunification. In B. A. Pine, R. Krieger, & A. N. Maluccio (Eds.), *Together again: Family reunification in foster care* (pp. 141–54). Washington, DC: Child Welfare League of America.

Grealish, M., Piña, V., & Vandenberg, J. (1995, August). *Ground rules for parent-professional partnerships.* Dona Anna County Child and Adolescent Collaborative and the National Resource Network for Child and Family Mental Health Services, training presented by the Community Partnerships Group, Las Cruces, NM.

Greenberg, L. S., & Pinsof, W. M. (1986). Process research: Current trends and future perspectives. In L. S. Greenberg & W. M. Pinsof (Eds.), *The psychotherapeutic process: A research handbook* (pp. 3–20). New York: Guilford Press.

Grimely, D., Prochaska, J. O., Velicer, W. F., Blais, L. M., & DiClemente, C. C. (1992). The transtheoretical model of change. In T. M. Brinthaupt & R. P. Lipka (Eds.), *Changing the self: Philosophies, techniques, and experiences* (pp. 201–28). Albany: State University of New York Press.

Gutierrez, L., GlenMaye, L., & DeLois, K. (1995). The organizational context of empowerment practice: Implications for social work administration. *Social Work, 40,* 249–58.

Gutierrez, L. M. (1990). Working with women of color: An empowerment perspective. *Social Work, 35,* 149–54.

Hardy, K. V., & Laszloffy, T. A. (1995). The Cultural Genogram: Key to training culturally competent family therapists. *Journal of Marital and Family Therapy, 21,* 227–80.

Hartman, A. (1978). Diagrammatic assessment of family relationships. *Social Casework, 59,* 465–76.

Hartman, A., & Laird, J. (1983). *Family-centered social work practice.* New York: Free Press.

Hess, P. M., & Proch, K. O. (1988). *Family visiting in out-of-home care: A guide to practice.* Washington, DC: Child Welfare League of America.

Hill, R. (1949). *Families under stress.* New York: Harper and Row.

Hill, R. (1958). Generic features of families under stress. *Social Casework, 49,* 139-50.

Hodges, V. G. (1991). Providing culturally sensitive intensive family preservation services to ethnic minority families. In E. M. Tracy, D. A. Haapala, J. Kinney, & P. J. Pecora (Eds.), *Intensive family preservation services: An instructional sourcebook* (pp. 95–116). Cleveland: Case Western Reserve University, Mandel School of Applied Social Sciences.

Illinois Department of Children and Family Services. (n.d.). *Child endangerment risk assessment protocol.* Chicago: Author.

Imber-Black, E. (1988). Creating a new relationship between a family and larger systems: Ongoing work. In *Families and larger systems: A family therapists guide through the labyrinth* (pp. 163–83). New York: Guilford Press.

Kinney, J. (n.d.) *The cards: Deciding who you are and where you're going.* Tacoma, WA: Home, Safe.

Kinney, J., Strand, K., Hagerup, M., & Bruner, C. (1994). *Beyond the buzzwords: Key principles in effective frontline practice.* Falls Church, VA: National Center for Service Integration.

Kirk, R., Reed, K., & Lin, A. (1995). *North Carolina Family Assessment Scale and user's guide.* Chapel Hill: University of North Carolina at Chapel Hill, School of Social Work, Human Services Research and Design Laboratory.

Lee, J. A. B. (1996). The empowerment approach to social work practice. In F. J. Turner (Ed.), *Social work treatment: Interlocking theoretical approaches* (4th ed., pp. 218–49). New York: Free Press.

Leigh, J. W. (1998). *Communicating for cultural competence.* Boston: Allyn and Bacon.

Lindbald-Goldberg, M., Dore, M. M., & Stern, L. (1998). *Creating competence from chaos: A comprehensive guide to home-based services.* New York: Norton.

Lloyd, J. (1984). *Basic family-centered curriculum.* Iowa City, IA: National Resource Center on Family-Based Services. Wendy Deutelbaum Associates.

Madsen, W. C. (1999). *Collaborative therapy with multi-stressed families.* New York: Guilford Press.

Maes, W. R., & Sanfilipo, N. (1997). *PATH: Family genealogy and the strengths model in family preservation.* Albuquerque, NM: Southeast Heights Renaissance Project.

Martinez, S., Henry, J., Dudley, V., Gonzales, P., Lovelace, B., Watts, C., Luna, A., Baca, J., Valenzuela, J., Sansom, D., Nyergers, H., Nalder, S., Workman, S., Miller, M., Gass, V., Satz, E., Cunningham, C., Kahn, Y., Burrows, J., Thomas, N., Jackson, E., Curley, C., Gomez, C., Dickens, R., & Romancito, M. (n.d.). *New Mexico Family-Centered Assessment Tool.* Las Cruces: New Mexico State University, School of Social Work.

McCroskey, J., & Meezan, W. (1997). *Family preservation and family functioning.* Washington, DC: Child Welfare League of America.

McCubbin, H., & Patterson, J. M. (1983). The family stress process: The double ABCX model of adjustment and adaptation. In H. McCubbin, M. Sussman, & J. Patterson (Eds.), *Advances and developments in family stress theory and research* (pp. 7–37). New York: Haworth.

McCubbin, H. I., Thompson, A. I., & McCubbin, M. A. (1996). *Family assessment: Resiliency, coping, and adaption: Inventories for research and practice.* Madison: University of Wisconsin Publishers.

McCubbin, H. I., Thompson, A. I., & McCubbin, M. A. (n.d.) *Family assessment: Resiliency, coping, and adaption: Inventories for research and practice.* Madison: University of Wisconsin Publishers.

McCubbin, H. I., Thompson, E. A., Thompson, A. I., & Fromer, J. E. (Eds.). (1998). *Stress, coping, and health in families: Sense of coherence and resiliency.* Thousand Oaks, CA: Sage.

McGoldrick, M., & Gerson, R. (1985). *Genograms in family assessment.* New York: Norton.

Merkel-Holguin, L. (1998). Implementation of family group decision making processes in the U.S.: Policies and practices in transition? *Protecting Children, 14* (4), 4–10.

Meyer, B. L. (1999, July). Implementing actuarial risk assessment: Policy decisions and field practice in New Mexico. *Proceedings from the Twelfth National Round Table on Child Protective Services Risk Assessment* (pp. 103–117). Englewood, CO: American Humane Association.

Miller, W. R., & Rollnick, S. (1991). *Motivational interviewing: Preparing people to change addictive behavior.* New York: Guilford Press.

Minuchin, S. (1974). *Families and family therapy.* Cambridge: Harvard University Press.

National Resource Center on Family Based Services. (n.d.). *Reframing/Relabeling/Redefinition Exercise.* Iowa City, IA: Author.

Olson, D. H. (1989). *Circumplex Model of Family Systems VIII: Family assessment and intervention.* New York: Haworth Press.

Olson, D. H., Portner, J., & Lavee, Y. (1985). *FACES-III.* St. Paul: University of Minnesota.

Oriti, B., Bibb, A., & Mahboubi, J. (1996). Family-centered practice with racially/ethnically mixed families. *Families in Society: The Journal of Contemporary Human Services, 77,* 573–82.

Overton, A., Tinker, K. H., & Associates. (1959). *Casework notebook.* St. Paul: Family-Centered Project.

Pearpoint, J., O'Brien, J. O., & Forest, M. (1992). *PATH (Planning Alternative Tomorrows with Hope): A workbook for planning better futures.* Toronto: Inclusion Press.

Prochaska, J. O. (1994). Strong and weak principles for progressing from precontemplation to action on the basis of twelve problem behaviors. *Health Psychology, 13* (1), 47–51.

Prochaska, J. O., DiClemente, C. C., & Norcross, J. C. (1992). In search of how people change: Applications to addictive behaviors. *American Psychologist, 47,* 1102–14.

Rapp, C. A. (1998). *The strengths model: Case management with people suffering from severe and persistent mental illness.* New York: Oxford University Press.

Ronnau, J. (1995). *Family Preservation Institute: A family preservation approach to assessing and using family strengths.* Las Cruces: New Mexico State University, Department of Social Work.

Rooney, R. H. (1992). *Strategies for work with involuntary clients.* New York: Columbia University Press.

Saleebey, D. (Ed.). (1992). *The strengths perspective in social work practice.* New York: Longman.

Sandau-Beckler, P. (1998). *Family Preservation Institute: A family preservation approach to engaging and strengthening families.* Las Cruces: New Mexico State University, School of Social Work.

Sandau-Beckler, P. (1999). *New Mexico Family-Centered Tool research report.* Las Cruces: New Mexico State University, School of Social Work.

Saunders, B., Wilkinson, C., & Towers, T. (1996). Motivation and addictive behaviors: Theoretical perspectives. In F. Rotgers, D. S. Keller, & J. Morgenstern (Eds.), *Treating substance abuse: Theory and technique* (pp. 241–85). New York: Guilford Press.

Schroeder, C., & Sandau-Beckler, P. (1997, December). *Family-based outcomes training outline.* Paper presented at the Eleventh Annual Conference of the National Association for Family-Based Services, Minneapolis.

St. Luke's Innovative Resources. (n.d.-a). *Five-Column Approach.* Bendigo, Australia: Author.

St. Luke's Innovative Resources. (n.d.-b). *Progress indicators.* Bendigo, Australia: Author.

Thompson, R. A. (1995). *Preventing child maltreatment through social support: A critical analysis.* Thousand Oaks, CA: Sage.

Tomm, K. (1987). Interventive interviewing: Part II. Reflexive questioning as a means to enable self-healing. *Family Process 26,* 167–83.

Tracy, E. M., & Whittaker, J. K. (1990). The social network map: Assessing social support in clinical practice. *Families in Society: The Journal of Contemporary Human Services, 71* (8), 461–70.

Turnbull, A. P., Summers, J. A., & Brotherson, M. J. (1983). *Working with families with disabled members: A family systems approach.* Lawrence: University of Kansas.

U.S. Marine Corps Family Advocacy Program. (1997). *A guide to conducting spouse abuse assessments.* Duluth, MN: Author.

Vega, W. A., Patterson, T., Sallis, J., Nader, P., Atkins, C., & Abramson, I. (1986). Cohesion and adaptability in Mexican-American and Anglo Families. *Journal of Marriage and the Family, 48,* 857–67.

Veeken, J., & Deal, R. (1999). *Strength Cards and Strength Cards for Kids.* Bendigo, Victoria, Australia: St. Luke's Innovative Resources.

6 Well-Being and Family-Centered Services

The Value of the Developmental Assets Framework

MARC MANNES

Child welfare and the newer umbrella term, child and family services, have consistently articulated three goals: (a) safety, (b) permanency, and (c) well-being. Interest in and support for these goals have waxed and waned over time as politicians, child and family professionals, advocates, and special interests that lobby for groups, such as foster and adoptive parents, have sought to influence service system policies and procedures by securing federal legislation to emphasize one particular goal more than the others. During the middle and late 1970s, passage of the Child Abuse Prevention and Treatment Act of 1974 riveted professional and service system attention on the issue of safety. Several years later, the Adoption Assistance and Child Welfare Act of 1980 shifted delivery system emphasis to the goal of permanency. The creation of the Family Preservation and Support Services Program in 1993 continued to stress the importance of permanency but also paid major attention to the well-being of biological families via family preservation and the promotion of family support. The more recent Adoption and Safe Families Act (ASFA) of 1997 moves the spotlight squarely back to the issue of safety, presses the time frame for permanency decision making, and reinforces the adoptive permanency option.

While one particular goal may receive greater attention during a period of time, the interrelatedness among the three stated goals needs to be kept in mind. For example, many have welcomed the passage of ASFA and the reassertion of safety as the bedrock of child and family services without attempting to appreciate or understand the larger context. Besharov and Laumann (1997) remind us that when the child welfare system focuses on safety it responds almost exclusively to the physical dimension of well-being. Even though outside child and family services well-being typically is defined more broadly than just the avoidance of harm, little attention is paid to how the economic, cognitive, and affective dimensions of well-being might affect both safety and permanency. A more expansive definition of well-being encompasses having basic needs met, being in good health, and functioning properly in a range of areas (Griffin, 1990).

The narrowness of the prevailing mindset regarding well-being and the limited means by which the system responds are understandable, yet they remain disturbing in light of both the prevalence of poverty in child welfare cases (Pelton, 1993) and the consequences of that poverty for young people (Duncan, Brooks-Gunn, & Klebanov, 1994). The lack of an adequate response likely stems from the ongoing imbalance between supply of (in the form of staff and financial resources) and demand for child protective services. Perhaps it is all a by-product of the residual nature of child welfare services (Lindsey, 1994), of which more will be said later. Or it may just be an unfortunate consequence of a policy decision made in 1969 that mandates the separation of financial and social services in the states' administration of foster care, which eventually meant that

in effect, the ability of public agencies to provide services for families not yet experiencing problems extreme enough to warrant intervention by a child welfare unit was largely lost. (U.S. Department of Health and Human Services, 1997, p. 3)

This chapter suggests that the status of family-centered services is compromised and its advancement impeded as long as the prevailing political, legal, regulatory, and service system environment concentrates on physical safety, adoptions, and timely permanency decisions and pays only marginal attention to the well-being of young people and their natural parents. The chapter goes on to make the case that one of the ways in which family-centered services can respond successfully to this set of circumstances is by crafting a broader definition of well-being and by forging programs and practice that optimize child and adolescent development.

The first part of the chapter illustrates how emphasizing either safety, permanency, or well-being generates very different types of service system orientations and professional activities, and considers how family-based reforms have affected the delivery system and case practice in the past and how they might influence the future. The second part describes the genesis and content of the developmental assets framework and its relationship to adolescent thriving, and makes the case for the framework's relevance to child and adolescent well-being. Finally, the third section highlights why and how the developmental assets framework can make family-centered services more responsive to well-being, more inclined to provide skill building and growth experiences for children and adolescents, and more likely to emphasize the positive development of young people.

SOME IMPLICATIONS AND EFFECTS OF ATTENDING TO SAFETY, PERMANENCY, AND WELL-BEING FOR CHILD AND FAMILY SERVICES

The degree to which safety, permanency, or well-being are emphasized during a particular time period helps set the direction for professional work and influences how it actually is conducted. When the child and family service system emphasizes safety to the virtual exclusion of other goals, it enforces a child-centric perspective consistent with many traditional approaches in the helping professions. These traditional approaches are grounded in social psychology and are attentive to individual risk factors, and tabulate success and failure on the basis of the risk-producing behavior of individuals (Goodman, Wandersman, Chinman, Imm, & Morrissey, 1996). Moreover, concentrating on safety serves to reinforce residual policy premises (Lindsey, 1994; Wilensky & Lebeaux, 1965) wherein government services are viewed as marginal and are brought to bear only when an emergency appears and there are breakdowns or failures in the operation of primary systems, such as family. Use of a residual mentality logically leads to programs that emphasize treatment and to a practice that is problem focused.

When the service system moves beyond safety and begins to address the issue of permanency, it retains aspects of child-centric and social psychology as it stretches to incorporate a family-based, family systems perspective. This is because all the different expressions of permanency take into account the idea and structure of family. Regardless of whether practitioners are looking to reunify, attempting to place a young person with kin long term, or seeking an adoptive placement, they are considering "the best interests" of the child or adolescent in terms of family. When permanency gets factored into the child and family equation one has moved toward acknowledging more institutional (Wilensky & Lebeaux, 1965) or structural (Kammerman & Kahn, 1995) policy premises wherein governmental action is seen as appropriate and necessary to meet the needs of citizens. Structural policy premises accept that in complex and interdependent societies, social service/welfare programs have a more normalizing role to play. The introduction of a normalizing perspective legitimizes supportive and supplementary services for parents (Kadushin & Martin, 1988). It also encourages the emergence of prevention programs that are more accepting of strengths-based assessments (Van Den Berg & Grealish, 1996) and more amenable to a strengths-based practice (Saleebey, 1996).

When the system shifts its attention to a multifaceted conceptualization of well-being, it retains both the child-centric and the family-centered dimensions, but it has stretched even further and retains the possibility of considering the larger social ecology of human development (Bronfenbrenner, 1979). Programs can begin to incorporate a "promotional" orientation attuned to developmental factors (Furstenberg, Cook, Eccles, Elder, & Sameroff, 1999), and practice can shift from being strengths based to being thriving oriented.

When well-being serves as the focal point of the system, there is the potential to adopt universal policy premises wherein all citizens can attain self-fulfillment. The expression of universalistic policies remains stifled, however, because a majority of voters appear unwilling to accept the tax consequences of public policies that would result in cash transfers, child subsidies, and government-financed parental leave policies, which are standard child and family investment strategies throughout much of the rest of the industrialized world (Mannes, 1997). More hopeful signs are evident in the program and practice arenas. There are many examples of promotional initiatives in the child and adolescent fields (Roth, Brooks-Gunn, Murray, & Foster, 1998), and some of the concepts and content useful to developing a thriving-based practice reside in the developmental assets framework (Benson, Leffert, Scales, & Blyth, 1998).

The association among system goals, service orientation, and theoretical frameworks is summarized in figure 6.1. The implications of the different child and family system goals for policy, program, and practice are shown in table 6.1.

FAMILY-CENTERED REFORMS AND CHILD AND FAMILY SERVICES

Those who advocated child welfare reform and helped build family-centered services made a major contribution to differentiating between a child-centered system and a family/community-centered system. Reformers recognized that a child-centric approach to child maltreatment is short-sighted, because maltreatment is influenced by broader ecological forces manifest in neighborhoods and communities (Garbarino, 1976). They understood that although reductions in individual risk-associated behaviors are valuable and should be desired, individual-level changes often depend on modifications in the larger social ecology (Goodman et al., 1996).

FIGURE 6.1. Relationship Among Child and Family System Goals, Service Orientation, and Theoretical Approaches

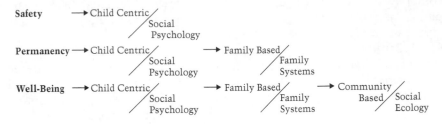

TABLE 6.1. Comparing System Goals, Policy Premises, Program Orientations, and Practice Methods

Child and Family System Goals	Policy Premises	Program Orientation(s)	Practice Methods
Safety	Residual	Treatment	Problem Centered
Permanency	Structural	Supportive Supplementary Substitute and Prevention	Strengths Based
Well-Being	Universal	Promotion	Thriving Focused

They were aware that wellness needs to be considered from an ecological perspective (Green & Potvin, 1996). Reformers encouraged elected officials who set policies and practitioners who offer interventions to think beyond the needs of the individual, or as a social ecologist would say, to think about the needs of the individual in context (Bronfenbrenner, 1979).

Family-centered service reforms also helped make the important distinction between a worker-driven system and a family-driven system. In a family-driven system the family is viewed as the primary experts on issues needing to be dealt with, and family members are actively involved in setting the terms and conditions of a case plan in order to secure progress.

These two reforms, (a) a family/community-centered system as opposed to a child-centered system and (b) a worker-driven system in contrast with a family-driven system, are combined in figure 6.2 to illustrate how family-centered reforms have sought to modify both child and family system orientation and practice. The intent has been to make several system transitions: first, from Quadrant I, the traditional child-centered and worker-driven system, to the revised system in Quadrant II, which is more family and community friendly but remains worker driven; second, from

FIGURE 6.2. Influence of Family-Centered Reforms on Child and Family Services

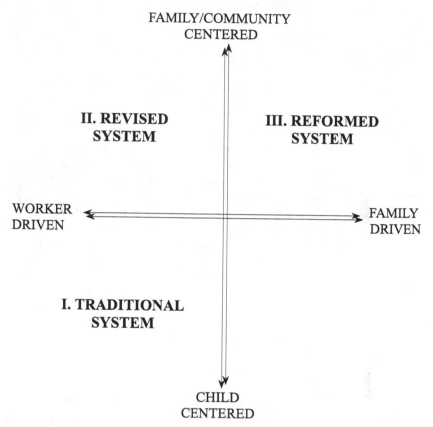

the Quadrant II revised system to the more reformed system in Quadrant III, which is both family/community focused and family driven.

Although family-based reforms have helped raise consciousness and understanding of an ecological perspective and have sought to create a different balance of power between worker and family, implementation has been complicated and problematic. The continued expansion of family support has been thwarted by the new federal allocation criteria spelled out in ASFA (Mannes, 1998). The research of Gleeson, O'Donnel, and Bonecutter (1997) suggests that permanency planning for children in kinship care fails to secure the meaningful involvement of key family members, whose involvement is essential for consistency with the tenets of family-centered practice. Yet even with a checkered implementation record, family-based reformers can point to a number of significant accomplishments, including more family-focused child welfare services, increased community-based prevention programming, and the expanded use of strengths-based practice. Future progress, however, necessitates a theoretical grounding more consonant with an ecological perspective, policies and programs more attentive and responsive to a broader definition of well-being, interventions more congruent with the promotion of human development, and a practice rooted in thriving.

Progress on all these fronts depends on coming to terms with the difference between prevention and promotion (Dunst, Trivett, & Thompson, 1990). According to Furstenberg et al. (1999), "promotive strategies foster children's talents and opportunities, and prevention strategies reduce children's exposure to various types of dangerous circumstances" (p. 71). Prevention strategies encourage young people to avoid costly behaviors and minimize their exposure to risky situations. Promotion strategies support investment in experiences and opportunities that will help young people tap their talents and develop skills and competencies. In the field of medicine, an analogous distinction is made between disease prevention and health promotion or wellness. In the same way that the absence of disease does not necessarily confer wellness to people, child and family prevention programming does not automatically translate into promotional benefits.

The next section suggests how the developmental assets framework can articulate a more expansive and ecological conceptualization of well-being for family-centered services. It establishes the content validity of the developmental assets framework and examines the framework's relationship to the concept of thriving.

THE EMPIRICAL BASIS FOR THE DEVELOPMENTAL ASSETS FRAMEWORK

Search Institute uses the developmental assets framework to establish a set of benchmarks for positive child and adolescent development and to serve as a taxonomy of developmental targets that require both family and community engagement (Benson, Leffert, et al., 1998). The developmental assets framework concentrates on the second decade of life, encompassing the middle and high school years. The original framework consisted of thirty developmental assets (Benson, 1990). In 1996, ten additional constructs were added to expand the framework to forty developmental assets. This expansion was based on an analysis of data gathered from a quarter of a million students, ongoing synthesis of child and adolescent research, and consultation with researchers and practitioners.

The framework's intellectual foundations are rooted in empirical studies of child and adolescent development, as well as in the more applied literature of prevention, protective factors, and resiliency (Benson, Leffert, et al., 1998). The research synthesis is used to identify the assets intended to integrate developmental experiences that are widely known to inform three types of health outcomes: (a) the prevention of high-risk behaviors (e.g., substance abuse, violence, sexual intercourse, school dropout); (b) the enhancement of thriving outcomes (e.g., school success, affirmation of diversity, the proactive approach to nutrition and exercise); and (c) resiliency, or the capacity to rebound in the face of adversity (Benson, Leffert, et al., 1998). The objective was to identify the developmental factors that were particularly robust in predicting health outcomes and that seem to possess predictive utility across sex, race-ethnicity, and family income (Benson, Leffert, et al., 1998).

The developmental assets were also conceived to reflect core developmental processes. They encompass the kinds of relationships, social experiences, social environments, patterns of interaction, norms, and competencies over which a community has considerable control. The assets are more about the primary processes of socialization than about the equally important arenas of economics, services, or physical infrastructure of a setting (Benson, Leffert, et al., 1998).

The forty developmental assets are both a theoretical and a research framework (Benson, Leffert, et al., 1998). Because the framework also is intended to have practical significance for the mobilization of communities around positive child and adolescent development, the forty assets are categorized to maintain conceptual integrity, and also so they can be easily described and readily understood by members of a community. Figure 6.3 illustrates the grouping of twenty external assets (i.e., health-promoting features of the environment) and twenty internal assets (e.g., commitments, values, and competencies).

The external assets represent the adult provisions of positive developmental experiences of relationships and opportunities. Research suggests that the assets emerge through ongoing exposure to informal interactions with supportive adults and peers, and that a larger network of community institutions reinforces them (Benson, Leffert, et al., 1998). The internal assets are competencies, skills, and self-perceptions that young people gradually acquire over time as a result of numerous experiences. Communities can mobilize and act in ways that will increase the likelihood that young people have external assets.

In figure 6.3 you will see that both internal and external assets are organized into four categories. The external groupings are (a) support, (b) empowerment, (c) boundaries and expectations, and (d) constructive use of time. The four internal categories are (a) commitment to learning, (b) positive values, (c) social competencies, and (d) positive identity. Scales and Leffert (1999) reviewed more than 800 studies in order to provide the scientific foundations for the eight categories and each of the forty assets.

FIGURE 6.3. Search Institute Forty Developmental Assets

External Assets

Category	Asset Name and Definition
Support	1. **Family support**—Family life provides high levels of love and support.
	2. **Positive family communication**—Young person and her or his parent(s) communicate positively, and young person is willing to seek advice and counsel from parent(s).
	3. **Other adult relationships**—Young person receives support from three or more nonparent adults.
	4. **Caring neighborhood**—Young person experiences caring neighbors.
	5. **Caring school climate**—School provides a caring, encouraging environment.
	6. **Parent involvement in schooling**—Parent(s) are actively involved in helping young person succeed in school.
Empowerment	7. **Community values youth**—Young person perceives that adults in the community value youth.
	8. **Youth as resources**—Young people are given useful roles in the community.
	9. **Service to others**—Young person serves in the community one hour or more per week.
	10. **Safety**—Young person feels safe at home, at school, and in the neighborhood.

Internal Assets

Category	Asset Name and Definition
Commitment to Learning	21. **Achievement motivation**—Young person is motivated to do well in school.
	22. **School engagement**—Young person is actively engaged in learning.
	23. **Homework**—Young person reports doing at least one hour of homework every school day.
	24. **Bonding to school**—Young person cares about his or her school.
	25. **Reading for pleasure**—Young person reads for pleasure three or more hours per week.
Positive Values	26. **Caring**—Young person places high value on helping other people.
	27. **Equality and social justice**—Young person places high value on promoting equality and reducing hunger and poverty.
	28. **Integrity**—Young person acts on convictions and stands up for her or his beliefs.
	29. **Honesty**—Young person "tells the truth even when it's not easy."
	30. **Responsibility**—Young person accepts and takes personal responsibility.
	31. **Restraint**—Young person believes it is important not to be sexually active or to use alcohol or other drugs.

Boundaries and Expectations

11. **Family boundaries**—Family has clear rules and consequences and monitors the young person's whereabouts.
12. **School boundaries**—School provides clear rules and consequences.
13. **Neighborhood boundaries**—Neighbors take responsibility for monitoring young people's behavior.
14. **Adult role models**—Parent(s) and other adults model positive, responsible behavior.
15. **Positive peer influence**—Young person's best friends model responsible behavior.
16. **High expectations**—Both parent(s) and teachers will encourage the young person to do well.

Constructive Use of Time

17. **Creative activities**—Young person spends three or more hours per week in lessons or practice in music, theatre, or other arts.
18. **Youth programs**—Young person spends three or more hours per week in sports, clubs, or organizations at school and/or in the community.
19. **Religious community**—Young person spends one or more hours per week in activities in a religious institution.
20. **Time at home**—Young person is out with friends "with nothing special to do" two or fewer nights per week.

Social Competencies

32. **Planning and decision making**—Young person knows how to plan ahead and make choices.
33. **Interpersonal competence**—Young person has empathy, sensitivity, and friendship skills.
34. **Cultural competence**—Young person has knowledge of and comfort with people of different cultural/racial/ethnic backgrounds.
35. **Resistance skills**—Young person can resist negative peer pressure and dangerous situations.
36. **Peaceful conflict resolution**—Young person seeks to resolve conflict nonviolently.

Positive Identity

37. **Personal power**—Young person feels he or she has control over "things that happen to me."
38. **Self-esteem**—Young person reports having a high self-esteem.
39. **Sense of purpose**—Young person reports that "my life has a purpose."
40. **Positive view of personal future**—Young person is optimistic about her or his personal future.

Source: From *A Fragile Foundation: The State of the Developmental Assets Among American Youth* (p. 3) by P. L. Benson, P. C. Scales, N. Leffert, and E. C. Roehlkepartain, 1999, Minneapolis: Search Institute. Copyright 1999 by Search Institute. Adapted with permission.

A reduced set of sources presented in this article to validate the asset categories is drawn from Benson, Leffert, et al. (1998).

The support assets cover a number of opportunities for experiencing affirmation, approval, and acceptance within multiple socializing settings (family, intergenerational relationships, neighborhood, and school) (Benson, Leffert, et al., 1998). These interactions include young people experiencing relational support and having warm and caring environments (Scales & Gibbons, 1996; Zimmerman & Arunkumar, 1994).

The empowerment assets capture a host of factors that encourage children and adolescents to become active within their community, with a special emphasis on adolescents feeling valued and useful (Zeldin & Price, 1995). The asset of safety is seen as strongly related to empowerment.

Early models for understanding child and adolescent development often focused on the singular effects of the family environment. Recent explanations have become increasingly ecological and have suggested that broader community socialization strategies are of equal importance to adolescent development (e.g., Furstenberg, 1993; Sampson, 1997). The boundaries and expectations assets recognize the importance of youth receiving clear and consistent messages from a number of different sources, including families, with which adolescents are involved. These assets also affirm the presence of adults and peers who model positive and responsible behaviors (Benson, Leffert, et al., 1998).

The constructive use of time assets highlight a meaningful array of constructive opportunities that should be available to all young people, particularly in the 10-to-18-year-old range. Ideally, these are settings that allow caring adults to help nurture adolescent skills and capacities (e.g., Blyth & Leffert, 1995; Carnegie Council on Adolescent Development, 1992; Dubas & Snider, 1993). Even though most communities of faith have become as age segregated as the rest of society, religious institutions are one of the few remaining intergenerational communities to which youth have access. An extensive scientific literature suggests, after controlling for family background, that religious participation more broadly enhances caring for others and helps reduce multiple forms of risk-taking behavior (e.g., Donahue & Benson, 1995).

The commitment to learning assets encapsulate a combination of personal beliefs, values, and skills that are linked to enhanced academic success (Scales & Leffert, 1999). They include an engagement in learning activities, a sense of belonging to the school environment, the motivation to do well, and expectations for success (e.g., Eccles & Midgley, 1990; Wentzel, 1993). Factors such as parental attitudes, encouragement, involvement, and modeling are key aspects of commitment to learning. Schooling also appears to matter through its formal and informal curricula. Peer group and community norms that encourage high attention to educational tasks also appear instrumental (Benson, Leffert, et al., 1998).

The six positive values assets represent prosocial and personal character values (e.g., Brooks-Gunn & Paikoff, 1993; Chase-Lansdale, Wakschlag, & Brooks-Gunn, 1995; Eisenberg, Miller, Shell, & McNalley, 1991). These six are indicative of a public consensus on values. They also appear to have a role in health promotion (Scales & Leffert, 1999).

The social competencies assets reflect a set of personal skills that are helpful in dealing with the myriad choices, challenges, and opportunities presented to young people in complex societies. These assets are indicative of adaptive functioning in which the individual can successfully call on personal and environmental resources (Peterson & Leigh, 1990; Waters & Sroufe, 1983). Lerner (1987) makes the case that social competence develops within social contexts and is composed of planning and decision-making skills, interpersonal and cultural competence, resistance skills, and the ability to resolve conflicts peacefully (e.g., DuBois & Hirsch, 1990; Mann, Harmoni, & Power, 1989; Zimmerman, Sprecher, Langer, & Holloway, 1993).

Identity formation is basic to successful adolescent development (Erikson, 1968). The positive identity assets address young people's views of themselves in relation to their future, self-esteem, and sense of purpose and power (e.g., Diener & Dweck, 1980; Garmezy, 1985; Harter, 1990).

THE BASIS FOR DEFINING THRIVING OUTCOMES

Search Institute has identified seven outcomes of adolescent well-being that represent thriving. Thriving is a concept that not only incorporates the absence of problem behaviors or other signs of pathology but also demonstrates signs or indicators of healthy development. The seven thriving indicators are (a) school success, (b) leadership, (c) helping others, (d) maintenance of physical health, (e) delay of gratification, (f) valuing diversity, and (g) overcoming adversity (Scales, Benson, & Leffert, 2000). These indicators are thought to be important aspects of adolescent well-being for several reasons. An extensive review of literature pertaining to the forty developmental assets has shown the thriving indicators to be generally related to other positive outcomes during the course of adolescence, in addition to more distal outcomes of early adulthood (Scales & Leffert, 1999).

Scales et al. (2000) detail the empirical association between the thriving indicators and adolescent well-being. School success has been linked to reduced use of alcohol and other drugs (e.g., Hawkins, Catalano, & Miller, 1992), leadership opportunities are related to positive mental health (e.g., Komro et al., 1996), and helping others is thought to contribute to self-esteem (e.g., Conrad & Hedin, 1981). In addition, physical health is tied to positive school performance (U.S. Congress Office of Technology Assessment, 1991), and the ability to control impulses or delay gratification is connected to decreased levels of delinquency (Patterson & Stouthamer-Loeber, 1984) and increased ability for self-regulation (Kurdek & Fine, 1994). Although valuing diversity and being culturally competent have been studied less, they appear to be related to peer acceptance (Parkhurst & Asher, 1992) and increased problem-solving ability (Mott & Krane, 1994). Also, the thriving constructs represent some of the fundamental developmental tasks associated with adolescence (Hamburg, 1989).

MEASUREMENT OF THE DEVELOPMENTAL ASSETS AND THRIVING INDICATORS

Search Institute makes use of a 156-item survey instrument, Profiles of Student Life: Attitudes and Behaviors (PSL-A&B), to measure each of the forty developmental assets and the thriving indicators (the survey also measures high-risk behaviors). Basic demographic information regarding age, grade, gender, race/ethnicity, family structure, and parental education is gathered as well. The survey is administered anonymously in a classroom setting in middle and high schools. Students complete the survey, and the forms are mailed to Search Institute for processing and for the production of a report, which is then sent back to the community.

Varying numbers of items are used to measure each of the forty assets. Thirteen are measured with single items, precluding any assessment of internal consistency. Nineteen demonstrate reliability coefficients above .60, four between .50 and .59, and four less than .50 (Leffert et al., 1998). By assessing all forty developmental assets, thriving indicators, and risk behaviors simultaneously and within the limits of a classroom period, Search Institute sacrifices measurement precision but is able to capture a broad description of young people's development and life experiences. This breadth allows the institute to uniquely map the relationships and connections between many of the major dimensions of young people's lives.

Each thriving indicator is measured with one survey question on the PSL-A&B. Strategies of using single-item measures often are used for survey research with large samples. According to Scales et al. (2000), two recent examples of common secondary analysis data sets that use numerous single-item measures are the National Education Longitudinal Study (Manlove, 1998) and the National Household Survey of Drug Abuse (Hoffman & Johnson, 1998). The thriving indicators retain sufficient construct validity because the single items used to measure them reflect salient elements of the construct as derived from the literature (Scales et al., 2000).

Search Institute also constructed a thriving index, composed of summing the responses to each thriving item, standardized to a mean of 0 and a standard deviation of 1. This allowed for analysis of individual thriving items and the index. The internal consistency of the thriving index, as measured by Cronbach's coefficient alpha, is .49 (Scales et al., 2000). According to Scales et al. (2000), there are several possible explanations for the relatively low reliability of the thriving index. One could make the case that the single item measures that make up the index may themselves be unreliable. Alternatively, one could argue that they each require very different response frameworks that may not reliably support summation. Also, keep in mind that the individual items that compose the index were not intended to statistically represent a single construct called "thriving." Instead, thriving was understood and conceptualized as multidimensional. Accordingly, the low reliability of the seven summed items is not surprising, because the act of summing implicitly assumes a more unidimensional construct of thriving.

As Scales et al. (2000) make clear, individual variation in interests and capabilities must also be taken into account. An adolescent could be highly successful in school, demonstrate the ability to delay gratification, and maintain his or her physical health, but not allocate his or her time to formal volunteering or to formal leadership positions. Most observers— including the adolescent—would still consider such a young person to be thriving. Scales et al. (2000) go on to suggest that some might even consider an adolescent to be thriving if she or he volunteered and was a leader but did not get As in school, maintain good nutrition and exercise habits, or have the ability to delay gratification.

There is clearly much conceptual and empirical work to be done in clarifying what thriving really means for adolescents; and forging greater clarity remains essential to the quality of a focus on well-being, promotional programs, and a practice seeking to optimize child and adolescent development.

FINDINGS RELATED TO THE DEVELOPMENTAL ASSETS FRAMEWORK AND THRIVING INDICATORS

These findings are based on the responses of 99,462 sixth-to-twelfth-grade youth in 213 communities who completed the PSL-A&B survey during the 1996–1997 school year (Benson, Scales, Leffert, & Roehlkepartain, 1999). This sample is not nationally representative but is large and somewhat diverse.

On average, a young person experiences only eighteen of the forty assets. Sixty-four percent of youth report experiencing twenty or fewer of the assets. Also, twenty-seven of the assets are experienced by 50 percent or less of the young people surveyed. The distribution of developmental assets among the sample is presented in figure 6.4. The data suggest that the foundation that young people need in order to be healthy, caring, and competent is fragile (Benson, Leffert, et al., 1998).

Most adolescents do not report experiencing even a simple majority of the thriving indicators (Scales et al., 2000). The typical adolescent represented in Search Institute's aggregate sample indicates that he or she possesses fewer than four of the seven; the thriving indicators appear to co-occur, with youth who report one thriving indicator more likely to experience additional positive thriving indicators (Scales et al., 2000).

Correlational analysis shows the relationship between the developmental assets and the thriving indicators. Youths reporting a greater num-

FIGURE 6.4. Youth Who Report Experiencing Each Level of Assets

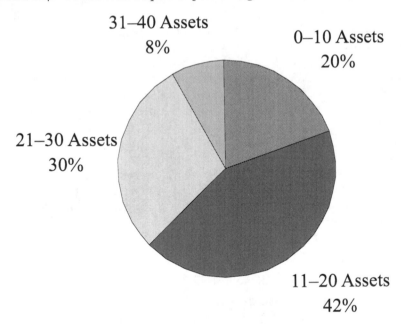

(Note: Numbers do not add to 100% due to rounding.)

Source: From *A Fragile Foundation: The State of the Developmental Assets Among American Youth* (p. xii), by P. L. Benson, P. C. Scales, N. Leffert, and E. C. Roehlkepartain, 1999, Minneapolis: Search Institute. Copyright 1999 by Search Institute. Adapted with permission.

ber of assets are much more likely to engage in the thriving behaviors than are youths reporting less. This pattern is illustrated in table 6.2.

Regression analysis of the sample was performed to see how specific clusters of developmental assets might explain the experience of thriving outcomes across different racial-ethnic groups of youths. Separate stepwise regressions for each racial-ethnic group (American Indian, Asian American, African American, Hispanic, and Caucasian American) were run and were controlled for the demographic variables (maternal education, gender, and grade) that literature has suggested mediate or moderate levels of developmental assets or thriving indicators (Scales & Leffert, 1999).

The developmental assets accounted for a considerable amount of the variance explained in the thriving index (47 to 54 percent across ethnic groups) and for moderate amounts of variance (10 to 43 percent across ethnic groups and beyond the contribution of demographic variables) in explaining the individual thriving indicators (Scales et al., 2000). Scales and his associates at Search Institute also found that the developmental assets seem to have moderate explanatory power for six of the seven thriving outcomes (valuing diversity, school success, physical health, helping others, leadership, and delay of gratification). Less of the variance is accounted for in overcoming adversity, for which the developmental assets, over and above the contribution of demographic variables, explained only 10 to 17 percent of the variance. The implication is that the measure used to assess the ability to overcome adversity may be less adequate than the other thriving measures for three reasons (Scales et al., 2000). First, the question used to assess the thriving outcome of overcoming adversity may require a com-

TABLE 6.2. The Power of Developmental Assets

Thriving Behavior	Definition	0–10 Assets	11–20 Assets	21–30 Assets	31–40 Assets
Succeeds in School	Gets mostly As on report card.	7%	19%	35%	53%
Values Diversity	Places high importance on getting to know people of other racial/ethnic groups.	34%	53%	69%	87%
Helps Others	Helps friends or neighbors one or more hours per week.	69%	83%	91%	96%
Exhibits Leadership	Has been a leader of a group or organization in the past twelve months.	48%	67%	78%	87%

Source: From An Asset Builder's Guide to Service Learning (p. 12), by E. C. Roehlkepartain, T. Bright, and B. Margolis-Rupp, 2000, Minneapolis: Search Institute. Copyright 2000 by Search Institute. Adapted with permission.

plex cognitive frame of reference for responding (i.e., involving adolescents' perception of how people who know them well would describe them). There is likely to be a great deal of variability in an individual adolescent's ability to respond to such a question. Second, the ability to overcome adversity may be better described by domain-specific measures instead of by the unidimensional measure used for this inquiry. Third, it is plausible that the developmental assets may be better predictors of the ability to overcome adversity in contexts or circumstances not assessed by this measure.

According to Scales et al. (2000), the regression analyses explained similar proportions of variance in the outcomes found in other studies. Scales et al. (2000) cite several examples. A comprehensive array of demographic, individual, family, and school variables together explained 7 to 30 percent of the variance in the majority of health risk outcomes among 12,000 students in grades seven to twelve (Resnick et al., 1997). Similarly, in a study of middle school environmental effects on academic motivation and achievement among 1,000 seventh-grade students, Roeser and Eccles (1998) reported that 11 to 30 percent of the variance in most dependent variables was explained (which included academic self-concept, valuing of education, and self-esteem). Garmezy (1991) posits that protective factors, unlike risk factors, might affect adolescents more indirectly than directly, and could result from their interaction with and modification of risk factors. Therefore, the unique contribution of positive-protective factors may be more difficult to identify. Although there was some variation in the patterns of assets that meaningfully predict various thriving outcomes across different racial-ethnic groups, the strongest predictors were remarkably similar and mostly consistent with the literature (Scales et al., 2000).

Despite limitation in the crafting of thriving constructs and with the reliability and validity of how they were measured, the findings presented here will hopefully stimulate additional research. Conceptualizing and measuring positive adolescent outcomes are deserving of scientific attention, which has most often been reserved for risk and problematic outcomes.

ADAPTING THE DEVELOPMENTAL ASSETS FRAMEWORK TO CHILDREN

The developmental assets framework was designed originally to focus on the second decade of life. It is reasonable to surmise that the developmental assets framework is built on a foundation established in childhood, and that the asset language might offer a helpful lens for understanding issues pertaining to well-being during the first decade of life. To adapt the asset framework and include children from birth to age 11, Search Institute used the existing framework, consulted child and youth practitioners, and reviewed the developmental research literature. As a result, the first-decade-of-life portion of the framework would be grounded firmly in what is known about healthy development but would also communicate clearly to parents and practitioners (Leffert, Benson, & Roehlkepartain, 1997). The first decade framework represents a preliminary step in conceptualizing the developmental assets for children from birth to age 11. Search Institute is comfortable with this initial step because it sees the developmental assets framework as well-grounded in life-span developmental psychology (Benson, Leffert, et al., 1998). Since Search Institute has not yet developed tools to measure assets in children, the application of the framework to children is for now exploratory in nature.

Figures 6.5 and 6.6 show the framework of developmental assets and its hypothesized progression from infancy through adolescence across four developmental age periods: (a) infancy-toddler, (b) preschool, (c) middle childhood or the elementary school age, and (d) adolescence (Leffert et al., 1997). Although Search Institute has chosen to maintain the external-internal distinction as a way to understand clearly the asset categories, we acknowledge that it does not apply directly to infants and young children. Search Institute's review of the literature suggests that during infancy and early childhood, all the assets would externally surround the child through important relationships, with the primary responsibility for building the assets resting with parents and other caregivers (Benson, Leffert, et al., 1998). The building of developmental assets in infants and young children is based on their being cared for in a sensitive and responsible manner and being exposed to many situations that are developmentally sound. Additional work also needs to be conducted to ascertain how thriving concepts and constructs are applicable to children ages 0 to 11.

THE IMPORTANCE OF APPLYING THE DEVELOPMENTAL ASSETS FRAMEWORK TO FAMILY-CENTERED SERVICES

The next generation of family-centered programs and practice needs to rigorously promote the positive and productive development of young people so they can experience their full potential. The developmental assets framework is a research-grounded and ecologically oriented approach that focuses on the social, emotional, and psychological aspects of well-being and is designed to optimize child and adolescent development. It is consistent with the philosophy of family-based work and is responsive to the spectrum of family-centered services, from intensive family preservation through family support. The developmental assets framework can contribute to how we think about and how we respond to the developmental well-being of young people throughout the first two decades of life. Its infusion will not necessarily be easy.

FIGURE 6.5.

Asset Type	Infants and Toddlers (birth to age 2)	Preschoolers (ages 3 to 5)	Elementary-Age Children (ages 6 to 11)	Adolescents (ages 12 to 18)
EXTERNAL ASSETS				
Support				
1.	Family support			
2.	Positive family communication			
3.	Other adult resources		Other adult relationships	
4.	Caring neighborhood			
5.	Caring out-of-home climate		Caring school climate	
6.	Parent involvement in out-of-home situations		Parent involvement in schooling	
Empowerment				
7.	Children valued		Community values children	Community values youth
8.	Children have roles in family life	Children given useful roles		Youth as resources
9.	Service to others			
10.	Safety			
Boundaries and Expectations				
11.	Family boundaries			
12.	Out-of-home boundaries		School boundaries	
13.	Neighborhood boundaries			
14.	Adult role models			
15.	Positive peer observation	Positive peer interactions		Positive peer influence
16.	Expectations for growth			High expectations
Constructive Use of Time				
17.	Creative activities			
18.	Out-of-home activities	Child programs		Youth programs
19.	Religious community			
20.	Positive, supervised time at home			Time at home

Source: From *Starting Out Right: Developmental Assets for Children* (p. 24), by N. Leffert, P. L. Benson and J. L. Roehlkepartain, 1997, Minneapolis: Search Institute. Copyright 1997 by Search Institute. Adapted with permission.

Given the community orientation implicit in family-based reforms, one would expect family-centered services to readily incorporate an ecological perspective into their interventions. Yet the most widely employed and well-known family-based interventions have been more tied to family systems or crisis intervention theory (Nelson and Landsman, 1992). This occurs despite the existence of a body of theoretical and empirical examples of ecological influences on children, adolescents, and parenting. According

FIGURE 6.6.

Asset Type	Infants and Toddlers (birth to age 2)	Preschoolers (ages 3 to 5)	Elementary-Age Children (ages 6 to 11)	Adolescents (ages 12 to 18)
INTERNAL ASSETS				
Commitment to Learning				
21.	Achievement expectation		Achievement motivation	
22.	Engagement expectation		School engagement	
23.	Stimulating activity		Homework	
24.	Enjoyment of learning		Bonding to school	
25.	Reading for pleasure			
Positive Values				
26.	Family values caring		Caring	
27.	Family values equality and social justice		Equality and social justice	
28.	Family values integrity		Integrity	
29.	Family values honesty		Honesty	
30.	Family values responsibility		Responsibility	
31.	Family values healthy lifestyle and sexual attitudes		Healthy lifestyle and sexual attitudes	Restraint
Social Competencies				
32.	Planning and decision-making observation	Planning and decision-making practice	Planning and decision making	
33.	Interpersonal observation	Interpersonal interactions	Interpersonal competence	
34.	Cultural observation	Cultural interactions	Cultural competence	
35.	Resistance observation	Resistance practice	Resistance skills	
36.	Peaceful conflict resolution observation	Peaceful conflict resolution practice	Peaceful conflict resolution	
Positive Identity				
37.	Family has personal power		Personal power	
38.	Family models high self-esteem		Self-esteem	
39.	Family has a sense of purpose		Sense of purpose	
40.	Family has a positive view of the future		Positive view of personal future	

Source: *Starting Out Right: Developmental Assets for Children* (p. 25), by N. Leffert, P. L. Benson and J. L. Roehlkepartain, 1997, Minneapolis: Search Institute. Copyright 1997 by Search Institute. Adapted with permission.

to Benson, Leffert, et al. (1998), Zigler (1990) pointed out young peoples' heavy involvement in social institutions, and Lerner (1986, 1992) explained how ecology informs development and in turn how adolescents affect social context. Garbarino (1976) painted a portrait of the community context for problems associated with parenting. Belsky (1984) proposed an ecological model of parenting that takes into account the multiple interactions of parent, child, and the environment. Broderick (1993) established a transactional/interactional model of family dynamics that goes beyond linear approaches to get at transcybernetic processes, and that takes into account biological, structural, and cultural factors. Luster and Mittelstaedt's (1993) research of teenage motherhood concluded that issues are not tied to the age at which a young mother bears a child, but are linked to the ecology in which she lives. Finally, Benson (1997) discussed the community's role in raising healthy young people.

The significance of positive human development has been acknowledged in the family-centered services arena. Wells and Tracy (1996) argue that even intensive family preservation services should stop being implemented as a tertiary placement prevention strategy, and instead should be reoriented to meet primary and secondary prevention purposes. According to their argument, based on an analysis and interpretation of available research, intensive family preservation services would have greater beneficial impact by promoting child development and by minimizing the potential for maltreatment in families where risk factors are present than by actually preventing placements themselves.

According to Pecora, Fraser, Nelson, McCrosky, and Meezan (1995), most parenting interventions in family-based programs strive to increase knowledge of proper parenting, create more informed beliefs about child rearing, accept behavioral expectations that are age appropriate, secure a deeper understanding of child development, and obtain ideas along with opportunities to practice more appropriate discipline. The primary intent has been to improve role performance (Pecora et al., 1995).

There is evidence that paying attention to developmental well-being and promoting human development can make a difference in the lives of children and adults. According to Vondra and Belsky (1993),

> In summary, the effects of a troubled and/or problematic childhood for parenting difficulty and dysfunction appear to depend very much on opportunities to rework poor relationship experience. When children have alternative relationship models available to them and/or can participate in a supportive relationship amidst the stressors of their childhood, when young adults can rework relationship issues by their long-term involvement (whether personal or professional) with a caring and supportive individual, the relationship they create with their own children need not mirror the hardships of their upbringing. (p. 24)

Benson, Galbraith, and Espeland (1998) and Roehlkepartain and Leffert (2000) have given program designers and practitioners a wealth of ideas about developmental well-being. The information contained in these resources can give direction to the design of promotional programs and can provide content ideas for a thriving-oriented practice in support of promotional programming. It can offer tips and ideas for service staff's engagement with families and children in order to jointly set case goals that are related to increasing well-being, and to give guidance to parents and adolescents regarding how they can build developmental assets in their children and siblings.

The applicability of the developmental assets framework needs to be kept in perspective. It does not address the political or economic aspects of well-being, which inevitably must also be reckoned with. For all its promise and potential, the framework is not an antipoverty remedy.

While this chapter has paid much attention to the future utility of the developmental assets framework, it is important to note that public agencies and their phalanx of associated service providers can currently make use of the framework to help meet many of the "core children's service outcome indicators" associated with well-being and family support (Casey Outcomes and Decision-Making Project, 1998). This suggests that the developmental asset framework may also be beneficial under existing political, legislative, and regulatory conditions.

More important, it remains possible for federal policy and the child and family system to focus on well-being, as the brand-new Foster Care Independence Medical Act of 1999 demonstrates: many of its provisions embrace economic and psychosocial aspects of well-being for young people being served by independent living programs (Child Welfare League of America, 1999). Imagine if that same approach were applied not just to older adolescents aging out of the service system but also to the developmental well-being of all the members of less-advantaged families, and especially to children who are at risk of entering foster care. Such an approach would spark a renaissance for family-centered services, and the developmental assets framework could fuel the activity.

REFERENCES

Belsky, J. (1984). The determinants of parenting: A process model. *Child Development 55*, 83–96.

Benson, P. L. (1990). *The troubled journey: A portrait of 6th–12th grade youth.* Minneapolis: Search Institute.

Benson, P. L. (1997). *All kids are our kids: What communities must do to raise caring and responsible children and adolescents.* San Francisco: Jossey-Bass.

Benson, P. L., Galbraith, J., & Espeland, P. (1998). *What teens need to succeed.* Minneapolis: Free Spirit Press.

Benson, P. L., Leffert, N., Scales, P. C., & Blyth, D. A. (1998). Beyond the "village" rhetoric: Creating healthy communities for children and adolescents. *Applied Developmental Science, 2*, 138–59.

Benson, P. L., Scales, P. C., Leffert, N., & Roehlkepartain, E. C. (1999). *A fragile foundation: The state of the developmental assets among American youth.* Minneapolis: Search Institute.

Besharov, D. J., & Laumann, L. A. (1997). Don't call it child abuse if it's really poverty. *Journal of Children and Poverty, 3* (1), 5–36.

Blyth, D. A., & Leffert, N. (1995). Communities as contexts for adolescent development: An empirical analysis. *Journal of Adolescent Research, 10,* 64–87.

Broderick, C. B. (1993). *Understanding family process: Basics of family systems theory.* Newbury Park, CA: Sage.

Bronfenbrenner, U. (1979). *The ecology of human development.* Cambridge: Harvard University Press.

Brooks-Gunn, J., & Paikoff, R. L. (1993). "Sex is a gamble, kissing is a game": Adolescent sexuality and health promotion. In S. G. Millstein, A. C. Petersen, & E. O. Nightingale (Eds.), *Promoting the health of adolescents: New directions for the twenty-first century* (pp. 180–208). New York: Oxford University Press.

Carnegie Council on Adolescent Development. (1992). *A matter of time: Risk and opportunity in the non-school hours.* Washington, DC: Author.

Casey Outcomes and Decision-Making Project. (1998). *Assessing outcomes in child welfare services: Principles, concepts, and a framework of core outcome indicators.* Denver: American Humane Association Children's Division.

Chase-Lansdale, P. L., Wakschlag, L. S., & Brooks-Gunn, J. (1995). A psychological perspective on the development of caring in children and youth: The role of the family. *Journal of Adolescence, 18,* 515–56.

Child Welfare League of America. (1999). *The Foster Care Independence Act: Summary of provisions.* Washington, DC: Author.

Conrad, D. E., & Hedin, D. (1981). National assessment of experiential education: Summary and implications. *Journal of Experiential Education, 4,* 6–20.

Diener, C. I., & Dweck, C. S. (1980). An analysis of learned helplessness: II. The processing of success. *Journal of Personality and Social Psychology, 39,* 940–52.

Donahue, M. J., & Benson, P. L. (1995). Religion and the well-being of adolescents. *Journal of Social Issues, 51,* 145–60.

Dubas, J. S., & Snider, B. A. (1993). The role of community-based youth groups in enhancing learning and achievement through nonformal education. In R. M. Lerner (Ed.), *Early adolescence: Perspectives on research, policy, and intervention* (pp. 159–74). Hillsdale, NJ: Lawrence Erlbaum Associates.

DuBois, D. L., & Hirsch, B. J. (1990). School and neighborhood friendship patterns in Blacks and Whites in early adolescence. *Child Development, 61,* 524–36.

Duncan, G. J., Brooks-Gunn, J., & Klebanov, P. (1994). Economic deprivation and early child development. *Child Development, 65,* 296–318.

Dunst, C. J., Trivette, C. M., & Thompson, R. (1990). Supporting and strengthening family functioning: Toward a congruence between principle and practice. *Prevention in Human Services, 9* (1), 19–43.

Eccles, J. S., & Midgley, C. (1990). Changes in academic motivation and self-perception during adolescence. In R. Montemayor, G. R. Adams, & T. P. Gullotta (Eds.), *From childhood to adolescence: A transitional period? Ad-*

vances in adolescent development (Vol. 2, pp. 134–55). Thousand Oaks, CA: Sage.

Eisenberg, N., Miller, P. A., Shell, R., & McNalley, S. (1991). Prosocial development in adolescence: A longitudinal study. *Development Psychology,* 27, 849–57.

Erikson, E. H. (1968). *Identity: Youth and crisis.* New York: Norton.

Furstenberg, F. (1993). How families manage risk and opportunity in dangerous neighborhoods. In W. J. Wilson (Ed.), *Sociology and the public agenda* (pp. 231–53). Newbury Park, CA: Sage.

Furstenberg, F. F. Jr., Cook, T. D., Eccles, J., Elder, G. H. Jr., & Sameroff, A. (1999). *Managing to make it.* Chicago: University of Chicago Press.

Garbarino, J. (1976). A preliminary study of some ecological correlates of child abuse: The impact of socioeconomic stress on mothers. *Child Development,* 47, 178–85.

Garmezy, N. (1985). Stress-resistant children: The search for protective factors. In J. E. Stevenson (Ed.), *Journal of Child Psychology and Psychiatry book supplement no. 4: Recent research in developmental psychopathology* (pp. 213–33). Oxford, England: Pergamon.

Garmezy, N. (1991). Resiliency and vulnerability to adverse developmental outcomes associated with poverty. *American Behavioral Scientist,* 34, 416–30.

Gleeson, J. P., O'Donnel, J., & Bonecutter, F. J. (1997). Understanding the complexity of practice in kinship foster care. *Child Welfare,* 76 (6), 801–26.

Goodman, R. M., Wandersman, A., Chinman, M., Imm, P., & Morrissey, E. (1996). An ecological assessment of community-based interventions for prevention and health promotion: Approaches to measuring community coalitions. *American Journal of Community Psychology,* 24 (1), 33–61.

Green, L. W., & Potvin, R. L. (1996). Ecological foundations of health promotion. *American Journal of Health Promotion,* 10, 270–81.

Griffin, J. (1990). *Well-being: Its meaning, measurement, and moral importance.* Oxford, England: Clarendon Press.

Hamburg, D. A. (1989). *Early adolescence: A critical time for interventions in education and health.* New York: Carnegie Corporation of New York.

Harter, S. (1990). Processes underlying adolescent self-concept formation. In R. Montemayor, G. R. Adams, & T. P. Gullotta (Eds.), *From childhood to adolescence: A transitional period? Advances in adolescent development* (Vol. 2, pp. 205–39). Newbury Park, CA: Sage.

Hawkins, J. D., Catalano, R. F., & Miller, J. Y. (1992). Risk and protective factors for alcohol and other drug problems in adolescence and early childhood: Implications for substance abuse prevention. *Psychological Bulletin,* 112 (1), 64–105.

Hoffman, J. P., & Johnson, R. A. (1998). A national portrait of family structure and adolescent drug use. *Journal of Marriage and the Family,* 60, 633–45.

Kadushin, A., & Martin, J. A. (1988). *Child Welfare Services* (2nd ed.). New York: Macmillan.

Kammerman, K., & Kahn, A. (1995). *Starting right: How America neglects its youngest children and what we can do about it.* New York: Oxford University Press.

Komro, K. A., Perry, C. L., Murrah, D. M., Veblen-Mortensen, S., Williams, C. L., & Astine, P. S. (1996). Peer-planned social activities for preventing alcohol use among young adolescents. *Journal of School Health, 66,* 328–34.

Kurdek, L. A., & Fine, M. A. (1994). Family acceptance and family control as predictors of adjustment in young adolescents: Linear, curvilinear, or interactive effects? *Child Development, 65,* 1137–46.

Leffert, N., Benson, P. L., & Roehlkepartain, J. L. (1997). *Starting out right: Developmental assets for children.* Minneapolis: Search Institute.

Leffert, N., Benson, P. L., Scales, P. C., Sharma, A. R., Drake, D. R., & Blyth, D. A. (1998). Developmental assets: Measurement and prediction of risk behaviors among adolescents. *Applied Developmental Science, 2,* 209–30.

Lerner, R. M. (1986). *Concepts and themes of human development* (2nd ed.). New York: Random House.

Lerner, R. M. (1987). A life-span perspective for early adolescence. In R. M. Lerner & T. T. Foch (Eds.), *Biological-psychological interactions in early adolescence* (pp. 9–34). Hillsdale, NJ: Lawrence Erlbaum Associates.

Lerner, R. M. (1992). Dialects, developmental contextualism, and the further enhancement of theory about puberty and psychosocial development. *Journal of Early Adolescence, 12,* 366–88.

Lindsey, D. (1994). *The welfare of children.* New York: Oxford University Press.

Luster, T., & Mittelstaedt, M. (1993). Adolescent mothers. In T. Luster & L. Okagaki (Eds.), *Parenting: An ecological perspective* (pp. 69–99). Hillsdale, NJ: Lawrence Erlbaum Associates.

Manlove, J. (1998). The influence of high school dropout and school disengagement on the risk of school-age pregnancy. *Journal of Research on Adolescence, 8,* 187–220.

Mann, L., Harmoni, R., & Power, C. N. (1989). Adolescent decision making: The development of competence. *Journal of Sociology, 44,* 868–96.

Mannes, M. (1997). The evolution and implications of reforms for public child welfare and community-based family support. In *Summary of Proceedings, 1997 National Roundtable Series on Family Group Decision Making* (pp. 69–77). Denver: American Humane Association Children's Division.

Mannes, M. (1998). Promoting safe and stable families: Is it a renewed—or a new—Title IV-B, Subpart 2? *Prevention Report, 1,* 2–4.

Mott, P., & Krane, A. (1994). Interpersonal cognitive problem solving and childhood social competence. *Cognitive Theory and Research, 28,* 127–41.

Nelson, K. E., & Landsman, M. J. (1992) *Alternative models of family preservation: Family-based services in context.* Springfield, IL: Charles C Thomas.

Parkhurst, J. T., & Asher, S. R. (1992). Peer rejection in middle school: Subgroup differences in behavior, loneliness, and interpersonal concerns. *Developmental Psychology, 28,* 231–41.

Patterson, G. R., & Stouthamer-Loeber, M. (1984) The correlation of family management practices and delinquency. *Child Development, 55,* 1299–1307.

Pecora, P. J., Fraser, M. W., Nelson, K. E., McCrosky, J., & Meezan, W. (1995). *Evaluating family-based services.* New York: Aldine De Gruyter.

Pelton, L. (1993). The role of material factors in child abuse and neglect. In *Neighbors helping neighbors: A new national strategy for the protection of children* (pp. 110–13). Washington, DC: U.S. Advisory Board on Child Abuse and Neglect.

Peterson, G. W., & Leigh, F. K. (1990). The family and social competence in adolescence. In T. P. Gullotta, G. R. Adams, & R. Montemayor (Eds.), *Developing social competency in adolescence. Advances in adolescent development* (Vol. 3, pp. 97–138). Newbury Park, CA: Sage.

Resnick, M. D., Bearman, P. S., Blum, R. W., Bauman, K. E., Harris, K. M., Jones, J., Tabor, J., Beuhring, T., Sieving, R. E., Shew, M., Ireland, M., Bearinger, L. H., & Udry, J. R. (1997). Protecting adolescents from harm: Findings from the National Longitudinal Study on Adolescent Health. *Journal of the American Medical Association, 278* (10), 823–32.

Roehlkepartain, J. L., & Leffert, N. (2000). *What young children need to succeed: Working together to build assets from birth to age 11.* Minneapolis: Free Spirit.

Roeser, R. W., & Eccles, J. S. (1998). Adolescents' perceptions of middle school: Relation to longitudinal changes in academic and psychological adjustment. *Journal of Research on Adolescence, 8,* 123–58.

Roth, J., Brooks-Gunn, J., Murray, L., & Foster, W. (1998). Promoting healthy adolescents: Synthesis of youth development program evaluations. *Journal of Research on Adolescents, 8* (4), 423–59.

Saleebey, D. (1996). The strengths perspective in social work practice: Extensions and cautions. *Social Work, 41* (3), 296–305.

Sampson, R. J. (1997). Collective regulation of adolescent misbehavior: Validation results from eighty Chicago neighborhoods. *Journal of Adolescent Research, 12,* 227–44.

Scales, P. C., Benson, P. L., & Leffert, N. (2000). Contribution of developmental assets to the prediction of thriving among adolescents. *Applied Developmental Science, 4,* 27–46.

Scales, P. C., & Gibbons, J. L. (1996). Extended family members and unrelated adults in the lives of young adolescents: A research agenda. *Journal of Early Adolescence, 16,* 365–89.

Scales, P. C., & Leffert, N. (1999). *Developmental assets: A synthesis of the scientific research on adolescent development.* Minneapolis: Search Institute.

U.S. Congress, Office of Technology Assessment. (1991). *Vol. I: Summary and policy options. Adolescent health* (DHHS Publication No. OTA-H-468). Washington, DC: U.S. Government Printing Office.

U.S. Department of Health and Human Services, Children's Bureau. (1997). *National study of protective, preventive, and reunification services delivered to children and their families.* Washington, DC: U.S. Government Printing Office.

Van Den Berg, J. E., & Grealish, E. M. (1996). Individualized services and supports through the wraparound process: Philosophy and procedures. *Journal of Child and Family Studies, 5,* 7–22.

Vondra, J., & Belsky, J. (1993). Developmental origins of parenting: Personality and relationship factors. In T. Luster & L. Okagaki (Eds.), *Parenting: An ecological perspective* (pp. 1–33). Hillsdale, NJ: Lawrence Erlbaum Associates.

Waters, E., & Sroufe, L. A. (1983). Social competence as a developmental construct. *Developmental Review, 3,* 79–97.

Wells, K., & Tracy, E. (1996). Reorienting intensive family preservation services in relation to public child welfare practice. *Child Welfare, 75* (6), 667–92.

Wentzel, K. R. (1993). Motivation and achievement in early adolescence: The role of multiple classroom goals. *Journal of Early Adolescence, 13,* 4–20.

Wilensky, H., & Lebeaux, C. (1965). *Industrial society and social welfare.* New York: Free Press.

Zeldin, S., & Price, L. A. (1995). Creating supportive communities for adolescent development: Challenges to scholars—An introduction. *Journal of Adolescent Research, 10,* 6–14.

Zigler, E. (1990). Preface. In S. J. Meisels & J. P. Skonkoff (Eds.), *Handbook of early childhood intervention* (pp. ix–xiv). New York: Cambridge University Press.

Zimmerman, M. A., & Arunkumar, R. (1994). Resiliency research: Implications for schools and policy. *Social Policy Report, 8,* 1–18.

Zimmerman, R. S., Sprecher, S., Langer, L. M., & Holloway, C. D. (1993). Adolescents' perceived ability to say "no" to unwanted sex. *Journal of Adolescent Research, 10,* 383–99.

7 Interventions

Hard and Soft Services

Elizabeth M. Tracy

  This chapter provides a description and analysis of the various types of interventions used by home-based, family-centered workers. The overall intent of the chapter is to focus on what family preservation workers actually do with families, how they and the families perceive these services, how interventions have been categorized, and what we know (or do not know) about the relative contributions of different types of services to the overall work with a family. Case examples will illustrate the use of hard and soft services at various stages of work, as well as particular interventions in the context of the total work with a family.

While this chapter draws from several empirical studies of family preservation services, it is *not* a comprehensive review of family preservation models across model types and populations served (see, for example, the following research reviews for that content: Bath & Haapala, 1994; Blythe, Salley, & Jayaratne, 1994; Fraser, Nelson, & Rivard, 1997; and Littell, 1997). Additionally, while a variety of intervention techniques are described, the chapter itself does *not* constitute "training" in any one family-centered model. Becoming a successful family-centered practitioner requires much more detailed preparation, practice, and supervision than can be achieved from reading alone. The case examples, however, will describe the experience of this form of service provision from those closest to it—the workers and families.

The chapter opens with definitional issues that surround home-based, family-centered intervention in general and family preservation services in particular, then goes on to describe the basic features and typical job responsibilities of home-based workers. Definitions and categories to describe hard and soft services are then explored. Research on family preservation interventions is briefly reviewed, followed by several detailed case examples. The chapter concludes with reflections on service provision in family preservation practice in the future.

DEFINITIONAL ISSUES

Defining Home-Based Family Preservation Services

Family-centered services of all types are grounded in a common set of principles, including maintaining the welfare and safety of children and other family members and making the services family-focused, community-based, accessible, flexible, and intensive enough to meet the families' needs (U.S. Department of Health and Human Services, 1994).[1] Yet no definition of a family preservation program or intervention has been consistently applied. A number of typologies have been proposed (Nelson, Landsman, & Deutalbaum, 1990; Pecora, Fraser, Haapala, & Bartlomé, 1987; Stroul, 1998) based on (a) the site of service delivery—home-based versus office-based, (b) the duration of services—short-term versus long-term, (c) the intensity of service—number of hours spent with families each week, and (d) the treatment characteristics, model, or theory, such as multisystemic family therapy (Henggeler, Melton, Smith, Schoenwald, & Hanley, 1993), structural family therapy (AuClaire & Schwartz, 1986), and cognitive-behavioral therapy (Kinney, Haapala, & Booth, 1991).

Among the most widely cited definitions of services to preserve families is the one formulated by the Child Welfare League of America. The *Standards for Services to Strengthen and Preserve Families with Children* (Child Welfare League of America, 1989) classifies services into two types: (a) family resource, support, and education (i.e., services to support adults in their roles as parents) and (b) family centered (i.e., services to support families who are experiencing problems that may threaten their stability). The latter category contains what are called family-centered casework services, such as case management, and intensive family-centered crisis services, such as services for families with a child at risk of out-of-home placement or a child who is returning from care.

According to the league's definition of intensive family-centered crisis services, such services have the following features:

1. They are intended for families with one or more children at risk of imminent placement.
2. They are available to families twenty-four hours a day.
3. Most of the services involve direct contact with families.
4. Workers serve no more than six families at a time.
5. Families are seen by workers on an average of eight to ten hours per week.
6. Services are provided from four to a maximum of twelve weeks.

A worker contacts a family within forty-eight hours of the family's referral for service. These features reflect many of the defining aspects of the Homebuilders[2] program (Kinney, Madsen, Fleming, & Haapala, 1977), an early family preservation program whose model has been disseminated widely (Kinney et al., 1991). This intensive model will be the primary focus of this chapter.

While no all-encompassing definition of home-based interventions exists, a number of principles for effective frontline practice have been drawn from the experience of home-based and family-centered service programs (see table 7.1), and a number of competencies and training curricula for home-based family preservation practice have been developed to meet the staff development needs (see table 7.2). Home-based services can be found within a wide variety of social service programs—from broad-based family support early intervention programs to structural family therapy models (Berry, 1997). Home-based services also have been shown to contribute to the prevention and treatment of child maltreatment (Cohn & Daro, 1987;

TABLE 7.1. Principles for Effective Intervention

Effective workers
1. emphasize client strengths, rather than client pathology, and use client strengths and resources in problem solving
2. view their clients holistically, and their treatment plans encompass a broad range of factors
3. join with their clients as true partners in a collaborative problem-solving effort
4. tailor treatment plans to meet the needs and goals of their clients
5. work together with clients to create very specific, short-term, measurable goals for treatment
6. display certain skills and attitudes, including the ability to engage clients in a trusting working relationship, to express appropriate empathy, and to facilitate learning of a broad range of life skills.

Source: Beyond the Buzzwords: Key Principles in Effective Frontline Practice (p. 9), by J. Kinney, K. Strand, M. Haberup, and C. Bruner, 1994, Falls Church, VA: National Center for Service Integration. Reprinted with permission of Child and Family Policy Center, Des Moines, IA.

TABLE 7.2. Family Preservation Competencies

1. Frames problems in solvable, acceptable ways and employs techniques and skills that build on each family's unique strengths and motivate the family to attain self-sufficiency.
2. Engages family, agencies, and community systems in genuine partnership and teaches skills necessary to attain the family's goals.
3. Understands, respects, and practices within the family's cultural context, experience, and history as the framework for family preservation practice.
4. Is knowledgeable and respectful of, and sensitive and responsive to, issues of human diversity in the course of working with families.
5. Applies knowledge of human growth and behavior, systems theory, and multiple change strategies to develop systemic options for each unique family system.
6. Integrates and applies the values and techniques of family preservation (services and practices) based on a commitment to the core belief in the importance of the family system.
7. Joins in partnership with the family to facilitate empowerment of the family while supporting the family preservation values and using the family preservation change process to enable the family to meet its goals by whatever means necessary.

Source: "The Challenge and Potential of Family Preservation Services in the Public Child Welfare System," by A. L. Sallee and J. C. Lloyd, 1994, *Protecting Children, 10* (3), p. 6. Reprinted with permission from the American Humane Association, Children's Services.

Leventhal, 1996). One study of family preservation found that the amount of time the worker spent in the home was related to successful outcomes (Berry, 1992). Service delivery in the home is a hallmark of family preservation services; yet reviews of research have noted that many evaluations fail to include sufficient detail on interventions employed (Berry, 1997; Pecora, Fraser, Nelson, McCroskey, & Meezan, 1995; Tracy, 1995). Therefore, a closer examination of home-based family preservation interventions is warranted.

Defining Social Work Intervention

The definition of *intervention* in the *Social Work Dictionary* is "interceding in or coming between groups of people, events, planning activities or an individual's internal conflicts" (Barker, 1987, pp. 82). Intervention includes all the activities and roles used to solve or prevent problems or to achieve agreed-upon goals. Typical worker intervention activities would include, among others, counseling, therapy, skill training, advocacy, mediation, social planning, and community development and organization. Intervention activities shared with clients could include observation, role-play practice, behavioral rehearsal, and homework or reading assignments.

Interventions must be guided by the assessment of the situation and should be selected on the basis of their relevancy and proven efficacy. Interventions must also make sense to clients, be targeted to the correct system for change (individual, family, school, community), be culturally and developmentally relevant, and be delivered in sufficient intensity as warranted by the situation (Hepworth & Larsen, 1993).

Hallmarks of Home-Based Interventions

While family preservation interventions share many features with social work interventions in general, worthy of note are a number of additional defining features:[3]

1. A broad spectrum of comprehensive services is offered.
2. Traditional professional and bureaucratic boundaries are regularly crossed.
3. Staff members and program structures are fundamentally flexible.
4. The child is seen in the context of family and the family is seen in the context of its surroundings.
5. Professionals are perceived as caring and trustworthy; clients are viewed as colleagues.
6. Services are sought that meet the needs of families, crossing bureaucratic lines when needed.
7. Professionals provide services in nontraditional settings, venturing beyond their own office surroundings.
8. Professionals redefine their roles to respond to many more family needs, both clinical and concrete.
9. Interventions make full use of family and community strengths and resources.

That family preservation services use the home as the primary site for intervention is an important feature. Families are seen in their own homes and neighboring surroundings; home-based workers interact in whatever settings are comfortable for the family and are relevant to the agreed-upon goals of service (e.g. McDonald's, playgrounds, schools). A number of benefits are thought to be related to this "in-environment" method of service delivery (Berry, 1997).

Engagement, assessment, and goal setting may proceed more smoothly and quickly if the family is seen in the home. The home provides many more opportunities for teaching and modeling new behaviors, at the point and place in time they are most needed. These "teachable moments" (Kinney et al., 1991) allow for a greater transfer of learning to occur than if parenting skills, for example, were taught and practiced in an office setting. More members of the family or of its social network can be contacted when services are delivered in the home, such as family members who may have been reluctant to come to an office setting or neighbors who could provide support to the family. The family may more easily become involved in working on change goals when services are convenient and accessible. The degree to which individual family goals are achieved is an important predictor of overall program success (Fraser, Pecora, & Haapala, 1991); thus, getting families actively involved is a critical first step. Finally, the home-based worker is able to assess the social and physical environment of the family—both its strengths and challenges—and then more comprehensive and responsive interventions can be offered (Kemp, Whittaker, & Tracy, 1997).

A final hallmark of home-based services worthy of discussion and consideration is its value base. Although all social work interventions are derived from a value base, family preservation and home-based services are unique in their explicit statement of values and beliefs (Whittaker, Kinney, Tracy, & Booth, 1990). Home-based workers are challenged to act in a manner consistent with their beliefs, thereby demonstrating their values in a tangible way to families. For example, several value statements of the Homebuilders program, such as "clients are our colleagues," "do no harm," "it is our job to instill hope," and "clients are doing the best they can," serve to guide worker-client interactions through all phases of intervention with a family (Kinney et al., 1991).

THE HOME-BASED WORKER'S INTERVENTION TASK

The following is a basic job description for an intensive home-based counselor position in one urban family preservation program. Examining this job description may provide some clues to the ways in which home-based workers apply the intervention principles valued by the programs in which they work. In this sample program, the home-based worker's job comprises the following:

1. Provide in-home crisis-oriented treatment and support to families, which includes but is not limited to family and individual counseling, substance abuse counseling, family education, family and individual skill training, advocacy, information and referral, transportation, other services necessary to the enrichment of the family environment, and alcohol/drug education.
2. Formulate a goal-oriented treatment plan with a step-oriented process to prevent recurrence of crisis and to stabilize the family.
3. Keep thorough client records, and submit and use a goal-attainment scale or other approved system to allow for supervision and evaluation of the success of the treatment plan. The worker is also responsible for timely termination/evaluation letters.
4. Participate in ongoing supervision and staff training.

5. Provide advocacy and liaison work with schools, the justice system, social services, health service, and like agencies as needed.
6. Provide backup support to other staff members as directed.
7. Provide evening and weekend coverage as needed.[4]

This job description presumes that the home-based worker is a versatile and flexible service provider, capable of assuming a variety of roles and functions in relation to the family's circumstance. Berry (1997) points out that while no clear consensus exists on the educational characteristics required for home-based work, there is often a clear consensus on personal qualities desired: "Programs want workers who can provide therapeutic as well as case management services in work situations that are demanding, stressful, unstructured, unpredictable, and potentially dangerous" (p. 108). The job description also assumes a comprehensive knowledge of a variety of change theories, intervention strategies, and approaches to working with families. Other home-based models, grounded in one or more specific theoretical or treatment approaches, also may require knowledge in other fields of practice or theory.

Yet even with such a detailed job description, it is unlikely that the new worker can fully comprehend ahead of time the range of interventions and the amount of time and energy typically required for home-based work. In a typical service period—perhaps one to three months or more (as defined by the particular program or model)—home-based workers will conduct joint family sessions; individual sessions with children and adults; skills-based learning activities on a wide variety of social and life skills for family members of differing ages and developmental levels; collateral contacts with formal and informal service providers; referral, outreach, and advocacy efforts with other agencies and community groups; concrete services; and crisis intervention services on an as-needed basis. Regardless of the theoretical model employed by a particular family preservation program, many of the services are organized by central themes important to the family: stress management, anger management, behavior management, homemaker services, and respite care, with the overall intent to increase parenting skills, improve family relationships, decrease stress, increase supports and resources, and enhance developmental outcomes for all family members (Berry, 1997).

To gain a deeper appreciation for the job responsibilities of a home-based worker, we also need to consider other job tasks in addition to the intervention responsibilities and activities mentioned above: travel time; completion of paperwork for assessment, record keeping and reimbursement purposes; correspondence with funders of the home-based services, which may include a managed-care, private, or public service agency; and ongoing training and supervision. Managing one's own life while at the same time becoming closely involved with the lives of up to four or more families in crisis is also a balancing act for many home-based workers (Tracy, Bean, Gwatkin, & Hill, 1992).

CATEGORIES OF HOME-BASED INTERVENTIONS

Several research studies have attempted to track the number and types of interventions typically used in home-based practice (Berry, 1992; Fraser et al., 1991; Schuerman, Rzepnicki, & Littell, 1994; McCroskey & Meezan, 1997). Because early evaluations of family preservation programs generally did not provide much detail about the exact content and range of interventions, it has been difficult to replicate the service, to attribute outcomes to specific services, or even to compare one study with another. Tables 7.3 and 7.4 illustrate one way to categorize successfully interventions used in a large-scale research study, based on whether they represent concrete or clinical services (Fraser et al., 1991). Measurement instruments for clinical use by family preservation workers also are being developed (Craig-Van Grack, 1997).

Hard versus Soft Services

A major distinction often is made between *hard* and *soft* services. Hard, or concrete, services include the provision of material goods or financial assistance—providing transportation for a family, helping with housework or home repair, and providing food are all examples of concrete services. Soft, or clinical, services include, for example, assessment, counseling, and

TABLE 7.3. Concrete Services

Provide transportation	Help obtain utility benefits
Provide recreation activities	Help secure child care
Help client get a job	Arrange life-skills classes
Do housework with client	Help obtain housing
Arrange recreation activities	Help secure clothing
Help secure financial assistance	Provide household goods
Provide child care	Help obtain household goods
Give financial assistance	Help obtain legal aid
Provide food	Provide clothing
Help get food	Move client to new location
Help with transportation	Provide a job
Help obtain medical/dental services	Help arrange cleaning services
Provide toys or recreation equipment	

Source: Families in Crisis: The Impact of Intensive Family Preservation Services (p. 94), by M. W. Fraser, P. J. Pecora, and D. A. Haapala, 1991, New York: Aldine de Gruyter. Copyright 1991 by Walter de Gruyter, Inc. Reprinted with permission.

TABLE 7.4. Clinical Services

Listen to client	Build self-esteem	Give and accept
Encourage client	Track/chart behaviors	feedback
Offer support/	Clarify family roles	Teach use of leisure
understanding	Handle frustration	Social skills
Relationship building	Process of change	Assertiveness
Use reinforcement	Refer to other	Anxiety management
Set treatment goals	counseling	Values clarification
Reframing	Problem ownership	Relaxation
Natural/logical	Build structure/routine	Conversational skills
consequences	Negotiation skills	Family council
Clarify problem	Time-out	Provide paper/pencil
behaviors	Problem solving	tests
Child development	Environmental controls	Track emotion
Provide literature	De-escalating	Develop informal
Rational-emotive	Behavior rehearsal/role	supports
therapy concepts	play	Fair fighting
Build hope	Use of crisis card	Money management
"I" statements	Refer to other	Appropriate sexual
Anger management	counseling	behavior
Monitor clients	No-lose problem	Recognize suicide
Consult with other	solving	potential
service agencies	Meet with other	Time management
Clarify family rules	providers	Attend/testify at court
Improve compliance	Accepting "no"	Teach job hunting
Active listening skill	Self-criticism reduction	Academic skills
Defuse crisis	Depression	Territoriality concepts
Provide reinforcers	management	Protect from sexual
Make treatment plans	Pleasant events	abuse
Rational-emotive	Impulse management	How to use journal
therapy techniques	Advocate with schools	Advocate with utilities
Track behaviors	Refer to social service	Multiple-impact
		therapy

Source: Families in Crisis: The Impact of Intensive Family Preservation Services (pp. 96–97), by M. W. Fraser, P. J. Pecora, and D. A. Haapala, 1991, New York: Aldine de Gruyter. Copyright 1991 by Walter de Gruyter. Reprinted with permission.

parent training. Typically, families receive a mix of hard and soft services depending on their needs and goals; thus, services are highly individualized and flexible. One of the defining features of family preservation intervention is the high proportion of concrete services provided to families. Lewis (1991) reported that concrete services, especially transportation, accounted for nearly one-quarter of the service time for intensive family preservation workers using the Homebuilders model. Family preservation workers frequently help families fix broken windows, shop for food, obtain furniture, and care for their home and children (Schuerman et al., 1994).

Concrete services typically are offered in the early stages of work with a family, both to reduce the immediate crisis and to form a relationship with the family. But concrete services are not intended exclusively for poor families (Lewis, 1991). Families who otherwise are financially able to pay for services may find it difficult to access services for a variety of reasons. In these situations, "enabling services" (Berry, 1997) intended to link the family with needed formal and informal supports may be most helpful. The provision of concrete services correlates highly with "success" in family preservation (i.e., goal attainment and the child remaining in the home) (see Berry, 1997, for a review of the efficacy of hard versus soft services).

Families often perceive the provision of hard services as evidence that the worker accepts them where they are and will offer help that is valuable. For many families, hard services represent a new way of helping, dramatically different from the "talking" help (e.g. counseling, therapy, groups) that they received from other programs. Concrete services demonstrate support for the family in a tangible way. Hard services also help reduce environmental problems and barriers facing families and improve household conditions. Several studies have found that overall living conditions at termination were predictive of placement prevention (Berry, 1992; Fraser et al., 1991), and that the adequacy of basic supports for the family (e.g., income, social, health) contributes to improved outcome for children (McCroskey and Meezan, 1997). As a case example, near the end or termination of service, hard services may be provided to help solidify the changes made by a family; a move to stable, safe housing near the end of service may help ensure that other changes made by the family will endure over time (such as avoidance of further substance abuse). Family preservation services can address the environmental problems that make parenting and family life more difficult to manage, although traditional child welfare case plans have been criticized for relying almost exclusively on clinical (person-oriented) services even in the face of environmental deficits and stressors (Tracy, Green, & Bremseth, 1993).

Safety Planning and Clinical Skills Training

Another major distinction in service types provided by family preservation workers can be made between services and activities intended to reduce violence and ensure safety during the service period and the clinical services intended to change behaviors, attitudes, knowledge, or interactions. Family preservation programs typically work with families that have a high potential for violence; therefore, safety for everyone is the first priority. Interventions to defuse violence and establish safety rules are early agenda items for home-based work. Kinney et al. (1991) suggest a range of strategies to keep people safe: preparation and mindset (e.g., gathering information about the potential for violence), practical tips (e.g., park close to the home), and clinical interventions (e.g., structuring techniques to maintain contact and safety from one visit to another). A number of "clinical skills," such as active listening, serve well to reduce the potential for violence escalation. Most programs require a signed safety contract prior to beginning work with the family. This contract establishes safety ground rules and expectations. Individualized crisis plans often are used to deal with specific situations, such as what to do if relapse occurs. Most programs have arranged other administrative procedures when safety issues are of high concern, such as having a coworker attend a visit, calling a supervisor upon arrival at the home, or arranging for a neutral but convenient meeting place other than the home itself.

Among the wide variety of clinical interventions used by home-based workers, a large percentage is educational or skills-building (e.g., modeling parenting skills, teaching family care and housekeeping skills, and showing families how to access services). These appear to hold the most promise for family preservation (Berry, 1997). Home-based workers often play the role of teachers of the adults as well as the children in the family. People tend to learn best from people they like and respect. People tend to dislike learning if they feel put down or stupid. Therefore, all the techniques that family preservation workers use to engage with the family, such as active listening, looking for strengths, and working from the family's agenda, perhaps also place them in a position in which the knowledge and skills they bring will be valued and adopted by the family.

Targets of Intervention

Home-based intervention can be examined on the basis of the target of intervention. While home-based services are typically referred to as family-centered, the home-based worker interacts with more than just the family. Home-based workers may meet with individual family members separately. They also may work with the family in its entirety. The family's social network may be assessed and convened or otherwise mobilized as a supportive resource for the family (Tracy & Whittaker, 1990; Tracy, Whittaker, Pugh, Kapp, & Overstreet, 1994). In cases of isolated families, the worker may develop new links with formal and informal support systems. Berry and Cash (1998) describe the use of psycho-educational groups as a way to provide a safe and supportive network for a family. Finally, home-based workers are in contact with other community agencies and services, making referrals, advocating for services, modeling interactions, or in other ways streamlining the process for families.

CASE EXAMPLES

The Hogan Family

The family consists of Mary (33), Eric (16), Robby (13), Andy (6), and Alex (6). One year ago, Andy disclosed that Eric had sexually molested him on several occasions. An investigation concluded that Eric also had molested Alex and that six years ago he molested Robby.

Consequently, Eric was removed from the home. He lived with an uncle for three months, then was placed for six months in a Crisis Residential Center. During that time, the family participated in family counseling, and Eric attended a group for juvenile sex offenders.

Three months ago, Eric returned home. Mary stated that she reluctantly agreed to his return, based on her belief that the family would receive daily, in-home counseling. She reported that the service she actually received was "babysitting" while she was at work. She explained that the counselor arrived at 4:30 A.M. when Mary left for work, and supervised the children all day so that Eric had no opportunity to be alone with them. However, in the early morning the counselor slept downstairs while the children slept upstairs. Mary felt that this was not enough protection for the twins.

Mary expressed great fear that Eric would reoffend. She did not believe the twins were safe or that the support services the family received were adequate. She said she felt exhausted by having to transport the boys to counseling in the South County, when she lives in the North County. She felt that Eric would get more help if he were placed in a group home setting. She requested that Eric again be placed. Family preservation was offered as an alternative. The home-based worker established a number of goals with the family:

1. Create as safe an environment as possible to reduce the likelihood of future sexual abuse within the family.
2. Improve communication between family members (decrease amount of verbal harassment between family members).
3. Develop a plan and make appropriate referrals for services after family preservation.

A number of services were provided to address safety issues: the family preservation worker listened to the mother's concerns about Eric's presence at home; purchased locks for bedroom and bathroom doors and monitored the routine use of them; established "safety rules" for family members and ensured that they were understood and enforced; taught the difference between appropriate and inappropriate touch (using coloring books, Spider-man comics, and puppets) to the twins and assessed their ability to understand the information; taught the twins what to do if they were inappropriately touched (including assertive statement and telling responsible adults). With safety issues addressed, a number of clinical skills training services could be offered to deal with the communication concerns in this family: they were taught "feeling words" and "I" messages. In addition, a number of concrete enabling services were offered: helping Eric set up individual counseling; referring the twins to a group for 5-to-7-year-old victims; and referring Robby to a group of teenage victims (excerpted from Morgan & Marckworth, 1991).

Discussion. This family case presents for consideration a number of assessment issues that highlight the value base of family preservation practice. Should Eric be at home? Why, or why not? Clearly, the family must balance the safety of the younger siblings with the importance of Eric being at home. A number of services addressed the safety issues present in this family; services to address safety can be viewed as a prerequisite to other clinical and concrete services. The role of clinical skills training, enabling concrete services, the timing of both, and their relative importance to the overall intervention can also be considered.

The Clark Family

A public health nurse referred the Clark family to Homebuilders.[5] The nurse requested that the Homebuilders intervention coincide with the release of the Clark's infant daughter from the hospital. The baby had been born prematurely and had spent the first three months of her life in the hospital.

The nurse requested intensive services because she was concerned about the family situation. The Clark's 3-year-old son recently had been diagnosed as hyperactive and as having some brain damage. In addition, Children's Protective Services and the nurse were questioning three concussions the boy had experienced over the last year. The nurse and CPS were certain that unless Homebuilders was available to see the family, both children would have to be placed in foster care.

The nurse discussed her concerns with the parents, who consented to allow a Homebuilders therapist come to their home. The family had no phone, so the therapist dropped by unannounced for a visit. Mrs. Clark was home at the time, so the therapist asked if she could stay awhile and talk.

After sitting down, the first thing the therapist noticed was the smell of gas leaking from the furnace. Mrs. Clark agreed that she had smelled gas. The therapist suggested that Mrs. Clark dress herself and the children warmly, open the window and turn the furnace down. While she did that, the therapist went to a public phone and called the landlord to send out a repairman.

When the therapist returned, Mrs. Clark talked about her situation. She said she had been very depressed since the baby's birth, and that she often felt that the child did not belong to her. She was also extremely upset about her son's "wild" behavior. She wondered if the boy had a "bad seed" in him like his uncle who was in prison. She began to think she might kill him rather than watch him grow up to be a murderer like his uncle.

Mrs. Clark was very thin, pale, and weak. She had a chronic cold and had lost her front teeth due to poor health. Now 22, she had given birth to three children and had four miscarriages in five years of marriage. She also said she was very lonely. Her husband was usually away from the house from midmorning to late at night. He worked as an insurance salesman, but he had not sold a policy in five months. The woman told the therapist that every other counselor they saw told her that her husband was "rotten," and she should leave him. She said she loved him and that he didn't beat her. The family had moved to Washington from Idaho several months previously so they could remain married, yet still be eligible for state aid. They were currently receiving funds from the WIC (Women, Infants and Children) program.

The next day the therapist approached a local charitable organization and received the $25 needed to have a telephone installed. She also obtained two old bed sheets that could be nailed up as curtains, since Mrs. Clark had expressed fears about sitting alone at night with no curtains for privacy. She told the therapist that recently a strange man had been peering in her window at night. She had been raped once before and was scared that it might happen again.

During the next home visit, they focused on the 3-year-old son. Mrs. Clark said she did not love him and described a variety of his behaviors that she labeled as self-destructive and wild. She reported incidents such as him throwing himself backwards off furniture, touching the hot stove and laughing, turning on the kitchen burners, banging his head against the wall until he passed out, and biting, scratching, and hitting other people. Although he was 3, he still had not started talking. She was concerned that Children's Protective Services would think she was abusing him because he hurt himself so much, and because they locked him in his room at night. The Clarks did this because the boy slept only two or three hours at a stretch, and if he was not locked in his room, he would go into the kitchen and eat until he vomited. She said CPS thought she should put him in an institution because she couldn't handle him. He would not kiss or show any affection to people. She said Children's Protective Services in Idaho had removed him from the home the previous year when she had "a nervous breakdown" and was hospitalized. Since moving to Tacoma, the parents had already voluntarily placed the boy once for seventy-two hours because the mother felt she "couldn't cope" with him any longer. She also was afraid she might harm him because he made her so angry sometimes.

Before leaving for the day, the therapist made a list with Mrs. Clark of what Mrs. Clark could do if she felt her son's behavior was so bad that she would want to place him again. The Homebuilder let her know she thought it was a good idea to lock him in his room sometimes, and explained the concept of time-out. The list also included calling the Homebuilder (the family's phone was to be installed the next day). Then they made an appointment to take the son to Mary Bridge Children's Hospital Learning Center to see about enrolling him in a special school program. Finally, the therapist talked with the mother about making some free time for herself and volunteered to baby-sit for several hours later that week. Mrs. Clark accepted the offer.

Later that week, the Homebuilder was alone with the children for five hours while she was baby-sitting. She learned a lot about the young boy. She observed him engage in some of the behaviors Mrs. Clark had reported. By the end of the day, however, she determined that he responded to positive reinforcement and time-out. During the afternoon she taught him to play a kissing game. The information gathered that day was invaluable. It was evidence for both the therapist and the mother that the little boy could change, and that he did care about people. His mother cried the first time they played the kissing game.

During the second week of the intervention, Mrs. Clark began to talk more freely about her discontent with her marriage. She said she knew her husband wasn't really working all the times he was gone. She expressed resentment over the fact that he dressed nicely, while she had only one outfit. He was free to play all day and night, while she stayed confined in their apartment. He would not let her get a driver's license, but he would not drive her places. Feeling she had reached a teachable moment, the Homebuilder began to talk about territoriality and assertiveness training. The Homebuilder also called the woman's Department of Social and Health Services caseworker and obtained authorization to replace her front teeth.

Mr. Clark was beginning to get curious about what was happening. One day he stayed home to meet the therapist. While his wife was at the dentist, he and the Homebuilder spent several hours talking. He shared his own frustrations about having to be on welfare. The Homebuilder told him she wanted him to be a part of the counseling process, and he agreed to attend the next session. After their discussion, he seemed more willing to participate.

During the last weeks of the intervention, the therapist focused primarily on teaching the parents some behavioral child-management skills. The son had begun attending the Mary Bridge School Program, and Mrs. Clark rode the bus with him every day. The Homebuilder was pleased to see this change, because it gave the mother a chance to watch the teachers and to make friends with the staff there. Mrs. Clark reported having some positive feelings about her son and no longer feeling that she should send him away. She also began to feel much better about herself. She had temporary caps on her teeth and began to smile more. She also began to gain a little weight.

As the end of the intervention approached, the therapist and Mrs. Clark explored possibilities for her to continue counseling. She decided she wanted to go back to a counselor at the mental health center. She had seen the counselor a couple of times right after the baby was born last summer and thought she could trust her. She made an appointment.

During her last week with the family, the therapist helped the Clarks move to a better apartment in the neighborhood where they felt safer. It wasn't until after the move that the family found that the Mary Bridge bus would no longer be able to transport the boy to school. Mrs. Clark became very upset but quickly deescalated herself and began to problem solve. She talked with the counselors at Mary Bridge and followed their suggestion to see if the boy could be transferred to Child Study and Treatment Center's day care program. There were no openings at the center, but he was put on the waiting list.

A follow-up call with this family several months later revealed that although there had been a number of upsetting events after the Homebuilder left, they were still together as a family. Mrs. Clark had been seeing her counselor and had continued to work on being more assertive. She and her husband also were going for marital counseling. Mr. Clark had quit selling insurance and was enrolled in a job-training program. The son was attending the new school, and the mother was participating in a parent education program required by the school. The Clarks reported that their son was starting to talk and no longer seemed "wild." The infant daughter was doing fine.

Discussion. This case is noteworthy in the amount that was accomplished within just the first week of intervention. It clearly demonstrates how active the worker can be in meeting concrete needs and dealing with the environment (gas, phone, curtains, babysitting, dental care), while at the same time being sensitive to the family's needs and pace. There was an explicit focus on the mother as an individual, not solely as a parent, yet a great deal of time was spent generating a behavior management plan that would improve both the child's behavior and the parent-child relationship. Moreover, the Homebuilder worked with whoever was available at the time of the visit. The case was not terminated until all family members were actively involved. Finally, the worker dealt with the child's school placement and set up needed, ongoing counseling.

The Johnson Family

Marilyn Johnson freely admitted her addiction to crack. The ninety-eight-pound, 31-year-old mother of four was selling her food stamps to support her habit. The authorities suspected that drug trafficking took place in her home; and these suspicions were aggravated by the burly man who monitored admittance to her two-story house and the hovering presence of numbers of men and women on the premises. Marilyn's younger children were unkempt. Her 13-year-old daughter hadn't attended school for six months, had engaged in physical brawls with Marilyn, and had run in the streets with her boyfriend, a drug "roller." The police told Marilyn that she had twenty-four hours to rid her home of drug traffic, and the Children's Protective Services threatened to remove her children.

The case was referred to Families First and the Ennis Center for Children, a new program in Detroit that specialized in the treatment of high-risk families. When the Families First worker visited Marilyn the day the referral was made, Marilyn was obviously high but insisted that she wanted help in keeping her family together.

Prior to her drug addiction, Marilyn lived a conventional, comfortable life. She was married, worked as a restaurant manager, and owned a house and car. Her drug use began when her husband urged her to try heroin, and it became a daily habit. As her addiction progressed, she turned to crack, and her marriage floundered; she lost her job and was forced to sell her home, furniture, appliances, clothing, and car to support her drug habit. She became the pawn of dealers who beat her and demanded that she sell drugs from her home.

When Families First arrived, she had been using crack for two years and was illegally "squatting" in a house with broken windows, falling plaster, and bullet holes in the walls. Listening to her story, the caseworker offered understanding and compassion, carefully avoiding judgment or criticism.

When the worker explained to Marilyn that the goal of the Families First intervention was to keep families together, Marilyn made the commitment to work with the program. The worker identified three goals for the intervention: to find new housing, to obtain drug treatment, and to rebuild a relationship with her 13-year-old daughter. The worker helped to alter supervision arrangements so that she could be satisfied that the children would be protected without being removed from the home.

The caseworker encouraged Marilyn to take the initiative in looking for housing; the worker provided such support services as Realtor lists and transportation. While driving around looking for housing, they talked. The caseworker actively reinforced Marilyn's determination and motivation and encouraged the positive steps she was taking to regain control of her life. The Families First worker often spent all day, every day, with Marilyn, helping in the search for a new house and securing emergency goods and clothing. Because Marilyn had no money or means of transportation, the worker's provision of these concrete needs was an important part of the intervention process.

It was impossible for Marilyn to enroll in a drug treatment program until housing and furniture were secured, so the caseworker devised alternatives to help Marilyn refrain from using drugs until her treatment could begin. They worked out several emergency tactics, such as "crisis cards" with substitute activities, the use of "self-talk," and the twenty-four-hour availability of her caseworker by phone. On a few occasions, when Marilyn relapsed and smoked crack, she was very upset and called her Families First worker to discuss it. Another ongoing concern was the continued drug trafficking in her home. It was difficult for Marilyn to admit the risk to her children posed by the drug sales, but eventually she acknowledged the need to detach herself from her drug-involved friends and environment, as well as from her husband and male friends who remained on drugs.

By the end of the six-week intervention, with the help of emergency funds from the state, Marilyn had moved to a four-bedroom house, complete with furniture, appliances, and utilities. She enrolled in a women's drug treatment facility that specialized in the needs of women and their families and included a program for preschool children to attend along with their mothers. Six months after the program's conclusion, Marilyn's improved sense of self-worth was reflected in her appearance. She gained weight, began to dress fashionably, and used makeup. Her relationships with her children, especially her 13-year-old daughter, improved dramatically after counseling, and her daughter began to attend school every day. Marilyn attended Narcotics Anonymous meetings daily, learned money-management skills, and applied for employment through Vocational Rehabilitation Services (excerpted from Edna McConnell Clark Foundation, 1993).

Discussion. This case example illustrates the challenges of family preservation in the context of substance abuse problems in the family. Consider the definition of "recovery" and the response to "relapse." Would this family have been terminated from more traditional services? Family preservation programs have had to integrate substance abuse treatment practice and principles into their work, such as assessment of the stage of change and motivational interviewing techniques. This case also illustrates the use of concrete services and social network resources to support the families' growth and safety. The worker spent a great deal of time with the family, thereby demonstrating the advantages of a small caseload and flexible work schedule.

FUTURE ISSUES

In spite of the broad-based support for family preservation programs, we have limited knowledge of the ways in which home-based interventions function, and with what effects (Pecora et al., 1995; Rossi, 1992). Critical issues facing family preservation services in the coming century can be found in such areas as research and program evaluation, practice issues, and program administration.

Research and Evaluation

Among the more critical research and program evaluation issues are identifying the proper role for such services (Berry, 1991; Rossi, Schuerman, & Budde, 1994; Wells & Tracy, 1996) within the child welfare system and other child-serving systems (Dore, 1991, 1993; Leavitt & McGowan, 1991); understanding the effectiveness of programs and the extent to which gains made in treatment can be maintained over time (Fraser et al., 1991; Littell, Schuerman, Rzepnicki, Howard, & Budde, 1993; Wells & Biegel, 1991, 1992; Wells & Whittington, 1993); and gaining a better understanding of what services are most effective for which presenting problems (Littell, Schuerman, & Chak, 1994). Research must continue its focus on multiple measures of outcome, beyond placement alone (McCroskey & Meezan, 1997). Finally, more process and qualitative studies are called for both to describe the services offered and provided to families and to explore how families experience the service (Drisko, 1998). Perhaps the methods for acquiring research findings and knowledge will be facilitated by the Internet. With more and more agencies and organizations developing Web sites, it will be faster and easier to access information about a specific program model.

Program Administration

Among the program administrative issues are the development of effective approaches to the preparation and supervision of family preservation workers (Whittaker et al., 1990); organizational supports to sustain programs over time (Blythe, Tracy, Kotovsky, & Gwatkin, 1992); defining and determining the target population for family preservation (Tracy, 1991); and learning how best to work with managed care and insurance agencies that still tend to view and pay for services on the basis of one identified client versus the whole family.

Practice Issues

A survey conducted by Denby, Curtis, and Alford (1998) suggests significant bias against targeting family preservation services to children of color. Yet many principles of family preservation are thought to be consistent with culturally competent practice (Carter, 1997; Fong, 1994; Hodges, 1991). Among the most pressing practice issues will be gaining a better understanding of how best to respond to what will be an increasingly diverse American population. Learning how to integrate various treatment approaches, including those for treatment of substance abuse or domestic violence, into individual family preservation programs (Tracy, 1994; Blythe, Jiordana, & Kelly, 1991) also will be a continuing need. As the social service system works toward the development of family-centered, community-based, integrated services, family preservation programs will need to collaborate closely with the continuum of services available in a community (Corrigan & Bishop, 1997). In addition, family preservation practice may need to incorporate family and community development intervention strategies along with individual change strategies, if it is to deal successfully with the larger-scale social problems confronting referred families.

NOTES

1. Thanks are extended to Kathleen Wells, who helped conceptualize and write this section.
2. Homebuilders is the trademark of Behavioral Science Institute. References to Homebuilders throughout this chapter should be regarded as implicitly carrying the registered trademark.
3. From *Intensive family preservation services: An instructional sourcebook* (pp. 2–13), by E. M. Tracy, J. Kinney, D. Haapala, and P. Pecora (Eds.), 1991, Cleveland: Mandel School of Applied Social Sciences. Copyright 1991 by publisher. Adapted with permission.
4. One-page job description from Parents and Children Together Program— PACT, Bellefaire/Jewish Children's Bureau, Cleveland, Ohio.
5. The Clark family case example is from *Reaching High-Risk Families: Intensive Family Preservation in Human Services* (pp. 60–63), by J. K. Whittaker, J. Kinney, E. M. Tracy, and C. Booth (Eds.), 1990, New York: Aldine de Gruyter. Copyright 1990 by Walter de Gruyter, Inc., New York. Reprinted with permission.

REFERENCES

AuClaire, P., & Schwartz, I. (1986). *An evaluation of the effectiveness of intensive home based services as an alternative to placement for adolescents and their families.* Minneapolis: Hennepin County Human Service Department and the University of Minnesota, Hubert H. Humphrey Institute of Public Affairs.

Barker, R. L. (1987). *The social work dictionary.* Silver Springs, MD: National Association of Social Workers.

Bath, H. I., & Haapala, D. A. (1994). Family preservation services: What does the outcome research really tell us? *Social Service Review, 68* (3), 386–404.

Berry, M. (1991). The assessment of imminence of risk of placement: Lessons from a family preservation program. *Children and Youth Services Review, 13,* 239–56.

Berry, M. (1992). An evaluation of family preservation services: Fitting agency services to family needs. *Social Work, 37,* 314–21.

Berry, M. (1997). *The family at risk: Issues and trends in family preservation services.* Columbia: University of South Carolina Press.

Berry, M., & Cash, S. J. (1998). Creating community through psychoeducational groups in family preservation work. *Families in Society, 79* (1), 15–24.

Blythe, B. J., Jiordana, M. J., & Kelly, S. A. (1991). Family preservation with substance abusing families: Help that works. *Children, Youth and Family Services Quarterly, 14* (3), 12–13.

Blythe, B. J., Salley, M. P., & Jayaratne, S. (1994). A review of intensive family preservation services research. *Social Work Research, 18* (4), 213–24.

Blythe, B. J., Tracy, E. M., Kotovsky, A., & Gwatkin, S. (1992). Organizational supports to sustain intensive family preservation programs. *Families in Society, 73* (8), 463–70.

Carter, C. (1997). Using African-centered principles in family-preservation services. *Families in Society, 78* (5), 531–38.

Child Welfare League of America. (1989). *Standards for services to strengthen and preserve families with children.* Washington, DC: Author.

Corrigan, D., & Bishop, K. K. (1997). Creating family-centered integrated service systems and interprofessional educational programs to implement them. *Social Work in Education, 19* (3), 149–63.

Craig-Van Grack, A. (1997). A taxonomy and recording instrument for process measurement of family preservation services. *Child Welfare, 76* (2) 349–71.

Denby, R. W., Curtis, C. M., & Alford, K. A. (1998). Family preservation services and special populations: The invisible target. *Families in Society, 79* (1), 3–14.

Dore, M. (1991). Context and structure of practice: Implications for research. In K. Wells & D. Biegel (Eds.), *Family preservation services: Research and evaluation* (pp. 121–37). Newbury Park, CA: Sage.

Dore, M. (1993). Family preservation and poor families: When Homebuilding is not enough. *Families in Society, 74* (9), 545–56.

Drisko, J. W. (1998). Utilization-focused evaluation of two intensive family preservation programs. *Families in Society, 79* (1), 62–74.

Edna McConnell Clark Foundation. (1993). *Keeping families together: Facts on Family Preservation Services.* New York: Author.

Fong, R. (1994). Family preservation: Making it work for Asians. *Child Welfare, 73* (4), 331–41.

Fraser, M. W., Nelson, K. E., & Rivard, J. C. (1997). Effectiveness of family preservation services. *Social Work Research, 21* (3), 138–53.

Fraser, M. W., Pecora, P. J., & Haapala, D. A. (1991). *Families in crisis: The impact of intensive family preservation services.* New York: Aldine de Gruyter.

Henggler, S., Melton, G., Smith, L., Schoenwald, S., & Hanley, J. (1993). Family preservation using multisystemic treatment: Long-term follow-up to a clinical trial with serious juvenile offenders. *Journal of Child and Family Studies, 2* (4), 283–93.

Hepworth, D. H., & Larsen, J. A. (1993). *Direct social work practice: Theory and skills* (4th ed.). Pacific Grove, CA: Brooks Cole.

Hodges, V. G. (1991). Providing culturally sensitive intensive family preservation services to ethnic minority families. In E. M. Tracy, D. A. Haapala,

J. Kinney, & P. J. Pecora (Eds.), *Intensive family preservation services: An instructional sourcebook* (pp. 95–116). Cleveland: Case Western Reserve University, Mandel School of Applied Social Sciences.

Kemp, S., Whittaker, J. K., & Tracy, E. M. (1997). *Person-environment practice: The social ecology of interpersonal helping.* New York: Aldine de Gruyter.

Kinney, J., Haapala, D., & Booth, C. (1991). *Keeping families together: The Homebuilders model.* New York: Aldine de Gruyter.

Kinney, J. Haapala, D., Booth, C., & Leavitt, S. (1990) The Homebuilders model. In J. K. Whittaker, J. Kinney, E. M. Tracy, & C. Booth (Eds.), *Reaching high-risk families: Intensive family preservation in human services* (pp. 31–64). New York: Aldine de Gruyter.

Kinney, J., Madsen, B., Fleming, T., & Haapala, D. (1977). Homebuilders: Keeping families together. *Journal of Consulting and Clinical Psychology, 45,* 667–73.

Kinney, J., Strand, K., Hagerup, M., & Bruner, C. (1994). *Beyond the buzzwords: Key principles in effective frontline practice.* Falls Church, VA: National Center for Service Integration.

Leavitt, S., & McGowan, B. (1991). Transferring the principles of intensive family preservation services to different fields of practice. In E. M. Tracy, D. A. Haapala, J. Kinney, & P. J. Pecora (Eds.), *Intensive family preservaton services: An instructional sourcebook* (pp. 51–70). Cleveland: Case Western Reserve University, Mandel School of Applied Social Sciences.

Leventhal, J. M. (1996). Twenty years later: We do know how to prevent child abuse and neglect. *Child Abuse and Neglect, 20* (8), 647–53.

Lewis, R. E. (1991). What are the characteristics of intensive family preservation services? In M. W. Fraser, P. J. Pecora, & D. A. Haapala, *Families in crisis: The impact of family preservation services* (pp. 93–107). New York: Aldine de Gruyter.

Littell, J. H. (1997). Effects of the duration, intensity, and breadth of family preservation services: A new analysis of data from the Illinois Family First experiment. *Children and Youth Services Review, 19* (1, 2) 17–39.

Littell, J. H., Schuerman, J. R., & Chak, A. (1994). *What works best for whom in family preservation? Relationships between service characteristics and outcomes for selected subgroups of families* (Discussion Paper 054). Chicago: Chapin Hall Center for Children.

Littell, J. H., Schuerman, J. R., Rzepnicki, T. L., Howard, J., & Budde, S. (1993). Shifting objectives in family preservation programs. In R. K. Grigsby & E. S. Morton (Eds.), *Advancing family preservation practice* (pp. 99–116). Newbury Park, CA: Sage.

McCroskey, J., & Meezan, W. (1997). *Family preservation and family functioning.* Washington, DC: Child Welfare League of America.

Morgan, L. J., & Marckworth, P. (Eds.) (1991). *Intensive family preservation services: Resource book.* Cleveland: Mandel School of Applied Social Sciences.

Nelson, K. E., Lansman, M., & Deutalbaum, W. (1990). Three models of family-centered placement prevention services. *Child Welfare, 69,* 3–21.

Pecora, P., Fraser, M., Haapala, D., & Bartlomé, I. (1987). *Defining family preservation services: Three intensive home-based treatment programs.* Salt Lake City: University of Utah, Social Research Institute.

Pecora, P. J., Fraser, M. W., Nelson, K. E., McCroskey, J., & Meezan, M. (1995). *Evaluating family-based services.* New York: Aldine de Gruyter.

Rossi, P., Schuerman, J., & Budde, S. (1994). *Understanding child placement decisions and those who make them.* Chicago: University of Chicago, Chapin Hall Center for Children.

Rossi, P. H. (1992). Assessing family preservation programs. *Children and Youth Services Review, 14,* 77–97.

Schuerman, J. R., Rzepnicki, T. L., & Littell, J. H. (1994). *Putting families first: An experiment in family preservation.* New York: Aldine de Gruyter.

Stroul, B. (1988). *Series on community-based services for children and adults who are severely emotionally disturbed: Vol. 1. Home-based services.* Washington, DC: Georgetown University Child Development Center.

Tracy, E., Green, R., & Bremseth, M. (1993). Meeting the environmental needs of abused and neglected children: Implications from a statewide survey of supportive services. *Social Work Research and Abstracts, 29* (2), 21–26.

Tracy, E. M. (1991). Defining the target population for family preservation services. In K. Wells and D. E. Biegel (Eds.), *Family preservation services: Research and evaluation* (pp. 138–58). Newbury Park, CA: Sage.

Tracy, E. M. (1994). Maternal substance abuse: Protecting the child, preserving the family. *Social Work, 39* (5), 534–40.

Tracy, E. M. (1995). Family Preservation Services. In *Encyclopedia of Social work,* (19th ed.). National Association of Social Workers Press.

Tracy, E. M., Bean, N., Gwatkin, S., & Hill, B. (1992). Family preservation workers: Sources of job satisfaction and job stress. *Research on Social Work Practice, 2* (4), 465–78.

Tracy, E. M., Kinney, J., Haapala, D., & Pecora, P. (1991). Intensive family preservation services: A strategic response to families in crisis. In E. M. Tracy, J. Kinney, D. Haapala, & P. Pecora (Eds.), *Intensive family preservation services: An instructional sourcebook* (pp. 2–13). Cleveland: Mandel School of Applied Social Sciences.

Tracy, E. M., & Whittaker, J. K. (1990). The social network map: Assessing social support in clinical social work practice. *Families in Society, 71* (8), 461–70.

Tracy, E. M., Whittaker, J. K., Pugh, A., Kapp, S., & Overstreet, E. J. (1994). Support networks characteristics of primary caregivers in family preservation services: An exploratory study. *Families in Society, 75* (8), 481–89.

U.S. Department of Health and Human Services. (1994). *Program Instruction. Family preservation and support services.* Washington, DC: Administration on Children, Youth and Families.

Wells, K., & Biegel, D. E. (Eds.). (1991). *Family preservation services: Research and evaluation.* Newbury Park, CA: Sage.

Wells, K., & Biegel, D. E. (1992). Intensive family preservation services research: Current status and future agenda. *Social Work Research and Abstracts, 28* (1), 21–27.

Wells, K., & Tracy, E. (1996). Re-orienting family preservation services to public child welfare practice. *Child Welfare, 75* (6), 667–92.

Wells, K., & Whittington, D. (1993). Child and family functioning after intensive family preservation services. *Social Service Review, 67* (1), 55–83.

Whittaker, J. K., Kinney, J., Tracy, E. M., & Booth, C. (Eds.). (1990). *Reaching high-risk families: Intensive family preservation in human services.* New York: Aldine de Gruyter.

8 Formal and Informal Kinship Care

Supporting the Whole Family

Gary R. Anderson

The stresses on families and the complexity of challenges facing families underscore the need for social support. This support is typically and powerfully provided by a range of persons and activities through a family's natural and informal interactions and through more formal, organized efforts. The power of informal social supports is evidenced in daily practice with at-risk children and families. For example, a young mother pulled her car into a gas station at an expressway exit and ordered her 8-year-old daughter to go to the bathroom. When the daughter entered the bathroom, the mother returned to her car and drove off, abandoning her daughter at the station. The attendants called the police, and the girl called her grandmother. Arriving almost simultaneously with the child protective services worker and the police were a collection of aunts, uncles, and grandparents to enfold the young girl. Offering to help find the mother and providing information about the mother's behavior and condition, the family encircled the girl and took her into their familiar custody for protection and care (Anderson, 1994).

The importance of informal social supports is demonstrated through research. Numerous studies have affirmed the importance of and preference for family members and friends as sources of help (Burnette, 1997;

Keller & McDade, 1997; Potts, 1997). Such sources include peers and community members, as well as family members. The support provided by kinship networks has been described as a resilient response to a child and family crisis, particularly in the African American community (Scannapieco & Jackson, 1996).

FORMAL AND INFORMAL SUPPORT

Formal family support services are defined as

> . . . community-based services to promote well-being of children and families designed to increase the strength and stability of families (including adoptive, foster, and extended families), . . . to afford children a stable and supportive family environment, and to otherwise enhance child development. (Geballe, 1995, p. 159)

These services can include home visits, parent support groups, respite care, structured activities to improve parent-child relationships, drop-in family centers, information and referral services, and early developmental screening for children (Geballe, 1995).

Formal supports are provided by entities developed and funded by a system or organization to provide some service to an identified population. The formality connotes an intentionality of *purpose*, the *planning* for service delivery, and the *process* of developing a structure for the provision of some form of support. Formal supports often are delivered in a predetermined manner, through a planned and standardized process of application, at set times or places, and by qualified providers. There is often a degree of accountability, requiring some form of documentation of service and some degree of financial support for the products, services, and structure of the organization (Bonecutter & Gleeson, 1997). There may be some stigma on individuals or families receiving assistance from formal social support systems. Formal supports are provided by educational and school-based services, family preservation and child welfare services, mental health counseling, legal and court system services, and health care organizations.

Informal supports typically were not developed or created for the sole purpose of providing a service to an identified population. They have no clearly articulated structure or process for the delivery of a product or service. Boundaries of time and place are looser than in formal systems of support. Providers of service are not subject to educational or accreditation standards. Documentation of effort is not required because accountability is less often externally scrutinized, and there are few reporting requirements. There is often mutuality of support, and such assistance is relatively free from stigma. Informal supports are provided by family members, friends, neighbors, and persons with whom one might share some attachment or affiliation due to membership in a faith community, racial/ethnic group, club, or other association (Bonecutter & Gleeson, 1997).

Family-centered services often are most prominently identified by or feature those services provided by formal support systems. The resources provided by the informal system oftentimes are overlooked or misjudged and consequently are underappreciated and underutilized by formal systems. There also may be situations in which families have few informal supports, and this should be recognized as a significant challenge to the formal systems of support.

At the center of family-centered services is the social support provided by relatives and kinship networks. According to Hegar (1999), more than 2.5 million families in the United States were maintained by grandparents with one or more grandchildren living with them, comprising 7 percent of all U.S. families with minor children. This support, particularly in the child welfare system, has been and will increasingly be relied on to provide the most intensive forms of assistance for its vulnerable members. In this chapter the special resource of extended family members will be identified in relation to both the informal and formal systems of support. Kinship networks provide significant support to family members but in turn require a range of supports themselves.

KINSHIP FAMILY CARE

Informal Kinship Care

The existence and prominence of extended family and other individuals who may not be related by blood but have a role and position as family members has been well documented, particularly in the African American community (Hegar, 1999; Stehno, 1988). A more inclusive definition of family, and consequently kinship, is recognized by the Kinship Care Policy and Practice Committee of the Child Welfare League of America, which states that family caregivers include members of one's tribe or clan, godparents, stepparents, or "other adults who have a kinship bond with a child" (Child Welfare League of America, 1994, p. 2). The value of kinship care among other cultural groups also is affirmed but less well documented. For example, the importance of family and family support in Latino households is affirmed by a study of Latino grandmothers in New York City who provide care for their grandchildren and receive significant support from other children (Burnette, 1997).

This informal system provides support to family members by providing respite care and the long-term nurturing of grandchildren, nieces, nephews, and other children. Older adult relatives and caregivers provide a home for children whose parents are unable to provide a safe, nurturing environment due to illness, economic hardship and relocation, involuntary separations (child welfare or court intervention or both), or abandonment. These arrangements are negotiated by family members in the community without the intervention of formal systems. Children are sent to or taken in by family in response to a need for their care and protection. There are no agency actions or applications for service processed.

Caregivers give a number of reasons for undertaking kinship care, and they experience numerous rewards. Relative caregivers report that when a child in their extended family is in need of short-term or long-term care, they expect to be a resource to that child. This responsibility is seen as a duty and obligation—as part of what it means to be in a family. It may not even be considered a choice: "Of course I would care for my grandchild or other related child in need." There is the satisfaction of acting in concert with one's values and of doing "what is right," and the conviction that family members should respond in this sacrificial manner for one another. In addition to the sense of duty and the affirmation of one's values and convictions, there may be an experience of pleasure that comes with the child and a return to a parenting role. There may be a sense of enjoyment in raising children, experiencing their affection and bond, and sharing certain life experiences. For some relatives it may be their only direct experience in parenting; for others it may be a chance to parent again at a different stage in their lives with the benefit of further life experience. A sense of family is affirmed, and a pleasure in parenting is rekindled. There is also the sense of relief and satisfaction that a vulnerable child has not been "lost to the family" or been at risk among unknown families in distant and unconnected neighborhoods. The kinship caregiver has affirmed a positive, loving family connection and prevented a troubling, unknown fate for the child.

In addition to the merits for the caregiver, research on kinship care, particularly in the formal system, has demonstrated the benefits for the child within the extended family. The dynamic of being held and nurtured within one's family can be operationalized in a number of ways. The traumatic effects of separation from one's biological parents are perhaps buffered through the experience of something *familiar* when the child is cared for by familiar persons with familiar names, in a familiar setting, and with a shared history, habits, and heritage (e.g., language, food, rituals, holidays). An informal transition from one's parent to one's aunt or grandfather may be less searing than a court-involved investigatory process and involuntary removal. *Continuity* with one's family and culture is preserved. The child is more likely to remain with his or her brothers and sisters because a kinship caregiver is more likely to accept responsibility for raising an entire sibling group. There is at least a de facto permanence, because the child is with family members with the promise and potential of lifelong attachments. These attachments are not jeopardized by the child turning 18 or outgrowing a formal system's brokered relationship. Moreover, within kinship care the child's place in society is not as marginalized—living with a relative would seem to be a more acceptable social status than living in unrelated foster care or group care (Beeman & Boisen, 1999). The child with special challenges may find more tolerance among family members than among nonrelated caregivers.

The acceptance of a relative into one's home also can precipitate or heighten a number of issues (Crumbley & Little, 1997). First, the relative caregiver, usually a female, has now assumed a new or regained status of parenting. This may pose a number of challenges: (a) understanding child raising; (b) responding to disciplinary challenges; (c) coping with demands on one's time, attention, and supervision; (d) handling dilemmas with regard to child and adolescent behavior; and (e) dealing with particular emotional or learning challenges the child might have possessed before placement or that might be heightened by the child's experience with the absent parent and the separation process.

This new role also involves the relative caregiver in formal systems that may be unfamiliar or may have been experienced some time ago and under different circumstances. The new caregiver will have to negotiate the educational system in order to place the child in school, respond to school expectations, and cope with the child's adjustments and requirements posed by the educational process. The caregiver and the child may experience these multiple adjustments and new settings while also attempting to cope with feelings of loss, change, separation, and adjustment to multiple new environments. The new caregiver will be involved with medical services in order to obtain school-required immunizations and physical examinations, to treat the child's illnesses and accidents, and to respond to dental and other related care and emergencies. The new caregiver may also become involved with the mental health system if the child requires counseling or medication to respond to psychosocial issues or specific disorders that affect the child's ability to function in the home, school, or community.

All these challenges related to the new parenting role pose other potential complications for the caregiver. Caregivers may have a preexisting physical or medical condition that already complicates their lives. Such conditions may be further taxed by the demands of child care and supervision. Consequently, the caregiver's involvement with the medical or health care systems would continue and perhaps intensify. The caregiver might be faced with questions of legal custody or guardianship with regard to educational placements and securing medical treatment for the child, requiring some involvement with the legal system. There may be other legal complications with regard to the status of the child in the caregiver's home and an uncertainty, if not struggle, between older caregivers and their adult children with regard to custody of children.

The provision of adequate living space may be difficult, if not impossible. An aunt caring for her own children may be confronted with the need to find space for two or three additional children in her already fully occupied apartment. Grandparents may live in a small space that suits them but now must accommodate several more children (Draimin, Hudis, & Segura, 1992). Providing food, shelter, clothes, educational supplies, medical care, recreational activities, and other required services is expensive. The need for financial assistance would increase, and this might involve the caregiver with the financial assistance services in the community, including food stamps, Social Security, Temporary Assistance for Needy Families (TANF), and child-support agencies. There would be additional parenting demands on the caregiver to furnish a place for the child in the new home, provide transportation to various sites, supervise and entertain the child, provide necessary meals, and respond to the child's emotional needs.

The caregiver's life might, in fact, have additional complications. It is possible that rather than caring for only one child in need of a home, a caregiver will be confronted with an entire sibling group that requires nurturance and protection. It is also possible that the caregiver is raising additional children from other family members, caring for an older relative, or supporting an adult child in crisis. It is also possible that the parent who can no longer care for the child or children may be in the neighborhood and may be making demands on the relative caregiver or be engaged in some form of ongoing conflict with family members, including the caregiver.

Caring for adolescents may pose particular challenges. Older relatives, while willing to care for younger children, may be more reluctant to take into their home an adolescent who is perceived to be a troublemaker (Draimin, 1995). A kinship care arrangement that seemed secure when the children were elementary school age may face new challenges as children enter adolescence. These challenges may have subtle differences from those faced by other parents raising adolescents, because family members may be coping with issues of pronounced grief, anger, abandonment, and separation, in addition to the typical stressors of adolescence. Kin caregivers with adolescent children may have a particular need for social and educational support (Starr, Dubowitz, Harrington, & Feigelman, 1999).

The new caregiver may face a number of emotional and psychological challenges. He or she may face the dual task of dealing personally with the loss of the loved one and at the same time responding to children who also are experiencing a grieving process (Draimin, 1995). The caregiver may feel some measure of guilt if an adult child is unable or unwilling to care for his or her children. This guilt could be compounded if the adult child has an illness, such as AIDS, has been imprisoned, or is involved in substance abuse. The new caregiver may be frustrated or angry with the adult child for in some way failing to adequately parent, resulting in these new demands on the relative caregiver (Crumbley & Little, 1997). These reactions may be complicated by a sense of shame and depression that may heighten social isolation. These strains introduce additional complications because the children in care may be affected by the anger or other reactions of the new caregiver toward the caregiver's adult child. The strains of new caregiving and the responses of the caregiver may create or heighten some measure of interpersonal conflict between a couple or between other family members. One researcher noted,

> Some of these women, no matter how willing and devoted they are, will be unable to continue to bear the escalating burdens of illness, emotional exhaustion, poverty, or the severity of the children's behavior or academic problems. (Levine, 1995, p. 194)

As informal kinship care introduces a number of challenges for these new caregivers—including bringing them into contact with a number of formal systems and potentially increasing the stress within the family— there are a number of opportunities for the kinship family to confront the formal child welfare system. This system could be conceptualized as a continuum of structures and services calibrated to respond to different levels of family stress and child endangerment. This continuum, conceptualized on the basis of intrusiveness and level of formal involvement in the life of the family, includes family support services, family preservation services, child abuse prevention responses, child protective services, shelter and emergency care, foster care, group home and residential care, and adoptive services.

There are times when the kinship care process briefly intersects with the formal child welfare and legal systems. The need for child placement might be identified during a child protective investigation in response to a report of neglect or maltreatment. Relatives are identified by the child, by the parent(s), by their own presence on the scene, or by a worker's investigation. When a relative accepts responsibility for the care of the child, the formal system may withdraw. The child welfare system may remain involved with the family, either by legally sanctioning the placement or, more marginally, through a diversion strategy that maintains the family on a caseload while not providing formal foster care status and payments.

There are multiple merits to informal kinship care. These include the advantages gained for the child and the caregiver and family by keeping the child within the family system. They also include the avoidance of the complications introduced by the formal system. These complications include (a) some demands for formal evaluation processes such as psychological or psychiatric interviews, foster parent training, physical exams, and follow-up interviews with court and agency personnel; (b) some schedule of meetings and ongoing negotiations with agents of formal systems, such as child welfare workers (who may change frequently due to staff turnover) or representatives of the family court; (c) possibly some scrutiny and demands with regard to one's home, its size or configuration, and resources; (d) monitoring the child's education; (e) some measure of oversight with regard to family travel plans, particularly out-of-state travel; (f) experiencing some questioning with regard to one's parenting aptitude and capacity; (g) criminal and other background checks; (h) some provision of financial resources with accompanying fiscal accountability; and (i) the general experience that one's control of a family and its decisions is not free from second-guessing, advice, or at times overt countercommands. It is no surprise that many kinship caregivers report a desire to avoid involvement with formal systems, particularly the child welfare system, and approach such contacts with ambivalence, at best.

There are additional complications and questions that could be reasonably raised with regard to informal kinship caregiving. These issues can be divided into two general categories, involving the social and economic support of kinship arrangements and involving concerns for the safety and well-being of children.

Social and Economic Support

Providing food, clothing, and shelter, in addition to addressing the social, educational, and recreational needs of children, requires a certain amount of financial resources. Informal kinship care oftentimes is not a planned experience and may be established quickly in response to a family crisis or emergency. There often has not been time to prepare financially for such a responsibility. In addition, many caregivers already experience marginal financial status before the introduction of new members to the household. Economic support for informal kinship caregivers may not exist. Even when some financial assistance does exist, it may be very limited, difficult to procure, stigmatizing, or unknown or inaccessible to the caregiver. The caregiver's financial resources may be further taxed if the child now in his or her care requires mental health counseling or has physical and medical conditions that require special treatment and medications. The transportation and related demands pose additional financial stress and costs related to caregiver time and energy. This is multiplied with the care of a sibling group. Essentially on their own, there are few sources of financial assistance for caregiver families. The caregiver also may need legal advice and services.

Oftentimes there is equal need for social supports. The caregiver's preexisting social network may not be able or adequate to provide the emotional, psychological, spiritual, logistical, and educational support needed to meet the new challenges of parenting one's grandchildren or nieces and nephews. Caregivers may not have ready access to the support provided by a friend or sympathetic neighbor, and they may not have the knowledge of or access to formal supports for themselves or for the children in their care. There is also a need for respite care. Oftentimes there is a need for day care and other child care to help a caregiver who is maintaining some level of employment. Other family members may provide this support and backup. Caregivers also draw on their formal faith communities and inner spiritual resources to cope with the challenges of kinship care. The social support needs of the caregiver may supersede any financial needs. The formal system of care—particularly the child welfare system—provides a measure of financial support and potentially some degree of social support.

Safety and Well-Being of Children

The process of formal child welfare agency placement (including such features as background checks) is designed to address the safety and well-being of children placed away from their biological parents. In informal placements there is no formal assessment of the caregiver's background, capacity and temperament, and resources for parenting. In addition, in informal care oftentimes there are not the same fiscal and other supports for families as in the formal system. So it is possible that a child informally placed with a relative could be living with a caregiver who does not have the material resources to care for the child, and in a few cases may not have the capacity and experience to provide quality nurturance and ensure the child's safety. The assumption that all relatives are able to care for other relatives at all times may be questioned. Some of the child's relatives may not present a familiar person or place for the child. There may be additional safety risks in informal situations if a parent who has abused or neglected the child has continuing ready access to the child and the child is inadequately supervised and protected. In informal care, risks to a child's safety may not surface unless the child becomes the subject of a child protective services report or the kin caregiver terminates the placement and the child is placed informally with other relatives or comes to the attention of the child welfare system.

How does one identify relatives for the purpose of informal placement? First, families generally are quite aware of their own networks and ties. These are facilitated by geographic proximity, oftentimes with multiple generations living within the same household or neighborhood. Informal placements by their nature are arranged by family members within the existing family structure and culture. Consequently, the identification and placement is subject to the coalitions, patterns, and systemic dynamics of the extended family and kin relationships. These networks and patterns can to some extent be identified by social service professionals who interview key informants within the family; knowledge of family resources oftentimes resides with the children in the family.

There are several more formal paths to the identification of extended family resources for caregiving. One means of identifying kin that is used increasingly in the United States is family group conferencing. These processes, also called family group decision making, are based on a model from New Zealand (discussed in greater detail by Lisa Merkel-Holguin in Chapter 9). Usually triggered by a child protective services investigation, a facilitator or coordinator is assigned to a family to work with the parents in order to convene a family group meeting. These meetings optimally will include the whole family and other adults who are similar to blood relations; they are held to consider the risk factors and allegations with regard to the child's safety and to construct a plan to ensure the child's safety and well-being. The coordinator works with the parents to construct an invitation list for the meeting. This meeting may last several hours and includes an information stage to apprise the family of the child's situation, a discussion period during which the family constructs a plan for the child's care and safety, and a time of negotiation, clarification, and planning with the professionals involved in the situation. There are a number of models for family group conferencing. One of the most consistent outcomes of these conferences is the involvement of kin in providing a home for the vulnerable child and participating in a service plan for the parent and family. In the United States, family group conferencing is used most frequently in the child-protection process at the early stages of child placement (Merkel-Holguin, 1996).

Informal kinship care is a resource to families and communities. But as this review of the challenges facing kinship caregivers demonstrates, the caregiver still needs a support system. The informal supports needed and used by kinship care providers include (a) other relatives (particularly adult children) who provide concrete assistance, backup, and emotional support; (b) friends and neighbors who similarly provide a variety of assistance; (c) faith communities and other religious groups; and (d) senior groups and centers (Burnette, 1997).

Today in the United States millions of children are cared for in the homes of their grandparents, aunts, uncles, older siblings, or other close kin. The great majority of these arrangements were made informally between family members, some in response to emergencies, others in an extended, planned manner, and many with an informality and fluidity that make it difficult to label such arrangements as a "placement." Involvement with somewhat less intrusive formal systems, such as the educational or health care systems, is negotiated with varying degrees of difficulty and complications. Some kinship caregivers, however, were specifically identified, recruited, and drafted by agents of the child welfare system or law enforcement and enlisted to take care of relative children. A number of these recruited relatives later returned to informal status, but as caregivers of a grandchild or other relative. A number of these caregivers remain in the formal child welfare system with reimbursement as approved foster parents. The role of kinship care in the formal system raises a number of issues for society and for the social service system. Many of these issues have implications for the informal caregivers as well.

FORMAL KINSHIP CARE

In the United States, the fastest growing form of out-of-home placement is kinship foster care (Bonecutter & Gleeson, 1997). Based on more than twenty years of experience with kinship homes being defined as foster care placements, a number of qualities have consistently emerged in research and practice:

1. Children in kinship foster care have longer stays in foster care status because children are less likely to return to their biological parents (Bonecutter and Gleeson, 1997) and are less likely to be adopted than are children in traditional, nonrelated placements (Barth, Courtney, Berrick, & Albert, 1994; Thornton, 1991).

2. Kinship care providers are most frequently female, grandmothers or aunts, and are more likely to be single parents and less likely to have completed high school or own their own homes than are nonrelated caregivers. Kin caregivers have lower incomes and poorer health, in general, than nonrelated caregivers (Scannapieco, 1999).

3. The primary reason for child placement in a kinship foster home is parental neglect of the child, often involving drug exposure (Berrick, Barth, & Needell, 1994).

Formal kinship foster care highlights a number of issues:

1. *Permanency status.* Is a placement with a relative by definition a permanent placement so that a child can remain in long-term kinship foster care without an agency being required to pursue other goals, such as family reunification and adoption? What are the implications of the Adoption and Safe Families Act of 1997, which, for example, provides the possibility of a time limit exception for children in kinship care at the option of the state? What is the relationship between permanency goals and definitions and financial service supports for kin caregivers? Is subsidized guardianship a viable option to provide income support and to step down or eliminate the kinship family's tie to the formal child welfare system?

2. *Relative adoptions.* Are kin caregivers prospective adoptive parents? Some studies have suggested that kin are reluctant to adopt related children in their care (Berrick et al., 1994; Thornton, 1991); others have

concluded that kin caregivers are as willing to consider adoption as are other caregivers (Gebel, 1996) and that lower adoption rates may be explained by the failure of workers to present the adoption option (Gleeson, O'Donnell, & Bonecutter, 1997).

3. *Funding.* What mechanisms are available to reimburse relatives for providing kinship care in general, and specifically kinship foster care? What requirements are attached to these funding sources; for example, if public assistance dollars are used does the amount of assistance decrease per child based on the size of a sibling group? In addition, if TANF funds are used to support kinship care, to what extent are older relatives required to comply with requirements associated with TANF, such as work requirements? How adequate are these sources of financial and service support? To what extent is kinship foster care used as income support by parents and their relatives? To what extent should family preservation and family support funds be used to support kinship arrangements before a placement or as a follow-up to leaving placement (Danzy & Jackson, 1997)? Is it possible to provide emergency financial assistance (including food, furniture, and clothing) that can move to a lesser or greater level of support over time? State and local governments are developing a range of mechanisms to support kinship care outside the child welfare system, such as (a) use of TANF funds for financial and service support (e.g., Colorado, California, Missouri, Florida), (b) use of adoption subsidies for relatives in the child welfare system and outside the formal system (e.g., Georgia), and (c) family preservation and family support funds (e.g., Michigan).

4. *Standards and licensing.* To what extent should kinship foster care placements be treated the same as nonrelated foster care placements—including licensing requirements, training requirements for foster parents, training expectations for workers supervising kinship homes, and degree and intensity of agency supervision? If certain requirements are applied to kinship care, are those requirements implemented with flexibility and creativity? For example, is there a variety of training models so that kinship caregivers can have relevant content delivered in an accessible manner?

5. *Practice.* How does one ensure the safety of the child in a kinship placement? To what extent is visitation between parents and children allowed or encouraged, and how are boundaries determined and enforced? To what extent do workers get involved in the life and dynamics of an extended family system?

6. *Culture.* Are workers and agencies knowledgeable of the values, beliefs, and cultural practices of kinship caregivers? In addition to knowledge, is there respectful practice, comfort, and insight with regard to workers' own assumptions and prejudices? Are workers capable of flexible thinking, so that they can recognize that people from other cultures may think or act differently than people in their own culture? Is there an ability to re-

spond with flexibility to support a child and family in a culturally sensitive manner (Pinderhughes, 1997)?

7. *Preference.* How does one judge between the preference for placement with kin and the need for a placement that has the capabilities of meeting a child's special needs and ensuring his or her well-being? Are all relatives candidates for caregiving, and how are choices made when multiple relatives present themselves as preferred caregivers? How can relatives be identified early on in a case so that wrenching decisions involving young children who have been in nonrelated care can be reduced?

8. *Justice.* Is the use of kinship care an attempt to save government funds (in a manner that may overburden older adults living at or below the poverty level), and does this strategy create different levels of care for children based on whether they are with kin or in unrelated homes?

POLICY ISSUES

The examination of kinship care, including kinship care within foster care systems, raises a number of issues and implications for practice and policy. A number of these issues translate into practice-focused responses to increase the safety and well-being of children.

Broaden the definition of "family." In American society and in the English language, the word *family* frequently connotes a relationship between two adults joined by marriage and includes the children from that marriage (Parsons, 1943). Based on the conceptualization of family from a variety of cultures and in recognition of the reality of the structure and characteristics of families, service providers need to understand family in a broader sense so that the word includes the full array of people defined by the family as family. This includes the recognition that family might include individuals who are not related by blood ties but have a role and place in the family as family members. In addition, a child might be raised by multiple relatives rather than by a single caregiver, either in a multifamily household or in another arrangement crafted by the family:

> Children may spend all or part of days, weeks, or months with mother and father and an aunt or grandmother and an older sibling and a neighbor in seemingly limitless combination and permutation . . . . these plans are often hidden from outside or official view. (Nagler, Adnopoz, & Forsyth, 1995, p. 78)

Even when individual workers understand and appreciate a broad definition of family, the reporting documents and paperwork required by formal systems may force a nuclear-family focus. When "team meetings" involve providers and family members, is the scope of intended and invited family members limited to parents? What family members are invited to and included in family visitation? Consequently, there should be a continual focus on the appreciation of the full family, and to the extent possible a modification in the paperwork and practice that shapes investigations, assessments, and service planning.

Identify extended family members. If the extended family and kinship network is a resource to a child and a strength to be recognized in assessments and service planning, then workers need to ask about extended family to facilitate the identification of family resources early in the life of the experience with a family. Formal structures such as family group conferencing are not commonly available, so the identification of kinship resources will continue to rely primarily on the worker's awareness, interview skills, and respectful inquiry.

Identify multiple relatives and family subsets. In the identification of kinship relationships and resources workers risk identifying only a subset of possible relatives. For example, a worker might identify only the child's mother and her relatives as possible resources (Gleeson et al., 1999). The tendency to overlook paternal relationships has been noted, and it results in the constricting of family resources. For a number of reasons, certain relatives may not be appropriate caregivers, but these decisions should be based on an assessment rather than the disqualification of whole groups of relatives without cause. Concerns about the identification of fathers and the location of fathers are receiving increasing attention. For example, protocols are being developed on the use of DNA testing to establish paternity in child welfare cases. Parent locator services in the child support payment system are increasingly at the disposal of child welfare agencies to help locate absent parents (usually fathers) for the purpose of gaining paternal involvement with children, identifying paternal relatives and resources, or securing relinquishments to facilitate adoption. The integration of child support and social service systems in order to facilitate the identification of fathers and the assessment and engagement of fathers and their families is a continuing challenge.

Family members as resources for support. The focus on relatives as a resource has frequently highlighted issues related to informal or formal foster care and accompanying issues. The identification, assessment, and recruitment of family members as agents of *family support* have received less attention. Reasonable efforts to prevent the placement of children in any type of foster care arrangement should include the assessment and use of relatives as respite care providers and as providers of emotional, spiritual, and financial assistance. In a crisis that precipitates family preservation intervention, a focus on the family unit in need is understandable, but a vision that includes the larger family system provides information and resources for the short-term challenges and perhaps the best hope for longer-term safety and stability. Strategies such as family group conferencing have rarely been applied to work with families before they have come to the attention of a child protection agency.

Linking child welfare and aging through kinship care. Addressing kinship care has been a stimulant for collaboration between the field of child welfare and the field of aging. State departments of aging and child welfare departments have been and increasingly can be resources to one another. The formal aging network provides a range of community-based resources, including senior community centers, meals programs, health screening, and financial assistance. Organizations such as the American Association of Retired Persons (AARP) have provided local and national leadership on issues of concern to older adults in caregiving roles. This collaboration can be particularly fruitful at the level of family support services so that an array and continuum of community-based services are available to older adults and kin caregivers. However, this also highlights a complication facing a number of kinship caregivers. Some of the services funded are categorically available only to adults over a certain age. Eligibility may be restricted to those over the ages of 65 or 55. For example, a bill pending in the U.S. Senate (Bill 1536, August 1999) would establish a National Family Caregiver Support Program and would define "grandparents or older individual who is a relative caregiver" as a person who is "60 years of age or older." Yet a significant number of kinship caregivers are under the age of 60. It is possible to be a grandparent and not yet have achieved the age of 50. So in addition to the challenge of collaborating across departmental and field boundaries—such as child welfare and aging—there is the challenge of providing services through the aging network to caregivers who do not meet age eligibility requirements. Exceptions for kin care should be explored.

Strengthening other collaborative systems. Collaborations with other systems should be strengthened. For example, collaboration with the criminal justice system is an area for further development. Fifty percent of children whose mothers are incarcerated are placed with grandparents and an additional 25 percent with relatives or friends in informal placements (Seymour, 1998). With rising numbers of women in prison, working with prisons (minimum and maximum security), probation and parole, and other criminal justice systems is increasingly required for the support of children and families.

As another example of collaboration, the formal social service system should recognize the value of informal systems in their support of kinship care providers. For example, the duty to one's family and love for one's family is oftentimes integral to a caregiver's value system. This value system is further informed and shaped by the caregiver's spiritual life and religious beliefs. Family-centered perspectives require an understanding of and appreciation for the family's inner resources and the social and spiritual sustaining role of formal faith community affiliations.

Siblings raising siblings. Another group of kinship care providers that may go undetected and unserved, either through professional inattention or deliberate attempts to remain unrecognized due to fear of separation or other negative consequences, are older siblings raising younger brothers and sisters. A New York City study of adolescents in families in which a parent had AIDS found that in 10 percent of the families, older adolescents assumed guardianship of their younger siblings. The primary motive for this assumption of parenting responsibility was the children's desire to stay together and the fear that no family member or traditional foster care arrangement would accept the full sibling group (Draimin et al., 1992).

Prevalence of kinship care. The importance and prevalence of kinship care in the African American community has been noted in a number of studies. For example, according to the 1990 U.S. Census 12 percent of African American children were living with grandparents (with higher percentages in some urban areas such as Detroit, New York, and Oakland). In contrast, 5.7 percent of Hispanic children and 3.6 percent of white children were living with relatives (Levine, 1995). Although the percentages are lower, the real numbers of white and Hispanic children are still significant, and these communities of kin caregivers should not be overlooked.

The legal concept of permanency planning. The concept of permanency planning, as developed by the Adoption Assistance and Child Welfare Act of 1980 and the Adoption and Safe Families Act of 1997, underlines the central importance of a secure and safe lifetime relationship for children. The 1980 legislation did not directly identify kinship care. The 1997 legislation supports the use of kinship care and recognizes the need to study and better understand this crucial form of family support. The Adoption and Safe Families Act also strongly prioritizes safety for children and focuses on adoption as a permanency goal for which states would be rewarded. The pressure on kinship families to adopt children in order to achieve permanency may be reinforced by this new initiative to support and reward adoption outcomes. As noted earlier, kinship families may be more willing to adopt related children than first believed, but there may be the danger of coercing families to adopt in response to adoption outcome rewards. The development of permanency options and related financial and social support continue as policy challenges. The provision of financial support outside of licensed foster care and support for a range of recognized arrangements with relatives seem to be viable directions.

□ □ □

The value of kinship care is well established. The support provided by a whole family to its most vulnerable members is the primary means of social and financial support in our society. Family-centered services provided by the formal system of agencies and organizations may strengthen and supplement the extended family. In some cases, where no extended family or kin seem to be available, formal systems may attempt to provide similar supports and build connections so that a family-like resource is available to an at-risk child or family. Effective family-centered services will recognize the central role of an extended family in providing support but also the need for kinship caregivers to find assistance within their families and from respectful formal support services.

REFERENCES

Anderson, G. (1994). *Beyond survival: Resiliency and children with HIV/AIDS* (Monograph). Chicago: University of Illinois at Chicago.

Barth, R., Courtney, M., Berrick, J., & Albert, V. (1994). *From child abuse to permanency planning: Child welfare services, pathways, and placements.* New York: Aldine de Gruyter.

Beeman, S., & Boisen, L. (1999). Child welfare professionals' attitudes toward kinship foster care. *Child Welfare, 78*, 315–38.

Berrick, J., Barth, R., & Needell, B. (1994). A comparison of kinship foster homes and foster family homes: Implications for kinship foster care as family preservation. *Children and Youth Services Review, 16*, 33–63.

Bonecutter, F., & Gleeson, J. (1997). Broadening our view: Lessons from kinship foster care. In G. R. Anderson, A. S. Ryan, & B. R. Leashore (Eds.), *Challenge of permanency planning in a multicultural society* (pp. 91–119). New York: Haworth Press.

Burnette, D. (1997). Grandmother caregivers in innercity Latino families: A descriptive profile and informal social supports. In G. R. Anderson, A. S. Ryan, & B. R. Leashore (Eds.), *The challenge of permanency planning in a multicultural society* (pp. 125–39). New York: Haworth Press.

Child Welfare League of America. (1994). *Kinship care: A natural bridge.* Washington, DC: Author.

Crumbley, J., & Little, R. (1997). *Relatives raising children: An overview of kinship care.* Washington, DC: Child Welfare League of America.

Danzy, J., & Jackson, S. (1997). Family preservation and support services: A missed opportunity for kinship care. *Child Welfare, 76*, 31–44.

Draimin, B. (1995). A second family? Placement and custody decisions. In S. Geballe, J. Gruendel, & W. Andiman (Eds.), *Forgotten children of the AIDS epidemic.* New Haven: Yale University Press.

Draimin, B, Hudis, J., & Segura, J. (1992). *The mental health needs of well adolescents in families with AIDS.* New York: NYC Human Resources Administration.

Geballe, S. (1995). Toward a child-responsive legal system. In S. Geballe, J. Gruendel, & W. Andiman (Eds.), *Forgotten children of the AIDS epidemic* (pp. 140–64). New Haven: Yale University Press.

Gebel, T. (1996). Kinship care and non-relative family foster care: A comparison of caregiver attributes and attitudes. *Child Welfare, 75,* 5–18.

Gleeson, J., O'Donnell, J., & Bonecutter, F. (1997). Understanding the complexity of practice in kinship foster care. *Child Welfare, 76,* 801–26.

Hegar, R. (1999). The cultural roots of kinship care. In R. Hegar & M. Scannapieco (Eds.), *Kinship foster care: Policy, practice, and research* (pp. 17–27). New York: Oxford University Press.

Keller, J., & McDade, K. (1997). Cultural diversity and help-seeking behavior: Sources of help and obstacles to support for parents. In Anderson et al., *The challenge of permanency planning in a multicultural society* (pp. 63–78). New York: Haworth Press.

Levine, C. (1995). Today's challenges, tomorrow's dilemmas. In S. Geballe, J. Gruendel, & W. Andiman (Eds.), *Forgotten children of the AIDS epidemic* (pp. 190–24). New Haven: Yale University Press.

Merkel-Holguin, L. (1996). Putting families back into the child protection partnership: Family group decision making. *Protecting Children, 12,* 3–4.

Nagler, S., Adnopoz, J., & Forsyth, B. (1995). Uncertainty, stigma, and secrecy: Psychological aspects of AIDS for children and adolescents. In S. Geballe, J. Gruendel, & W. Andiman (Eds.), *Forgotten children of the AIDS epidemic* (pp. 71–82). New Haven: Yale University Press.

Parsons, T. (1943). The kinship system of the contemporary United States. *American Anthropologist, 45,* 22–38.

Pinderhughes, E. (1997). Developing diversity competence in child welfare and permanency planning. In G. R. Anderson, A. S. Ryan, & B. R. Leashore (Eds.), *The challenge of permanency planning in a multicultural society* (pp. 19–38). New York: Haworth Press.

Potts, M. (1997). Social support and depression among older adults living alone: The importance of friends within and outside of a retirement community. *Social Work. 42,* 348–62.

Scannapieco, M. (1999). Kinship care in the public child welfare system. In R. Hegar & M. Scannapieco (Eds.), *Kinship foster care* (pp. 141–54). New York: Oxford University Press.

Scannapieco, M., & Jackson, S. (1996). Kinship care: The African American response to family preservation. *Social Work, 41,* 190–96.

Seymour, C. (1998). Children with parents in prison: Child welfare policy, program, and practice issues. *Child Welfare, 77,* 469–94.

Starr, R., Dubowitz, H., Harrington, D., & Feigelman, S. (1999). Behavior problems of teens in kinship care. In R. Heger & M. Scannapieco (Eds.), *Kinship foster care* (pp. 193–207). New York: Oxford Press.

Stehno, S. M. (1988). Public responsibility for dependent black children. *Social Service Review, 62,* 485–501.

Thornton, J. (1991). Permanency planning for children in kinship foster homes. *Child Welfare, 70,* 593–601.

9 Family Group Conferencing

An "Extended Family" Process to Safeguard Children
and Strengthen Family Well-Being

LISA MERKEL-HOLGUIN, WITH CONTRIBUTIONS FROM
KIMBERLY RIBICH

Family group conferencing is a new approach to working with
families engaged with the child welfare system. The goal of this approach
is to allow families greater control over the decisions and plans made to
ensure the safety and well-being of their children and to foster greater cooperation, collaboration, and communication between child welfare professionals and the families they work with. In addition to being used to
resolve concerns of abuse and neglect, family group conferencing approaches are being applied in cases of youth crime, school truancy, neighborhood conflict, adult offending, and family maintenance. This chapter,
however, will focus solely on the practice, policy, and evolution of family
group conferencing from a child welfare perspective.

HISTORICAL ROOTS IN NEW ZEALAND

Prior to becoming a formalized process, family group conferencing origi-
nated with the Maori—the indigenous people of New Zealand.[1] In their
language, it is referred to as *Whanau Hui*, or family meeting. *Whanau Hui*
is a broad term that can refer to any type of family gathering (Atkin, 1988–
1989). In the context of child welfare, the *Whanau Hui* is a family meeting
that focuses on resolving issues about a child's care and protection.

In Maori society, the *Whanau*, or family, is the most important social structure. *Whanau* incorporates the nuclear family, extended family members, and sometimes also those who are related through marriage. Unwritten codes of conduct and values apply to all family members. *Whanau* means loyalty, unity, mutual interdependence and help, mutual responsibility, and duty (Walker, 1996). Membership in a *Whanau* obligates each person to uphold these values.

Children are important to Maori society. To whom the children are born is not an important issue. Immediately after birth, the *Whanau* is expected to care for and nurture the child; and as the child grows, so does the expectation and responsibility of the *Whanau*. In this way, interdependence is fostered and continued through each generation (Walker, 1996).

Family meetings are an integral part of maintaining interdependence and cooperation. Family meetings also reinforce the Maori's core goal of maintaining balance and connection between the physical, psychological, emotional, and spiritual. When conflicts arise, meetings are held. All family and community members take responsibility to restore the balance and harmony that have been disrupted.

When New Zealand was colonized more than 150 years ago, a new set of values began to conflict with those of New Zealand's indigenous people. Decisions that affected their future were made without their consultation. Thus, a rather patriarchal history in which government assumed authority for the people was introduced. Traditional Maori society and Maori families were weakened and balance and harmony disrupted as the tribes accepted less responsibility for their people.

As an agency of the government, the Department of Social Welfare employed professionals to make social welfare decisions for New Zealanders. All too frequently, however, professional staff did not have the appropriate training or qualifications to make appropriate decisions about cultural issues. Moreover, Maori children were coming into institutional care and not being returned to their families of origin in ever increasing numbers (Hardin, 1996). This government involvement further disrupted families and complicated or thwarted their ability to make decisions for themselves and their children. Therefore, the Maori had special interest in the legislation that affected their families and children, and their political input was a major force behind the changes in social welfare practice and policy (Hardin, 1996).

NEW ZEALAND'S LEGISLATIVE PRECEDENCE

In 1985, a ministerial committee was charged with the task of investigating and reporting on the operations of the Department of Social Welfare from the Maori point of view. The report, known as *PUAO-TE-ATA-TU*, was presented to the minister of social welfare in 1986 with thirteen recommendations. In it, the committee identified areas of concern and explained the cultural underpinnings of family decision making (Ministerial Advisory Committee, 1988). The committee also challenged the Department of Social Welfare to address institutional racism and monoculturalism (Wilcox et al., 1991).

As the initial report was published, family decision-making processes became a part of social work practice, especially in dealing with care and protection cases. These early family decision-making projects were summarized in an internal report, *Whakakpakiri Whanau! Family Decision Making*, in 1988 (Hardin, 1996), which supported the feasibility of wider family involvement in decision making.

Both reports had an impact on attitudes and actions, thus providing the catalyst for enacting the Children, Young Persons and Their Families Act in 1989 (Wilcox et al., 1991). With this act, New Zealand first saw family group conferencing emerge into law and become a mandatory requirement for child welfare cases.

Since the law was enacted, New Zealanders have made substantial progress in addressing the relevant policy and practice issues. Moreover, the historical context inspired a new type of social work practice worldwide—one grounded in a strengths-based, culturally relevant, and family-centered philosophy.

EVOLUTION OF FAMILY GROUP CONFERENCING

The general issues concerning child well-being, including child abuse and neglect, have always existed on various levels of the public consciousness. When our societal climate and conditions change, so do our attitudes, views, and responses to these issues. These tandem changes often spur new developments or refinements in the systems, policies, and practices that support child well-being. Family group conferencing is a good example of this. Given the dynamic nature of these changes, family group decision making has continued to evolve, spawning worldwide developments in Australia, Canada, England, Sweden, South Africa, and the United States. Interestingly enough, in all of these worldwide developments, the same underlying themes exist.

The evolution of family group conferencing has revolved around two primary realizations or themes: (a) children do better when they can maintain strong connections to their primary caregivers and family of origin, including extended family networks, and (b) child welfare interventions that assume the primary responsibility for care of children can often be disempowering to a family and do more harm than good (Connolly & McKenzie, 1999; Marsh & Crow, 1998). These realizations are acknowledged internally and are based in part on the following trends:

1. A growing number of children are being placed in out-of-home care.
2. A growing number of children are spending greater lengths of time in these out-of-home settings, including foster care and residential care.
3. The services provided to children and families often are not culturally relevant.
4. Children need permanency in a more timely manner.

These themes and resulting trends foster a new collective response to the issues of child abuse and neglect and how to ensure child well-being. A shift in the underlying core values and beliefs about families drives this collective response. In the last decade, legislative processes and mandates also have supported these responses. Internationally, all these factors are converging to produce the momentum around developing family group conferencing initiatives. This applies not only to the child welfare system but also to juvenile justice, mental health, and educational systems. Essentially, family group conferencing philosophies embody the values emerging worldwide. How this translates into practice, however, depends on how it is engaged within various systems.

THE PRACTICE OF FAMILY GROUP CONFERENCING

The practice of family group conferencing espouses the value that children are best protected in the context of their families, and families are best supported in the context of their communities. Protecting children must be viewed as a shared responsibility—not one placed solely on the child welfare agency, but one that encompasses various governmental agencies at the federal, state, and local level, as well as nonprofit local organizations, community leaders, citizen groups, neighbors, and most important the family.

Family group conferencing builds on family-centered practice and strengths-based, empowerment, and participatory theories. As paraphrased by Vesneski (1998), and according to Dunst, Deal, and Trivette (1994), family-centered approaches should (a) create opportunities for family members to become more competent, independent, and self-sustaining; (b) strengthen both families and their natural support networks while bolstering their decision-making abilities; and (c) emphasize enhancing the competencies families need to independently mobilize and sustain their support networks.

Communities commonly follow four phases when implementing family group conferencing approaches:

- □ *Phase 1.* Referral to hold a family group conference
- □ *Phase 2.* Preparation and planning
- □ *Phase 3.* The family group conference
- □ *Phase 4.* Follow-up

The following sections describe the family group conferencing process in the context of best practice standards based on theories and international research.

Phase One: Referral to Hold a Family Group Conference (FGC)

The referral phase addresses two primary questions: (a) When should a family be referred for a family group conference? and (b) What type of cases should be referred? In most U.S. communities, the public agency social worker most intimately involved with the family refers the case to an FGC coordinator. The referring worker's role in the FGC process is to help identify other professionals involved with the family, present information at the conference, work with the family to detail the agreed-upon plan, and in some instances, assist with plan implementation. This professional typically has the authority to reject plans that compromise a child's safety and well-being.

The underpinning philosophy of this approach recognizes that all families can use their experiences, knowledge, strengths, and wisdom to make good decisions, when they are presented with accurate and timely information. Families find identity, historical connections, and security within their social networks that result in their increased commitment to, and investment in, other members. Belief in this philosophical construct translates to FGCs having universal application for all families and in all cases. The need to control the types of cases referred contradicts various philosophies of FGCs, an approach that inherently values and trusts decision-making abilities of families.

The principle of universality is supported by New Zealand's legislation that mandates FGCs to be held in cases where an investigator has determined that a child or young person is in need of care or protection. Independent of the country implementing this approach, the referral process commences after a public child welfare agency social worker's abuse-and-neglect investigation documents child safety and well-being concerns. The case is then referred to a coordinator whose responsibility it is to arrange the FGC.

In New Zealand, the legislative framework and strong political forces have created an expectation that all families with child abuse and neglect concerns are entitled to make decisions through the FGC process. In the

United States, implementation of the FGC model is voluntary, with communities establishing varying principles and standards of practice.

One dramatic departure from FGC cornerstone philosophies is the automatic exclusion of certain types of cases—in particular, those that involve domestic violence and child sexual abuse—from FGC processes. Professionals' perceptions of families—their abilities, strengths, knowledge, and functionality—contribute to their determination of family appropriateness for this approach.

New Zealand's experience has shown that the FGC can be used in child sexual abuse cases if the proper supports and guidelines are instituted to ensure the safety and confidentiality of all participants involved in the conference. Newfoundland's demonstration project reports similar findings using the FGC in cases involving domestic violence (Pennell & Burford, 1997). Family group conferencing must not revictimize or disempower family members or others involved in the process. Careful and comprehensive preparation must occur to lessen legitimate safety concerns of participants. It is the coordinator's responsibility, in partnership with the family, to promote safe and effective participation of all participants. Only when this standard cannot be achieved should an FGC not be convened. Although organizing an FGC may seem like a simple task, it is in fact a lengthy, detailed process that involves comprehensive preparation.

The responsibilities and roles of the coordinator are well defined, but the qualifications for and structure of this position are not so clear. Some would argue that it is the coordinators' skills and philosophical beliefs, not the professional qualifications or credentials, that determine the success of FGCs. A coordinator's ability to engage all members of the family, mobilize family capabilities to make decisions, and model conflict resolution techniques during the FGC process are a few of the most important skills. Coordinators' knowledge of child abuse and neglect, family dynamics, substance abuse issues, and domestic violence can also be helpful. The question that is being tested in European countries implementing the FGC model is whether volunteers with the appropriate knowledge and skills can serve as coordinators. In the United States, a variety of factors (e.g., confidentiality laws) have limited the number of communities experimenting with volunteers in the coordinator capacity. Likely, the results from Europe will demonstrate that the coordinator role can be deprofessionalized, as long as the person has the necessary skills and knowledge.

With regard to structure, in New Zealand the coordinator function is housed in and funded by a public agency, the Children, Young Persons and Their Families Service. In the United States some public agencies support this as an internal function, as a way to systematically transform child welfare practice and policy, creating the opportunity for philosophical shifts to occur. In other U.S. locales, the public child welfare agency is outsourcing the coordinator function to a community-based organization for multiple reasons: (a) the inflexibility sometimes found in public agencies caused by union structures; (b) the intensity of Child Protective Services workers' existing workloads and the impact on conducting quality FGC processes; and (c) preference to locate this critical function in an agency that conveys a family-friendly, supportive atmosphere to people in the community. Without a mandated and funded structure, both approaches have merit and will depend on community-specific cultures and objectives.

Phase Two: Preparation and Planning for a Family Group Conference

Research demonstrates that both the coordinator's ability and the quality of preparation and planning correlate with the overall success of the conference (Maxwell & Morris, 1993; Paterson & Harvey, 1991). Although the amount of time it takes to adequately prepare a family varies based on case- and family-specific circumstances, data from communities worldwide suggest that an average of twenty-two to thirty-five hours per family group conference is necessary to undertake the comprehensive activities in this phase (Burford & Pennell, 1995; Crow & Marsh, 1999; Gunderson, 1998).

Nonetheless, for a number of reasons this preparation and planning phase appears most vulnerable to being corrupted and shortchanged. First, fiscal constraints, political pressures, and the need to produce outcomes can result in the organization of FGCs without thorough preparation. Second, when service providers reconfigure the coordinator role as one of solely a logistics coordinator, the preparation activities that can transform the service provider–family relationship to reflect partnership, empowerment, and participatory philosophies are overlooked. Third, coordinators' skills to remain detached and objective influence their ability to intensely engage with a family to prepare for the conference.

Without thorough and intensive preconference planning, the FGC approach reflects more traditional case-planning methods. Preparation is one distinctive element of FGCs that demonstrates to families the service providers' commitment to a process that strengthens and sustains family support networks, builds on family abilities, and refocuses the primary responsibility for children back on the family where it belongs. Kook and Sivak (1998) suggest that families' histories of oppression, retribution, and punishment with formal systems will cause them to proceed with caution, as they become partners in such decision-making processes. The coordinator therefore must have adequate time to complete the preconference activities described in the following section.

Defining Family

One of Kook and Sivak's (1998) basic principles is that "nuclear families are a part of the whole family" (p. 37). Too often, only family members within the local community are considered family, which misrepresents the multigenerational, extended family network. Kook and Sivak (1998) suggest working with families to develop their definition of family, which is likely to transcend the obvious kinship network to include neighbors, friends, and others. When "family" is defined broadly, social isolation decreases while social supports increase. Pennell and Burford (1995) substantiated this notion when they discovered that family members had broader social networks than they originally believed. For coordinators to get at the notion of family—which will be different in every case—it is important to ask the family, "How do you define family?" or "Who do you consider part of your family?" The definition should be based on the family's perceptions, not those of the coordinator or other professionals involved in the case. Burford and Pennell (1995) quoted a family member as follows:

> I think we should have more family members present. This gives us more input in coming up with solutions. It shouldn't just be immediate family. Having more friends and family around would be a big help. (p. 24)

Inviting "Family" Members

Given that FGC philosophies emphasize that children belong to families and that families are responsible for the care and protection of their children, it logically flows that anyone who fits the definition of "family" is invited to the FGC, unless his or her attendance presents safety concerns. In fact, New Zealand's legislation provides the coordinator authority to invite to the meeting any individual within the extended family network who can provide support to or be a resource for the family. In the United States, some communities are using state confidentiality statutes to limit the attendance of extended family members at an FGC. Although in some instances, these child abuse laws would need minimal redefinition or creative interpretation, some progressive U.S. communities embrace the philosophy that the child belongs to the family and community, not solely to the parent. In these instances, local policies have been reconfigured to create the most inclusive process possible.

Expectedly, family members have a natural proclivity to invite individuals who are supportive and understanding (Burford & Pennell, 1995). Embarrassment, shame, unresolved conflicts, underestimation of their support network, and lack of involvement with certain family members are some of the reasons for parents wanting to limit attendance. However, despite parental objections, in concert with family-centered practice, the

FGC must involve the wider family network. Otherwise, the plans devised are less likely to capture all potential supports, resources, and suggestions that could resolve the concerns presented at the conference. In support of an inclusive policy, Nixon, Taverner, and Wallace (1996) quoted a family member as follows:

> My family don't always keep in touch, but they came together because we were at crisis point. When they heard what was going on, they decided it had to be worked out. (p. 50)

Exclusion policies remove family members from the FGC when participant safety is jeopardized by threats of violence, when individuals exhibit a mental disturbance or drug addiction, or when a person's participation would unduly stress the abused (American Humane Association, 1997; Pennell & Burford, 1994).

Likely, family members are not familiar with the family group conferencing process. Through conversations and written materials (e.g., brochures), coordinators begin to educate those who may be involved in the FGC about the intent and process. The coordinators also need to communicate with members of the extended family network to describe the incident that prompted the FGC. With an understanding of the case facts, family members can concentrate on the purpose, process, and their roles during the FGC. When coordinators withhold or neglect to communicate any critical information, the power imbalance between professional and client is reinforced. Clear and consistent messages to all invited family members increase the partnership path between the service provider and family.

Building Relationships with the Extended Family Network
Inviting individuals to and explaining the FGC are stepping-stones in the process. Family group conferencing, based on family-centered and strengths-based philosophies, incorporates relationship building into the preparation phase, wherein the coordinator talks with family members to define their strengths, concerns, and available resources. All too often, this important activity is sidestepped because the time between the referral and the FGC is condensed, or the coordinator's workload prohibits this level of involvement. Yet this communication process between the coordinator and different family members, which typically occurs over a three-to-four-week period, serves to overcome a family's distrust of the process, improves the coordinator's understanding of the family dynamics and interaction patterns, and facilitates a family's active participation during the conference. The opportunity to connect with family, to be graced by oral histories, and to mobilize the family to rebuild its support network is lost when the coordinators are unable to capitalize on the family's willingness to en-

gage. Putting families at the center of this partnership requires more than telephoning some members of the extended network and mailing invitations to others.

Protecting Physical and Emotional Safety During the Conference

Building relationships with the family also provides the coordinator the opportunity to assess the possibility of violence occurring both during and after the conference. Although FGCs can blend accountability, responsibility, and healing—benefiting both the abused and abuser—criteria must be established regarding perpetrator participation and attendance, and support for the victims. Individuals responsible for the concern can be positively involved in developing and implementing solutions. In preparations with the family, however, the coordinator must be assured that the survivors of violence are not revictimized during this process. Burford and Pennell (1995) quoted one FGC coordinator as follows:

> The two uncles who attended the meeting were people the Dad had respect for and he wanted their approval. It was imperative that they be present at the FGC as this ensured the Dad's attendance and his good behavior. It was they who made him feel shame about what he had done, not the officials present. (p. 14)

A number of strategies can be employed to maximize individual participation while at the same time protecting attendees from further harm. First, support people for abusers and survivors, children and adults alike, can be appointed to provide emotional and physical support and safety and at times represent their perspective. In the case of abusers, the support person also plays a role in neutralizing inappropriate behaviors or diminishing their tendencies to act out in a way that is counterproductive to the conference (e.g., violent outbursts). Second, when it is determined that the abuser's participation would be damaging to the process or to the survivor, thereby justifying exclusion, various methods (e.g., letters, videotapes, audiotapes, statements in advance) can be integrated into the process to provide information for the family to consider during the conference. In developing these forms of communication, it is likely that the individual will need the coordinator's assistance to craft language that provides strengths-oriented information that families can use when developing a plan.

Involving Children and Young People

Independent of a child's physical presence at an FGC, children must be included in the preparation phase. Coordinators must commit enough time to dialogue with the child to elicit his or her perspective. During the preparation phase, the coordinator—in partnership with the family—can determine the child's or young person's capability to participate in the conference as well as the family's assurance that the child will not be scapegoated. Although both professionals and family members want to protect children from reexperiencing conflict, rejection, and pain, FGCs present the opportunity for children to contribute their perspective, share their family wisdom, and refocus the group's energy on creating workable plans that protect them and improve the functioning of their family.

This practice is linked to New Zealand's historical context. In traditional Maori society, children are always allowed to attend and participate in family meetings. The belief is that family meetings are a way for children to learn adult problem-solving processes and to learn who supports and cares for them (Walker, 1996).

Burford and Pennell (1998) suggest that when children's voices are heard, feuding families are less likely to exploit them during the conference. Children's perspectives can be relayed through invitations they draw, statements presented by them or their support person, or even through displaying a picture of themselves at the conference venue. The coordinator must determine the children's comfort level in participating and identify a support person who can provide emotional and physical support during the conference process. As Marsh and Crow (1998) write, child participation can be "painful, but appropriate" (p. 103). Since children are an essential part of the family system from a theoretical perspective, their involvement can redirect the family's plan and can rebuild the social support networks that cross generations. Burford and Pennell (1995) quoted a child participant as follows:

> It was good in the sense that I became aware of people who cared about me. At the same time, I was scared to see how family members would react to what had happened. I was glad I was allowed to stay outside of the circle but still be a part of it. (p. 19)

Managing Unresolved Family Issues

The intent of the FGC process is not to resolve long-standing inter- and intrafamilial conflicts, and during preparation conversations, the coordinator guides the families to put aside differences on behalf of the children. Family group conferencing builds partnerships but doesn't strive to reconcile parties, particularly on issues that are not related to the presenting concerns. Nonetheless, coordinators' understanding of unresolved conflicts within a family system will aid them in facilitating the conference. Nixon et al. (1996) quoted a family member:

> It was like a wedding reception. You knew there were going to be people there that you didn't like but it was important to go. (p. 52)

Defining and Communicating Professionals' Roles

Child welfare professionals worldwide have difficulty with their roles being redefined from expert to information giver and resource organizer (Burford & Pennell, 1995; Crow & Marsh, 1997). Families are recast as the experts, with their knowledge and experiences of family functioning being paramount in the child protection partnership with service providers. The formation of any workable partnership takes time whereby mutual respect is developed and fostered, trust is established, and expertise is shared. Once this alliance flourishes, professionals and family members are better able to work together in developing and implementing plans.

Similar to their work with family members, coordinators also educate professionals about the purpose and process of FGCs, helping them to redefine their roles and alleviating their concerns. Before the conference occurs, the coordinator partners with each professional to discuss both the content and delivery of his or her presentation during the information sharing stage of the FGC. How information is presented to the extended family network can support the partnership building between family and service provider, reflect family-centered philosophies, or cause irrevocable harm to the FGC process. Professionals must be willing to replace their opinions with trust that the family has the capacity and the right to make care and protection decisions.

Coordinating Logistics for the Meeting

The family should determine the time and date, location, and food for the conference, but the coordinator facilitates the logistical operations. Transportation, accommodation for out-of-town guests, child care, and interpreter services are some of the logistics that the coordinator arranges in consultation with the family.

Family group conferencing embodies family-centered practice when the extended family network makes the logistical decisions. If FGCs are convened to accommodate professionals' schedules, a message is delivered that defies partnership building and minimizes the family's contribution— undercutting the family's responsibility for its children. The FGC belongs to the family, and disregarding that principle demonstrates lack of respect for the family.

Phase Three: The Family Group Conference

Once all the preparation has been completed, the FGC is convened. Regardless of the purpose, in traditional Maori society, the family meeting process is structured and often follows the same phases and rituals—an opening, a discussion, a resolution, and a closing. Similarly, the FGC model follows four distinct stages: (a) introduction, (b) information sharing, (c) private family time, and (d) decision and planning. If the FGC is truly a family-centered process, then each meeting will be unique with regard to the number of participants, their relationship to the child, and the length of meeting.

A number of studies have documented the FGC process. The average number of FGC participants has ranged from nine to fourteen (Burford & Pennell, 1995; Marsh and Crow, 1998; Paterson & Harvey, 1991). Even more important than the total number of participants is their relationship to the family. The body of worldwide research shows that biological family members are likely to outnumber both support people and professionals attending. Although Burford and Pennell's (1995) study found that biological family members were more likely to be invited and attend, the roles of the extended family network, including friends and neighbors, could not be overlooked. As Marsh and Crow (1998) noted, in more than one-fourth of eighty conferences reviewed, fictive kin (e.g., friends and neighbors) were present.

There should be no time limits for FGCs. A rigid schedule contradicts the spirit and nature of family conferencing, which should support family creativity, flexibility, and partnership building. Family history, quality of the preparation, leadership within the family, the nature of the case, and decision-making styles are just a few factors that influence the length of the FGC. Interestingly, the average duration of the FGC varied significantly between projects. Marsh and Crow (1998) clock the average FGC time at 2.5 hours, Burford and Pennell (1995) at 6 hours, Sundell (1998) at almost 3 hours (for the private family time only), and Paterson and Harvey (1991) at 3.5 hours.

In principle the FGC belongs to the family. Therefore, coordinators must permit the family to claim ownership of the process through its members' actions and words. If the theories supporting FGCs—including participatory, empowerment, and family strengths—are not manifested in practice, the intent and purpose of the approach is corrupted. This section, therefore, will describe various methodologies for interweaving family-centered practices into the FGC process.

Introductions

The introductions stage sets the tone for the FGC. During the preparation phase, the coordinator must determine if the family has any traditional, cultural, or religious rites to begin a family meeting (e.g., a song or prayer) and identify the family member who should formally welcome the attendees. Family-driven rituals and welcomes immediately help characterize this as the family's process. Conference attendees introduce themselves by their relationship to the child, reemphasizing the reason the family has united—for the safety and well-being of the children.

The coordinator should describe the FGC process, including the agency's policy regarding plans developed during the conference. In addition, the coordinator should clarify his or her role as a facilitator for parts of the conference. In this facilitative role, the coordinator must remain neutral to the content but be able to guide the process. Active listening will be an important skill. Two of the most critical facilitative goals during the introductions stage are (a) to reach agreement about the purpose of the meeting with the family and (b) to work with the family to establish ground rules that detail acceptable actions and behaviors during the conference. Ground rules provide a framework for refocusing and create a mechanism for accountability during the conference.

Finally, whoever hosts the FGC—whether a family member, the co-ordinator, a support person, or another—must create a comfortable environment. This person identifies venue logistics (e.g., bathrooms), offers food, and avails himself or herself to the group should a participant need something during the conference.

Information Sharing

The purpose of the information sharing stage is for professionals to present the basic facts about the case and other related information to the participants. "When professionals go beyond that purpose—presenting their opinions and making recommendations to the family about the case—they re-exert their control over decision-making processes that belong to the family" (Merkel-Holguin, 1998, p. 9). According to Lupton and Stevens (1997), this is a likely occurrence when professionals view their new role of information giver only as challenging their competency and revoking their decision-making authority. Hassall and Maxwell (1991) also identified concerns about the quality of the information provided to families both before and during the conference, and the potential negative influence on the families' decisions.

In addition to the content and quality of the information, the manner of professionals' presentations affects the process. Professionals should incorporate the family's strengths—stated behaviorally and specifically—into their presentation of concerns. Effective coordinator facilitation holds professionals accountable by asking them to reframe information that is deficit-oriented or jargon-loaded and to refrain from presenting irrelevant information. Coordinators can equalize the power imbalance by encouraging families to question the "authorities." This questioning and clarification function belongs only to the extended family network. Professionals should not be allowed to follow up or clarify other professionals' comments, unless asked by the family.

Families should be invited to identify their own strengths and concerns. This practice visibly demonstrates that the family-generated information, based on intimate history and knowledge, is just as valuable as that presented by professionals. It repositions family at a time during the conference that might otherwise be disempowering and discouraging. Lupton and Stevens (1997) found that family members tended to feel uncomfortable during the information sharing stage of the meeting, and methods that mobilize their strengths and expand their perspectives—thereby redistributing power—are likely to increase their comfort with this process.

There is a growing debate as to whether professionals also should share potential resources with the extended family network during this stage of the process. Some believe that families would not be able to construct plans without knowing the types and availability of services and resources. Others believe that providing even a listing of services stunts family creativity when it is developing a plan and decreases the likelihood of extended family networks mobilizing their own resources.

Philosophically, the practice of resource sharing empowers the professionals as experts because an underlying inherent assumption is that their assessment of the case is accurate. It may provide an unnecessary avenue for professionals to reexert control over the family.

Private Family Time

After information sharing, the FGC process moves to the next stage of the conference, private family time. All the concerns, strengths, and other pertinent information must be presented so the family has the right information on which to base its decision. During private family time, all professionals, service providers, and other nonfamily members leave the room, and the family formulates its service plan (and backup plans), which it presents back to the professionals during the decision stage of the conference. Professionals, including the referring social worker and other information givers, may disperse, agreeing to return after a certain period of time or providing pager or mobile phone numbers to the family so they can return after the family completes this stage. The coordinator stays nearby in case the family requests any assistance.

The literature cites a number of reasons for including only family members in the deliberation process. Family members are not as likely to reveal family secrets in the presence of nonfamily members and others. Furthermore, professional involvement during this time often results in a facilitated or dominated process, which counters the family-centered and strengths-based principles on which FGCs are based.

Without private family time, research shows and history documents that power will not be shared, and the imbalance will persevere. Family members know their strengths, weaknesses, and unspoken secrets—knowledge that is critical in formulating plans that better protect children. When there are no "external" experts to defer to, family members rely on their own expertise and knowledge.

In theory, both professionals and families embrace the idea of private family time. However, it can be difficult to practice. For professionals, particularly the information givers, their anxieties relate to (a) productive use of the time, (b) curiosity about the discussions with concerns that social workers will be blamed and children scapegoated, and (c) potential for violence (Barker & Barker, 1995). Overall, Marsh and Crow (1998) found professionals to support private family time. Those who have experienced it indicate that despite their anxieties, they also found relief in giving much of the responsibility over to the family.

Families may also question their decision-making ability and understanding of resources necessary to develop a plan. Their anxieties are lessened, however, when (a) adequate preparation occurs, (b) a family recorder is appointed before the beginning of private family time, (c) they are reminded that the professionals and support people will work with them to finalize and resource the plan, and (d) the coordinator and other professionals make themselves available to the family should they have questions or need clarification. Although unrelated conflicts can surface during this time, the ground rules developed by family consensus can refocus the participants on the purpose. It can be an intimidating process (Gilling, Patterson, & Walker, 1995), particularly for families who have been disempowered by formal systems, but families have indicated that decision making is easier without the presence of professionals (Lupton, Barnard, & Swall-Yarrington, 1995).

Private family time is an essential component of family group conferencing. When it is absent, the process mirrors one of traditional case planning. When families are respected and trusted, as modeled by private family time, child welfare practice can be radically transformed.

Decision

Once the family has arrived at a plan, it invites the professionals and support people back into the room. During this stage, a family spokesperson presents and explains the family's rationale for its plan and contingency options. Then, the whole group fleshes out the plan—outlining specific activities, time frames and frequencies, responsibilities, availability of resources, and methods of accountability and monitoring. The coordinator facilitates this process, which Marsh and Crow (1998) documented as the most difficult to manage. For families, this is the conclusion of an intensive process; for professionals, this reemphasizes their role as resource provider based on family-driven needs. The outcome of the decision-making stage is to achieve agreement on the plan, which may include modifications based on the large group discussion. Reaching agreement between the family and professionals reinforces participatory decision-making styles.

At the conclusion, the coordinator asks participants to state their level of agreement with the plan. Only a few participants, however, have the authority to veto the family's plan. New Zealand law gives that right only to the parents, guardians, referring social worker, and the child's lawyer. When coordinators have this authority—which is occurring in some U.S. communities—their neutrality and objectivity is lost, significantly diminishing their ability to facilitate a fair process. Those with veto authority must be present during the decision stage to provide a family with immediate feedback. If professionals have concerns about the plan, family-centered practice would suggest that the family be encouraged to reengage in private family time to further debate the safety concerns. This practice of reconvening fosters competency building in decision making and family independence.

Family plans are rarely vetoed, which demonstrates that when the circle is widened to include the extended family network with authority and freedom to use its wisdom and creativity, families make good plans that safeguard their children. In a New Zealand study, 5 percent of the plans were vetoed (New Zealand Department of Social Welfare, 1993). In the Newfoundland and Labrador study, there were no vetoes (Burford & Pennell, 1995). In the United Kingdom baseline data for 1994–1996, only 2 percent of plans were vetoed (Lupton & Stevens, 1997). In addition to reflecting solid family decision-making abilities, these minimal percentages also highlight FGC policies that allow professionals to veto only the plans that do not protect children's safety—a demonstration that family-driven plans are respected, as are the families who created them, even if those plans differ from the plans that would have been generated by the professionals.

Phase Four: Follow-Up
After the family plan is developed, agreed to, and copies provided to all participants, implementation begins. Two essential elements in the implementation process are resourcing and monitoring the plans. This practice method includes a more intimate role for extended family members with the family's case plan, from an implementation, informal support, and monitoring perspective.

Resourcing
Issues of resources are important to discuss in the context of family-centered practice. When policymakers view the FGC as a cost-neutral or reduction approach, family-created plans with identifiable needs are likely to be ignored. Plans developed through FGCs, just as with other approaches, need resources to be successful. Family members are likely to

extend their own resources to support the plan, but formal resources also must be available to assist the family.

Lupton et al. (1995) compared a group of families who participated in FGCs with families who didn't participate in conferences and discovered that the FGC-participating families are more likely to utilize "support and resources" from larger family systems. The greater use of extended family resources in FGC plans fosters family independence and reliance on the support network. Various researchers have documented this occurrence. Vesneski's (1998) study of one hundred FGCs in Washington state indicated that families bring existing resources to the conferences. Of the FGCs reviewed in a study by Crow and Marsh (1997, p. 15), 90 percent resulted in family members offering supportive resources to the child's immediate family.

In addition to the resources that families provide for plan implementation, research clearly demonstrates families' need for formal services. Lupton and Stevens (1997) found that even though FGCs utilize family resources at a greater rate, this did not reduce the agency resources and supports provided. In fact, in their study, agencies were responsible for 60 percent of the plan components, with families responsible for the remaining 40 percent.

While FGCs can facilitate family self-sufficiency through their network-resourcing plans, formal resources must also be accessible. Communities implementing FGCs must have flexible structures to use existing resources differently or as Nixon et al. (1996) suggest, to create vastly different resources based on family-expressed needs. Through FGCs, families become not only the plan generators but also the drivers of service delivery. This notion epitomizes family-centered, empowerment, and participatory theories.

Monitoring

After the plan has been implemented and resources are in place, follow-up and monitoring are required to ensure its effectiveness in achieving child safety, functioning, and well-being. Monitoring is a useful vehicle to create continued partnerships between agencies and families to ensure progress and attainment of goals. One premise is that family involvement in decision making and plan development will also increase the likelihood that extended family members will monitor the plan. The quality of monitoring or review procedures, however, is continually being called into question (Lupton & Stevens, 1997; Renouf, Robb, & Wells, 1990). Essentially, who is responsible for monitoring progress and ensuring that everyone follows through on his or her commitments?

In New Zealand, both Paterson and Harvey (1991) and Rimene (1993) indicated that a number of plans are not implemented. In fact, Paterson and Harvey (1991) found that "decisions were not carried out, reviews were not carried out, and family/Whanau members were unclear about, or did not carry out, their individual responsibilities after the FGC" (p. 46). Lupton and Stevens (1997) found that families and social workers monitored approximately one-half of the plans in both years of their study. Pennell and Burford (1997) also found that key components of the plan were not implemented.

The follow-up stage is undoubtedly the weakest link in this family-centered process. When family members or professionals do not deliver plan components, the probability increases that families will need traditional forms of intervention. The results from research so far demonstrate a need to develop a structure for formal monitoring and review.

Outcomes

Arguably the practice of family group conferencing blends family-centered, empowerment, participatory, and strengths-oriented theories to increase child safety and family well-being, but can outcomes support this innovative approach?

Pennell and Burford (1997) found that families participating in FGCs, as compared with those receiving traditional interventions in the child welfare system, experienced "decreases in substantiated child abuse/neglect, emergency responses to crises, and indicators of woman/wife abuse; and increases in indicators that family members were safe at home" (p. 3). In addition, the project participants reported that the FGCs improved family functioning through an enhancement of family unity, improved care for children, decreased family violence, and reduced drinking problems (Pennell & Burford, 1997).

The increased likelihood that children would be placed with extended family (Crow & Marsh, 1997; Connolly, 1994; Vesneski, 1998) supports FGCs as building partnerships and support networks within family units to protect children, while also honoring their culture and history. Marsh and Crow (1998) concluded from their research that FGC plans both protect and benefit children, as demonstrated by indicators on the at-risk register and re-abuse rates.

Although these results are very promising, additional research that further explores issues of child permanency; child and family safety, functioning, and well-being; and family stability is needed to support family group conferencing as an approach for the twenty-first century.

□ □ □

Due to a legislative framework, family group conferencing is the way child abuse and neglect concerns are resolved in New Zealand. Although other communities and countries, experimenting with the FGC model, have designed policies and protocols, conducted training, and designed evaluation initiatives, there is growing debate about how best to sustain this practice approach. Various funding streams in the United States are currently being used to implement FGCs, including foundation support, Title IV-E, Medicaid, welfare reform, and other juvenile justice and child welfare public dollars. However, much of this funding is structured in such a way that FGC initiatives are demonstration-oriented or time-limited.

As Merkel-Holguin (in press) stated:

> Whether a legislative framework would hinder or help the advancement of family group conferencing in the United States is questionable. New Zealand's law establishes the FGC process, outlines the structure for its conduct, clarifies jurisdictional authority, defines practice standards, provides policy directions, and endows resources to the implementing agencies. Yet shepherding legislative change at the federal or state level can be a risky endeavor.

Nonetheless, "practice guidelines and standards, supported by formal or legislated policy, are needed to ensure the efficacy of family group conferencing."

NOTES

1. This section is from "Origins of Family Decision Making: Indigenous Roots in New Zealand," by K. Ribich, 1998, *Protecting Children*, 14 (4), pp. 21–22. Copyright 1998 by the American Humane Association. Adapted with permission.

REFERENCES

American Humane Association. (1997). *Innovations for children's services for the 21st century: Family group decision making.* Englewood, CO: Author.

Atkin, W. R. (1988–1989). New Zealand: Children versus families—Is there any conflict? *Journal of Family Law*, 7 (1), 231–42.

Barker, S. O., & Barker, R. (1995). *A study of the experiences and perceptions of "family" and "staff" participants in family group conferences* (Cwlwon Project). Gwyneddd, Wales: Medra.

Burford, G. & Pennell, J. (1995). *Family group decision making project implementation report summary.* Newfoundland, Canada: Memorial University of Newfoundland.

Burford, G., & Pennell, J. (1998). *Outcome report: Vol. 1. Family group decision making project.* Newfoundland, Canada: Memorial University of Newfoundland.

Connolly, M. (1994). An act of empowerment: The Children, Young Persons and Their Families Act. *British Journal of Social Work*, 24 (1), 87–100.

Connolly, M., & McKenzie, M. (1999). *Effective participatory practice: Family group conferencing in child protection.* New York: Aldine De Gruyter.

Crow, G., & Marsh P. (1997). *Family group conferences: Partnership and child welfare.* Sheffield, United Kingdom: University of Sheffield.

Crow, G., & Marsh, P. (1999). *The Swindon and Wiltshire family group conference project evaluation report.* Sheffield, United Kingdom: University of Sheffield

Dunst, C., Deal, A., & Trivette, C. (1994). *Methods, strategies, and practices: Vol. 1. Supporting and strengthening families.* Cambridge, MA: Brookline Books.

Gilling, M., Patterson, L., & Walker, B. (1995). *Family members' experiences of the care and protection family group conference process.* Wellington, New Zealand: Social Policy Agency.

Gunderson, K. (1998). Pre-conference preparation: An investment in success. *Protecting Children 14* (4), 11–12.

Hardin, M. (1996). *Family group conferences in child abuse and neglect cases: Learning from the experience of New Zealand.* Washington, DC: ABA Center on Children and the Law, American Bar Association.

Hassall, I., & Maxwell, G. (1991). The family group conference. In G. M. Maxwell (Ed.), *An appraisal of the first year of the Children, Young Persons and Their Families Act 1989* (pp. 1–13). Wellington, New Zealand: Office of Commissioner for Children.

Kook, T., & Sivak, P. (1998). The Stanislaus model of family conferencing: Basic principles, practice, and structure. In *Summary of Proceedings: 1998 National Roundtable on Family Group Decision Making* (pp. 35–43). Englewood, CO: American Humane Association.

Lupton, C., Barnard, S., & Swall-Yarrington, M. (1995). *Family planning: An evaluation of the family group conference model* (Report No. 31). Portsmouth, United Kingdom: University of Portsmouth.

Lupton, C., & Stevens, M. (1997). *Family outcomes: Following through on family group conferences.* (Report No. 34). Portsmouth, United Kingdom: University of Portsmouth.

Marsh, P., & Crow, G. (1998). *Family group conferences in child welfare.* London: Blackwell Science.

Maxwell, G., & Morris, A. (1993). *Family group conferences: Key elements.* Paper presented at the Mission of St. James and St. John, Melbourne, Australia.

Merkel-Holguin, L. (1998). Implementation of family group decision making in the U.S.: Policies and practices in transition. *Protecting Children 14* (4), 4–10.

Merkel-Holguin, L. (in press). Diversions and departures in the implementation of family group conferencing in America. In G. Burford and J. Hudson (Eds.), *Family group conferences: Perspectives on policy, practice, and research.* New York: Aldine de Gruyter.

Ministerial Advisory Committee on a Maori Perspective for the Department of Social Welfare. (1988). *PUAO-TE-ATA-TU (daybreak): The report of the Ministerial Advisory.* Wellington, New Zealand: Author.

New Zealand Department of Social Welfare. (1993). *Statistics report.* Wellington, New Zealand: Author

Nixon, P., Taverner, P., & Wallace, P. (1996). "It gets you out and about"— children and family veiws of FGCs. In K. Morris and J. Tunnard, (Eds.),

Family group conferences: Messages from UK practice and research. London: Family Rights Group.

Paterson, K., & Harvey, M. (1991). *An evaluation of the organization and operation of care and protection family group conferences.* Wellington, New Zealand: Department of Social Welfare, Evaluation Unit.

Pennell, J., & Burford, G. (1994). Widening the circle: The family group decision making project. *Journal of Child and Youth Care, 9* (1), 1–12.

Pennell, J., & Burford, G. (1995). *Family group decision making implementation report.* St. John's, Newfoundland: Memorial University.

Pennell, J., & Burford, G. (1997). *Family group decision making: After the conference—progress in resolving violence and promoting well being.* Newfoundland, Canada: Memorial University of Newfoundland.

Renouf, J., Robb, G., & Wells, P. (1990). *Children, Young Persons and Their Families Act: Report on its first year of operation.* Wellington, New Zealand: Department of Social Welfare.

Rimene, S. (1993). *The Children, Young Persons and Their Families Act 1989, from a Maori perspective.* Unpublished master's thesis, Victoria University of Wellington, Wellington, New Zealand.

Sundell, K. (1998). The Swedish family group conference study. *Protecting Children, 14* (4), 32.

Vesneski, W. M. 1998). *Placing Washington state's family group conference program in context: A theoretical and empirical review.* Unpublished master's thesis, University of Washington, Seattle, WA.

Walker, H. (1996). Whanau Hui, family decision making, and the family group conference: An indigenous Maori view. *Protecting Children, 12* (3), pp. 8–10.

Wilcox, R., Walker, H., Smith, D., Ropata, M., Moore, J., Monu, L., Hewitt, A., Featherstone, T., & Allan, G. (1991). *Family decision making: Family group conferences: Practitioners' views.* Lower Hutt, New Zealand: Practitioners' Publishing.

10 Targeting the Right Families for Family-Centered Services

Current Dilemmas and Future Directions

Ramona W. Denby

Family-centered services are currently under attack. The arguments against family-centered services appear to be multidirectional. Some question whether family-centered services have been evaluated with sound, appropriate, and clinician-driven research rigor (Heneghan, Horwitz, & Leventhal, 1996; Wells & Biegel, 1990, 1992). On a more fundamental level, some argue that family-centered programs have not been proven to produce any real, discernable differences (especially long-term) between those children and families who receive the services and those who do not (Feldman, 1991a; Schuerman, Rzepnicki, Littell, & Chak, 1993; Yuan & Struckman-Johnson, 1991). Moreover, there are those who present the notion that arguments related to program effectiveness are irrelevant at this juncture because of a lack of clear definitions of who should receive the services (Walton & Denby, 1997; Wells & Biegel, 1990). Similarly, researchers have also questioned the effectiveness and receipt of family-centered services by different subpopulations, such as children of color (Denby, Curtis, & Alford, 1998; National Association of Black Social Workers, 1992). Some opponents of family-centered services seem to be philosophically opposed to the ideology, policy, and practice of family-centered services (Lindsey, 1994; MacDonald, 1994; Pelton, 1992). Finally, and most disturbing, is the contention that instead of bringing about real change in children's lives, family-centered programs jeopardize their safety (Bernard, 1992; Gelles, 1996; Ingrassia & McCormick, 1994; Seader, 1994).

Despite the increasing anti–family-centered-services rhetoric, there is still a significant voice that asserts the merits of family-centered programming (Berg, 1994; Cole, 1995; Early & Hawkins, 1994; Hartman, 1993; Maluccio, Pine, & Warsh, 1994; Mannes, 1993; Nelson, 1994; Pecora, 1994). Some scholars maintain that much of the slanderous campaign against family-centered services is the result of a political agenda spawned by the ever increasing threat of depleted social service spending, reform, and insufficient resources (Hartman, 1993; Maluccio et al., 1994). In addition, significant reports have demonstrated the success of family-centered services in increasing family functioning, safeguarding children, and preserving family units (Feldman, 1991b; Hayes & Joseph, 1985; Magura & Moses, 1984; Pecora, Bartlome, Magana, & Sperry, 1991; Spaid, Fraser, & Lewis, 1991; Walton, 1998; Walton, Fraser, Lewis, Pecora, & Walton, 1993).

Regardless of the family-centered efficacy debate, the need for reflection and program examination is clear. The necessity to explore the need for change, define new program approaches, and ensure program integrity by way of program examination is ongoing.

This chapter considers the future direction of family-centered services as it relates to the manner in which children and families are selected for services. In doing so, the chapter provides readers with a critical assessment of how the lack of clear definitions of target populations in family-centered services adversely affects program outcomes. The chapter also proposes targeting criteria that have the potential to aid practitioners, program managers, and other decision makers in their attempt to match appropriate clients to needed services.

Intensive family preservation services—a major family-centered program type—will serve as the primary basis of discussion throughout the chapter. Additionally, most of the discussion concerning family-centered services will draw upon the practices and experiences of the child welfare system. However, relevant examples of the targeting problem in other family-centered domains (e.g., the juvenile justice system, mental health system, disability system) will also be given.

The chapter is divided into three major parts. Part 1 provides a historical context of the targeting dilemma. In this section, readers will gain an understanding of the manner in which the eligibility structure has evolved in family-centered services. The author distinguishes between the formal (officially stated) method for selecting children and families for services and the informal (unstated) method of client selection.

Part 2 projects a plausible future direction in improving the process for targeting children and families for family-centered services. In this section, the author provides a synthesis of the current literature, which presents the need for a reconceptualization of the intended client population in family-centered services. Readers are provided with a summary of the research and literature that have questioned the accountability and demonstrable success of family-centered services. Most significant to this portion of the chapter is a delineation and a critical analysis of ten probable strategies for targeting family-centered services. This section discusses the current and future service priorities in family-centered programs. Finally, part 2 proposes potential service priority tiers that can be used in decisions to select client families for family-centered work.

Part 3 concludes the chapter by exploring the structural change needed in order for family-centered officials to incorporate the ten suggested targeting strategies/service priorities into their programs. Recommended reform is examined in terms of theoretical changes, changing practice models, policy changes, and new research agendas.

PART 1: THE EVOLUTION OF TARGETING PRACTICES IN FAMILY-CENTERED SERVICES

Formal Eligibility Criteria

Theory

By original design, family-centered services were intended to strengthen and maintain families in their own homes by providing a combination of necessary concrete and therapeutic services. In child welfare, family-centered services developed as a measure used to prevent family dissolution and the out-of-home placement of children. Intended client groups included families assessed to be in a state of crisis or emergency (Hutchinson & Nelson, 1985) or families whose children were considered to be at risk of out-of-home placement (Whittaker & Tracy, 1990).

As family-centered services evolved and became more professionalized and structured, the formal criteria used to determine a family's eligibility for services became the designation of "imminent risk." The chief architects of family-centered programs intended families who have "one or more children at imminent danger of placement" to be the targets of services (Kinney, Haapala, Booth, & Leavitt, 1990). As a theoretical construct, a child considered to be in imminent danger or risk is one whose current familial circumstances warrant his or her placement in substitute care if emergency services are not delivered immediately. Although widespread disagreement existed over both the importance of imminent risk as a service criterion and the feasibility of applying the imminent risk standard, the notion was viewed as the official method of selecting families for services.

Legislation and Policy

In addition to theoretical constructs, family-centered service eligibility has also been determined by prevailing legislation and policy. Because a significant portion of the funding for family-centered services has historically been tied to public—as opposed to private—entities, the selection of children and families was often dictated by federal and state legislation. For example, Title IV-E of the Social Security Act had as a major aim the prevention of undue separation of children from their families of origin. Likewise, the Adoption Assistance and Child Welfare Act of 1980 encouraged states to lessen their reliance on the use of foster care placement and to increase permanency planning by providing a monetary incentive structure. In an attempt to comply with federal mandates, family-centered service officials geared the program-eligibility structure accordingly.

A more recent federal mandate, the Family Preservation and Support Services Act (Subpart 2 of Title IV-B of the Social Security Act) of the Omnibus Budget Reconciliation Act of 1993, also sets general parameters for client selection in family-centered services (see Early & Hawkins, 1994; Ahsan, 1996, for a summary and analysis of the act). This act instructed states to provide "five-year plans" that could demonstrate their strategy for strengthening and supporting families. Consequently, the Administration on Children, Youth and Families specified that those states that did not spend at least 25 percent of their funds on family preservation or family support services had to provide a written rationale (Kaye, 1997). Such wording influenced the manner in which services were delivered and the way that clients were selected.

Informal Eligibility Criteria

Workers' Practices

Program philosophy, agency policy, program start-up considerations, expectations of stakeholders, public-agency versus private-agency status, geographic catchment areas, and financial and staff resources are all elements that play an official role in determining the manner in which clients are targeted for family-centered services (Feldman, 1990). In addition, the theoretical constructs (e.g., imminent risk), policies, and legislation (e.g., Public Law 96-272, the Family Preservation and Support Services Act) discussed above also play a tremendous role in official case selection. However, official case selection points, theoretical constructs, policies, and legislation all share one main commonality—ambiguity. It is the sense of ambiguity experienced by workers that has led to the emergence of informal methods of targeting families for services. Moreover, workers' case selection methods are compromised by biases, personal ideology, and profound subjectivity (Denby, 1995). As a result of unclear policy direction and workers' subjectivity, an informal client eligibility structure has emerged in family-centered programs. This client eligibility structure may also be the result of the nature of work encompassed in the delivery of family-centered services. Because their jobs involve enormous responsibility, workers often must make decisions in the face of great pressure, complex cases, difficult choices, and depleted resources. Adding to this difficulty, workers are further handicapped by the lack of scientific methods concerning case selection.

Studies have shown that workers are hindered as the result of using formal ways of selecting cases such as the "imminent risk" criteria (Denby, 1995; Budde, 1995). Instead of employing objective means of case selection, children and families are targeted for services in an arbitrary manner. In a study of frontline practitioners, Miller and Fisher (1992) discovered several significant obstacles to effective case investigation and decision making. These obstacles were the result of the nature of the cases themselves, the workers' lack of a knowledge base, and the lack of professional support available to aid workers in decision making. The most salient obstacles to worker decision making found by Miller and Fisher (1992) included the following: (a) the numbers of children and the complexity of family systems, (b) adults who were intimidating, (c) mitigating factors such as the workers' difficulty in understanding cultural norms and the workers' tendency to apply middle-class values and ideas to clients' situations, (d) an insecure knowledge base, and (e) limited help in terms of supervision and assessment support.

In addition, Gambrill (1994) asserts that workers' discretion in the implementation of agency policy can compromise goal attainment. Gambrill maintains that when workers' discretion produces client harm or renders ineffective service delivery, it should be avoided. Gambrill has advanced the notion that unwanted worker discretion occurs when the following conditions are in operation: (a) a lack of required attitude, knowledge, and skills, (b) a lack of needed resources to deliver services, (c) a dysfunctional incentive system in place, and (d) a vague objective.

Finally, in her study of social workers in medical and protective service settings, Hamilton (1992) found that workers' personal characteristics (e.g., education, ethnicity, sex, age, marital status, children, socioeconomic status, time in the field, personal experiences with corporal punishment, and working experiences in child abuse) help inform their decision making and the choices they make about clients.

Other Decision Makers and Stakeholders

In addition to the tremendous importance of workers' practice in the establishment of informal eligibility structures, two other elements play a critical role: (a) the discretion used by states in the interpretation of federal guidelines and the implementation of programs and (b) the significance of reigning and established program models. First, like individual workers, states have been inconsistent in the interpretation of federal guidelines in relation to program operations. Within the family-based services arena, states are freer to use their judgment in establishing program specifications such as eligibility because federal regulations tend to be somewhat ambiguous. With children, the mentally ill, and the elderly as examples, Burt and Pittman (1985) were able to demonstrate how local authority over the implementation of federal policy had an adverse impact. Stein (1994) and others argue that the national government must establish clearly stated directives for states to use in the implementation of programs. In reference to the implementation of the Adoption Assistance and Child Welfare Act, Stein asserts that failure at the federal level to provide clear objectives led to weak implementation at the state and local levels. States, as major decision makers and stakeholders, have played a significant role in the evolution of informal client eligibility categories. Because of the great leeway given to states and localities in interpreting federal law, inconsistent eligibility standards exist throughout all states.

Second, the dominance of particular program models also shares a place in the evolution of informal client eligibility categories. Homebuilders—also known as the Crisis Intervention Model (Kinney, Haapala, & Booth, 1991)—is arguably a significant program prototype within the family-centered services arena. Incorporating a time-limited, empowerment-oriented, and strengths-focused philosophy, Homebuilders has become one of the reigning family-centered treatment models within the family preservation field. Like the formal eligibility category, the Homebuilders model is purposely mentioned again under the informal eligibility category because some (Adams, 1994) would argue that the manner in which we decide what families are eligible for services has not so much to do with policy, formality, or proven effectiveness as much as it has to do with the monopolization of one specific model within the family-centered services market. Adams demonstrates that a major, private funding entity, the Edna McConnell Clark Foundation, supports only Homebuilder types of programs. As a result, both a formal and informal culture has developed due to many programs' attempts to meet grant funders' specifications by stating officially that they subscribe to the Homebuilders model, while unofficially servicing non–imminent risk cases, self-referrals, and the like (Adams, 1994). Other family-centered treatment models, such as the Home-Based Model/ FAMILIES (Bryce, 1978; Bribitzer & Verdieck, 1988; Leeds, 1984; Lloyd & Bryce, 1984; Maybanks & Bryce, 1979; Pearson & King, 1987; Reid, Kagan, & Schlosberg, 1988) and the Family-Treatment Model (Alexander & Parsons, 1982; Barton, Alexander, Waldron, Turner, & Warburton, 1985; Showell, 1985; Showell, Hartley, & Allen, 1988; Lantz, 1985; Tavantzis, Tavantzis,

Brown, & Rohrbaugh, 1985), do not appear to have had the same impact on the family-centered field as has Homebuilders. In a review of the most prevalent family-centered intervention models, Nelson, Landsman, and Deutelbam (1990) found many similarities in the three models. When service eligibility is geared around the practices of one particular model, criteria are set according to that model, even if alternative approaches are parallel, more successful, or more client appropriate.

PART 2: FUTURE DIRECTION OF TARGETING PRACTICES IN FAMILY-CENTERED SERVICES

Reconceptualization of the "Intended" Client Population

The targeting issue (i.e., inability of family-centered services to definitively assert a specific client population) seems to be a significant problem hindering family-centered programs today. There exist no universal method of case selection, no clear definition of those for whom family-centered services are best suited, and no systematic categories or criteria on which workers and other decision makers base their rationale for service delivery.

The previous section explored how and why the client eligibility structure has evolved within the family-centered arena. Such an evolution and the resulting inconsistency in how children and families are targeted for services has recently prompted great discussion. The lack of clear target populations seems to be a point at which some researchers (Wells & Tracy, 1996) have leveled their criticisms against family-centered services. Moreover, many researchers have articulated a concern regarding the fact that family-centered officials are unable to predict a target population clearly (Rossi, 1992; Schuerman, Rzepnicki, Littell, & Budde, 1992; Tracy, 1991). Others have discovered that family-centered workers do not agree with, and therefore do not target, intended client populations (Denby, 1995; Denby et al., 1998). Budde (1995) found that many families served by family preservation programs do not meet the target criteria.

In the absence of specific guidelines for identifying families most appropriate for family-centered intervention, family-centered workers are given the nearly impossible task of working miracles with clients who are extremely dysfunctional. Nonetheless, the targeting problem is being studied and addressed in at least three significant ways: (a) a call to target special populations, (b) a voice that prompts a new and concise way of putting into operation the concept of imminent risk, and (c) a suggestion that family-centered services should abandon the "prevention of out-of-home placement" as their primary goal.

First, based on the significant body of research that reports the devastating circumstances that children of color face within the child welfare system, researchers are beginning to examine whether these children and other special populations should be the target of family-centered services (Denby et al., 1998; Dodson, 1983; Gray & Nybell, 1990; Hodges, 1991; Morisey, 1990; Pinderhughes, 1991; Stehno, 1990). Second, because the concept of imminent risk is unclear, value laden, and susceptible to great worker bias, it has been suggested that more objective criteria (e.g., cases where a court has ruled in favor of the removal of the children from the home) be applied to the term (Rzepnicki, 1994). Third, some researchers suggest that deciding on the appropriate target for family-centered intervention is related to the selection of clear and appropriate service rationales. Wells and Tracy (1996) suggest that the service rationale of prevention of out-of-home placement be replaced. Target populations should not necessarily be composed solely of children at immediate risk of out-of-home placement.

Accountability and Program Success

The targeting issue (as discussed above) is of great concern to family-centered practitioners because of its direct implications for achieving and measuring program success. Family-centered programs have lacked credibility in their assertions regarding program efficiency, given the inability to ascertain whether services are reaching the intended client populations. The targeting issue is one example of the current problems surrounding program accountability and success. This section will explore other key issues related to program success within the family-centered arena.

Family-centered services are not lacking for critics or those advocating reform (Berliner, 1993; Bernard, 1992; Drake et al., 1995; Gelles, 1996; Ingrassia & McCormick, 1994; Lindsey, 1994; MacDonald, 1994; Pelton, 1992; Rossi, 1994; Schuerman, Rzepnicki, & Littell, 1994; Seader, 1994; Wald, 1988; Wells & Biegel, 1990; Wells & Freer, 1994; Yuan, McDonald, Wheeler, Struckman-Johnson, & Rivest, 1990). Criticism should not necessarily be shunned, and program administrators must be somewhat self-critical. By the same token, program criticism should be constructive and oriented toward seeking alternatives. This section will attempt to synthesize pertinent aspects of the family-centered literature regarding program shortcomings. In a more prudent manner, this section will consider the merits of the criticism and begin to chart a new and feasible course of action. In general, discussion concerning the efficacy of family-centered services can be organized into the following categories:

1. The measure of program success should be improved family functioning, not the avoidance of placement.
2. Research and evaluation methods lack substance and quality and are not often appropriate, or program outcomes for families who

receive services are really no different from those that do not, and program effects are not long lasting.

3. Programs fail to protect children from abusive parents who are not able to be rehabilitated.

4. Services are limited and insufficient in meeting client needs, and programs are able to reach only about one-half of those families who need services.

5. Services give, at best, Band-Aid solutions and never really address the root causes (e.g., poverty, substance abuse) of clients' problems.

A selling point of family-centered services has traditionally been the assertion that services prevent unnecessary out-of-home placements and help to divert children from institutional placements. Many programs have used decreased foster care rates as their primary measure of success. Although a decreased out-of-home placement rate has long been an indicator of success, it is now becoming a point for which family-centered programs are scrutinized. Some family-centered services evaluators (Wald, 1988) are questioning whether placement rate, as a measure of success, should be replaced by improved family functioning. Another perspective on this issue is the notion that the prevention of out-of-home placement is a necessary outcome measure, given the fact that family-centered programs are touted as placement-prevention services (Rzepnicki, 1994).

A second issue surrounding accountability in family-centered services concerns service effectiveness and the manner in which effectiveness has been measured and researched. As an example, research conducted by Schuerman et al. (1994) and Rossi (1994) on family preservation services has recently become a popular point of illustration in the claim that family-centered services are not effective. These studies report little or no difference between families that received intensive, in-home services and control groups that did not. In the case of the Illinois study (Schuerman et al., 1994), findings indicate slight, but more improved, gains and outcomes on the side of the control group families. In a review of the literature related to family preservation research and effectiveness, Wells and Biegel (1992) report that in cases where there exist positive family outcomes, the outcomes are short-lived, and the families remain vulnerable.

A related issue concerning the research conducted on family-centered services is the research method itself. Family-centered evaluations are often criticized because they do not employ experimental methods (Wells & Biegel, 1990). Wells and Freer (1994) believe that family-centered services should be evaluated with qualitative methods so that outcomes that do not lend themselves to quantitative designs can be fully understood.

The most serious scrutiny directed at family-centered services concerns whether children truly can be protected from harm while receiving services. A growing and resounding voice questions whether parents who mistreat their children can actually be changed or rehabilitated. Berliner (1993) maintains that abusive parents often fail to complete their case plans and reabuse their children in a substantial number of cases. Similarly, Bernard (1992) reminds us that one of the most violent institutions in America is the "institution of family." Bernard believes that maintaining children in their family settings may not be in their best interest. Finally, by illustrating the deaths of children at the hands of their own parents, Ingrassia and McCormick (1994) assert that family-centered services are a failure, and they decry the emphasis on the preservation of families.

Service limitation and insufficiency is a fourth area of scrutiny often heard in critiques of family-centered services. When making charges against the programs, opponents of family-centered services often cite the programs' inability to serve significant numbers of children and families, their funding insufficiencies, and other limitations. Seader (1994) cites the limitation of available community resources as problematic in the delivery of family-centered services. In addition, by reviewing three experimental studies, Wells and Biegel (1992) offer evidence of the limitations of family-centered services by suggesting that only one-half of the children who are truly at risk of out-of-home placement actually receive services.

Finally, family-centered services have been accused of superficial intervention. Stated another way, critics argue that family-centered services never fully remedy the clients' core problems and the sources of family dysfunction. For example, Lindsey (1994) believes that family preservation is a "residual approach" that uses individual treatment and behavioral approaches to tackle major child welfare issues that are really the consequence of poverty. Likewise, Lindsey (1994), Pelton (1992), Dore (1993), and others of like mind espouse the notion that family-centered services fail when they offer individual treatment for a social or societal problem, namely, poverty.

Targeting Criteria and Service Priorities

Thus far, this chapter has explored both early and current targeting practices within the family-centered services arena. The chapter has established the fact that the inability to target and provide services precisely to the intended client populations has been extremely problematic in the delivery of family-centered services. The author has also provided examples of other current problems faced by family-centered service providers, researchers, and evaluators. As discussed, careful attention must also be given to the other problem areas. However, the intent of the author is to concentrate primarily on the issue of targeting. Issues such as whether family-centered programs employ rigorous measures of evaluation or whether these services should be researched with qualitative or with quantitative methods are really secondary to the more fundamental problems, namely, deciding and proving who should receive family-centered services. Moreover, if the community of scholars can ever definitively establish clear targeting categories, other problematic issues such as "Can children be safely protected in their homes?" and "Should we measure family functioning or placement avoidance?" may become more clear. Perhaps new methods of targeting client populations will conclude that families at immediate risk of losing their children are not those clients truly suited for family-centered services.

This portion of the chapter will provide a listing and analysis of ten key factors that must be considered when establishing new targeting categories. These factors represent priorities that have been derived from conceptual theories, practice models, policy intentions, and research. A synthesis of the literature yields the following ten categories as areas that constitute the most effective targeting strategies: (a) child safety issues, (b) client overrepresentation, (c) service equity/most underserved, (d) risk factors (environment, parent, and child), (e) cost avoidance, (f) problem severity, (g) service appropriateness; (h) psychological adjustment, (i) systems-level data, and (j) success factors. Salient studies and researchers who have contributed significantly to our understanding of the role of the aforementioned factors on targeting decisions are summarized in table 10.1.

Child Safety Issues/Risk Factors

Both opponents and proponents of family-centered services agree that children's safety must be the foremost consideration in devising new methods of targeting children and families for family-centered services. Paradoxically, while all agree that child safety is the first priority in developing targeting criteria, few agree on methods of deciding which children are unsafe if left in the home. For example, DePanfilis and Scannapieco (1994) demonstrated, in their review of ten risk assessment models used in forty-two states, a general consensus that existing models for judging child safety are premature and not well received. Some researchers (Zuravin & Taylor, 1987) used incidence rates and mapping techniques to shed light on neighborhoods that have a strong likelihood of housing families that are experiencing child maltreatment. These mapping techniques enabled researchers to predict which neighborhoods are most at risk for child maltreatment (Deccio & Horner, 1994; Garbarino & Sherman, 1980). Other researchers suggested tiers of client characteristics and a menu of risk indicators (Campbell, 1991; Jones & McCurdy, 1992; Waterhouse & Carnie, 1992; Zuravin, Orme, & Hegar, 1994). Finally, many have used case characteristics as a basis for deciding child safety: (a) the frequency and severity of past abuse (Graham, 1978; Meddin, 1984), (b) the child's age (Meddin, 1984), (c) behavior exhibited by the mother (Boehm, 1962, 1968), and (d) environ-

TABLE 10.1. Targeting Criteria and Service Priorities

Child Safety	Client Over-representation	Service Equity	Risk Factors	Cost Avoidance
Boehm 1962, 1968	Billingsley, 1968	Close, 1983	Bath & Haapala, 1993	Daro & Cohn, 1998
Campbell, 1991	Day, 1979	Denby, Curtis, & Alford, 1998	Campbell, 1991	Froelich, 1992
DePanfilis & Scannapieco, 1994	Gustavasson & Segal, 1994	National Association of Black Social Workers, 1992	Deccio & Horner, 1994	Hutchinson, 1982
Graham, 1978	McRoy, 1994		Dirom, 1992	Landsman et al., 1993
Jones & McCurdy, 1992	National Black Child Development Institute, 1989	National Black Child Development Institute, 1989	Doueck, Bronson, & Levine, 1992	McCrowskey & Meezan, 1993
Meddin, 1984	National Association of Black Social Workers, 1992	Pinderhughes, 1991	Doueck, Levine, & Bronson, 1993	Nelson et al, 1996
Waterhouse & Carnie, 1992		Stehno, 1990	Eamon, 1994	Szykula & Fleischman, 1985
Zuravin, Orme, & Hegar, 1994	W. K. Kellogg Foundation, 1995		Gaudin, 1993	University Associates, 1993
			Johnson, 1994	
			Jones & McCurdy, 1992	
			Pecora, 1991	
			Pelton, 1991	
			Schuerman, 1994	
			Thieman & Dail, 1992	
			Waterhouse & Carnie, 1992	
			Wald & Wooverton, 1990	
			Zuravin, Orme, & Hegar, 1994	

mental factors (Meddin, 1984). Safety criteria are numerous, varied, and nonsystematic. Given that family-centered workers are predicting human behavior (an imprecise science), this writer is not hopeful that the family-centered community will ever definitively and unanimously formulate a sound predictor of child safety. As family-centered officials begin to consider new targeting criteria that take into account child safety, the old notion of selecting families with children who are at immediate risk, immediate danger, or imminent risk may have to be abandoned. In fact, research indicates that family preservation workers do not actually aim

TABLE 10.1. *(continued)*

Problem Severity	Service Appropriateness	Psychological Adjustment	Systems Level Data	Success Factors
Dalgleish & Drew, 1989 DePanfilis & Scannapieco, 1994 Phillips et al., 1971 Wells & Tracy, 1996	Bath & Haapala, 1993 Cimmarusti, 1992 Eamon, 1994 Hutchinson, 1982 Nelson, Landsman, & Deutelbaum, 1990 Nelson et al., 1996 Pelton, 1994	Cowger, 1992 DeJong & Miller, 1995 MacDonald, 1992 Reid, Kagan, & Scholsberg, 1998 Saleebey, 1991 Weick et al, 1989	Denby, 1995 Derezotes & Snowden, 1990 Kamerman & Kahn, 1993 Melton, 1997 Stevenson, Cheung, & Lueng, 1992	Gaudin et al., 1990 Katz & Robinson, 1991 Reid, Kagan, & Scholsberg, 1988 Tracy, 1990 Whittaker & Tracey, 1991

services at imminent-risk cases (Budde, 1995; Denby, 1995). Imminent or immediate risk of removal implies a level of risk that may no longer be tolerable if we truly honor our desire to hold child safety above all other considerations.

Client Overrepresentation

Children of color have been and still remain the most overrepresented client population within the child welfare system (Billingsley, 1968; Day, 1979; Gustavasson & Segal, 1994; National Black Child Development Institute, 1989; W. K. Kellogg Foundation, 1995; McRoy, 1994; National Association of Black Social Workers, 1992). The plight of children of color as the result of foster care drift, adoption disruption, and differential foster care exit rates is also a well-established phenomenon (Barth, 1996; Barth et al., 1986; Finch & Fanshel, 1985; Finch, Fanshel, & Grundy, 1986; Jenkins et al., 1983; McMurtry & Lie, 1992; Olsen, 1982; Seaburg & Tolley, 1986).

As discussed earlier in this chapter, decreased out-of-home placement rates have long been a goal of family-centered services. Despite calls for the elimination of this goal, it appears that family-centered services will need to continue to demonstrate that a major goal of service delivery is the decrease of out-of-home placement rates. Unlike foster care provision and child abuse and neglect investigation, family-centered interventions and family preservation are not services that are mandated and funded as priorities. These services are seen as more of a luxury—preventative and ancillary. Family-centered services that employ targeting criteria with the potential to decrease the overrepresentation of specific client populations will need to become the priority.

Service Equity/Most Underserved

Rhetoric concerning the desire to relieve the child welfare system of the great numbers of children who are overrepresented (e.g., children of color) has long existed. Many saw family-centered services, and family preservation in particular, as a new beginning and held out hope that these services would bring about change in the lives of children of color who remain trapped within service systems. However, the promise that many held for family-centered services in relation to children of color has not materialized. The nonreceipt of services and the bias against children of color in family-centered services is evident (Close, 1983; Denby et al., 1998; National Association of Black Social Workers, 1992; National Black Child Development Institute, 1989; Pinderhughes, 1991; Stehno, 1990). In a search for effective, new targeting criteria, family-centered services will need to take into account the issue of service equity to address the history of underservice experienced by children of color.

Assessment of Risk Factors: Environment, Parent, and Child

There is a need to consider again the topic of child safety in our exploration of the role that risk factors will serve in a new era of family-centered service delivery. The child safety section established the fact that environmental, parental, and child characteristics have historically been the manner in which we judged child home safety. In addition, the child safety section suggested that new targeting criteria reconsider the long-standing goal of targeting imminent-risk families, or families in which there exists the immediate threat of the removal of children from the home. Now it is important to consider the method (e.g., risk forms, computer-based expert systems, screening teams, worker narratives, worker/supervisor case conferencing) with which we decide the level of risk. The literature is composed of disparate methods for how environmental, parental, and child characteristics have been assessed. Each method has its strengths and weaknesses.

Risk Assessment Forms. Risk assessment forms have been criticized for not being scientific and for not being effectively implemented (Doueck, Levine, & Bronson, 1993; Doueck, Bronson, & Levine, 1992; Wald & Woolverton, 1990). Thieman and Dail (1992) report the failure of a major family risk scale in identifying acute risk characteristics and risk for out-of-home placement among 995 families. Guadin (1993), reviewing nine structured assessment scales widely used with neglectful families, concludes that in spite of the benefits and merits of the scales, they should not replace sound, clinical conclusions and should never be used as a sole decision-making measure. Similarly, Pecora (1991) provides a discussion of four major types of risk assessment systems: (a) the matrix approach, (b) an empirical predictors method, (c) family assessment scales, and (d) child at-risk fields. Pecora concludes that in spite of the many gains (e.g., structuring worker documentation, helping workers assess risk not only at intake but throughout the life of the case) made through the use of risk assessment scales, these measures still suffer in three main ways: (a) some risk systems are incorrectly used, (b) child neglect may be minimized, and (c) complex cases are not assessed adequately.

Computer-Based Expert Systems. Computer-based expert systems are computer programs that incorporate the knowledge base of experts in the field in order to render decisions about children and the assessment of risk (Schuerman, 1994). They make use of statistical findings and incorporate the results of intensive worker interviews. The systems, although currently in an embryonic stage of development, have the benefit of offering experienced expertise to inexperienced workers (Schuerman, 1994). They are limited in that they do not inform users of the "standard of correctness" (Johnson, 1994). In other words, to date we are still undecided on the specific case criteria that should be used in defining whether workers make correct decisions in child removal situations and in the assessment of risk.

Screening Teams, Worker Narratives, Worker/Supervisor Case Conferencing. It seems that recommendations concerning the appropriate manner in which to assess client risk have come full circle. Originally, the "soft" ways (i.e., worker observation and impression) of measuring client risk were criticized for their level of subjectivity and the fact that they lack scientific rigor. From the subjective approach we evolved to the "hard" approaches to risk measurement (i.e., risk assessment scales and computer-generated models). Currently, there is increased frustration with the "hard" approaches, and attention is being given to the weaknesses inherent in those models. Now, seemingly, a call is being made for the revival of old-fashioned clinical impression. However, it appears that a recommendation is being made for more study of the use of clinical impression models that employ a large degree of intersubjectivity (i.e., screening teams, peer-reviewed worker narratives, and case conferencing). Also, there is a call for the study of multidimensional methods, that is, methods that employ both quantitative risk scales and qualitative teams of decision makers (Doueck et al., 1992; Thieman & Dail, 1992). Finally, it has been suggested—and research has demonstrated—that there are benefits to assessing client risk through pairing child protection investigators and family preservation workers at the onset of service delivery (Walton, 1997).

Cost Avoidance

The issue of cost saving has been long touted as a major benefit of family-centered services. Significant studies have demonstrated the cost effectiveness of family-centered services (Hutchinson, 1982; Landsman et al., 1993; Nelson, Landsman, Tyler, & Richardson, 1996; University Associates, 1993). Savings have been calculated in terms of the number and length of substitute care placements averted, the amount of Title IV-B funds made available for prevention services through unused Title IV-E funds, and the administrative expenses spared.

Moving into an era of program reform, proponents of family-centered services will no longer be able to market such services solely on the basis of their cost effectiveness. Cost-saving patterns accompanied by low placement rates, low rates of subsequent maltreatment, and positive changes in client functioning will need to be clearly demonstrated. For example, Nelson, Landsman, and Deutelbaum (1990) highlight the results of a three-site study of intensive family services where six-month programs cost $255 more per family than shorter programs but save an average of $1,212 in placement costs during the first year following service. The site that experienced the significant cost savings also reported that only 12 percent of its clients experienced a subsequent placement during the one-year follow-up phase.

Problem Severity

The issue of children's risk for further maltreatment is critical in deciding which families are most appropriate for family-centered services; therefore, it warrants further consideration. Problem severity, including the duration of the current problem, its intensity, and a family's potential for long-term sustainability in the eradication of the problem situation, must be considered. As discussed in the risk factor section above, most risk measures of all types attempt to ascertain the degree to which a child is at risk for out-of-home placement and the degree to which there exists a potential for further harm. Reformed targeting criteria will have to be informed by discernable answers to questions regarding problem severity. It has been suggested that perhaps cases that present intense, prolonged problem situations, with no apparent indicators that a long-term positive effect will occur, should not be targeted for placement prevention (Wells & Tracy, 1996). However, even if the community of decision makers could agree that families possessing the aforementioned characteristics should not be the target of service delivery, the task of identifying these families remains to be accomplished.

Service Appropriateness

Essential in determining which families are most appropriate for receiving family-centered services is the study of service appropriateness. Decisions regarding service appropriateness include consideration of the following: (a) service or intervention models, (b) service length, and (c) cultural specificity. This chapter has considered three main family-centered intervention types (i.e., Homebuilders, Home-Based/FAMILIES, and the Family-Treatment Model). The Homebuilders model is oriented to crisis-intervention theory, is short term, and emphasizes psychoeducational services (Nelson et al., 1990). Home-Based/FAMILIES is similar to Homebuilders but uses longer treatment periods, and its intervention base derives from family systems theory. Family-Treatment Models place less emphasis on concrete, supportive service delivery and more focus on therapeutic programming.

In determining the most appropriate families for family-centered intervention, caseworkers must evaluate carefully the appropriateness of the three program types mentioned above in terms of service orientation, service length, and the degree to which the models are culturally compatible. Relevant questions include the following: (a) What clients benefit most from short-term and long-term program models? (b) Do certain ethnic groups respond more favorably under particular theoretical models? and (c) Do client conditions such as poverty warrant the implementation of certain program models? Other researchers have posed similar questions. For example, Eamon (1994) and Pelton (1994) raise the question "Does poverty contribute to child maltreatment?" These researchers and others speculate that poverty does contribute to child maltreatment, and they raise the possibility that family-centered interventions may never be suitable for significant numbers of impoverished families.

Nelson et al. (1996) maintain that specific family-centered models are more effective with certain populations than they are with others. Specifically, they discovered that subpoverty populations have concrete and therapeutic service needs best served by comprehensive program models that include "teamed services, smaller caseloads, case management as well as treatment services and flexible funds." Similarly, they observed in a study of families that have younger children and are low income that African American families that are newly referred child abuse and neglect cases or are chronically neglecting cases have higher subsequent placement rates. Finally, this same study resulted in a discovery that longer service models may be more beneficial to clients whose families have adults who suffer from emotional problems or have children who suffer from behavioral problems.

Research conducted by Bath and Haapala (1993) adds credence to the author's belief that service appropriateness must become a main consideration in deciding which families should be the target of family-centered services. In an examination of intensive family preservation services, Bath and Haapala discovered that children from neglectful families and multiple maltreating families have the most dismal outcomes. In addition to the above categories, the field of family-centered services will need to develop closer approximations concerning the nature of program delivery that is best suited to families facing issues of substance abuse.

In short, targeting the right families for family-centered services will demand that those considering the matter discover what family types benefit most from programs that adhere to particular features.

Psychological Adjustment

Three psychological adjustment issues are worthy of exploration in our efforts to know which families benefit most from family-centered services: client motivation, client maturity, and the acknowledgment of problems. Many family-centered clinicians suspect that client motivation is a major indicator of how successful families will be in reaching their service goals. However, research attention is rarely given to this facet of the maltreating parent's level of psychological adjustment. When it has been given, it has been done in a nonimpressionist manner. More study of the role of client motivation in predicting service readiness is sorely needed. Perhaps a key issue in this line of inquiry might spring from the therapeutic interviewing technique suggested by MacDonald (1992), who speculates that clients who are able to approach their problems from a solution-focused standpoint and can imagine the consequences of their current predicament from a future standpoint have the potential to make great therapeutic strides.

Additionally, client maturity may be an area of psychological adjustment that is worthy of investigation. Chronological age and emotional maturity may both be significant in ascertaining the role played by this category of adjustment in clients' readiness for service.

Finally, the ability to concede that one has a problem seems to be a psychological adjustment factor for which there should be screening when decisions are made regarding the targeting of clients for family-centered services. In fact, research suggests that clients who can acknowledge a family problem are less likely than those who cannot do so to experience the out-of-home placement of a child (Reid et al., 1988).

Client motivation, client maturity, and the ability to acknowledge the presence of a problem all seem to be strengths on the part of potential family-centered clients. Significant works have been written about the therapeutic benefit of engaging clients from a strengths perspective (Cowger, 1992; DeJong & Miller, 1995; Saleebey, 1992; Weick, Rapp, Sullivan, & Kisthardt, 1989). The presence of these strengths may indicate those families who are most appropriate for family-centered services.

Systems-Level Data

Akin to the category "service appropriateness," in order to move closer to identifying the families that are best suited for family-centered intervention, family-centered programs will be forced to undertake serious examination of the systems in which they operate. Not only do systems-level data include specification of program/intervention types (previously discussed), but they also include other structural issues, such as program capacity, program experience, and available resources. Prior to deciding which families will be the target of service delivery, family-centered programs must undergo considerable examination of their infrastructure and decide whether they are equipped to handle the client situations that may present themselves. In a study of the significance of two main service criteria (i.e., imminent risk and special populations) on workers' decisions to target family preservation services, Denby (1995) discovered that workers are hindered from providing services to either of these two groups because of the lack of available community resources to aid service delivery. Underfunded, understaffed programs with limited experience may not be the best match for some of the client populations that appear to be in need of family-centered services.

Success Factors

Traditionally, family-centered services have screened and selected families for services based on case characteristics associated with service failure— for example, the presence of parental mental illness (Katz & Robinson, 1991). However, the assumption that the opposite of the negative state will yield positive client results is limiting. Instead, prudent research should seek to discover combinations of client characteristics that are associated with success. For instance, few child behavior problems, the presence of all significant family members at intake conferences, and fewer critical incidents have been shown to be correlates of client success in home-based programs (Reid et al., 1988). Moreover, the presence and mobilization of social networks appear to be factors associated with client success (Gaudin, Wodarski, Arkinson, & Avery, 1990). In addition, Whittaker and Tracy (1990) and Tracy (1990) have provided insights into the importance of social networks in intervening with intensive, family-based client populations. Selecting the right families for family-centered intervention will require further exploration of success factors such as those mentioned above.

The above section highlighted ten key areas that require further research. Among the many challenges that family-centered programs will face during the next century is deciding which families and client populations are most suitable for family-centered services. The ten criteria and service priorities discussed above are essential components in matching the right families to the right forms of family-centered intervention. In order to create the most optimal program conditions, family-centered services must include a closer examination of the feasibility of targeting the following types of cases: (a) cases in which a child's safety can be reasonably ensured, (b) cases involving overrepresented groups, (c) cases involving groups that are most underserved, including special populations and children of color, (d) cases involving client groups whose risk factors are not insurmountable, (e) cases involving clients who stand to render the greatest cost savings, (f) cases in which the problem severity lends itself to limited treatment modalities, (g) cases in which clients exhibit maturity and motivation and in which adult caregivers are able to concede that problems exist, (h) cases involving clients whom programs can fully serve, given the limitations imposed by systems (including the program itself), and (i) cases that clearly show evidence of the presence of empirically derived indicators of success.

Service Tiers

This section will attempt to address issues surrounding the implementation of the ten targeting criteria described above. As demonstrated, significant research can be found to provide a rationale and justification for the use of the above criteria as a base for targeting. However, little is known about how the targeting priorities should be implemented within family-centered programs. It seems reasonable that if family-centered programs are to avoid some of the programming mistakes that have plagued the programs in the past, the community of decision makers must come to some consensus regarding what the service priority is for family-centered programs. Moreover, in addition to the value statement, principles, and goals that are now the foundation of all family-centered programming, we must decide in a systematic and universally applicable way what populations we believe to be the priority for service delivery. In this chapter ten service priority areas have been suggested. However, even the specificity of these defined areas may be too broad to be adopted as guidelines for determining which populations can be most effectively and consistently served. Nonetheless, if we are to gain anything from the current knowledge base, it seems that at least five of the service priorities discussed have the potential to become universally adopted. Issues regarding child safety, service equity, problem severity, service appropriateness, and cost avoidance are too significant to ignore as potential universal service priorities.

Family-based programs will need service tiers. In the first service tier, programs throughout the nation can agree to the above service priorities. In the second service tier, programs would then devise local implementation strategies that target client groups based on the unique needs of their respective service areas and locations. Stated another way, a pool of eligible clients can be gathered by adhering to the five service priorities discussed above. From that pool of clients, individual family-centered programs can further decide who is eligible for services, given the unique needs of their geographic area. In fact, this tier approach has been recommended through neighborhood mapping techniques (Zuravin & Taylor, 1987). From this second tier, the third and final service tier is created. Individual family-centered programs can triage cases for service delivery.

PART 3: PUTTING THE TARGETING CRITERIA INTO ACTION

Implementation of the targeting criteria and service tiers described above will require that family-centered officials reassess existing procedures and processes. More specifically, successful targeting practices have implications for current and future family-centered theory, practice, policy, and research. This section provides a discussion of what will be required of the aforementioned family-centered entities in regard to the creation of more precise targeting criteria.

Theory

Above all, family-centered practitioners will require new "socialization" regarding the proposed targeting criteria. Family-centered service reformers will have to engage practitioners in dialogues about the very nature of the targeting criteria, the rationale for their use, and how they are to be implemented. At the root of this task is a major paradigm shift. Practitioners, programmers, and the like will need to collaborate and seek to discover new or revised theories that can successfully undergird the implementation of the proposed targeting criteria. Theoretical shifts must be accomplished through extensive education and training. For example, Cimmarusti (1992) writes about the development of the "multisystems approach" and the evolution of this approach from many reformed theoretical premises. Similarly, family-centered officials must seek to reform existing theories that do not conform to the ten case-selection targeting criteria described here. Education and training will need to begin in baccalaureate-level and master's-level social work programs and extend to agency-based training. Child welfare sequences, direct practice, and macro education tracks must begin to expose students to the ten targeting criteria by way of course content and curricular aims. Pecora (1990) provides a basis by which human service education programs can begin to revise their administration curricula so that students become acclimated to the design of family preservation services.

Practice

The practice implications of the ten targeting criteria are many. For instance, successful implementation of the targeting criteria will require that family-centered programmers (a) profile the type of workers they desire, (b) seek professional support and endorsement of their programs, and (c) build and deliver culturally competent program models. Service delivery methods, agency practices, and the overall culture of the program must be conducive to the implementation of the ten targeting criteria. In fact, the most often cited primary obstacle to program reforms is failure to support and adopt new ways of doing things (Melton, 1997). Kamerman and Kahn (1993) have also summarized some barriers to reform and have made specific recommendations for the implementation of alternative models. If the ten targeting criteria are to be implemented, programs will be forced to employ workers who have been indoctrinated in the ten principles and workers whose value and belief systems support the ten targeting objectives. Moreover, family-centered program managers need to seek contracts and endorsements from only those collateral agencies that subscribe to the targeting principles and objectives. Program managers will not want to enter into contracts with referring agencies that will not conform to the ten targeting criteria. Finally, because the targeting criteria seek to serve those populations that are traditionally underserved and those clients who are most overrepresented in the child welfare system (e.g., children of color and their families), family-centered programs will have to operate from culturally specific program models. Culturally specific intervention is necessary because research has shown that differences exist regarding the ways that racial groups communicate, function, raise their children, and view problems (Derezotes & Snowden, 1990). In some cases, the delivery of culturally specific services will require that programs throw out their old models entirely and institute new interventions that are completely culturally driven (e.g., located in indigenous neighborhoods, run by indigenous communities, implemented by workers trained in the culture of their client group). Stevenson, Cheung, and Leung (1992) provide a review of ethnic-sensitive models of intervention.

Policy

Recent critical changes in federal policy have implications for the ten targeting criteria described here. In family preservation we have recently witnessed the reissuance of the Family Preservation and Support Services Program (FPSSP) under the new Adoption and Safe Families Act of 1997—Promoting Safe and Stable Families Program (PSSFP). Although the continuation of the programs supported by FPSSP (now under the auspices of PSSFP) is good news, the new legislation will require that states beef up their adoption and reunification efforts while simultaneously maintaining family preservation and support programs. What makes this challenge even more difficult is that these new directives were accompanied by only a modest increase in funding. Some family-centered scholars (e.g., Mannes, 1998) have observed that the new legislation places family preservation and reunification services in precarious positions. Mannes (1998) raises the critical question of what the philosophical orientation of the new programs (programs that seek to balance the many objectives of PSSFP) will be, and whether they will be truly family centered.

The ten targeting criteria described in this chapter will require a continued policy emphasis on family preservation and family support. The implementation of the targeting criteria will require the help of advocacy groups who are very vocal about the needs of the children and families whom the criteria seek to identify. Lobbying for national and local support will be required if the ten targeting criteria are to be adopted. Significant advocacy and lobbying should be carried out at the local level. Family-centered programmers and practitioners will need to galvanize support for the targeting criteria. In fact, the advocacy role of direct-service workers is extremely critical but often unrealized (Herbert & Mould, 1992). Finally, because PSSFP will probably result in greater limits on funding family preservation programs, it will be even more imperative that family-centered officials get a clear perspective on the target of these precious services. Likewise, because the pendulum appears to be swinging to the back end of services, as opposed to the front end (namely, prevention efforts), family-centered officials will need to become even more diligent in marketing services.

Research

The ten targeting criteria described here have tremendous implications for family-centered research. Many researchers have called for new or revised approaches to research in family-centered services. For example, Blythe (1990) believes that new research should involve the "personal scientist" (i.e., a person who can engage in practice and research simultaneously). Wells and Freer (1994) assert that family-centered programs must make greater use of qualitative methods of inquiry. Bath and Haapala (1994) counter all the recent, negative commentary being directed at family preservation programs by calling for more small-scale evaluations that can better handle the internal validity issues that were contained in the California (Yuan et al., 1990), New Jersey (Feldman, 1991), and Illinois (Schuerman et al., 1993) studies.

The obvious conclusion readers may gather from this chapter is that the recommended ten targeting criteria will need to undergo extensive research. Although certain criteria have been tested, the fit of all ten criteria will need to be proven. Demonstration projects that make use of the above three research suggestions may be appropriate in the early testing of the ten targeting criteria.

□ □ □

As child welfare workers move into a new era of family-centered service delivery, it behooves officials to continue to scrutinize themselves and to engage in dialogue regarding program improvements. This chapter has demonstrated that family-centered programs are indeed asking questions about the need to reshape various aspects of programming, including the measure of program success (placement avoidance or improved family functioning), research and evaluation methods, programs' ability to truly protect children from abusive parents, and the limitations and insufficiency of services. However, this chapter has attempted to demonstrate that the more fundamental problem of "targeting" must be the first focus of all dialogue concerning program reform. A ten-point targeting plan has been developed and accompanied by suggestions on how the plan might be successfully implemented.

REFERENCES

Adams, P. (1994). Marketing social change: The case of family preservation. *Children and Youth Services Review, 16* (5, 6), 417–31.

Ahsan, N. (1996). The family preservation and support services program. *Future of Children, 6* (3), 157–60.

Alexander, J. F., & Parsons, B. V. (1982). *Functional family therapy.* Monterey, CA: Brooks/Cole.

Barth, R. P. (1996). The juvenile court and dependency cases. *Future of Children, 6* (3), 100–110.

Barth, R. P., Snowden, L. R., Broeck, E., Clancy, T., Jordan, C., & Barusch, A. S. (1986). Contributors to reunification or permanent out-of-home care for physically abused children. *Journal of Social Service Research, 92* (2, 3), 31–45.

Barton, C., Alexander, J. F., Waldron, H., Turner, C. W., & Warburton, J. (1985). Generalizing treatment effects of functional therapy: Three replications. *American Journal of Family Therapy, 13,* 16–26.

Bath, H. I., & Haapala, D. A. (1993). Intensive family preservation services with abused and neglected children: An examination of group differences. *Child Abuse and Neglect, 17* (2), 213–25.

Bath, H. I., & Haapala, D. A. (1994). Family preservation services: What does the outcome research really tell us? *Social Service Review, 68* (3), 386–404.

Berg, I. K. (1994). *Family-based services: A solution-focused approach.* New York: Norton.

Berliner, L. (1993). Is family preservation in the best interests of children? *Journal of Interpersonal Violence, 8* (4), 556–57.

Bernard, L. D. (1992). The dark side of family preservation. *Affilia—Journal of Women and Social Work, 7* (2), 156–59.

Billingsley, A. (1968). *Black families in white America.* Englewood Cliffs, NJ: Prentice Hall.

Blythe, B. J. (1990). Applying practice research methods in intensive family preservation services. In J. K. Whittaker, J. Kinney, E. M. Tracy, & C. Booth (Eds.), *Reaching high-risk families: Intensive family preservation in human services* (pp. 147–64). New York: Aldine de Gruyter.

Boehm, B. (1962). The community and the social agency define neglect. *Child welfare, 61* (1), 10–16.

Boehm, B. (1968). Protective services for neglected children. *Social work practice, proceedings of the National Conference on Social Welfare, 95th annual forum.* New York: Columbia University Press.

Bribitzer, M. P., & Verdieck, M. J. (1988). Home-based, family-centered intervention: Evaluation of a foster care treatment program. *Child Welfare, 67* (3), 255–66.

Bryce, M. E. (1978). *Client and worker comparison of agency organizational design and treatment techniques in an intensive home-based social service program for families.* Unpublished master's thesis, University of Iowa, Iowa City.

Budde, S. (1995). *Understanding the targeting problem in family preservation services: A study of child protection decision making.* Unpublished doctoral dissertation, University of Chicago, Chicago.

Burt, M. R., & Pittman, K. J. (1985). *Testing the social safety net.* Washington, DC: Urban Institute Press.

Campbell, M. (1991). Child at risk: How different are children on child abuse registers? *British Journal of Social Work, 21* (3), 259–75.

Cimmarusti, R. A. (1992). Family preservation practice based on a multisystems approach. *Child Welfare, 71* (3), 241–56.

Close, M. (1983). Child welfare and people of color: Denial of equal access. *Social Work Research and Abstracts, 19* (4), 13–20.

Cole, E. S. (1995). Becoming family centered: Child welfare's challenge. *Families in Society, 76,* 163–72.

Cowger, D. D. (1992). Assessment of client strengths. In D. Saleebey (Ed.), *The strengths perspective in social work practice* (pp. 139–47). New York: Longman.

Dalgheish, L., & Drew, E. (1989). The relationship of child abuse indicators to the assessment of perceived risk and the court's decision to separate. *Child Abuse and Neglect, 13,* 491–506.

Daro, D., & Cohn, A. H. (1988). Child maltreatment evaluation efforts: What have we learned? In G. T. Hotaling, D. Finkelhor, J. T. Kirkpatrick, & M. A. Strauss (Eds.), *Coping with family violence: Research and policy perspectives* (pp. 275–87). Newbury Park, CA: Sage.

Day, D. (1979). *The adoption of black children.* Lexington, MA: Lexington Books.

Deccio, G., & Horner, W. C. (1994). High-risk neighborhoods and high-risk families: Replication research related to the human ecology of child maltreatment. *Journal of Social Service Research, 18* (3, 4), 123–37.

DeJong, P., & Miller, S. D. (1995). How to interview for client strengths. *Social Work, 40* (6), 729–36.

Denby, R. W. (1995). *Targeting families for family preservation services: The decision-making process.* Unpublished doctoral dissertation, Ohio State University, Columbus.

Denby, R. W., Curtis, C. M., & Alford, K. A. (1998). Family preservation services and special populations: The invisible target. *Families in Society, 79* (1), 3–14.

DePanfilis, D., & Scannapieco, M. (1994). Assessing the safety of children at risk of maltreatment: Decision-making models. *Child Welfare, 73* (3), 229–45.

Derezotes, D. S., & Snowden, L. R. (1990). Cultural factors in the intervention of child maltreatment. *Child and Adolescent Social Work Journal, 7* (2), 161–75.

Dodson, J. E. (1983). *An Afro-centric manual: Toward a nondeficit perspective in services to families and children.* Knoxville: University of Tennessee, Office of Continuing Education, College of Social Work.

Dore, M. M. (1993). Family preservation and poor families: When "Homebuilding" is not enough. *Families in Society: The Journal of Contemporary Human Services, 74* (9), 545–56.

Doueck, H. J., Bronson, D. E., & Levine, M. (1992). Evaluating risk assessment implementation in child protection: Issues for consideration. *Child Abuse and Neglect, 16,* 637–46.

Doueck, H. J., Levine, M., & Bronson, D. E. (1993). Risk assessment in child protective services: An evaluation of the child at risk field system. *Journal of Interpersonal Violence, 18* (4), 446–67.

Drake, B., Berfield, M., D'Gama, L. A., Gallagher, J. P., Gibbs, M., Henry, S., & Lin, D. (1995). Implementing the family preservation program: Feedback from focus groups with consumers and providers of services. *Child and Adolescent Social Work Journal, 12* (5), 391–410.

Eamon, M. K. (1994). Poverty and placement outcomes of intensive family preservation services. *Child and Adolescent Social Work Journal, 11* (5), 349–61.

Early, B. P., & Hawkins, M. J. (1994). Opportunity and risks in emerging family policy: An analysis of family preservation legislation. *Children and Youth Services Review, 16* (5, 6), 309–18.

Feldman, L. (1990). Target population definition. In Y. Yuan & M. Rivest (Eds.), *Preserving families,* (pp. 16–38). Newbury Park, CA: Sage.

Feldman, L. H. (1991a). Evaluating the impact of family preservation services in New Jersey. In K. Wells & D. E. Biegel (Eds.), *Family preservation services: Research and evaluation* (pp. 47–71). Newbury Park, CA: Sage.

Feldman, L. H. (1991b). *Assessing the effectiveness of family preservation services in New Jersey within an ecological context* (Bureau of Research, Evaluation and Quality Assurance). Trenton: New Jersey Division of Youth and Family Services.

Finch, S. J., & Fanshel, D. (1985). Testing the equality of discharge patterns in foster care. *Social Work Research and Abstracts, 21* (3), 3–10.

Finch, S. J., Fanshel, D., & Grundy, J. F. (1986). Factors associated with the discharge of children from foster care. *Social Work Research and Abstracts, 22* (1), 10–18.

Froelich, P. K. (1992). *An analysis of change in placements and investigations associated with home based services.* Pierre: South Dakota Department of Social Services.

Gambrill, E. (1994). Does worker discretion in implementing agency policy compromise attainment of agency objectives? Yes. In E. Gambrill & T. J. Stein (Eds.), *Controversial issues in child welfare* (pp. 122–28; 133–35). Boston: Allyn and Bacon.

Garbarino, J., & Scherman, D. (1980). High-risk neighborhoods and high-risk families: The human ecology of child maltreatment. *Child Development, 51* (1), 188–98.

Gaudin, J. M. Jr. (1993). *Child neglect: A guide for intervention.* Washington, DC: U.S. Department of Health and Human Services, Administration for Children and Families.

Gaudin, J. M. Jr., Wodarski, J. S., Arkinson, M. K., & Avery, L. S. (1990). Remedying child neglect: Effectiveness of social network intervention. *Journal of Applied Social Sciences, 15* (1), 97–123.

Gelles, R. J. (1996). *The book of David: How preserving families can cost children's lives.* New York: Basic Books.

Graham, F. (1978). *A survey of caseworkers: Criteria for decision-making in abuse and neglect cases.* Trenton, NJ: Division of Youth and Family Services.

Gray, S. S., & Nybell, L. M. (1990). Issues in African American family preservation. *Child Welfare, 69,* 513–23.

Gustavasson, N. S., & Segal, E. A. (1994). *Critical issues in child welfare.* Thousand Oaks, CA: Sage.

Hamilton, J. (1992). *Child abuse: Factors influencing decision-making by social workers.* Unpublished doctoral dissertation, Yeshiva University, New York.

Hartman, A. (1993). Family preservation under attack. *Social Work, 38,* 509–12.

Hayes, J. R., & Joseph, J. A. (1985). *Home-based family centered project evaluation.* Columbus, OH: Metropolitan Human Services Commission.

Heneghan, A. M., Horwitz, S. M., & Leventhal, H. M. (1996). *Evaluating intensive family preservation programs: A methodologic review.* Unpublished manuscript, Albert Einstein College of Medicine, Bronx.

Herbert, M. D., & Mould, J. W. (1992). The advocacy role in public child welfare. *Child Welfare, 71* (2), 114–30.

Hodges, V. G. (1991). Providing culturally sensitive intensive family preservation services to ethnic minority families. In E. M. Tracy, D. A. Haapala, J. Kinney, & P. J. Pecora (Eds.), *Intensive family preservation services: An instructional sourcebook* (pp. 95–116). Cleveland: Case Western Reserve University, Mandel School of Applied Social Sciences.

Hutchinson, J. (1982). *A comparative analysis of the costs of substitute care and family based services.* Oakdale, IA: National Resource Center on Family Based Services.

Hutchinson, J. R., & Nelson, K. E. (1985). How public agencies can provide family-centered services. *Social Casework: The Journal of Contemporary Social Work, 66* (6), 367–71.

Ingrassia, M., & McCormick, J. (1994, April). Why leave children with bad parents? *Newsweek*, 52–58.

Jenkins, S., Diamond, B. E., Flanzraich, M., Gibson, J. W., Hendricks, J., & Marshood, N. (1983). Ethnic differentials in foster care placements. *Social Work Research and Abstracts, 19* (4), 41–45.

Johnson, W. (1994). Will computer-based expert systems improve decisions made about children? In E. Gambril & T. J. Stein (Eds.), *Controversial issues in child welfare* (pp. 114–21). Needham Heights, MA: Allyn and Bacon.

Jones, E. D., & McCurdy, K. (1992). The links between types of maltreatment and demographic characteristics of children. *Child Abuse and Neglect, 16,* 201–215.

Kamerman, S. B., & Kahn, A. J. (1993). If CPS is driving child welfare—where do we go from here? *Public Welfare, 51* (1), 41–43.

Katz, L., & Robinson, C. (1991). Foster care drift: A risk-assessment matrix. *Child Welfare, 70* (3), 347–58.

Kaye, E. (1997). Analysis of states' FY96 annual progress and services reports: The family preservation and family support implementation study (executive summary). *Prevention Report, 1,* 15–16.

Kinney, J., Haapala, D., & Booth, C. (1991). *Keeping families together: The Homebuilders model.* New York: Aldine De Gruyter.

Kinney, J., Haapala, D., Booth, C., & Leavitt, S. (1990). The Homebuilders model. In J. K. Whittaker, J. Kinney, E. M. Tracy, and C. Booth (Eds.), *Reaching high-risk families: Intensive family preservation in human services* (pp. 31–64). New York: Aldine de Gruyter.

Landsman, M. J., Richardson, B., Clem, M., Harper, C., Schuldt, T., & Nelson, K. (1993). *An evaluation of Families First of Minnesota.* Iowa City, IA: Institute for Social and Economic Development.

Lantz, B. K. (1985). Keeping troubled teens at home. *Children Today, 14* (3), 8–12.

Leeds, S. (1984). *Evaluation of Nebraska's Intensive Services Project.* Iowa City: University of Iowa, National Resource Center on Family Based Services.

Lindsey, D. (1994). Family preservation and child protection: Striking a balance. *Children and Youth Services Review, 16* (5, 6), 279–94.

Lloyd, J. C., & Bryce, M. E. (1984). *Placement prevention and reunification: A handbook for the family-centered service practitioner.* Iowa City: University of Iowa School of Social Work, National Resource Center on Family Based Services.

MacDonald, G. D. (1992). Accepting parental responsibility: "Future Questioning" as a means to avoid foster home placement of children. *Child Welfare, 71* (1), 3–17.

MacDonald, H. (1994). The ideology of "family preservation." *Public Interest, 115,* 45–60.

Magura, S., & Moses, B. S. (1984). Clients as evaluators in child protective services. *Child Welfare, 63* (2), 99–112.

Maluccio, A., Pine, B. A., & Warsh, R. (1994). Protecting children by preserving their families. *Children and Youth Services Review, 16* (5, 6), 295–307.

Mannes, M. (1993). Family preservation: A professional reform movement. *Journal of Sociology and Social Welfare, 20* (3), 5–24.

Mannes, M. (1998). Promoting safe and stable families: Is it a renewed—or a new—Title IV-B, Subpart 2? *Prevention Report, 1,* 2–4.

Maybanks, S., & Bryce, M. (1979). *Home-based services for children and families: Policy, practice, and research.* Springfield, IL: Charles C Thomas.

McCroskey, J., & Meezan, W. (1993). *Outcomes of home-based services: Effects on family functioning, child behavior, and child placement.* Los Angeles: University of Southern California School of Social Work.

McMurtry, S. L., Gwat, Y. L., & Lie, G. Y. (1992). Differential exit rates of minority children in foster care. *Social Work Research and Abstracts, 28* (1), 42–48.

McRoy, R. G. (1994). Attachment and racial identity issues: Implications for child placement decision-making. *Journal of Multicultural Social Work, 3* (3), 59–74.

Meddin, B. J. (1984). Criteria for placement decisions in protective services. *Child Welfare, 63* (4), 367–73.

Melton, G. B. (1997). Why don't the knuckleheads use common sense? In S. W. Henggeler, A. B. Albert, et al. (Eds.), *Innovative approaches for difficult to treat populations* (pp. 351–70). Washington, DC: American Psychiatric Press.

Miller, L. B., & Fisher, T. (1992). Some obstacles to the effective investigation and registration of children at risk—issues gleaned from a worker's perspective. *Journal of Social Work Practice, 6* (2), 129–40.

Morisey, P. G. (1990). Black children in foster care. In S. Logan, E. M. Freeman, & R. G. McRoy, *Social work practices with black families: A culturally specific perspective* (pp. 133–47). White Plains, NY: Longman.

National Association of Black Social Workers. (1992). *Preserving African American families: Research and action beyond the rhetoric.* Detroit, MI: Author.

National Black Child Development Institute. (1989). *Who will care when parents can't? A study of black children in foster care.* Washington, DC: Author.

Nelson, K. E. (1994). Do services to preserve the family place children at unnecessary risk? No. In E. Gambril & T. J. Stein (Eds.), *Controversial issues in child welfare* (pp. 67–71). Needham Heights, MA: Allyn & Bacon.

Nelson, K. E., Landsman, M. J., & Deutelbaum, W. (1990). Three models of family-centered placement prevention services. *Child Welfare, 69* (1), 3–21.

Nelson, K. E., Landsman, M., Tyler, M., & Richardson, B. (1996). Examining the length of service and cost-effectiveness of intensive family service. In National Resource Center for Family Centered Practice (Ed.), *Research Exchange* (pp. 13–17). Iowa City, IA: National Resource Center for Family Centered Practice.

Olsen, L. J. (1982). Predicting the permanency status of children in foster care. *Social Work Research and Abstracts, 18* (1), 9–20.

Pearson. C. L., & King, P. A. (1987). *Intensive family services: Evaluation of foster care prevention in Maryland: Final report.* Baltimore: Maryland Department of Human Resources.

Pecora, P. J. (1990). Designing and managing family preservation services: Implications for human services administration curricula. In J. K. Whittaker, J. Kinney, E. M. Tracy, & C. Booth (Eds.), *Reaching high-risk families: Intensive family preservation in human services* (pp. 127–45). New York: Aldine de Gruyter.

Pecora, P. J. (1991). Investigating allegations of child maltreatment: The strengths and limitations of current risk assessment systems. *Child and Youth Services, 15* (2), 73–92.

Pecora, P. J. (1994). Are intensive family preservation services effective? Yes. In E. Gambrill & T. J. Stein (Eds.), *Controversial issues in child welfare* (pp. 290–303). Needham Heights, MA: Allyn & Bacon.

Pecora, P. J., Bartlome, J. A., Magana, V. L., & Sperry, C. K. (1991). How consumers view intensive family preservation services. In M. W. Fraser, P. J. Pecora, & D. A. Haapala (Eds.), *Families in crisis: The impact of intensive family preservation services* (pp. 225–71). Hawthorne, NY: Aldine de Gruyter.

Pelton, L. H. (1992). A functional approach to reorganizing family and child welfare interventions. *Children and Youth Services Review, 14* (3–4), 289–303.

Pelton, L. H. (1994). Is poverty a key contributor to child maltreatment? Yes. In E. Gambrill & T. J. Stein (Eds.), *Controversial issues in child welfare* (pp. 16–22, 26–28). Needham Heights, MA: Allyn & Bacon.

Phillips, M. H., Shyne, A. W., Sherman, E. A., & Haring, B. L. (1971). *Factors associated with placement decisions in child welfare.* New York: Child Welfare League of America.

Pinderhughes, E. E. (1991). The delivery of child welfare services to African American clients. *American Journal of Orthopsychiatry, 61,* 599–605.

Reid, W. J., Kagan, R. M., & Scholsberg, S. B. (1988). Prevention of placement: Critical factors in program success. *Child Welfare, 67* (1), 25–36.

Rossi, P. H. (1992). Strategies for evaluation. *Children and Youth Services Review, 14,* 167–91.

Rossi, P. H. (1994). Reviewing progress in assessing the impact of family preservation services. *Children and Youth Services Review, 16,* 453–57.

Rzepnicki, T. L. (1994). Are intensive family preservation services effective? No. In E. Gambrill & T. J. Stein (Eds.), *Controversial issues in child welfare* (pp. 59–65, 71–72). Needham Heights, MA: Allyn & Bacon.

Saleebey, D. (Ed). (1992). *The strengths perspective in social work practice.* New York: Longman.

Schuerman, J. R. (1994). Will computer-based expert systems improve decisions made about children? Yes. In E. Gambrill & T. J. Stein (Eds.), *Controversial issues in child welfare* (pp. 109–12, 120–21). Boston: Allyn & Bacon.

Schuerman, J. R., Rzepnicki, T., & Littell, J. (1994). *Putting families first: An experiment in family preservation.* New York: Aldine de Gruyter.

Schuerman, J. R., Rzepnicki, T., Littell, J., & Budde, S. (1992). Implementation issues. *Children and Youth Services Review, 14,* 193–206.

Schuerman, J. R., Rzepnicki, T., Littell, J., & Chak, A. (1993). *Evaluation of the Illinois Family First Placement Prevention Program: Final report.* Chicago: University of Chicago, Chapin Hall Center for Children.

Seaburg, J. R., & Tolley, E. S. (1986). Predictors of the length of stay in foster care. *Social Work Research and Abstracts, 22* (3), 11–17.

Seader, M. B. (1994). Do services to preserve the family place children at unnecessary risk? Yes. In E. Gambrill & T. J. Stein (Eds.), *Controversial issues in child welfare* (pp. 59–65, 71–72). Needham Heights, MA: Allyn & Bacon.

Showell, W. H. (1985). *Biennial report of CSD's Intensive Family Services.* Salem: Oregon Children's Services Division.

Showell, W. H., Hartley, R., & Allen, M. (1988). *Outcomes of Oregon's Family Therapy Program: A descriptive study of 999 families.* Salem: Oregon Department of Human Resources.

Spaid, W. M., Fraser, M. W., & Lewis, R. E. (1991). Changes in family functioning: Is participation in intensive family preservation services correlated with changes in attitudes or behavior? In M. W. Fraser, P. J. Pecora, & D. A. Haapala, *Families in crisis: Findings from the family-based intensive treatment project* (pp. 131–48). Hawthorne, NY: Aldine de Gruyter.

Stehno, S. (1990). The elusive continuum of child welfare services: Implications for minority children and youths. *Child Welfare, 69,* 551–62.

Stein, T. J. (1994). Does state discretion in implementing federal policy compromise attainment of policy objectives? Yes. In E. Gambrill & T. J. Stein (Eds.), *Controversial issues in child welfare* (pp. 199–203, 208–10). Needham Heights, MA: Allyn & Bacon.

Stevenson, K. M., Cheung, K. M., & Leung, P. (1992). A new approach to training child protective services workers for ethnically sensitive practice. *Child Welfare, 71* (4), 291–305.

Szykula, S. A., & Fleischman, M. J. (1985). Reducing out-of-home placements of abused children: Two controlled field studies. *Child Abuse and Neglect, 9,* 277–83.

Tavantzis, T. N., Tavantzis, M., Brown, L. G., & Rohrbaugh, M. (1985). Home-based structural family therapy for delinquents at risk of placement. In M. P. Mirkin and S. Koman (Eds.), *Handbook of adolescent and family therapy* (pp. 69–88). New York: Gardner Press.

Thieman, A. A., & Dail, P. W. (1992). Family preservation services: Problems of measurement and assessment of risk. *Family Relations, 41* (2), 186–91.

Tracy, E. M. (1990). Identifying social support resources of at-risk families. *Social Work, 35* (3), 252–58.

Tracy, E. M. (1991). Defining the target population for family preservation services. In K. Wells & D. E. Biegel (Eds.), *Family preservation services: Research and evaluation* (pp. 47–71). Newbury Park, CA: Sage.

University Associates. (1993). *Evaluation of Michigan's Families First Program: Summary report.* Lansing, MI: Author.

W. K. Kellogg Foundation. (1995). *Families for kids of color: A special report on challenges and opportunities.* Battle Creek, MI: Author.

Wald, M. S. (1988). Family preservation: Are we moving too fast? *Public Welfare, 46* (3), 33–38.

Wald, M. S., & Woolverton, M. (1990). Risk assessment: The emperor's new clothes? *Child Welfare, 69* (6), 483–511.

Walton, E. (1997). Enhancing investigative decisions in child welfare: An exploratory use of intensive family preservation services. *Child Welfare, 76,* 447–61.

Walton, E. (1998). In-home family-focused reunification: A six-year follow-up of a successful experiment. *Social Work Research, 22,* 205–14.

Walton, E., & Denby, R. W. (1997). Targeting families to receive intensive family preservation services: Assessing the use of imminent risk of placement as a service criterion. *Journal of Family Preservation, 2* (2), 53–70.

Walton, E., Fraser, M. W., Lewis, R. E., Pecora, P. J., & Walton, W. K. (1993). In-home family-focused reunification: An experimental study. *Child Welfare,* 72 (5), 473–87.

Waterhouse, L., & Carnie, J. (1992). Assessing child protection risk. *British Journal of Social Work, 22* (1), 47–60.

Weick, A., Rapp, C., Sullivan, W. P., & Kisthardt, W. (1989). A strengths perspective for social work practice. *Social Work, 34,* 350–54.

Wells, K., & Biegel, D. E. (1990). Intensive family preservation services: A research agenda for the 1990s. *Final report: Intensive Family Preservation Services Research Conference.* (Proceedings of the Intensive Family Preservation Services Research Conference, Cleveland, Ohio, September 25–26, 1989). Iowa City: University of Iowa, School of Social Work, National Resource Center on Family Based Services.

Wells, K., & Biegel, D. E. (1992). Intensive family preservation services research: Current status and future agenda. *Social Work Research and Abstracts, 28* (1), 21–27.

Wells, K., & Freer, R. (1994). Reading between the lines: The case for qualitative research in intensive family preservation services. *Children and Youth Services Review, 16* (5, 6), 399–415.

Wells, K., & Tracy, E. (1996). Reorienting intensive family preservation services in relation to public child welfare practice. *Child Welfare, 75,* 667–92.

Whittaker, J. K., & Tracy, E. M. (1990). Family preservation services and education for social work practice: Stimulus and response. In J. K. Whittaker, J. Kinney, E. M. Tracy, and C. Booth (Eds.), *Reaching high-risk families: Intensive family preservation in human services* (pp. 31–64). New York: Aldine de Gruyter.

Whittaker, J. K., & Tracy, E. M. (1991). Social network intervention in intensive family-based preventive services. *Prevention in Human Services, 9* (1), 175–192.

Yuan, Y., McDonald, W., Wheeler, C., Struckman-Johnson, D., & Rivest, M. (1990). *Evaluation of AB 1562 In-Home Care Demonstration Projects: Final report.* Sacramento, CA: Office of Child Abuse Prevention.

Yuan, Y., & Struckman-Johnson, D. L. (1991). Placement outcomes for neglected children with prior placements in family preservation programs. In K. Wells & D. E. Biegel (Eds), *Family preservation services: Research and evaluation* (pp. 92–118). Newbury Park, CA: Sage.

Zuravin, S. J., Orme, J. G., & Hegar, R. L. (1994). Factors predicting an empirical investigation using ordinal probit regression. *Social Work Research, 18* (3), 131–38.

Zuravin, S. J., & Taylor, R. (1987). The ecology of child maltreatment: Identifying and characterizing high-risk neighborhoods. *Child Welfare, 60* (6), 497–506.

11 Walking Our Talk in the Neighborhoods

Going Beyond Lip Service in Service Delivery Improvement

KIM APPLE   DANIELE PRICE
SUE BERNSTEIN   KEITH ROBERTS
KATRINA FOGG   ROBERT SMITH
LARRIE FOGG   TASHA STEELE
DAVID HAAPALA   KATHY STRAND
EDITH JOHNSON   EDWIN TRENT
RICHARD JOHNSON   MARGARET TRENT
JILL KINNEY   VENESSA TRENT
JANICE NITTOLI   RON VIGNEC

REASONS WE NEED NEW APPROACHES TO HUMAN SERVICES DELIVERY

The late 1990s were difficult times in human services. Both workers and recipients were dissatisfied with the processes and outcomes of many of the models used to deliver services. Programs were too expensive. They didn't seem culturally relevant. All too often, models could not document that they had achieved the results they claimed. Taxpayers were often frustrated. Human services workers were often discouraged. Sometimes we felt overwhelmed by the problems we faced.

We searched for new models and had difficulty finding them. We did find some models that people liked. When we tried to replicate them, some groups welcomed them with open arms; others become defensive of their turf. Political battles ensued, taking valuable time and energy away from actually helping people. Attempts to improve the situation by "reforming" the health care and welfare systems may have benefits in the long run, but in the short term such efforts added to our feelings of helplessness, confusion, and vulnerability.

The problems of those we wished to help were getting worse, and our methods were not as effective as we would have liked. The funding streams were getting smaller; we had to do more with less. The polarization of solutions was increasing: some professionals advocated jail time and orphanages, and others continued to insist on the rights of biological parents to raise their children however they saw fit. We had to learn to deal with conflicts and move ahead. We had to do better at using all the resources available in our communities. Ultimately, we are all striving as individuals and communities to shift from blaming to helping, and to achieve a true, flexible, and mutually supportive collaboration.

Promising Directions

We were near consensus about promising ways to accomplish more with fewer resources. Certain buzzwords found their way into human services language, words that Charles Bruner called a "service mantra." They included such concepts as "empowerment" and "enhancing capacity." Principles included building on strengths; taking a holistic approach; individual tailoring; decision-making partnerships; setting short-term, specific goals; and emphasizing certain worker characteristics such as compassion and congruence (Kinney, Strand, Hagerup, & Bruner, 1994).

Some of the trendiest buzzwords were related to the shifting roles of professionals and to capitalizing on the existing strengths of neighborhood residents to get them involved in self-help, mutual aid, and mutual support. Pioneers such as Frank Reissman had put those concepts into practice for decades, but most of us were still struggling to figure out how to bring them alive in our work.

Purpose of This Chapter

The purpose of this chapter is to begin going "beyond the buzzwords" in terms of specifying issues and alternatives, to raise awareness of challenges and solutions, and to provide some concrete examples for the ways partnerships can work.

REASONS FOR FORMING PROFESSIONAL/NATURAL HELPER PARTNERSHIPS

Professionals and bureaucrats alone have not been able to solve problems facing our families. We had to include more people, more skills, and more resolve at more levels if we were going to make a difference.

Limitations of Overreliance on Professional and Bureaucratic Solutions

Overreliance on professional, formal agency, and system solutions can fail to create strategies that are fully relevant to and congruent with the needs of specific neighborhoods because those in charge may lack information and understanding. Overreliance can also be expensive. In the past, professionals' salaries were higher than we could afford, if an adequate amount of help was provided. Moreover, dollars spent for professionals sometimes ended up increasing the financial stability of people and organizations outside the community, rather than adding to local economic development.

Overreliance on professionals can send the message to community people that they cannot help themselves and must be rescued, thus attacking rather than enhancing their sense of self-efficacy. It can give people in the community implicit permission to wait until the professional provides the service or until there is money for the professional. The strategy can also create the belief that if help is successful, it is because the professional is good, and if the help doesn't work, it is because the recipient is inadequate, further demeaning the recipient's sense of self-efficacy.

Common Constraints on the Way We View Professionals and Natural Helpers

We often place unnecessary constraints on roles, making both professionals and natural helpers less effective. We usually think of professionals as addressing intrapsychic problems. Neighborhood workers have been assigned to "prevention," or problems that aren't too severe. They are regarded as appropriate chiefly for concrete issues, such as building speed bumps, getting streetlights installed, or getting drug houses closed.

Professional efforts to solve intrapsychic problems can often be hampered by conditions such as poverty and homelessness. However, laypeople often counsel one another on everything from marital problems and child rearing to thoughts of suicide. Just as we have learned about the irrevocable links between physical and mental health, we need to see distinctions between prevention and intervention as artificial. The distinctions we make between concrete services and psychological services are also artificial. And the distinctions between the types of help that require graduate degrees and the kind that can be done by friends and neighbors are, in many cases, arbitrary.

In fact, all the problems are interrelated. Residents and community workers and agency staff have different perspectives on the causes and resolutions of difficulties. We will all be more effective if we can share our perspectives and expertise to develop new strategies that will probably be more creative than any we could develop solely within our own frameworks.

REASONS WE NEED NATURAL HELPERS

The human services "system" and the community need natural helpers because they can provide a fresh outlook on helping in a particular community, because they can help us to learn to do better, and because they can achieve more with professionals' help than they can without it.

Strengths of Natural Helpers

Natural helpers understand their neighborhoods. They understand their own culture, and generally other cultures in the neighborhood, better than people who don't live there. They are usually more committed to resolving the issues because the challenges affect them personally. They generally have more trust and status within the neighborhood than do most outsiders.

Natural helpers are more likely than outsiders to hear about problems before they become so severe that intensive intervention is the only option. They are more likely to be available twenty-four hours a day to those they support, and this can decrease the possibility of people being harmed. They can be in a better position than most professionals to provide long-term support because they live within the community. They have different and necessary skills for helping. They are often more familiar with the intricacies of public bureaucracies than many professionals because their personal welfare has often depended on this understanding. They know which strategies work and which do not in their neighborhoods. They have mastered the ability to function in conditions that may be physically and emotionally frightening to professionals, sometimes to the degree that professionals refuse to enter or cannot function well.

Natural helpers are more likely to provide support in the recipient's natural environment. They can support families who have been or would be unable or unwilling to receive services in more traditional settings. This can allow for more effective and comprehensive monitoring of child safety. The monitoring is more likely to include all family members and, possibly, members of their support networks. Observation of participants in their natural environment allows for a more accurate and complete assessment. Family members, caseworkers, and other service providers know that helpers have the opportunity to observe firsthand family situations, problems, and progress on goals. This can increase helpers' credibility. The helper has continuous opportunities to model the use of new skills in real situations, and his or her presence eliminates the need for the recipient to transfer learning from one setting, such as an office, to another, such as a home.

Common Activities of Natural Helpers

As policymakers begin considering a shift from office-based talk therapy to neighborhood transformation, we can easily present the idea of natural helpers or indigenous workers as a new one. In fact, people have been helping one another before college degrees existed, before licensing existed, since people existed. Throughout time, even people with few resources have reached out to help one another. Table 11.1 lists common natural helper activities taking place in most of our communities now, usually off the radar screen and separate from the formal helping system.

Ways Natural Helpers Can Help Professionals

Some neighborhood helpers wish to work more closely with professionals. At the same time, they would like to raise the professionals' awareness of the best ways to be helpful. The following are some of their ideas.

Professionals need to keep thinking about communication, cooperation, and service to people in the community. They need to build, and keep, long-term positive relationships with kids and families in order to have a positive impact in the larger neighborhood. To build such relationships, they will need to value the gifts and resources that community members already have and to think of ways to encourage, support, recognize, and use them.

Being genuine and earnest is worth a lot. Professionals' good intentions can go a long way. They need to remember, though, that it will take time to develop relationships. They can't assume that once they have a few relationships, no further maintenance is required.

It would help if professionals would stop "putting themselves above other people" and work on building connections between and among us all. They need to realize the context for behavior, and really be present. If they get invited to private homes, they should go.

Professionals need to do more looking at an individual or family within the larger context of other people and the physical community. Some families move around but may still retain connections within the community, so it is important to realize that they may still be considered part of the community. If professionals are helping a family, they should seek suggestions from the family about who else might help.

Professionals also would benefit from understanding the cultural context and using that information to make culturally appropriate suggestions when they offer advice. One way of doing things will not work for everyone. Also, situations can frequently change. No one should allow their perceptions of the community and individuals within it to freeze in time. The situation changes and people change.

People in the community often need "translators" to explain how society's formal systems work—schools, Child Protective Services, and courts. Professionals can function as those translators. This may mean having to learn for themselves how things work, keeping in mind that even larger systems have variations that need to be understood and explained.

When trying to become familiar with a neighborhood or community, professionals should get to know "bridge people." Bridge people are individuals who can introduce a new professional helper to those key members of the neighborhood who have substantial influence with other community members. They often are not easy to recognize. Bridge people can be identified by contacting local churches, grocery stores, neighborhood centers, food banks, and community resident groups. The relationship with the bridge person should be a respectful one. In addition, professionals should not take one person's view of the community, family, or individual as necessarily the single and absolute truth.

Professionals need to recognize that the families and individuals they work with are key informants who can enlighten or offer advice. They should remember to be careful about asking for too much information on certain issues (gangs or drug selling, for example) for the sake of everyone's safety.

Professionals shouldn't assume that they must do all the community development in a neighborhood, or that it is wise to try. They should share resources with others to build a sense of partnership and to have a larger effect on the community. Recognizing others who have made a contribution to success and letting people know that they are parts of the larger group is beneficial. Individual or agency group vision should not interfere with the needs of the larger group or community.

REASONS WE NEED PROFESSIONALS

Advocates for neighborhood transformation and increased respect for natural helpers are often misinterpreted as saying professionals are not necessary. In fact, they are extremely necessary in many capacities.

Strengths of Professionals

Although some of the things professionals do could be done (and indeed, are being done) by natural helpers, many of their skills are invaluable in the change process. Some skills particularly valued by natural helpers include the following:

Grants management. Some professionals have had experience in grant writing, budgeting, and monitoring financial goals and objectives.

Conceptualizing issues. Professionals have some conceptual frameworks that can help others understand and address issues. Professionals have detailed knowledge of conceptual frameworks within which to assess and help resolve individual and family problems. Helpers can benefit from those frameworks in terms of organizing potentially overwhelming information and in setting and monitoring goals.

Training. Professionals know lots of ways to solve problems. Some are relevant for natural helpers and neighborhoods; some are not. Over time, it becomes easier to tell which is which. Professionals can educate natural helpers to assume more responsibilities, such as more training, mentoring, and direct help than they are already providing. They can help natural help-

TABLE 11.1. Some Activities of Natural Helpers: Five Categories

Skill Building
- Helping others learn to get and keep
  - Transportation
  - Child care/baby-sitting
  - Legal aid
  - Housing
  - Employment
  - Toys or recreational equipment
  - Clothing
  - Utility benefits or services
  - Medical and dental services
  - Furniture and household goods
  - Recreational opportunities
- Helping others get
  - Food and keep it available
  - Repair services
  - Financial aid
- Helping others learn to
  - Do housework and obtain homemaker services
  - Manage money
- Providing education, training, and information
  - Providing nutrition education
  - Giving the addresses and phone numbers of agencies to help with specific problems
  - Informing friends, neighbors, and relatives of their rights and responsibilities
  - Teaching professionals how better to help
  - Participating in statewide training: teaching educators the realities of living in poverty
- Serving as role models for others

Providing Emotional Support
- Listening
- Providing positive regard, without judgment
- Being available, spending time
- Avoiding gossip and manipulation
- Addressing issues of personal isolation by creating and sustaining a network of support for children, teens, and adults who want to use their learned knowledge to make more appropriate choices in their lives—especially relating to health, employability, and education
- Addressing issues of isolation from mainstream society by creating a chain of mentoring that will link families immersed in poverty with others in mainstream society

Community Leadership and Networking
- Organizing activities that help families form positive relationships with each other (potlucks, center work parties, and "parents' night out" sessions)
- Setting up skill and resource exchanges
  - Identifying tools, materials, skills, and expertise possessed by members of the center
  - Setting up and maintaining child care cooperatives

TABLE II.I. *(continued)*

- ○ Developing and running job clubs to share job leads and offer support to other parents looking for work
- ○ Establishing a "craft co-op" in which people make items together and split the profits between those who participate
- □ Setting up and managing laundry facilities
- □ Subscribing to area newspapers and posting classified ads for apartment rentals and help-wanted ads
- □ Contacting local police/sheriff's department about starting a neighborhood watch program
  - ○ On a large local map, chart out the location and times of crimes in the neighborhood
  - ○ Discuss the effects that a change in street lighting or police presence could have; begin discussion with police department about "community policing" in which officers walk (rather than drive) through the neighborhood or establish a "mini-station" of two to three officers in the neighborhood
- □ Contacting local rape prevention program for basic information about self-defense classes
  - ○ Contract with trainer to provide self-defense classes to Head Start parents
  - ○ Request funding for tuition and child care for parents to participate in a self-defense class offered locally
  - ○ Request funding for whistles as follow-up to self-defense class
  - ○ Bring in speaker on "victim advocacy" or victim restitution services
- □ Starting a child care co-op in which families exchange care services and each family contributes "co-op hours"
- □ Establishing a support group for families affected by substance abuse
- □ Contacting grocery store chains about the need for a store in the neighborhood (either to keep an existing store or to bring in a new one)
- □ Organizing weekly storytelling and plays by local artists
- □ Organizing tutoring
- □ Organizing arts and crafts classes
- □ Encouraging networking within the community through information sharing and group building
- □ Acting as a role model for professionals on interaction with residents
- □ Advising professionals on holding meetings or trainings
  - ○ Recommend the most appropriate place to hold the training—not only convenient to all, but also comfortable and accessible for subsequent activities
  - ○ Devise ways to make sure all trainees can attend trainings consistently (address baby-sitting needs—What will work best? Daytime programming with baby-sitting on-site? Nighttime programming with stipends for baby-sitting?)
- □ Initiating change by participating in coalitions and community activities that affect their neighborhoods and then planning small group trainings in their neighborhoods
- □ Joining boards and coalitions in order to educate decision makers on their neighborhood needs
- □ Volunteering for in-depth newspaper feature articles focusing on issues that affect the poor and on ways building strengths within the neighborhood can support long-term change

(Table continues)

TABLE 11.1. *(continued)*

Resource Acquisition
- ▢ Participation in focus groups developing public relations materials related to maternal health issues for inner-city women
- ▢ Knowledge about where to find transportation and housing
- ▢ Information about buying, selling, and trading—junk dealers, hock shops, garages, landlords, informal food and clothing banks, loan sharks

Concrete Help
- ▢ Baby-sitting
- ▢ Fixing things
- ▢ Braiding hair
- ▢ Gardening

Note: Some individuals may have assets in all five areas, but people who are strong in only one or two areas can still make important contributions.

These examples are presented to help service designers become aware of the resources that may already exist, so that those resources may be included in planning.

ers learn to provide training. They can work with natural helpers to adapt existing materials and develop new materials.

Evaluation. Professionals have often been trained to specify outcomes and to collect and analyze information. They have a systematic orientation and can understand controlled observation. Although natural helpers are sometimes annoyed with the system's insistence on this activity, they can usually accept it and continue to work hard to document what they are doing.

Identification of strengths. Professionals can help natural helpers become aware of just how much they do know and can encourage them to follow through on their beliefs.

Fund-raising. Professionals usually can write, and they know the language most funding sources use. They know people who make decisions about funding. They can help others learn to develop, fund, operate, and evaluate their own strategies.

Advocacy. Professionals can speak out on behalf of natural helpers. If professionals have spent time in neighborhoods, they can sometimes translate realities to policymakers and other professionals who have not been so fortunate.

Service delivery. Professionals can provide services themselves when necessary. They can provide specialized services in very difficult problem areas.

Problem solving. Professionals know multitudes of techniques for problem solving.

Mentoring. Professionals can make natural leaders aware of just how much they do know and encourage them to follow through on their own beliefs. They can help others learn to develop, fund, operate, and evaluate their own strategies.

Ways Professionals Might Help Natural Helpers

The skills of professionals are hard won through years of study and experience. But we must remember that nonprofessionals also are gaining skills and knowledge as they live. Some may even learn the same skills through life as professionals learned through college.

Some skills commonly thought to be the exclusive purview of professionals are inaccessible to laypeople only because of the jargon. We often talk of professionals' activities in special languages involving terms such as "borderline personality," "resistance," "denial," and "attention deficit disorder." Not everyone understands these professional words, and it is easy to become intimidated.

When one looks closely at the specific activities of professionals, it is possible to translate most words into regular English that can be understood by all, and laypeople can learn many of them, one by one, even if they don't have a particular degree. Some examples of activities professionals could teach natural helpers are shown in table 11.2.

Professional agency staff roles may need to change from "saving" neighborhoods and residents to enhancing the capacity of community workers and residents to provide more of their own help. At the same time, just as laypeople will never do brain surgery, there will always be especially difficult or violent situations that will require the help of those with many years of specialized training and experience. Our challenge is to determine what skills can be taught to many others and what capacities should rightfully be thought of as in the professional domain.

Professionals may gradually emphasize new roles for themselves, including helping paraprofessionals and others learn the tools instead of using the tools so directly themselves. Professionals can help others learn to provide training and to adapt certain materials to their situations. Professionals also may become more involved in helping others learn to develop, fund, operate, and evaluate their own models, and in providing specialized services for very difficult problem areas.

CHALLENGES IN DEVELOPING AND MAINTAINING
PROFESSIONAL/NATURAL HELPER PARTNERSHIPS

Although we can specify many potential advantages of professionals working more closely with natural helpers, we can also point out many potential challenges in doing so. We must continually remind ourselves that neither professionals nor natural helpers are homogeneous groups. Each relationship is unique, but some threads are likely to run through many attempts at partnerships.

TABLE 11.2. Possible Tools for Professionals to Use in Teaching Natural Helpers

---

Tools for Helpers to Conceptualize Helping and Problems
- Systems approaches
- Learning approaches
- Cognitive approaches
- Environmental approaches
- Philosophical and spiritual approaches
- Psychodynamic approaches

Tools for Helpers to Sustain Themselves
- Ways to assess what hurts
- Conceptual frameworks to design supports and solutions

Ways for Helpers to Keep People Safe
- Structure the situation before the helper arrives
- Structure the situation when the helper is helping
- Structure the situation between times the helper is there
- Help people learn how to assess the potential for violence
  - Assault
  - Homicide
  - Suicide
  - Child abuse
  - Domestic violence
- Help people learn not to trigger each other
- Develop safety plans
- Help people learn how to break the chain when triggering begins
- Help people learn how to get help when situations start to get out of control
- Childproof the home

Ways for Helpers to Engage Those They Wish to Help
- Meet people when and where they prefer to be met
- Greet people in ways that will show respect and help them feel comfortable
- Engage in culturally appropriate initial conversations
- Communicate that they understand the meaning as well as the words of what people are trying to say
- Respond to people's requests
- Listen without judging
- Affirm people's strengths, successes, and potential

Tools for Helpers and Those They Are Helping to Assess Situations
- Exercises to help people assess their values
- Exercises to help people identify their strengths and resources
- Exercises to help people clarify and prioritize their goals
- Ways to tell what happens before a particular problem occurs, perhaps triggering the problem
- Ways to tell what happens after a particular problem occurs, perhaps rewarding it
- Journals where people can safely tell what is going on

Ways Helpers Can Prevent Problems from Occurring
- Help people figure out how they spend their time
- Help people figure out which times cause them trouble

TABLE 11.2. *(continued)*

- □ Help people think of other ways to spend their time
- □ Help people actually do the other things
- □ Help people avoid danger
- □ Help people respond differently to the times that cause them trouble

Tools to Motivate People Toward Positive Change
- □ Show understanding of what people are trying to say—affirming the words, the feelings, and the meaning of what the person is saying
- □ Help the person find strengths and values—doing certain games or activities together
- □ Help the person feel more important
  - ○ Being respectful
  - ○ Spending time
  - ○ Noticing the good things
- □ Help the person feel more hopeful
- □ Help the person see that he or she is in charge
- □ Help the person see a positive vision of the future
  - ○ Imagining it
  - ○ Drawing a picture
  - ○ Making a collage
  - ○ Writing a letter
- □ Help the person see the difference between what is desired and where the current road leads
- □ Help the person feel more confident about being able to change
  - ○ Showing that others have problems, too
  - ○ Sharing something of your own background and struggles
- □ Help the person see that we can feel two ways about change—saying things that show both ways of feeling
- □ Help people decide where they are in terms of wanting to change
- □ Help people see why change might be good
  - ○ Noticing the things they say about why change would get them good things
  - ○ Adding on just a little to what they are saying, in the direction of change
  - ○ Rewarding them for little steps
- □ Help people see why not changing might be bad
  - ○ Noticing the things they say about bad things that will happen if they don't change
  - ○ Giving them information about some of the things that could happen or are happening
  - ○ Providing consequences when they don't try
- □ Help people remember times when they made changes
- □ Help them identify people like themselves who have made changes
- □ Share genuine beliefs in people's abilities to make changes
- □ Help people understand the process of change, and that it usually doesn't happen immediately

Tools to Help Others Make Changes in Certain Areas
- □ Parenting
  - ○ Learning to tell what is really happening: Who does what to whom?
  - ○ Noticing and rewarding kids doing the right thing

(Table continues)

TABLE 11.2. *(continued)*

- ○ Knowing when to ignore, distract, reward, and punish things kids do
- ○ Setting up the house so kids won't get in trouble
- ○ Getting clear what you expect from kids
- ○ Getting clear what will happen if they do or do not meet expectations
- ○ Having family meetings
- ○ Giving kids choices
- ○ Knowing how much supervision kids need
- ○ What to do when your kids are fighting
- ○ Helping kids respond to "no"
- ○ Showing your kids how you want them to be
- □ Managing feelings
  - ○ Figuring out what you are feeling (the "feeling thermometer")
  - ○ The faces chart
  - ○ Figuring out what might be causing the feeling
  - ○ How thinking can cause feelings
  - ○ How eating can cause feelings
  - ○ Things to do to conquer anger
    - —Crisis cards
    - —Changing thinking
    - —Doing something else
    - —Solving the problem
    - —Calling someone
    - —Practice being frustrated
  - ○ Things to do to stop being depressed
  - ○ Figure out what is causing depression
    - —Start doing different things
    - —Give credit for small steps
    - —Look at things that led to cheerfulness in the past
    - —Stop self-criticism
  - ○ Ways to stop being anxious
    - —Learning not to get anxious in the first place
    - —Things to do if it happens
  - ○ Tolerating being uncomfortable

Getting Along with Other People
- □ Learning social skills
- □ Learning problem solving
- □ Learning to be assertive
- □ Learning to listen
- □ Learning to negotiate
- □ Learning to make decisions
- □ Learning to say "no"
- □ Learning to tell others that what they do is bothersome
- □ Learning what to do when others say something you do is bothering them
- □ Controlling impulses
- □ Resisting pressure from others
- □ Accepting "no"

Tools for Helpers to Help Others Maintain Changes They Have Made
- □ Learning to predict slips
- □ Planning to prevent slips from happening

TABLE 11.2. *(continued)*

- □ Having a plan to get back on track
- □ Considering all possibilities to prevent slips
  - ○ Exercise
  - ○ Nutrition
  - ○ Prayer
  - ○ Acupuncture
  - ○ Meditation

Difficulties in Meeting One Another

Although it is possible that systems representatives may meet natural helpers as clients, it is very rare that they run into each other on equal grounds. They usually do not live in the same neighborhoods, attend the same churches, or participate in the same leisure activities. Administrators in the system have even fewer opportunities to meet natural helpers because they no longer see clients.

Lack of Awareness of a Different Culture

When they do meet, professionals and natural helpers are often doing essentially different dances, and they begin treading on one another immediately. Professionals have a fairly formalized way of greeting each other, making a few neutral comments about the weather or some news event, and then diving into a very linear agenda. Natural helpers do not separate their helping roles from themselves as people, so they are more likely either to plunge into an informality and warmth that is bewildering to professionals or to withdraw completely or react aggressively in response to methods of talking that seem to them to be forced and indirect.

Personal Histories

Natural helpers and professionals usually begin their relationships holding stereotypes about one another. Most have had direct personal contacts; all have heard about either hopeless clients or "uppity" professionals who have done significant damage to others. Natural helpers have had both good and bad relationships with professionals and may tend to divide them into those two categories. Their experiences with "the system" may have been bad. There can be a tendency to react negatively to "system-like" requirements, such as attention to cost effectiveness or guidelines about areas of focus and emphasis. Many such requirements are nonnegotiable, and angry reactions do nothing but distance natural helpers from the system they wish to change.

Emotional Reactions of Some Professionals

In any new venture anxiety, frustration, and confusion are likely. Some examples of particular triggers professionals may encounter include the following:

Cultural Differences

Professionals may literally be unable to understand the language, or the accent, or some of the phrases used by natural helpers. This is not a pleasant feeling. Differences in greeting behaviors, eye contact, formality, touch, and ways of expressing emotions can rapidly offend on a personal level when participants are not aware of their cultural differences.

Personal Safety

To meet natural helpers, professionals often will have to go into neighborhoods that can be frightening. In some areas, professionals will be more at risk than if they stayed in high-rise apartments downtown.

Job Security

Some professionals may worry that natural helpers will usurp their roles and endanger their job security. It is hard to feel great about someone who might leave you unemployed. They may risk credibility with their peers who may see them as betraying their profession and going over to the wrong side.

Professional Responsibility

There are few hard data about what natural helpers are accomplishing and what they would be able to accomplish if they had more training and support. There is always the risk that helpers may do harm instead of helping, and the professional may be blamed.

Schedules

Natural helpers usually do not keep schedules the same way professionals do. They are much more flexible in responding to immediate needs. Professionals may take offense at lateness or missed meetings, when it is a cultural difference rather than an insult. Because they often have fewer financial resources, natural helpers have fewer options in many emergencies. Cars are more likely to break down; airfares or tuition may not be available as planned. Professionals will likely become entangled in these predicaments and may need to provide transportation for natural helpers without cars. This takes additional time.

Emotional Reactions of Some Natural Helpers

Natural helpers may be likely to have their feelings triggered by interactions with professionals. They may be interacting with someone who is literally impossible for them to understand. Professional jargon, acronyms, and concepts often are not only totally foreign but can be insulting to those who believe many professionals have absolutely no idea what it is like to survive under difficult situations.

Inadvertently, and sometimes intentionally, professionals shut natural helpers out of decision-making processes. This can be done through lack of eye contact, a raised eyebrow, failure to invite individuals to meetings, and frequently, polite nods but no real understanding when natural helpers speak.

These exclusionary behaviors are particularly painful to natural helpers because it is now "trendy" to include them in the helping process. Forums, advisory boards, and new funding streams often advertise new principles involving "neighborhood-based" partnerships and helping people help themselves. But in many cases the real power rests with the same power brokers who have always had it. Natural helpers are aware of meetings held without them, token input, and being put on advisory boards instead of boards of directors. The discrepancy between what professionals say they do and what they actually do makes it difficult for natural helpers to respect them. It makes it difficult for natural helpers to keep trying to work with professionals. It makes it very difficult for natural helpers not to get angry.

Professionals might fail to understand the importance of a personal and long-term commitment to natural helpers and other residents of the neighborhoods where they work. Natural helpers are aware of the importance of finding professionals to whom they can relate. Those relationships are precious and have meaning beyond "business." If they end when the grant is over, or when someone gets promoted, it can be seen as another betrayal.

Language Differences Between Some Professionals and Some Natural Helpers

Professionals and natural helpers use different concepts, phrases, and words for talking and thinking about help. When one or the other language is selected, the other partners may feel slighted.

The first word that gets in the way is "partnership." Natural helpers tend to polarize over this concept, bouncing between a belief that at last they will have a voice equal to that of professionals and cynicism at having been betrayed in similar situations before. Professionals, on the other hand, often view the relationship as a "partnership" if they even consider natural helpers in their plans, or especially if they invite them to meetings or put them on advisory boards. The meaning of partnership needs to be clarified for all involved.

Many natural helpers have had either personal or close experience with the state public assistance, child welfare agencies, and housing authorities.

They may have felt humiliated and powerless in their interactions. In trying to develop partnerships, miscommunications may have occurred or promises may not have been kept. Allies or others with good intentions within public agencies may agree to work in partnership with natural helpers but may find they need to slow down or stop the process if it isn't politically feasible or the support they thought they had disappears. These experiences make it hard to expect the best from people and to develop the trusting relationships needed for a real partnership.

Other examples of professional mindsets that can irritate natural helpers include the word "project" because it implies something that comes and goes, while the helpers want their efforts to ripple across time. "Services" is problematic because it implies something done *for* someone rather than *with* them. Some natural helpers prefer "approach."

They often don't like "target population" because it implies something in the sights of a rifle. Many don't like "client" because it implies an expert/dependent relationship. "Case" is too unfeeling. Many natural helpers choose to talk about people and families. Some examples of the differences in basic assumptions about help are shown in table 11.3, and some differences in words and phrases we use to talk about helping are shown in table 11.4.

Lack of Clarity Regarding Roles

Tension Between Responsibilities and Values

People assume different roles within the natural helper and professional categories. It is a challenge for both professionals and natural helpers to acknowledge differences in authority and responsibility while still valuing inclusion, respect, and equality.

Inherent Power Differentials

It is unclear exactly what professionals' roles should be. Because professionals usually have more money, connections, and experience raising money, natural helpers may view them as people who can provide a job. It is easy for professionals to begin to take more responsibility than is helpful, given the partnership's values of self-reliance and independence. Both natural helpers and professionals need to be aware of this balancing act. Both sides need to be sensitive to cues that show when professionals are feeling too much pressure to take more responsibility, or when natural helpers think professionals have taken more control and responsibility than necessary.

The professionals in these partnerships will most likely have connections to funding sources and access to money. Many natural helpers are just barely making ends meet, increasing their likelihood of a financial

TABLE 11.3. Examples of Differences in Language Between Some Professionals and Some Natural Helpers

Some Professionals	Some Natural Helpers
Types of Help Provided	Types of Help Provided
Therapy	Education
Evaluation	Healing
Treatment	Moral and spiritual guidance
Aftercare	Resource development
	Advocacy
	Economic development
	Community organization
Who Decides What Type of Help Is Offered?	Who Decides What Type of Help Is Offered?
Federal government	Residents
State government	Neighborhoods
Agency professionals	Communities
Therapists	Recipients of help
Assessment triage team	Partnership
What Are the Vehicles for Help?	What Are the Vehicles for Help?
The fifty-minute hour	On-site informal connections
Group therapy	Changing neighborhood conditions
Evaluations	Self-help groups
Medications	
Who Needs Help?	Who Needs Help?
Dysfunctional people	All of us, depending on the time and day
Where Should Help Occur?	Where Should Help Occur?
In the office	In life, wherever it is happening

crisis from time to time. Professionals may feel pressured to respond to a financial crisis by giving pay advances or personally lending money.

Tension About Structure and Rigidity of Roles

Role constraints may limit one's ability to be an effective helper. On the other hand, a lack of constraint may mean a blurring of friendship, mentor, coworker, and family roles. As partnerships strive to use everyone's strengths, the roles of program managers or supervisors (whether those roles are filled by professionals or natural helpers) may be disregarded. Supervisors may have to remind people to let them know what's going on and keep information channeling through them.

Complexity of Individual Roles

Roles in professional/natural helper partnerships can get complex. A group of natural helpers may be made up of husband and wife teams, neighbors

TABLE 11.4. Examples of Differences in Wording Between Some Professionals and Some Natural Helpers

Some Professionals	Some Natural Helpers
Target population	People who need and want help
Case assignment	Who responds to which needs of this family?
Caseloads	How many families can we help together?
Cases	People
Client	Person, like me, who sometimes has problems in some areas
Service provider	People who help others, fellow person, neighbor, child of God
Vendor: "You will do what I want."	Partner: "We decide together"
Office hours	Whenever they need to talk, all the time
Nine to five weekdays	All the time
Hotline	Home phone
Supervision	Talking every day
Length of service	Defining moments/being there when needed
Service delivery	A helping hand
Client pathways	Figuring out a clear way to make things better
Therapy	Talking together, only no person has to have letters after their name
Diagnosis: What is this person?	What does this person want and need? How can I help?
Making an assessment	Getting to know one another
The child's needs	How can we help this kid to succeed?
Risk assessment	How can we help this kid to be okay?
Confidentiality	Secrecy
The "bumper" mentality, going at it alone	Reaching out
Being realistic	Having hope
	Poor adults can raise children properly
Having a job	Being called
Being objective and cool	Being personal
	Witnessing the pain
Keeping work and life separate	Work and life have big overlap
Following the rules	Forging a path, taking one step after another
People as recipients of service	People helping one another
The problem is in the person	Outcomes arise from complex interactions of factors
Services are "talking about problems"	Help is concrete—getting a snake out of the kitchen, making a "Beware of Wolf" sign
Public housing rules regarding number of people per room	Taking in a foster child

and other friends, and family members. Group members may switch among the roles of friend, family member, mentor, supervisor, boss, and coconspirator. For example, in a group called People Helping People (PHP), seven members are related to other group members, and all but one either are currently or have been married to or living with other group members. Most members also have personal relationships with one another and share many details of their lives.

It can be difficult for couples to stay in their coworker role. Buttons get pushed and people display more of their true relationships than they might like. Arguing in meetings may be commonplace.

Confusion in the Public Agency

The public agency may not be sure where a professional/natural helper partnership group fits into the spectrum of service providers. They may already have paraprofessionals who do housework or other concrete tasks. They may have transportation people, volunteers, and of course, all the professional agencies. They may not know how the partnership differs from these categories, and it can be difficult to clarify.

Financial Complexities in Professional/Natural Helper Partnerships

Confusion About Appropriate Matters for Payment

Natural helpers have worked with families and their neighborhoods free of charge, often for many years. Professional/natural helper partnerships can provide the opportunity for them to be paid for some or much of their work. For many, this can be confusing.

Personal expenses of natural helpers. In one partnership in Tacoma, Washington, a natural helper had been attending school for years to become eligible for a particular position in a new company there. A week before he was to finish, he found that public funding for his graduation fees had ended. He called his professional partner, requesting that she give him $400. She said that was outside the boundaries of the partnership, but that she had lots of work to be done around the house and that she would advance it to him if he would do the work. After she agreed to this, she was concerned that the roles were already complicated. It turned out the group member did the work well, and they became much closer and better able to work together as a result of their (some might say) rash and heedless disregard for boundaries.

Personal expenses of professionals. In another example, natural helpers wished to bill the organization sponsoring the partnership when a professional's dog damaged their hose.

Food. In order to work around many family, work, or school responsibilities, professional/natural helper partnership meetings may take place during mealtimes. It can be easy to spend a lot of money on food. Some partnerships have found it helpful to set a money limit per meeting. If hosts wish to go beyond that limit, it is up to them.

Goods for families being helped. Even though many natural helpers are living close to the edge with their own bills, they may not hesitate to buy shoes or give money to families they are helping. Often they could get the money another way if they were willing to use the "system" more. Many natural helpers are not accustomed to having expense accounts or keeping receipts.

Potential Loss of Public Assistance Because of Partnership Income

There can be some confusion about how much and what kind of money or goods can be earned without jeopardizing a natural helper's public assistance. It is clearly possible that by earning money, a person might get more than he or she earned deducted from his or her assistance, resulting in a net loss from working. It is also clear that increases in income can influence housing payments and eligibility.

Because contingencies will probably be different for each person, each one needs to negotiate with caseworkers or housing representatives. Then natural helpers can make their own decisions about payment.

Employee and Contractor Status

Partnerships will have to determine whether members are employees or contractors. Criteria from the Internal Revenue Service and state labor laws need to be examined. PHP originally designated most partnership members as contractors. After further examination of IRS criteria and legal consultation, the designation was changed to employees.

Lack of Clarity Regarding Basics of Payment

Other possible payment issues that need to be clarified include the following: How often will people get paid? Will people get pay advances when in tight financial spots? Is different work worth more or less money? For example, do those providing supervision and other management functions get paid more?

Budget Constraints and Other Pressures on Public Agency Staff

Most public agency staff are expected to do far too much with too little. Child deaths and staff problems seem to appear on the front page of the newspaper almost weekly. These problems make it difficult for staff to consistently find time to work on new directions, because so much is demanded of them in responding to prevent disasters.

Budgeting constraints also pose obstacles to developing pathways for natural helpers to get off public assistance by paying them for some of the work they do with families. If the public agency already has access to low-cost paraprofessionals and volunteers, and if the agency has financial problems, a primary motivation will be to save money. The agency may wish natural helpers to work for free, as they have before. If costs become comparable to those of paraprofessionals, the agency may find it easier to proceed with an already established service.

Categorization of Funding

Funding sources are often very restrictive about what kind of help they will pay for and what kind of credentials the staff must have in order to give a certain kind of help. Mental health, substance abuse treatment, and child welfare funding streams usually require specific training and credentials. Many of the specific tasks that mental health professionals, qualified chemical dependency counselors, or child welfare specialists do, though, are already being done by natural helpers or can be learned. These restrictions, and the underlying belief that all of these tasks can only be done by professionals, limit the ability of professionals to explore alternative ways to serve families.

Differences of Opinion on How to Be Helpful

The most painful experiences can arise when public agency recommendations and perceptions of events differ from those of natural helper partnerships. Natural helpers most often identify with the "clients" and their powerlessness over the system. Many will be very sensitive to stereotyping, a failure to perceive strengths, and any other interactions that may humiliate family members. At the same time, natural helpers may need the money and support of the public agency. They may realize that if they alienate public agency workers, they may not get more referrals. They can be caught between objecting to some practices and preserving their integrity.

Some public agency workers have been disappointed many times by the families they try to help. Some of them may tend to go into long, vague descriptions of "inadequacy," "diminished capacity," or "personality disorder" that probably will not sit well with natural helpers, especially when there is no acknowledgment of, or search for, the strengths that people may have.

Public agency workers may feel compelled to refer family members to mental health centers if they believe emotional problems are involved. Families are often referred to a number of different service providers. Public agency workers themselves provide many direct services. Even with efforts by all to pin down who is doing what, situations are always changing, and it may seem impossible to keep up with, and coordinate, all actors and interventions. This often results in fragmented services and families being torn in many directions. Natural helpers may feel insulted that public agency workers do not think they have anything to offer in helping people with problems such as depression, anxiety, or interpersonal relationships.

ONE EXAMPLE OF A PROFESSIONAL/NATURAL HELPER PARTNERSHIP

In 1994, Jill Kinney, a psychologist, wanted to meet with people who were leaders in Tacoma's Eastside community, who helped their neighbors as part of their daily lives, who were "natural helpers." She asked people who were working in the Eastside for contacts and was introduced to Margaret Trent. Margaret talked to her friends and family, who were also active in the community. They all met with Jill and began talking about how to help families. This group of people from varying backgrounds, cultures, professions, and callings kept talking and drinking coffee, and in 1995, formed the group mentioned earlier in the chapter, People Helping People.

PHP consists of people who have been helping their neighbors for years, as well as a few professionals who were interested in learning from, supporting, and enhancing this kind of help. The group attracted funding from the Annie E. Casey Foundation, the Edna McConnell Clark Foundation, the Levi Strauss Foundation, and the Washington State Division of Child and Family Services. It managed those funds through a private nonprofit organization called Home Safe.

PHP members created infrastructures and procedures to allow them to use one another's strengths systematically to change neighborhood conditions and help families. This included creating a system of checks and balances for themselves, and a communications system. They developed an accounting structure that would allow them to accept and manage additional funds. They received training on safety, motivational interviewing, and keeping themselves balanced, in addition to assessing people's needs and influencing behavior. They practiced the skills on themselves and each other. They scheduled times for mutual support and fun.

PHP's mission was to develop, test, and disseminate new ways of supporting families and neighborhoods via diverse partnerships and to produce healthier communities with more effective service delivery systems. Their goals were as follows:

□ To prevent and remedy child abuse and neglect
□ To prevent and remedy drug abuse
□ To disseminate what they learned

PHP served families in both formal and informal ways. The formal referrals came from a contract with the local public child protective agency and the Division of Developmental Disabilities. Informal referrals came from neighbors, friends of neighbors, or chance meetings with someone in trouble in grocery stores or other public places. PHP members have always helped families informally, but the partnership increased the support and resources available to these families. PHP documented its efforts with families in order to gather information on what works and what doesn't and to be able to disseminate its results.

PHP worked to educate the system about the needs of neighborhoods and people who live there and to combine professionals and natural helpers in a positive direction. PHP tried to be a model of effective ways for members to support each other, to become the "book of hard knocks" full of "dos" and "don'ts," and to help new sites be as different as they needed to be.

All PHP participants are responsible for constantly trying to intervene in a way that benefits the whole neighborhood rather than only an individual. They rely on participants and helpers together to brainstorm tasks related to changing conditions, and to prioritize them. Some, such as fixing someone's fence, will take only an hour or two. Others, such as painting a mural over graffiti, may take weeks or months. The following issues were grappled with and continue to be important to a professional/natural helper partnership.

Assurances of Safety for Children

Safety for children was the top priority in PHP. No natural helper began working with families without going through ten hours of training on keeping everyone safe. Safety of children has traditionally been the responsibility of professionals in child welfare. PHP believed that it is everybody's responsibility and that natural helpers play a critical role in child safety by decreasing risk and increasing protective factors. PHP staff all carried pagers, and families were given a list of the whole team. They were available on weekends, evenings, and in the middle of the night if needed.

PHP worked in a multitude of ways depending upon unique issues of individual families and helpers, intending to either provide, or provide access to, a variety of activities and support. Most risk and protective factors traditionally were seen as the role of the professional. PHP found that natural helpers can have a significant impact on these factors. PHP natural helpers used specific techniques related to self-esteem, child, family and worker safety, and drug abuse. Professionals in PHP provided supervision and backup in all areas.

Helping Others Build Self-Esteem

More and more research regarding behavior change suggests that a key concept is one's feelings of self-efficacy. If people don't believe they can change, if they don't have some hope, if they don't feel some sense of competence, the likelihood of change decreases greatly. Natural helpers are often particularly well positioned to help others improve their self-esteem. PHP saw this as a first step in helping people become better parents, stop drug abuse, and work more effectively with the system.

Keeping Children Safe

In order to reduce or prevent harm to children, PHP workers did many things to help create and maintain a climate of safety. When the helper was paired with a professional for backup and help in assessment and planning, all of the following could happen in the neighborhood.

General things they do all the time. PHP natural helpers advised others in the neighborhood of what was happening with their natural helper group. Neighbors often let PHP helpers know if they saw anything that caused them concern. They were out and around the neighborhood. The more others saw adults out, looking, and listening, the more it built a climate of safety and concern. PHP natural helpers were good neighbors. They knew their neighbors, talked to them, offered to help them, laughed with them, and did things with them.

To help keep children safe, PHP workers made friends with other families. When the helpers noticed a family with children that they did not know, they often greeted the family to get to know them. They developed relationships, making acquaintances and friends of strangers, listened to their stories, offered to help them if they wanted it. Helpers told about resources in the neighborhood—activities, services, and help—and engaged in activities with them, such as meals or walks. If natural helpers showed a genuine concern for residents as people, a relationship was possible.

Signs of problems with children at risk. Natural helpers sometimes set an example of working together by asking another family to help (for example, the helper would ask another family to let the helper know if her kids acted up, and she would offer to do the same for that family). They helped connect the family to the community and its activities, as a friendly gesture, not because of any suspicions. They provided information about existing services and how to get them. They listened to the parents' story. They asked permission of parents to help and if they agreed, got the parents involved. If family members wanted help, natural helpers usually offered to go with them to available services, introduced them, and made the first contact easier and more successful. If the family had extended family, natural helpers tried to talk to them about how they could help the parents with the kids.

What PHP did if there were problems, but they were not too severe. PHP natural helpers had a business card to give a family to identify themselves and let the family know that there were others to help families in the neighborhood. They offered to help if the parents needed a break from the children at times. They took the children with their own families on an outing. They watched the children for a while and helped connect the family with child care.

If the parent or child was upset, PHP natural helpers calmed things down. People are better able to think and act when their emotions are lower. PHP helpers listened to them without blaming or judging. They helped them understand what they were struggling with. They let them ventilate their anger without telling them to calm down.

PHP helpers gave advice to a family, when asked, about what family members could do differently. They let them know it was just an idea they had and that they were free to use the advice or not—it was up to them. They gave advice on health issues for children if they saw health hazards such as exposed wiring, dirty messes, or children with poor hygiene.

PHP natural helpers, in a concerned way, told a parent what problem behavior they would like changed. They would say, "I saw your daughter out on the street earlier, and I was worried because of the traffic sometimes. Is there any way you could think of to help keep her safe?" They also offered solutions such as, "I'd be willing to bring her into my yard when I see her, if you'd like."

When behavior or a situation contained enough risk to the child that helpers really thought they must prevent it, and they had tried other things such as advice and concern, they warned the family, caringly, of possible formal action if it didn't change.

Helping Everyone Learn to Stay Safe

PHP workers were trained to assess risks and address them to prevent negative consequences for children. Some ways to maximize the chances that everyone would be okay included frequent monitoring, changing the situation, structuring daily routines, contracts, crisis cards, and homework. These are issues that can be discussed even on the first visit. These and other methods helped family members keep their emotions and their situations under control, to protect children. These suggestions were not meant to solve problems over the long term (although this might happen). They were meant as immediate options that could help avoid trouble while all PHP participants had time with the family to work on longer-term options.

For example, one mom had been rough with her baby and was reported to Child Protective Services. Margaret, the PHP worker assigned to the family, found that the mother did not know what to do when she was overwhelmed with the many demands on her. Margaret worked with the mother to structure her day and prioritize her responsibilities. She also showed the mom how to write a crisis card that listed options for what to do before she got too overwhelmed. This mom reported feeling calmer and less overwhelmed. She reached out for help a number of times before she felt out of control.

Helping People Prevent and Eliminate Drug Abuse

Although many people were helped by drug treatment, many also refused it. Relapse is a big issue for many who complete treatment. PHP workers responded to people with drug problems in several ways.

Assessment. PHP workers were trained in the use of a comprehensive assessment process, as well as observation techniques including recognition of factors indicating drug abuse.

Enhancement of motivation. PHP workers were trained in motivational interviewing and other motivation enhancement techniques designed to help people move through stages of change—precontemplation, contemplation, determination, action, and maintenance. This process is done by acknowledging ambivalence, building feelings of self-efficacy, developing a positive vision for the future, and eliciting and supporting statements of self-motivation for change.

Developing an overall strategy for change. PHP workers helped family members understand the change process—that it wouldn't be easy and it wouldn't happen overnight. They helped families set realistic expectations and develop a menu of options for actually changing the behavior, including drug treatment and self-help groups. They helped people recognize triggers for their drug use and develop new ways of responding. They helped people develop new daily routines. They helped people cope with their feelings, find new ways of solving the problems the drugs were supposed to solve, and manage urges and other thoughts and feelings.

PHP workers also helped people understand and disengage from tendencies such as enabling, sabotaging, and codependency. They worked with extended family members on what they might do to help and helped the person in trouble develop positive friendships.

Maintaining progress. PHP workers helped people understand the causes of relapse and used specific techniques for relapse prevention. Also important was working toward helping people build a new life without drugs, including clarifying a sense of personal meaning, proper nutrition, and exercise.

A mother and daughter were referred to PHP to help the mother maintain her sobriety. Margaret, a natural helper, and Glenda, a professional, worked with the family. Margaret helped the mother get beds for her and her daughter and helped her develop a daily routine and identify interests and hobbies to enrich her new life without alcohol. Margaret was also available by telephone to talk at any time. Glenda worked with the mother to identify triggers for substance use, ways to avoid them, and alternative ways to respond to those triggers when they were unavoidable. Glenda also helped the mother write out a crisis card that listed options for what to do when she felt the urge to drink. This list included activities such as artwork and telephone numbers of people to call. Either Glenda and Margaret could have done any of these interventions. The decision-making process regarding "who does what" was based on their interest and comfort with each task, not on their natural helper or professional designation.

Roles

Roles in Relationship to the Families Seen

Wherever possible PHP encouraged development of new daily routines and interpersonal connections to sustain positive change, so that PHP helpers gradually became less necessary over time. At the same time, many members of PHP were neighbors of the families they were helping, and they will remain in their lives indefinitely. Special relationships were formed in this project, and lines between helpers and helpees at times were blurred. This challenges some professional assumptions about objectivity and professional distance. PHP helpers believed that what they gained in commitment and effectiveness would offset the time needed to continually clarify roles and goals as they proceeded. It was PHP's intent to strengthen connections, either formally or informally, with families and their family support centers, so that this resource would also continue to decrease their isolation over the long term.

When PHP started seeing families referred through the contract with the local Child Protective Services (CPS), a more formal paperwork process was required. The contract required an assessment and service plan, family contact notes, monthly summaries, and a closing summary. When the time came to write closing summaries, the professionals involved asked to schedule a closing meeting with the families to go over progress and to say good-bye. PHP natural helpers were amused by this concept, saying, "They are in our neighborhood. We will always run into them, there is no good-bye. The payment from CPS may have stopped, but the involvement with families does not stop." The professionals, consequently, decided to say goodbye to families on their own.

Roles in Relationship to Others in the Partnership

In most partnerships, roles are spelled out by previous training, education, and the traditions of various agencies. In its approach, PHP designed the responses to families and to neighborhoods based on the unique strengths, values, and needs of the real people involved, individually tailoring them according to the capacities of individual helpers as well as those being helped. Thus, interventions, and who did them, were a function of the demands of the situation, rather than of traditional roles and capacities. Responses were tailored from an extensive, flexible menu of options.

Whenever possible, tasks were carried out by family members and their existing informal support systems. When they did need help, decisions about who does what usually depended on the following criteria:

- [ ] Who does the family want to be involved?
- [ ] Who is available from the extended family and the informal system?
- [ ] Who on the team feels they have the time and skills to respond?
- [ ] What redefinition of roles will the neighborhood and other involved agencies tolerate?

PHP always tried to carefully evaluate potential sources of funds to avoid conflicts of values that could destroy its capacity to be responsive. Conflicts of values occurred nonetheless. With the public CPS agency contract, the redefinition of roles was more difficult than expected. The CPS agency contract emphasized the use of paraprofessionals and connections for informal, neighborhood resources, which seemed to fit the way PHP worked with families. Though PHP knew that interventions would need to be carefully documented using clinical language that the group did not like, members believed those issues could be overcome and would not affect the day-to-day work of the group.

After working with roughly eight families, the state contracts monitor was concerned that the professional involvement with some of the families was too low. The natural helpers or "paraprofessionals" appeared to be doing most of the work. Though the professionals did see every family, the intensity varied with the needs of each particular family. The professionals met with the natural helpers regularly, at least weekly, to go over progress and needs of the families. The contracts monitor did not think the professional involvement was high enough, saying the professional was to be the primary therapist, and the natural helper, or paraprofessional, was to only assist the primary therapist. Also, the contracts monitor and the Division of Children and Family Services caseworkers wanted PHP's paperwork in a narrative form using more clinical language. Since a number of the natural helpers did not have the writing skills to do that, the professional needed to be responsible for most of the paperwork.

These requirements affected the group in a number of ways. They gave more credibility and power to the professional. Families needed to be seen by people with credentials rather than by the person who might be able to best serve the family. The professional was supposed to lead the intervention and ask for help from the natural helper, rather than a professional/natural helper team deciding together how the family would be served. The natural helpers felt their credibility diminished and their strengths and skills not recognized. After many (heated) discussions, the group decided to focus on helping families in informal ways and look for more compatible and flexible funding sources. PHP continued with the contract but with only one professional/natural helper team.

Training

All PHP professionals and natural helpers received training in (a) safety, (b) CPS mandatory reporting, (c) drug treatment and prevention, (d) prevention of family violence, (e) conflict resolution, (f) parent training, and (g) building natural support systems. Training was provided by the professionals and the natural helpers in the group or by outside resources—depending on the skills and expertise available.

Referral Procedures

Referral procedures for informal families were informal. The natural helpers made it clear that formalizing the procedure would discourage many from asking for help. Informal families got in touch with PHP through word of mouth and chance meetings. PHP had a brochure but did not actively advertise because it received more than enough informal referrals. PHP used a more formal referral procedure for families referred by Child Protective Services. Caseworkers called a voice pager that was responded to immediately.

Location of Support

Natural helpers have always provided support for their neighbors in their own homes or the homes of the families they help. PHP members continued the process of providing support for all families in their homes and communities.

Intake and Assessment

Natural helpers were initially resistant to the more formal intake and assessment process required by the public agency contract. A process was designed whereby both professionals and natural helpers felt adequately informed as well as respecting the family and building rapport. A professional and a natural helper would go as a team on the initial visit. The purpose of this visit was to get the family's perspective on why it was referred to PHP and to identify the family's strengths. The team tried to visit the family at least two more times before the initial assessment was written for the public agency. A family self-assessment process was integral to this assessment. PHP saw assessment as ongoing and encouraged the family's input.

Duration of Help

Though specific contracts state how long formal help is provided, PHP natural helpers continued to run into the families they helped. They say that to state that a service is over is unnatural and unrealistic. Natural helpers were often neighbors to these families or they frequent the same social gatherings or service systems.

Writing About the Professional/Natural Helper Partnership

All of the articles and papers about PHP were written in partnership with the people involved. Each subject area was brought to the whole group and discussed, and notes were taken. Then the two professionals responsible for writing wrote drafts for review by the PHP group. Comments were incorporated into the next draft and reviewed by the PHP group again.

A FEW OF THE UNANSWERED QUESTIONS

In developing new approaches, it is as important for us to acknowledge and clarify what we do not know as well as what we are learning. A few of the questions we need to address include the following:

- Which tools commonly used by human services professionals can be transferred for use by neighborhood workers?
- How do those tools need to be adapted or supplemented by and for various cultural groups?
- How many of the techniques used within family-based services can be used by natural helpers and paraprofessionals in neighborhoods?
- How much can natural helpers learn to train their peers?
- How much of what neighborhood workers and residents are already doing can be packaged and transferred to professionals?
- Can some neighborhood workers make new careers as trainers?
- How well will neighborhood workers be able to design, develop, implement, and evaluate their own service strategies and models?
- What are the limits of neighborhood workers' capacity for providing their own help?
- What are the most cost-effective roles for professional workers and agencies in the future?

In this chapter, we discussed reasons for new approaches to social services and the advantages and challenges of developing professional/natural helper partnerships. We presented one example of a partnership, People Helping People, in Tacoma, Washington. We also identified questions that still remain. In the face of uncertainty, we could easily fall into limbo, waiting for the path toward the future to become more clear. This would be a sad error for us all, because it is precisely at these times of uncertainty, when the status quo is the most amenable to change, that we might make enormous changes for the better if we could find the energy, the hope, and the faith. We can build upon past successes and spread what we have learned far beyond what we originally hoped to reach. We have the opportunity to forge new partnerships that will allow us to combine knowledge from many perspectives, creating deeper insights and more creative alternatives.

NOTES

This chapter is about the challenges of true partnerships. It is about taking seriously the voices of the people we say we are trying to help, which often means giving up a lot of power and control. It means acknowledging the hard work, the great ideas, and the willingness of people to take risks and try out this partnership. Therefore, this paper has many authors. After working together in a professional/natural helper partnership and writing down the experiences and the ideas of the participants, two of the authors organized the ideas into a draft. The paper was distributed to the partnership members, changes were made, and more ideas were added. The authors with the professional writing experience could be seen as "translators" of the experience, rather than the sole authors. The ideas, insights, and conclusions came from many people. Therefore, all eighteen share the authorship.

In addition to Jill Kinney and Kathy Strand, the following people participated in creating this chapter: Kim Apple has extensive experience with office management and budgeting. She continues to assist with the financial management of the professional/natural helper partnership. Sue Bernstein has twenty years' experience working with churches and social service settings in neighborhoods. She has a bachelor's degree in education. Katrina Fogg has helped people in her neighborhood and church for many years. She has provided special meal preparation, companionship shopping, domestic budgeting, emergency child care, and backup clerical and office assistance. Larrie Fogg sees helping his community as part of his everyday life. Examples of help provided by Mr. Fogg include assessment of costs and materials needed to fix homes in serious disrepair, actual work fixing the homes, and accompanying people to Alcoholics Anonymous meetings. David Haapala is a licensed psychologist and cofounder of the nationally recognized Homebuilders program. Dr. Haapala is president of the National Association for Family-Based Services. Edith Johnson is employed part-time as a family advocate in Dixon Village, the community where she and her family live. She is a master teacher and has worked as a 4-H leader and a youth organizer with Washington State University. Ms. Johnson has an associate of arts degree from Tacoma Community College. Richard Johnson is interested in a holistic approach to health, child welfare, and management. His nontraditional approach has included teaching comparison shopping for used and new parts, accessing alternative funding, and helping install auto parts in an emergency situation. He is a certified respiratory therapist and has an associate of arts degree. Janice Nittoli is a senior associate for the Annie E. Casey Foundation. She was instrumental in conceptualizing the professional/natural helper partnership, allowing a flexible use of funds to create this evolving approach. Daniele Price is very active in her community. She helps her neighbors in many ways including bringing flowers, offering general legal knowledge and resources, library and Internet research, extending small loans for private objectives, advocating investment clubs, researching low-price airfare, and dog sitting. Ms. Price has an associate of arts degree from Evergreen University. Keith Roberts has served his community in many ways including helping someone fill out a do-it-yourself divorce kit, delivering the papers to court, fixing cars, and making witty remarks that defuse the tension in discussions. Tasha Steele helps mothers get health services for their children, talks people through crises, and provides transportation. She has extensive experience working with mentally ill and developmentally disabled people. Edwin Trent is particularly interested in helping other residents find employment and in providing support for men. He is state certified for Family Community Leadership and sits on the Board of Commissioners for Planning and Development for the city of Tacoma. Margaret Trent has thirty years' experience in Detroit, New York City, and Tacoma helping her neighbors connect with one another and use their strengths for mutual aid. She is a master teacher trainer and has done national-level training and consultation. Venessa Trent has developed and instructed a baby-sitting course to aid parents who cannot afford child care, helps mothers learn how to prepare low-cost meals, and drops by frequently to make sure small children are being supervised. Robert Smith emphasizes networking, administration, and mentoring of young boys. Examples of nontraditional services Mr. Smith has provided include arriving at a family's home to make sure the boys get on the bus, meeting the bus at school to make sure the boys make it into the building, and putting a bed together. Ron Vignec has a master of divinity degree. Pastor Vignec is a legend in the community for his wisdom, compassion, and vision of neighborhood transformation and development of new strategies for mutual support among people.

Financial support for the project described in this chapter was provided by the Annie E. Casey Foundation.

Portions of this chapter were previously published and adapted with permission. The following sources are acknowledged:

"Walking Our Talk in the Neighborhood: Building Professional/Natural Helper Partnerships," by K. Apple, S. Bernstein, K. Fogg, L. Fogg, D. Haapala, E. Johnson, R. Johnson, J. Kinney, J. Nittoli, D. Price, K. Roberts, T. Steele, K. Strand, E. Trent, M. Trent, V. Trent, R. Smith, and R. Vignec, 1997, *Social Policy*, 27 (4), p. 54–63. Copyright 1997 by Social Policy Corporation.

Wise Counsel: Redefining the Role of Consumers, Professionals, and Community Workers in the Helping Process (Resource Brief No. 8, pp. 41–55), by C. Bruner, E. S. Cahn, A. Gartner, R. P. Giloth, T. Herr, J. Kinney, F. Riessman, M. Trent, Y. Trevino, and S. L. Wagner, 1998, Falls Church, VA: National Center for Service Integration. Adapted with permission from the Child and Family Policy Center, Des Moines, IA.

Building Community Partnerships in Child Welfare (Brief Nos. 3 & 4), by Annie E. Casey, 1999, Baltimore, MD: Annie E. Casey Foundation.

REFERENCE

Kinney, J., Strand, K., Hagerup, M., & Bruner, C. (1994). *Beyond the buzzwords: Key principles in effective frontline practice.* Falls Church, VA: National Center for Service Integration.

12 Evaluation in a Dynamic Environment

Assessing Change When Nothing Is Constant

MARIANNE BERRY
MARIAN BUSSEY
SCOTTYE J. CASH

Since the passage of the Adoption Assistance and Child Welfare Act (Public Law 96–272) in 1980, the preservation of families through the prevention of unnecessary out-of-home placement has been a fundamental goal of family-centered services. Out-of-home placement can refer to foster care services provided by Child Protective Services (CPS); juvenile detention, jail, or boot camp in juvenile justice; hospitalization or residential care in mental health settings. All result in a major disruption in a child's and family's life, which has been found to predict many bad outcomes (Schorr, 1988).

The goal of family preservation—maintenance of family relationships through the prevention of child placement—thus applies across programs and policies in any family-centered system. This goal affects and frames practice, not only in regard to the attempt to make reasonable efforts to keep families together but in the constrained use of temporary foster care, continued contact with birth parents while children are temporarily out of the home or even placed in other permanent settings such as adoptive families, and the limited use of residential treatment or other more restrictive long-term out-of-home placements.

The preservation of families and family ties is therefore a philosophical tenet of all family-centered services (Lloyd & Sallee, 1994; Warsh, Pine, &

Maluccio, 1995). From an evaluative stance, this philosophical tenet becomes the ultimate objective. The primary objective of family-centered services, whether in child protection, juvenile justice, or mental health, is to prevent children from going into more formal or restrictive placements in the service system and to keep children out of foster care, out of jail, and out of residential treatment or hospitalization. This is a fairly distal goal, sometimes far removed from the more proximal treatment objectives that must be achieved first.

There are many specific means by which to achieve the goal of placement prevention, depending on the specific circumstances that propel the child and family toward placement. Placement as a distal outcome is multi-determined. Many different circumstances can lead to placement; further, sometimes they do, and sometimes they don't (i.e., there is seldom a direct link). Placement can be determined by family characteristics, service effectiveness, system influences (e.g., judicial decisions or placement availability), and community standards.

The systemic social and environmental influences on case and program outcomes are important and often neglected variables. And they are highly variable. The social and economic conditions of families in the United States are in flux and vary differentially for particular populations and in particular communities. Service components and effectiveness also vary by locale and change continually as certain service resources increase and decrease in availability or favor. Judicial and public concern for children, families, and their best interests continue to shift with public attention.

These shifting sands in the social terrain contribute to a highly dynamic environment in which family-centered services are embedded. Many different factors can influence whether families succeed (i.e., avoid bad outcomes; Schorr, 1988). When so many factors external to a program and external to a family can influence the primary outcome, internal validity—making a direct connection between services and outcomes—is of critical importance. To secure internal validity, it is necessary to ensure that a connection between treatment (the family-centered service) and outcome (avoidance of bad outcomes and attainment of better conditions) exists and is directly observable and measurable. Therefore, outcomes must become more proximal to the treatment process and more relevant to process goals; these components must be logically and directly related.

HISTORICAL DEVELOPMENT IN THE EVALUATION OF FAMILY-CENTERED SERVICES

Evaluation is concerned with whether programs achieve outcomes. Evaluation has been a critical element in the development and refinement of family-centered services for several reasons. First, findings from evaluations have been used to inform workers and administrators of what techniques or programs are helpful, thus optimally protecting clients from unethical or inappropriate treatment. For example, family preservation research has found that providing concrete services is related to good outcomes (Berry, 1994; Fraser, Pecora, & Haapala, 1991). Second, agencies have demonstrated treatment effectiveness to ensure funding for programs. This is becoming increasingly important as the fields of child welfare, mental health, and juvenile justice have moved to a managed care environment (Pecora, Massinga, & Mauzerall, 1997). Third, findings from evaluations have been used to help agencies plan for more effective and efficient utilization of staff and resources, through formative evaluations that define the structure and nature of services provided to families.

A specialized method of service delivery, which often goes by the name of intensive family preservation services (IFPS), is at present the most commonly evaluated form of family-centered services. In general, these are short-term intensive services provided to families at risk of imminent foster placement of their children, to try to reduce risks and enhance skills so that families can remain safely together. An addition to the service continuum, intensive family reunification services (IFRS), uses this form of service model to prepare and support the reunification of placed children with their families (Walton, 1991).

Distinguishing features of IFPS and IFRS relate to the structure and nature of service delivery. In terms of the *structure* of the model, the services provided by intensive family preservation and reunification programs are usually intensive and short-term, lasting at the most a few months. Caseworkers are typically available to the families twenty-four hours a day and seven days a week (Berry, 1992; Cole, 1995; Kinney, Dittmar, & Firth, 1990). Caseworkers thus carry a small caseload and have more face-to-face contact with families. In addition, large proportions of contact often take place in the client's home, instead of in the caseworker's office.

Although structured in ways that may seem a radical departure from traditional child welfare services, intensive family preservation services are actually based on an empirical and theoretical base of practice and service delivery that was established as effective and successful in the 1970s through several child welfare demonstration projects across the United States (Fein, Maluccio, Hamilton, & Ward, 1983; Lahti et al., 1978; Stein, Gambrill, & Wiltse, 1978). These demonstration projects to promote permanency and continuity for children, maintaining family ties when possible, used experimental designs and large samples and independently produced fairly similar and positive results.

While the structure of services is often heralded as the hallmark of intensive family preservation services, the *nature* of services and the underlying theoretical rationale are equally, if not more, important. The demonstration projects in the 1970s found that services were most effective (families were preserved) when services were family centered, when caseworkers and families established mutually agreed-upon goals, when services were multidimensional, involving collateral agencies and concrete assistance when required, when contracts between worker and family were used as a feature of service planning, and when clear indicators of case progress were identified and tracked by worker and family throughout the life of the case.

Building on this research base, founders of intensive family preservation programs in the 1970s asserted that short-term, cognitive-behavioral approaches provided to families in their homes could create lasting and generalizable improvements in parenting skills, family functioning, child behavior, and household safety (Kinney, Madsen, & Haapala, 1977). For example, the Homebuilders program used (and uses) many of the lessons learned in these demonstration projects to frame service delivery in a timely, quick, and efficient package. The *structure* of this service model as short term and intensive is predicated on its consistency with the *nature* of services as behavioral, contractual, concrete, and limited.

The remainder of this chapter will present an overview of the methods used in recent evaluation research in family-centered, family preservation services, primarily in the field of child welfare. The purpose will be to provide the reader with both an abstract conceptualization and concrete examples of the challenges and proposed solutions in the evaluation of family-centered services. These evaluations have incorporated and respected family-centered values and principles in the practice of program evaluation of family-centered services. A concrete discussion of evaluation techniques in this field will cover both the structural approaches necessary under dynamic conditions and the analysis and interpretation of resulting information to build the knowledge base, to inform the practice base on an immediate and relevant basis, and to advocate for programs when warranted. The practice of critical thinking by evaluators and consumers of resulting findings will be emphasized.

CURRENT APPLICATIONS: METHODS AND MEANINGS

Most evaluations and public discussions of family-centered services have focused on outcomes—and this trend will continue, without a doubt. On the whole, family preservation outcomes have been assessed by means of placement of children outside the home (Berry, 1997; Blythe, Salley, & Jayaratne, 1994; Heneghan, Horwitz, & Leventhal, 1996). Blythe et al. (1994), reviewing several existing family preservation evaluations, found placement prevention rates ranging from approximately 50 to 90 percent. Although several outcome studies of intensive family preservation services have reported placement prevention rates in this range, with many falling in the 75 to 95 percent range (Berry, 1997), these statistics are somewhat meaningless for three particularly important reasons related to the phenomenon of child placement.

First, the term *placement prevention* is somewhat misleading, given that it has not been established that placement is indeed prevented by these programs. Intensive family preservation services have not established that they are preventing placement among families who would have otherwise experienced placement without services, because the families who are not receiving services have also not experienced placement in many controlled studies (even though they were judged to be at equal risk of imminent placement of their children). Studies employing control groups have found that families in programs that did not offer placement prevention services also experienced placement in statistically equivalent proportions to those that offered placement prevention (Schuerman, Rzepnicki, & Littell, 1994; Yuan & Struckman-Johnson, 1991).

Second, the larger context and usage of child placement differs from locale to locale (Fraser, Pecora, & Haapala, 1991; Goerge, Wulczyn, & Harden, 1994, 1996; Kamerman & Kahn, 1989). A large multistate database on foster care placement rates and caseloads in California, Illinois, Michigan, New York, and Texas (five states that account for almost half of the U.S. population in foster care) finds large differences in placement rates and placement trends from state to state, and from region to region within states (Goerge, Wulczyn, & Harden, 1996). Comparisons between studies of placement prevention programs conducted in different states become exceedingly difficult when the overall incidence of placement in each state can be so variable and disparate. For example, the prevalence of foster placement in the state of Texas is notably lower than in other major states at 1 child per 1,000 children, compared to 3 to 6 children per 1,000 children in Illinois, Michigan, California, and New York (George, Wulczyn, & Harden, 1996). Incidence rates (first entry into foster care) in Texas are also the lowest of the five major states. Therefore, programs that strive to prevent placement in states that already use placement sparingly will have different outcomes than programs in states with a greater availability and use of foster care.

Third, the identified target populations served by family preservation programs also vary from locale to locale. An evaluation of Child Protective Services in Texas in 1988 (American Association for Protecting Children, 1988) identified the following formula to determine those services' target population: the Texas legislature funds Child Protective Services to provide services to only 60 percent of the families determined to be in need of services; and Child Protective Services in turn estimates that only 70 percent of eligible families actually need services in order to prevent reabuse or child placement. "Thus, the goal of the Department is to provide services to 42 of every 100 families [70 percent of 60 percent] in which abuse or neglect is confirmed or adjudicated" (American Association for Protecting Children, 1988, pp. 3–17). In actuality, only 29 out of 100 families in need were served during the year of the AAPC (1988) evaluation; these families can be expected to be at the highest relative risk of continued maltreatment. This trend is still present today in Texas (Texas Department of Protective and Regulatory Services, 1995). Other states or communities have differing approaches to definitions of the target population (Kalichman & Brosig, 1992) and therefore serve families at differing and perhaps lower levels of need.

Placement cannot be ignored as an outcome (although complex and fairly distal) because of its financial and emotional ramifications for children, families, and communities. But a focus on placement alone, or placement prevention alone, at any cost is dangerous and irresponsible. These placement options have their place in a service continuum that seeks to provide a range of appropriate and safe outcomes for families (Wells & Tracy, 1996).

Logic Models

Though any program or service *can* be evaluated without a clear theoretical model of how certain outcomes are expected to occur based on the nature of the services provided, "ideally, high-quality evaluations use theory as a way of guiding the choice of dependent and independent variables, as well as the research design and measures" (Pecora, Nelson, Meezan, McCroskey, & Fraser, 1995, p. 7).

Therefore, in addition to attention to placement outcomes and other family disruptions, evaluations will be best served by focusing on immediate and relevant outcomes, and on the best services by which to achieve those outcomes with these choices of services having a sound conceptual or theoretical framework. Services that have not been well defined are considered the "black box" (Staff & Fein, 1994) of family-centered services, in that if we don't know what different services are provided to different families, we cannot know (a) if services are indeed tailored to families and (b) which services provided by the program are effective (as determined by their association with positive outcomes).

Logic models, the result of logic modeling or program modeling, are a very useful format for planning and evaluating family-centered services (Alter & Egan, 1997; Alter & Murty, 1997). Alter and Egan (1997), in an overview of logic modeling in the evaluation of social work practice (and programs), delineate the seven basic elements to be explicated in a logic model:

1. Problem/need: what needs changing
2. Goal: the desired state to be achieved
3. Objectives: minigoals that will lead to goal achievement
4. Inputs: concrete and intangible resources needed
5. Methods: methods by which to use resources
6. Results: short-term impacts of inputs and methods
7. Outcomes: long-term outcomes of inputs and methods (p. 88)

In the field of family preservation services and evaluation, differing program models have led to differing evaluation methods. The original Homebuilders model (Kinney, Haapala, & Booth, 1991), for instance, based in part on the theory of crisis intervention and short-term, cognitive skill building to prevent out-of-home placements in families who were otherwise at imminent risk of placement, led to research models that measured placement rates as the ultimate outcome measure. A different model of services, designed for child welfare clients with more chronic conditions, and based on an ecological approach to strengthening family interactions and child-rearing skills (Meezan & McCroskey, 1996), led to a research model that emphasizes changes in family functioning (in addition to placement rates and types). Another more recent model of services, which uses a structured educational approach based on family systems theory, led to a research model that measured changes in child and family functioning, level of restrictiveness/length of stay of placements, and qualitative measures of client satisfaction (Raschick, 1997).

These examples highlight the following principles of evaluation that are based on incorporation of a logic model:

1. Goals, objectives, inputs, methods, results, and outcomes must be relevant to the problem/need that brought the family to the attention of the service system. All should be theoretically congruent and logically related.

2. All components must be systemically and ecologically relevant, in that the focus is truly family centered (not individual-pathologizing) and cognizant of environmental influences and supports.

3. Process and outcomes must build on previous knowledge. Certain methods and models of treatment for child abuse, child neglect, family dysfunction, depression, juvenile delinquency, and so on are more effective than others, more empirically sound. The empirical knowledge base should help guide the choice of inputs and methods.

4. Outcomes must be relevant to the structure and nature of inputs and methods (short-term versus long-term treatment, intensive versus low-level contacts, etc.).

Evaluation Methods: Designs and Samples

Intensive family preservation services have been and continue to be the subject of intense hyperbole and scrutiny (Gelles, 1996; Schuerman et al., 1994; Littell, 1995; Wald, 1988). Of the many evaluative studies conducted and published, most emphasize outcome achievement, with few incorporating an experimental research design. In recent years, methodological reviews have identified the strengths and weaknesses of this research base (Blythe et al., 1994; Heneghan et al., 1996).

The broader research base of family preservation consists primarily of information on client characteristics and case outcomes. A review of the evaluative research on intensive family preservation and reunification programs illuminates the preponderance of information on program inputs (such as client characteristics and problems) and outputs (primarily case outcomes, particularly child placement), with little information on the contents of the "black box" (Staff & Fein, 1994) or the structure and nature of services within these programs.

The following discussion of design, sampling, and measures reviews current applications in the evaluation of family-centered services, presents a critical analysis of what these current applications can and cannot contribute to the knowledge base guiding family-centered services, and provides further recommendations for the logical and valid evaluation of these types of services. Examples of family-centered evaluations clarify the problems and promise of evaluation in this field. The general theme of this discussion is that of "keeping it simple" or rather "keeping it logical," attending to the direct connection between the *goals* of the families in a family-centered program, the *services* by which those goals are expected to be achieved, and relevant and direct assessment of goal *achievement*.

Evaluation Design

Program evaluation can be used to answer a variety of questions of importance to different stakeholders (those who have an interest in the outcome of the evaluation) in the process. The important thing is to know what those questions are and to build them into the research design. There should be a logical developmental process in program evaluation, especially with new interventions, just as there should be with program implementation (Landsman, 1998). It would not make sense to do the same kind of program evaluation with a small pilot project just getting started in a community, for example, as would be done with a large-scale, ten-year-old program that has had experience with hundreds of clients (Knickman & Jellinek, 1997). At the very beginning of an evaluation, tempting though it is to ask immediately "Does it work?" it is often most productive to focus on the factors that will eventually lead to a program "working" or not.

Those factors may include a needs assessment, to thoroughly understand the nature of the problem and of the clients in a certain community, and a process evaluation, to look at how the program is being implemented—how staff are trained, who is served, what is actually done, and how consistently and faithfully staff implement the intervention (often referred to as *treatment integrity*).

Once it is established that (a) there is a need for a program, (b) it is reaching the targeted population, and (c) it is being implemented as designed, it is *then* appropriate to ask questions about outcomes. Researchers and practitioners are often most concerned with outcomes for individuals and families—has family, parent, and child functioning improved? Have children remained safely in their homes? Have family members learned and used new skills? Administrators and funding sources will also be concerned with cost-related outcomes—has the new service model reduced out-of-home placement costs relative to the costs of implementation? How do the costs of this model compare with those of other service models? Finally, policymakers may also be interested in community impact—over time, has the program improved the well-being of children and families in the target area? Are the community-level indicators, such as overall rates of abuse, school drop out, and prenatal services usage, changing?

Programs are expected to produce outcomes. The most persuasive program and outcome evaluation designs are those that use traditional experimental method—taking a large group of clients who need some kinds of service or treatment, and then randomly assigning them to either the treatment or control condition. Only with a control group can an evaluation have internal validity (i.e., determine that the intervention caused any change). In a classic experimental design, the control group receives no services at all, at least not until the research is completed. In reality, however, with the range and seriousness of the problems seen by Child Protective Services, research designs assigning clients to a no-treatment control group are rarely used. In some instances, usually with voluntary clients, demand for services may be so high that not all clients can be served when they ask for services, so there may be a natural "waiting list" control group. Because Raschick's (1997) study was with voluntary clients seeking services, and staff caseloads were full, his control group was formed from clients who could not be served because of a lack of treatment vacancies.

The more common type of experimental research design in the field of family-centered services is random assignment to either family preservation or to another form of service. This does not raise the same ethical questions as denial of treatment altogether, because until the research is actually done, program administrators cannot predict which form of services will result in the most gains for families and children. The control condition (actually a comparison condition rather than control) is often defined as traditional provision of services. At the conclusion of the evaluation, or at some specified interval of time, the clients who received the new program should, in theory, have made more progress on goals and functioning than the clients who were in the comparison group. With this design, it is theoretically not necessary to do a pretest and posttest, because there should be no differences between the clients initially assigned to the new program and those assigned to a comparison condition. The actual progress of the two groups, and the hypothesized differences between them, would show up in the postintervention measures. However, pretest measures are often used both to assess degree of change within each group and to test the assumption that both groups were equivalent at the start of the study. If the groups are found to differ, or if the assignment to treatment or control condition has not been random, it will be much harder to establish internal validity (i.e., to answer the question of program effectiveness). Rubin (1997) noted that over time, because of the way an agency may refer clients to treatment versus control—especially if the referral source has strongly held opinions on the relative value of a new program compared to other services—even a design that started out as experimental with random assignment may become nonexperimental.

Another real-world design problem that can and does have a large impact on interpreting the results of a program evaluation is the spread of the newer program goals and methods to comparison groups receiving traditional services. In some therapy research, it is the clients themselves, in the control or comparison condition, who may realize that another group is getting something new and may then decide to actively seek out some aspect of this different treatment. They may even try harder to show improvements out of a feeling of loyalty to their therapist or rivalry with the other group. In Child Protective Services, it could be the caseworkers who hear about what is being done in the new program (in this case, family-centered or family preservation services) and if they agree with the basic philosophy, put slightly more emphasis on using these new techniques that would be expected to strengthen families, and slightly less emphasis on a placement-reunification model. Diffusion of treatment effects has been mentioned as a possible explanation of the fact that in one of the largest randomized experimental studies so far, that of the Families First program in Illinois, few differences in placement rates were found between families assigned to the external family preservation services and those assigned to traditional agency-based services (Schuerman et al., 1994).

One way to compensate for the problem of diffusion of treatment, and a necessary step in any case, is to obtain a fairly thorough description of what both forms of service—family-centered and traditional services—actually entail, looking inside the "black box," as Staff and Fein (1994) did for reunification services. This may involve, at a minimum, some form of process recording by the service provider, or, in more depth, qualitative interviews with both service providers and families or videotaping and analysis of actual worker-family interactions. Several studies have attempted to provide more specificity to what family preservation services actually provide. Berry (1992), Craig-Van Grack (1997), Fraser, Pecora, and Haapala (1991), and Staff and Fein (1994) have designed forms to measure aspects of family preservation and family reunification services. However, there are still few published studies that describe the nature of family preservation services in much depth.

This kind of description of the process of family preservation services is equally important in quasi-experimental research designs, when random assignment to two different conditions is impossible. If a locality has made an administrative decision to refer all cases to family preservation, for instance, but still wants to know how effectively this is working, there are several alternative designs. One of the most straightforward is a one-group pretest-posttest design: clients are measured at intake and again at the end of service, on a variety of factors important to family functioning and the presenting problem. Any change in scores may be cautiously interpreted as due to the services received. There is always the possibility, however, that the clients would have improved even in the absence of these particular services. Since it is impossible to rule out that possibility, it must be dealt with as a possible threat to the validity of the findings. Evaluators can also compare the progress of clients in their sample with the progress (or possibly lack of progress) of clients in similar circumstances who were served by the agency before the new program was implemented. For an evaluation of family preservation services, for instance, this may mean searching agency records for statistics on placement rates, reabuse rates, or family functioning measures (if available) for clients in the one-year period prior to the implementation of family preservation services and comparing them with the same measures for clients who received family preservation services. The threat to validity with this design, however, is that the two cohorts (groups followed through time) experienced different historical influences and may have changed as a result of those outside influences, rather than as a result of the program. Other threats to validity are the possibility that people may be sensitized by taking a pretest and therefore change their answers on the posttest due to their reaction to the earlier test, not to actual attitude or behavior change, and the possibility that clients will try to make themselves appear particularly socially desirable, competent, or self-effective by minimizing their problems over time. Although an experimental design with a control group minimizes these possible threats to the validity of conclusions of research, quasi-experimental designs can build in ways to address them, both through thorough description of the clients, the program, and the research process and by use of

statistical controls (to compare clients on equivalence in other areas expected to impact their treatment progress).

Sampling

It is important to the logic of the treatment model that there be clear parameters for clients to be referred to family preservation services, and that
all clients who meet those requirements be in the pool of potential recipients. The families assigned to a family-centered program, when it is being
compared to other services, should be neither only the most functional and
motivated nor only the most troubled. They should be comparable—from
troubled to motivated—to families in the comparison group. Each program,
however, may have very different parameters for families defined as appropriate for family preservation or some other program. McCroskey and
Meezan's (1996) study of family preservation in Los Angeles, for instance,
had very few conditions that ruled families out as inappropriate for services.
Any family seen by Child Protective Services—whether for neglect, physical
abuse, or sexual abuse, whether or not there had been previous out-of-home
child placements, and whether or not placement was imminent—was accepted for the program (and then assigned randomly to either family preservation or traditional agency services) unless the family absolutely refused
or was incapable of understanding what was being asked. In contrast to this
broad definition of families appropriate for family preservation services, a
Nebraska family preservation program ruled out any family in which there
was refusal of services, sexual abuse, chronic psychosis, mentally retarded
parents, psychopathic or sociopathic family members, chronic substance
abuse, previous termination of parental rights, chronic problems, or no risk
of imminent placement (Leeds, 1984). Deciding which families are most
appropriate for family preservation services is not solely an evaluation
question (though evaluation may certainly help answer that question); it
is ultimately an administrative decision. What is noteworthy about both
of the evaluations just mentioned, different in scope though they be, is that
readers, and other administrators, have a very clear picture of exactly who
was served and can therefore interpret the findings accordingly. Just as in
the description of services provided, the more the researcher knows quan-
titatively and qualitatively about the clients served, the more useful the
evaluation data are in both replicating the program and understanding its
effectiveness.

Clearly, a variety and multiplicity of risk factors are found among families who have been reported for child abuse or neglect, which at times
warrants that the child be placed in foster care (Ronnau & Marlow, 1993).
Dore and Harnett (1995) provide the following characteristics of families
who are in the child welfare system: "In great distress, they frequently
suffer from multiple problems and needs. Parents often exhibit deficits in

caregiving capacity, problem-solving skills, knowledge of child development, and realistic expectations of child psychosocial functioning" (p. 67).

Some ambiguity exists, however, concerning precise criteria for risk, including imminent risk (i.e., identifying which children are in jeopardy of being placed outside the home) (Schuerman et al., 1994). Many family preservation programs, particularly the Homebuilders model, have used the criterion of imminent risk to screen clients for services. Many times imminent risk of placement is a judgment call based on the caseworker's subjective opinion (Doueck, Bronson, & Levine, 1992; Magura & Moses, 1986), although determinations of risk are better defined through the use of such structured tools as risk assessment inventories (Berry, 1992; Theiman & Dail, 1992). The reliability of such inventories is not well established, however (Berry, 1997; Doueck et al., 1992; Wald & Woolverton, 1990).

Evaluation Methods: Measurement Issues and Measures

Given adequate support and resources for agency personnel, a thorough evaluation of a family preservation or other family-centered program should include information on a family's intake characteristics, service provision, and a *variety* of case outcomes. Collection of reliable information in each of these three categories allows for a causal or associational analysis of each group of characteristics with the others, which is essential to planning (see table 12.1).

The collection of data on these elements presupposes adequate training for workers in the completion of data collection forms and incorporation of data collection into the service process (rather than separately adding it on to existing caseload requirements). Thus the most effective data collection instruments will be worker-friendly and will help guide individual case decision making and the tracking of individual case progress.

The information gathered in the three domains (i.e., client intake characteristics, service provision, and case outcomes) is intended to help individual caseworkers in their assessment, decision making, and tracking of case progress, regardless of its usage in a larger program evaluation. Such information, in aggregated form, will only be helpful to program planners, however, if collected on a sample of sufficient size and within an appropriately designed evaluation. A sound evaluation depends on careful choices of all three methods (design, sampling, and measures). Good data alone will not help caseworkers, administrators, or policymakers draw sound conclusions about families or programs.

Client Characteristics

Most families receiving family-centered services are in a crisis and, in family preservation programs, are said to be at imminent risk of having their

TABLE 12.1. Data Elements at Intake, During Service, and at Case Closure

Client Intake Characteristics	Service Provision	Case Outcomes
Family demographics □ Includes ethnicity and poverty level Nature and severity of maltreatment Family strengths/supports □ Personal qualities □ Knowledge/skills □ Social supports □ Income and material supports Family stressors □ History/chronicity of problems □ Environmental and household dangers □ Compounding problems (drug use, domestic violence, etc.)	Number of days case open Total time served Service intensity (time per day) Frequency and type of concrete services Frequency and type of educational services Frequency and type of clinical services Where services provided Use of psychoeducational groups Use of collateral helpers	Child placement while case open Maltreatment reports while case open Satisfactory case closure Gains in strengths/supports □ Family gains in intake factors while case open Reduction in family and environmental stressors Client satisfaction Family satisfaction Child placement after case closure Maltreatment reports after case closure Skill/knowledge/resource gains or losses between case closure and a follow-up point

child placed in foster care within twenty-four to forty-eight hours. In addition to a noted variability in the definition of imminent risk across studies (Blythe et al., 1994; Heneghan et al., 1996; Rossi, 1992), critics have identified other deficits in the research base in regard to client characteristics. Most notably, many studies have omitted or disregarded information regarding client ethnicity (Blythe et al., 1994), even though the phenomenon of disproportionate child placement rates for children of color is well established (Brown & Bailey-Etta, 1997; Pelton, 1989; Widom, 1988). Information on client financial resources or poverty level is another area often neglected in describing the clientele of family preservation and reunification services, despite the profound overrepresentation of families under the poverty line among clients of public Child Protective Services (Eamon, 1994; Pelton, 1989, 1993). Studies that have included information on economic resources and parental employment have found significant associations between these resources and successful family preservation (Berry, 1992; Smith, 1995) and family reunification (Fraser, Walton, Lewis, Pecora, & Walton, 1996).

An equally troubling omission from many studies of family preservation and child welfare services in general concerns the nature of the child maltreatment in the family (Daro, 1988; Lindsey, 1994). While many experts postulate that intensive services will be most effective with families whose risks are acute and not chronic, few studies report the chronicity of presenting problems or whether the families were treated for child abuse, child neglect, or both (Howing, Kohn, Gaudin, Kurtz, & Wodarski, 1992). Some studies on the differential effectiveness of family preservation with child abuse and child neglect have found greater effectiveness with physical abuse cases than with child neglect cases (Berry, 1992; Landsman, Nelson, Tyler, & Allen, 1990) because child neglect tends to be of a more chronic nature and is not as easily addressed by a short-term intervention.

Based on the previous research in understanding families and their situations, it is important to assess a range of client intake characteristics (see table 12.2). It is also important to measure intake characteristics in terms of things that can be changed during treatment, and not to focus entirely on the history of the family and factors that services cannot address or change. The focus of programs and evaluations must be on the changeable factors, factors to be addressed by services.

The most important data to collect is information regarding the family's strengths and the stressors that brought it to the family-centered program for help in the first place. Such information can be assessed through standardized or individualized means.

Standardized measures have the advantage of being tested and normed with other clinical or nonclinical populations. This allows a family-centered program to assess the comparison of its clients to clinical or non-

TABLE 12.2. Data Elements Assessed at Intake

Client characteristics

Family demographics
- Includes ethnicity and poverty level

Nature and severity of maltreatment

Family strengths/supports
- Personal qualities
- Knowledge/skills
- Social supports
- Income and material supports

Family stressors
- History/chronicity of problems
- Environmental and household dangers
- Compounding problems (drug use, domestic violence, etc.)

---

clinical norms of functioning. Table 12.3 provides a list of many standardized measures that have been used or recommended for use in evaluations of family-centered services. These tools assess family functioning, parent functioning, child functioning, and social support.

Individualized, nonstandardized measures and tools can also be used in the assessment and recording of family characteristics. Although they are often deemed beneficial to client populations that may exhibit non-standard characteristics (jeopardizing the utility of standardized norms), individualized measures also carry the deficit of having no established norms or reliability of the instrument used. Given the enormous problems of establishing internal validity discussed above, it is recommended that nonstandardized measures be avoided whenever possible.

TABLE 12.3. Standardized Measures for Use in Family Preservation Programs and Evaluations

Family Functioning	Family Adaptability Cohesion Evaluation Scales (FACES IV)
	Self-Report Family Inventory
	Family Environment Scale
	McMasters Family Assessment Device
	Index of Family Relations
	Child Well-Being Scales
	Family Systems Change Scale
	Family Assessment Form
	Family Risk Scales*
Child Functioning	Bayley Scales of Infant Development
	Denver Developmental Screening Test
	Peabody Picture Vocabulary Test (revised)
	Bzoch-League Receptive-Expressive Emergent Language Scale
	Standard Progressive Matrices
	System of Multicultural Pluralistic Assessment*
	Adaptive Behavior Social Inventory
	Child Behavior Checklist
	Youth Self-Report
	Vineland Adaptive Behavior Scales
	Conners Parent Symptom Questionnaire and Teachers Rating Scales
	Family Relations Test
	Children's Depression Inventory
	Coopersmith Self-Esteem Inventories
	Personality Inventory for Children
	State-Trait Anxiety Inventory for Children
	Home Observation for Measurement of the Environment
	Urban Childhood Level of Living Scale

(Table continues)

TABLE I2.3. *(continued)*

Parent Functioning	Adult-Adolescent Parenting Inventory
	Child Abuse Potential Inventory
	Parental Disposition Subscale of the Child Well-Being Scales
	Level of Living Scale*
	Parenting Stress Index
	Parental Locus of Control Scale
	Parental Acceptance-Rejection Questionnaire
	Child at Risk Field*
Social Support/ Community	Family Relationship Index
	Social Network Map
	Inventory Milardo Social Support
	Family Support Scale
	Inventory of Social Support
	Personal Network Matrix
	Life Event Scale**
	Interpersonal Support Evaluation List**

Source: Measures reviewed by Howing, Kohn, Gaudin, Kurtz, and Wodarski (1992) are indicated by a single asterisk (*). Those reviewed by Feldman (1991) are indicated by two asterisks (**). All others are reviewed by Pecora, Fraser, Nelson, McCroskey, and Meezan (1995). From *The Family at Risk: Issues and Trends in Family Preservation Services* (p. 178), by M. Berry, 1997, Columbia: University of South Carolina Press. Reprinted with permission.

The Structure and Nature of Services

Service provision has received to date the least attention in family preservation research (Bath & Haapala, 1994; Blythe et al., 1994). Given the variability in client populations and the variability in the context of child placement discussed above, a well-delineated, direct, and logical connection between service characteristics and case and program outcomes becomes particularly salient and critical to issues of program integrity and replication. It is only when outcomes can be directly connected to services that consumers of evaluation results can assess the nature of change among families, given all the variability external to a program and its families.

Better delineation and tracking of the structure and nature of service provision in intensive family preservation and family reunification services should strengthen three areas of the empirical base that supports or refutes these programs. First, a description of the structure and nature of services provided establishes treatment integrity, or the fidelity of a program to the stated service model. Second, clear delineation of services rendered in individual cases allows for testing of the validity of an individualized service plan based on the risk factors present in the individual family, a fundamental premise of the family preservation service model. Third, measurement and tracking of service provision allows for the analysis of the association of specific service components with case outcomes, controlling for the risk factors present.

Integrity of the treatment model. What do family-centered services look like? For example, what does the service model of intensive family preservation and intensive family reunification services really look like when implemented? Do agencies adhere to the short-term and intensive structure of services? Services provided in these models have been categorized as concrete services (provision and access to concrete resources, such as housing and financial assistance as well as household improvements) and educational and clinical services (including counseling and skills training). Do family preservation and family reunification services truly combine concrete with educational and clinical services in order to provide families with many resources that they can use to keep the family together?

The terms *short term* and *intensive* are the hallmarks of the structure of intensive family preservation services. The intent of the short duration of services is to motivate clients and workers to move and change expediently and also to contribute to cost-effective treatment, a major selling point of this method of service. The intensity of services, or the practice of large amounts of face-to-face contact between caseworker and family, is intended to contribute to effective and meaningful learning opportunities. Intensity allows caseworkers to assess families and their situations fully, and allows families to learn and practice skills with their caseworker in blocks of uninterrupted time.

> All of these aspects of the model—the rapid responses to referrals, the accessibility of workers at home during the evenings and weekends, the time available for families, the location of the services, the staffing pattern, the low caseloads, and the brief duration of services—produce a much more powerful intervention than one that utilizes only one or two of these components. It is impossible to have the intensity and flexibility we would like with a large caseload. It is impossible to maintain focus, responsiveness to crisis, and accessibility if the intervention drifts on for too long a period. We urge others considering replication of Homebuilders to try the whole package first, and tailor it to their communities if they encounter difficulties. If they eliminate one aspect, such as the short time frame or the low caseload, they are likely to decrease the power of the overall intervention far more than they can realize without first attempting the whole model. (Kinney et al., 1991, p. 53)

So, to what extent have intensive family preservation services been short term and intensive in actual practice? Intensive family preservation programs have proliferated across the country over the past decade, some modeled after Homebuilders, others with a different theoretical base. In general, programs have incorporated the structural elements of models to a greater degree than the content of a specific theoretical or practice model. This is not surprising, given that the structure of a program is more easily quantified, described, and thus transferred than is the content within that structure. Many program evaluations do not describe these service characteristics at all (Blythe et al., 1994; Heneghan et al., 1996). A small number of evaluations, however, have measured structural implementation of programs (see the review by Heneghan et al., 1996).

Feldman's (1991) evaluation of family preservation services reported an average of eleven hours contact per week per family, with service length ranging from seven to sixty-three days. This appears to be fairly intensive and short term, well within model guidelines. Similarly, Fraser, Pecora, and Haapala (1991) reported an average of thirty-seven hours of therapist contact per case, with service length averaging thirty days at the Washington study site and sixty-three days at the Utah study site (influenced by different program limits at each site).

Program structure becomes less short term and intensive in other sites or programs (which may be theoretically congruent with the nature of services, but this is often not established). For example, Meezan and McCroskey (1996) report service length of about three months in their study in Los Angeles, with one to three visits per week (at about two hours per week). Caseworkers carried ten to twelve cases at a time, so the intensity of services is questionable. Indeed, as Meezan and McCroskey note, these are "family-centered services rather than intensive family-centered services" (p. 14), an important and empirically sound distinction.

Staff and Fein's (1994) evaluation of services in a family reunification program in New England clearly found that the length of service was not short term (over two years per case), but was intensive. Reunified families in this program had received an average of twelve hours of service per week. This study is unique in its tracking of hours of service per case per week by each worker. The authors also note that such tracking is extremely burdensome on workers, and recommend this practice only for short studies.

Scannapieco's (1993) evaluation of "intensive worker involvement" (p. 511) in family preservation services in Minnesota found caseloads of nine families per worker and case time limits of six months. There was no description of service characteristics, however, making the proof of intensive worker involvement untestable. This was a secondary analysis of existing data, and service intensity information may have been unavailable. The program may be family centered, but it does not appear to be either short term or intensive. Categorizing it as intensive family preservation services is a common misattribution in the field between mission and method (Maluccio, Pine, & Warsh, 1994).

Other evaluations of programs are even less illuminating of the structure of services. The evaluation of intensive family preservation services across the state of Illinois in the early 1990s (Schuerman et al., 1994) laments the problem of "the black box and the million models" (p. 205), in that the program evaluated was implemented with such variability and creativity across sites (arguably an asset of the model) that summarizing or generalizing from study sites was difficult if not meaningless. While Charles Gershenson (1993) has called the Illinois study "an experiment in ambiguity," programs that claim to tailor service plans and service delivery to individual client needs are exceedingly difficult to measure and analyze by design.

In examining service implementation, previous research has focused in differing degrees on the concrete services, clinical services, and educational services provided to the families (Bath & Haapala, 1994; Blythe et al., 1994; Fraser, Pecora, & Haapala, 1991; Theiman & Dail, 1992). Some authors suggest that because family preservation services are intensive and time limited, the focus will necessarily be on providing concrete services rather than engaging the family in longer-term clinical or therapeutic processes (Fraser & Haapala, 1988), but few studies have tested this. Lewis (1991b) asserts that concrete services serve to engage clients; they improve the conditions facing families and therefore assist in building relationships with families. Concrete services should thus assist in the engagement of families by demonstrating the caseworker's understanding of the concrete circumstances facing families and their basic needs for safety, financial and material resources, and human comforts. This assertion must be tested.

In a study of family preservation services in New Jersey, Feldman (1991) used the Client Clinical Service Checklist and Concrete Services Checklist (developed by the Homebuilders program; Kinney et al., 1991) to describe the types of services that families received. These measures are appropriate, given that Feldman's study evaluated the implementation of a Homebuilders model program. The Client Clinical Service Checklist contains seven major categories: child management, emotional management, advocacy, interpersonal skills, clinical services, concrete services, and other services. Feldman found that over half of the 120 families served received services concerning child management and other clinical skills, while fewer than 10 percent received concrete services. Given the focus of the Homebuilders model on concrete helping and given the low socioeconomic status of families served in this study, "the low number of families receiving concrete services was surprising" (Feldman, 1991, p. 61).

Fraser, Pecora, and Haapala (1991), including Robert Lewis (1991a, 1991b), in a detailed evaluation of the Homebuilders program with 453 families, found that only one concrete service, the provision of transportation, was used by more than half of families served, while thirty-one clinical, or soft, services were commonly provided. Almost half of the clinical services provided were educational in nature, and centered around development of the treatment relationship, improving parenting effectiveness, modifying problem behaviors, teaching an understanding of child development, building self-esteem, and consulting with other services.

Using the Concrete Services Checklist (Fraser, Pecora, & Haapala, 1991), Lewis (1991a) found that about three-fourths of all families studied in Washington and Utah received some form of concrete services, with provision of transportation and recreational activities at the top of the list. Also common were helping clients get a job, doing housework with the client, arranging recreational activities, and helping to secure financial assistance. In cases receiving concrete services, those services accounted for an average of 25 percent of service time.

Berry's (1992) study of 367 families receiving intensive family preservation services in California measured the specific services provided in each case and the amount of time caseworkers expended on each service in each case. This study found that the most commonly provided services involved family assessment, parenting education, supplemental parenting (i.e., respite care), and teaching of family care—primarily educational or soft services.

Meezan and McCroskey (1996) also examined service provision through case files, agency management information systems, and client reports of service recipients. Worker reports of service provision and caregiver reports of service recipients were "remarkably similar" (p. 18). Services focused on child-rearing skills and family interaction.

Staff and Fein (1994) tracked two categories of services to families—activities and their purpose—in terms of the hours spent with the family. Direct clinical counseling was used by staff only 8 percent of the time, whereas concrete services were used 20 percent of the time, followed by travel (18 percent), and support groups (14 percent). The largest proportion of caseworker time (22 percent) was spent in staff meetings and supervision.

The ability to track collateral contacts is also salient in the provision of family preservation and family reunification services, given the ecological and multisystems orientation of this service model. Indeed, a rigorous experiment that compared the effectiveness of this service model with that of individual counseling (Borduin et al., 1995) found that 100 percent of cases receiving multisystemic treatment received interventions with collateral contacts (such as the school), compared to 10 percent of those receiving individual counseling.

Validity and relevance of individualized service delivery. Intensive family preservation service models have long argued that intensive services are intended to do whatever it takes to strengthen families and reduce the risk of child placement. Schuerman et al. (1995) have lamented the difficulty of evaluating individualized service delivery, calling it "the problem of the million models" (p. 205). The structure of services, giving workers great autonomy and flexibility in their time and services to families, is intended to support the development and implementation of a service plan that is related to the specific risks present in the family and consonant with goals developed in concert between the family and the worker. Program evaluations to date, however, have not adequately documented whether a "million model problem" (p. 205) does in fact exist.

Lewis (1991a) postulates that a noted variation in provision of services to families indicates a sensitivity in treatment provision to the needs of individual families. For example, Lewis notes that "only one [concrete] service, providing transportation, was provided in the majority of cases, which indicates the diversity of concrete services needed by families" (p. 93). Perhaps different workers approach clients with an array of services that are applied uniformly within worker caseloads. This alternative hypothesis is not tested in this study. Lewis (1991b) also notes that a wide range of clinical services provided is evidence of "the eclectic base of family preservation treatment" (p. 100). Although Lewis (1991b) does analyze the correlation of services to outcomes, or goal achievement, he does not test for the relevance of services to identified needs of clients.

In examining the amount of time spent with families, Berry (1992) found that intensive family preservation caseworkers spent more time with those families who had greater material and safety needs in the home. A higher intensity of service (contact time per day) was found among families with an emotionally disturbed, absent or physically handicapped parent. Services were provided for the longest duration of time to families experiencing child neglect or child emotional disturbance.

Finally, few studies have examined the differential effectiveness or structure of intensive family preservation and intensive family reunification services. Rates of foster care reentry after family reunification range from 18 to 28 percent in major states (Goerge et al., 1996), and foster care caseloads therefore contain large proportions of children from reunification breakdowns. The development of reunification programs addresses the need to secure and maintain reunified families (Hess, Folaron, & Jefferson, 1992; Maluccio, Fein, & Davis, 1994), but the effectiveness of these models is also not established (Fraser, Walton, et al., 1996).

To assess the structure and nature of services and to delineate and deconstruct the "black box" of services, we suggest the measures identified in table 12.4.

TABLE 12.4. Data Elements Assessed During Services

Service Provision
Number of days case open
Total time served
Service intensity (time per day)
Frequency and type of concrete services
Frequency and type of educational services
Frequency and type of clinical services
Where services provided
Use of psychoeducational groups
Use of collateral helpers

Distal Versus Proximal Outcomes

Most critics (Berry, 1992; Blythe et al., 1994; Rossi, 1992; Wells & Whittington, 1993) agree that child placement (or its prevention) is a woefully inadequate and misleading indicator of family preservation program effectiveness. Other critical indicators of program effectiveness suggested are changes in family functioning, changes in parenting and child behavior, and gains in material and social resources and supports. The measurement of *change* requires measures at more than one point in time. Therefore, the use of multiple points of assessment is critical in measuring change in families. This requirement leads to the important conclusion that most meaningful *outcomes* in family-centered programs are *changes* in those characteristics that brought the family to treatment. Therefore, the most meaningful outcome measures will take the form of repeated measures of intake levels of family functioning. Elements of family functioning that are addressed by treatment are logically most directly related to the success of the program in ameliorating those problems.

Several studies in the past few years have measured family functioning from pretest to posttest (Fraser, Pecora, & Haapala, 1991; Meezan & McCroskey, 1996; Scannapieco, 1993), and have found the provision of family preservation services to be related to decreases in risk factors (e.g., on Magura and Moses' [1986] Family Risk Scales; Pecora, Fraser, & Haapala, 1992) and increases in worker- or therapist-rated family functioning (Pecora et al., 1992; Scannapieco, 1993). Meezan and McCroskey's (1996) large-scale experiment in Los Angeles also found significant improvements in family functioning among families receiving intensive family-centered services, as reported by both caseworkers and caregivers using the Family Assessment Form, the Achenbach Child Behavior Checklist, and the Home Observation for Measurement of the Environment standardized instruments at case closure.

A small ($n = 42$) study of intensive family preservation services, incorporating a number of measures of family functioning, including many ratings of functioning by parents and by children (Wells & Whittington, 1993), found that both children and parents reported the resolution of many problems over the course of treatment. In addition, the study corroborated these positive consumer reports with statistically significant improvements on the therapist-rated Family Assessment Device and the Child Behavior Checklist.

Client satisfaction and other client-reported outcomes are additional areas of indicators of service effectiveness that have only recently developed in the evaluation of family preservation services (Meezan & McCroskey, 1996; Raschick, 1997; Wells & Whittington, 1993) and are producing divergent views of treatment results. Meezan and McCroskey (1996), in gathering assessments of family functioning and treatment goals from both caregiver and caseworker, identified a consistent difference, in that caregivers reported few problems, both at case opening and at case closing, while caseworkers reported families to have moderate problems in many areas of family functioning at case opening, with small but significant improvements by case closing. Improvements were reported by caregivers only in the areas of living conditions and financial conditions, while caseworkers reported improvements in living conditions, caregiver-child interactions, supports to the caregiver, and developmental stimulation of the child. This discrepancy between service providers and service recipients speaks to issues of reliability and validity regarding "whose truth" is assessed in family-centered services research, and the continued need for refinement and inclusion of *both* client-reported and worker-rated measures of family well-being.

As has been discussed, it is important, if not necessary, to measure not only placement (a distal outcome) but also proximal outcomes such as those outlined in table 12.5.

Drawing Meaning from Evaluation Methods

When data are gathered in all three domains (intake characteristics, service provision, and a variety of case outcomes) of family-centered services, a full range of analytical techniques can then provide a fairly thorough understanding of the interplay of these characteristics, services, and outcomes.

Reliability of Instruments

Reliability analysis will determine the internal consistency of separate instruments (used at discrete points of data collection). If instruments are not found to have good internal consistency within the particular service popu-

TABLE 12.5. Data Elements Assessed at Case Closure

Case Outcomes
Child placement while case open
Maltreatment reports while case open
Satisfactory case closure
Gains in strengths/supports
☐ Family gains in intake factors while case open
☐ Family gains in intake factors after case closure
Reduction in family and environmental stressors
Client satisfaction
Family reunification
Child placement after case closure
Maltreatment reports after case closure
Gains or losses between case closure and a follow-up point

lation or set of agency personnel, results regarding program effectiveness using data from these instruments will be unreliable and suspect. Thus reliability, or a lack thereof, must be established early in any evaluation process.

Description of Client Population

Prior to the examination of program effectiveness, it is useful to analyze family intake data by themselves, in order to acquire an adequate description of the population served.

Univariate analyses. Frequencies on the intake characteristics will provide an overall description of the population served by the program. Such information will include a ranking of the most common presenting problems experienced by program families, demographic profiles, common strengths possessed by families in the program, and common environmental stressors and compounding conditions. This will allow program planners, caseworkers, and families to assess the distribution of family strengths and stressors across the service population (including trends from year to year as stressors change).

Bivariate analyses. Bivariate statistical analyses such as cross-tabulations and t-tests will provide an associational analysis of which kinds of family stressors and strengths are most often found among families with certain presenting problems, such as child neglect. Such an analysis can provide workers and program planners with information on the clustering of characteristics or stressors among the service population. For example, do families with child neglect differ from families with child abuse in terms of income levels, external social supports, family constellation, and so on. Such analyses will go a long way toward supporting or breaking certain myths about this client population.

Multivariate analyses. Once a number of univariate and bivariate analyses have identified the key or most common presenting problems and demographic characteristics in the service population, one type of multivariate analysis, known as discriminant analysis, will help identify the relative weight of demographic characteristics in discriminating between families with a particular presenting problem and those without. For example, a number of demographic characteristics and family stressors could be entered into a discriminant analysis to distinguish between families referred for child neglect and those referred for child abuse. Such an analysis might identify material resource issues as key predictors of neglect, allowing program planners to focus service efforts on the provision of material supports to attempt to prevent or ameliorate child neglect in this population.

Examination of Case Outcomes and Program Effectiveness

Univariate analyses. A thorough univariate presentation of the case outcomes listed above will also provide a good first illustration of the effectiveness of the program being evaluated. Such a univariate analysis of the number of children removed, the number of subsequent reports of child maltreatment, and the condition of families at case closure will serve an important purpose for further analyses as well: evaluators can determine if there are enough cases in each condition (e.g., families preserved versus families experiencing placement) to allow for further bivariate and multivariate analyses. If all or most families are in one condition or another (e.g., few child removals), further statistical analyses comparing conditions or outcomes will not be supported for those outcomes.

Bivariate analyses. A key component of sound evaluative analysis is the correlation or prediction of outcomes, given certain characteristics of families or elements of services. Certainly, bivariate analyses that identify the key family and service correlates of child placement or child abuse in the service population are critical. In addition, paired t-tests between families' levels of stressors and strengths at intake and the same stressors and strengths at case closure will provide information on the gains (or losses) made by families while in the program and will be more specific than the global outcomes of child placement or repeated child maltreatment measured at case closure only.

If the evaluation design is experimental and involves random assignment of a pool of clients to either family preservation or some other services, the analysis will focus on differences in outcomes between the two groups. In addition, if there are also measures of process variables (length, intensity, and type of services) and of client characteristics (referral problem, socioeconomic factors, household composition, children's ages, for instance), additional multivariate analysis can assess the relative contribution of each of these client and service factors to improvement in outcome (measured relative to similar clients receiving different services), remembering that improvements mean change over time.

If the evaluation design involves pretest-posttest measures of one group of clients, then clients' improvement (or lack of improvement) at case closure is compared to their own baselines at intake. Again, if descriptions of client demographic characteristics and service characteristics are factored in, multivariate analysis can help define the client and service factors most closely correlated with successful (or unsuccessful) outcomes (improvements in family conditions). Berry's (1992) study of clients receiving family preservation services in Northern California, for example, found that the intensity of service provision (hours spent with the client) varied depending on severity of client needs, and that the provision of both concrete services (as opposed to therapeutic services) and services in the client's home (as opposed to from the office) were correlated with lower child placement rates at case closure and at repeated follow-up points.

Many authors have postulated an association between the provision of concrete and intensive services and client progress (Drisko, 1995; Lewis, 1991a; McCurdy, Hurvis, & Clark, 1996). It is suggested that concrete, intensive, home-based services are more relevant and immediately useful to clients than is psychological counseling or in-agency instruction. Some studies have indeed found an association between improvements and concrete services (Berry, 1992; Lewis, 1991a) or home-based service provision (Berry, 1992; Henggeler, Pickrel, Brondino, & Crouch, 1996), but these associations are not firmly established and are contradictory in the research base. The empirical validity of treatment outcomes is particularly critical in an era of managed care and established "treatment protocols" (Broskowski, 1997).

Many examples of the utility of bivariate analyses exist. For example, the intensity of service, or the proportion of time spent in the family's home, was associated with family preservation in Berry's (1992) study of 367 families. Most important, when greater than 50 percent of case time had been spent in the family's home, no children were placed in foster care, compared to a 28 percent placement rate among those families receiving less than half of their service time in their own home. Other correlations between intensity or duration of services and case outcomes are unavailable due to a lack of information in most studies regarding service variables (Blythe et al., 1994; Heneghan et al., 1996).

The structural component of time has not been analyzed to a large extent in intensive family preservation programs (Heneghan et al., 1996). This may be quite appropriate, given the complicated relationship between time and treatment outcomes (Berry, 1994). Particularly difficult cases can be served for a very short period of time (due to client dropout or expedient child removal and case closure) or may be served for an unusually long period of time (due to chronic problems or multiple needs), and with poor outcomes, often defined as child placement. Therefore, any simple correlations between duration of service and case needs or case outcomes are often found to be insignificant.

Lewis (1991b) found that one concrete service, "giving financial assistance," was associated with goal attainment of "establishing trust between therapists and families" (p. 230). In bivariate analyses, Fraser, Pecora, and Lewis (1991) found that the overall amount of time spent providing concrete services was significantly associated with reduced risk of placement. On the other hand, only one area of clinical services (time and money management) was associated with placement prevention. The other specific skills of listening to the client, encouraging the client, and providing literature were somewhat related to placement prevention, but not to a significant degree.

Multivariate analyses. Finally, multivariate analyses such as discriminant analysis will help identify the relative weight of a number of family and service characteristics in discriminating between success and failure of families in the program (remembering that success and failure can be defined in a number of ways in the analysis).

For example, in a multivariate analysis, concrete services have been found to be critically important (Fraser, Pecora, & Lewis, 1991). "Service success also was correlated significantly with the use of concrete services. Controlling for the behavior of the children and their parents plus goal achievement, families that received an enabling concrete service had a 32.8 percent lower risk of placement. Concrete services appear to be a critical ingredient in providing effective treatment . . . . More successful therapists appear to have trained family members to seek and obtain tangible help from community agencies" (p. 215).

Similarly, in the same study, the one characteristic of families at termination that predicted subsequent child removal, holding service, demographic, and social characteristics of clients constant, was the presence of serious environmental and structural problems in the household. It should be noted, however, that while concrete service provision was a statistically significant predictor of success in this sample using discriminant analysis, this variable lost its predictive ability in a more rigorous analysis using event history analysis (Fraser, Pecora, Popuang, & Haapala, 1992).

While Meezan and McCroskey (1996) do not report specific amounts of the types of service provided in their report, they do note that service factors were not as predictive of family improvements in their study as were family characteristics. However, the authors did find that "help in concrete areas was predictive of change in [the caregiver's] interpersonal relations" (p. 21), a correlation also found by Berry (1992) and Pecora et al.,

(1992). Meezan and McCroskey (1996) also report that concrete areas of change were sustained at follow-up, while improvements in interpersonal relations were not.

In a controlled study comparing multisystemic therapy with individual counseling (Borduin et al., 1995), the multisystemic group used more collateral contacts (usually schools, and sometimes peers) and produced more favorable improvements in family and individual functioning, specifically concerning increased family supportiveness, decreased family hostility, and improved adolescent behavior. The precise associations between these collateral contacts or other service characteristics and family improvements were not statistically tested in this report, however.

THE FUTURE IN EVALUATION OF FAMILY-BASED SERVICES— THE NEXT STEPS

As Warsh et al. (1995) and Wells and Tracy (1996) have outlined, intensive family preservation services are one specialized form of service delivery in a continuum of family-centered child welfare services. This method of service delivery has structural and natural elements specified in program models (Kinney et al., 1991; Nelson, Landsman, & Deutelbaum, 1990). Other models, such as that evaluated by Meezan and McCroskey (1996), may be less intensive but still embody the principles and purpose of family-centered services. As this review and others have shown, however, the adherence to structural and natural elements of models is often assumed and unaddressed in evaluations of programs (Blythe et al., 1994; Heneghan et al., 1996), raising questions as to the internal validity and comparability of study findings.

The small number of studies measuring structural and natural elements of intensive family preservation services finds much variability among programs in the duration and intensity of services and in the provision of concrete versus clinical services offered. As noted, the emphasis in these program models on tailoring services to family needs may account for such diversity, but this assumption needs to be tested empirically (Cavazos Dylla, & Berry, 1998).

The one fairly consistent finding in this small set of studies is a relationship between the provision of concrete services and workers' perceptions of enhanced client trust, oftentimes leading to better ultimate case outcomes. This is a correlation that intensive family preservation service models have hypothesized will occur; and, while needing further corroboration and explication, it provides additional support for attention to the concrete needs of families in crisis, whether served by Child Protective Services, juvenile services, or mental health services.

This chapter's discussion of family-centered services evaluation—research design, sampling, and measurement—has highlighted three critical issues in the field of evaluation: exploring the "black box" of services to discover and measure the actual structure and natures of those services, clarifying the distinction between distal and proximal goals, and using a logic model in the planning of services and their evaluation.

In many ways, these three issues are interrelated. An evaluation that starts with a theoretical model of how service is expected to change clients, then progresses to a description in some depth of the client families, the services offered, and how they are delivered, leads logically to the most appropriate, and potentially achievable, choice of outcome measures.

While many of the recent evaluations of family preservation services have used sound research designs involving large sample sizes, a control group, or pre- and posttest measures, and consistent trends have been found in some studies that link the provision of concrete services to positive outcomes, the lack of results found in other studies points to the need for more research on service process. We hope that the recommended design, sample, and measurement components enumerated here, linked in a framework logically related to the specific goals of any family-centered program, will provide firmer and more valid conclusions regarding change in a changing world.

REFERENCES

Alter, C., & Egan, M. (1997). Logic modeling: A tool for teaching critical thinking in social work practice. *Journal of Social Work Education, 33*, 85–102.

Alter, C., & Murty, S. (1997). Logic modeling: A tool for teaching practice evaluation. *Journal of Social Work Education, 33*, 103–17.

American Association for Protecting Children. (1988). *Child Protective Services program evaluation, Texas: Final report*. Denver, CO: American Humane Association.

Bath, H. I., & Haapala, D. A. (1994). Family preservation services: What does the outcome research really tell us? *Social Service Review, 68* (3), 386–404.

Berry, M. (1992). An evaluation of family preservation services: Fitting agency services to family needs. *Social Work, 37* (4), 314–21.

Berry, M. (1994). *Keeping families together*. New York: Garland.

Berry, M. (1997). *The family at risk: Issues and trends in family preservation services*. Columbia: University of South Carolina Press.

Berry, M., & Cavazos Dylla, D. J. (1997). Combining research and practice tools. In M. Berry, *The family at risk: Issues and trends in family preservation services* (p. 178). Columbia: University of South Carolina Press.

Blythe, B. J., Salley, M. P., & Jayaratne, S. (1994). A review of intensive family preservation services research. *Social Work Research, 18* (4), 213–24.

Borduin, C. M., Mann, B. J., Cone, L. T., Henggeler, S. W., Fucci, B. R., Blaske, D. M., & Williams, R. A. (1995). Multisystemic treatment of serious juvenile offenders: Long-term prevention of criminality and violence. *Journal of Consulting and Clinical Psychology, 63,* 569–78.

Broskowski, A. (1997, February). The role of risk-sharing arrangements. *Child and Family Focus, 3,* 2–5.

Brown, A. W., & Bailey-Etta, B. (1997). An out-of-home care system in crisis: Implications for African-American children in the child welfare system. *Child Welfare, 76,* 65–83.

Cavazos Dylla, D. J., & Berry, M. (1998). The role of consistency and diversity in building knowledge in family preservation. *Family Preservation Journal, 3,* 1–13.

Cole, E. S. (1995). Becoming family centered: Child welfare's challenge. *Families in Society, 76* (3), 163–72.

Courtney, M. E. (1997). Reconsidering family preservation: A review of Putting Families First. *Children and Youth Services Review, 19,* 61–76.

Craig-Van Grack, A. (1997). A taxonomy and recording instrument for process measurement of family preservation services. *Child Welfare, 76,* 349–70.

Daro, D. (1988). *Confronting child abuse: Research for effective program design.* New York: Free Press.

Dore, M. M., & Harnett, J. M. (1995). The role of the volunteer in family preservation services. *Families in Society, 76* (2), 67–75.

Doueck, H. J., Bronson, D. E., & Levine, M. (1992). Evaluating risk assessment implementation in child protection: Issues for consideration. *Child Abuse and Neglect, 16,* 637–46.

Drisko, J. W. (1995, March). *Clients strengthen programs: A utilization-focused evaluation of two intensive family preservation programs.* Paper presented at the Council on Social Work Education Annual Meeting, San Diego, CA.

Eamon, M. K. (1994). Poverty and placement outcomes of intensive family preservation services. *Child and Adolescent Social Work, 11,* 349–61.

Fein, E., Maluccio, A. N., Hamilton, V. J., & Ward, D. E. (1983). After foster care: Outcomes of permanency planning for children. *Child Welfare, 62,* 485–558.

Feldman, L. (1991). Evaluating the impact of intensive family preservation service in New Jersey. In K. Wells & D. E. Biegel (Eds.), *Family preservation services: Research and evaluation* (pp. 47–71). Newbury Park, CA: Sage.

Fraser, M. W., & Haapala, D. (1988). Home-based family treatment: A quantitative-qualitative assessment. *Journal of Applied Social Sciences, 12* (1), 1–23.

Fraser, M. W., Pecora, P. J., & Haapala, D. A. (1991). *Families in crisis: The impact of intensive family preservation services.* Hawthorne, NY: Aldine de Gruyter.

Fraser, M. W., Pecora, P. J., & Lewis, R. E. (1991). The correlates of treatment success and failure for intensive family preservation services. In M. W. Fraser, P. J. Pecora, & D. A. Haapala, *Families in crisis: The impact of intensive family preservation services.* Hawthorne, NY: Aldine de Gruyter.

Fraser, M. W., Pecora, P. J., Popuang, C., & Haapala, D. A. (1992). Event history analysis: A proportional hazards perspective on modeling outcomes in intensive family preservation services. In D. F. Gillespie & C. Glisson (Eds.), *Quantitative methods in social work: State of the art* (pp. 124–52). New York: Haworth Press.

Fraser, M. W., Walton, E., Lewis, R. E., Pecora, P. J., & Walton, W. K. (1996). An experiment in family reunification: Correlates of outcomes at one-year follow-up. *Children and Youth Services Review, 18,* 335–61.

Gelles, R. J. (1996). *The book of David: How preserving families can cost children's lives.* New York: Basic Books.

Gershenson, C. P. (1993). *Family First in Illinois: An experiment in ambiguity.* Washington, DC: Center for the Study of Social Policy.

Goerge, R., Wulczyn, F., & Harden, A. (1996, Summer). New comparative insights into states and their foster children. *Public Welfare, 24,* 12–25, 52.

Goerge, R. M., Wulczyn, F. H., & Harden, A. (1994). *Foster care dynamics, 1983–1992: A report of the multistate foster care data archive.* Chicago: Chapin Hall Center for Children.

Heneghan, A. M., Horwitz, S. M., & Leventhal, J. M. (1996). Evaluating intensive family preservation programs: A methodological review. *Pediatrics, 97,* 535–42.

Henggeler, S. W., Pickrel, S. G., Brondino, M. J., & Crouch, J. L. (1996). Eliminating (almost) treatment dropout of substance abusing dependent delinquents through home-based multisystemic therapy. *American Journal of Psychiatry, 153,* 427–28.

Hess, P.M., Folaron, G., & Jefferson, A. B. (1992). Effectiveness of family reunification services: An innovative evaluative model. *Social Work, 37,* 304–11.

Howing, P. T., Kohn, S., Gaudin, J. M., Kurtz, P. D., & Wordarski, J. S. (1992). Current research issues in child welfare. *Social Work Research and Abstracts, 28,* 5–12.

Kalichman, S. C., & Brosig, C. L. (1992). The effects of statutory requirements on child maltreatment reporting: A comparison of two state laws. *American Journal of Orthopsychiatry, 62* (2), 284–96.

Kamerman, S. B., & Kahn, A. J. (1989). *Social services for children, youth, and families in the United States.* Ann Arbor, MI: Annie E. Casey Foundation.

Kinney, J., Dittmar, K., & Firth, W. (1990). Keeping families together: The Homebuilders model. *Children Today, 19* (6), 14–19.

Kinney, J., Haapala, D. & Booth, C. (1991). *Keeping families together. The Homebuilders model.* New York: Aldine De Gruyter.

Kinney, J. M., Madsen, B., Fleming, T., & Haapala, D. A. (1977). Homebuilders: Keeping families together. *Journal of Consulting and Clinical Psychology, 45,* 667–73.

Knickman, J., & Jellinek, P. (1997). Epilogue: Four lessons from evaluating controversial programs. *Children and Youth Services Review, 19,* 607–14.

Lahti, J., Green, K., Emlen, A. C., Zadny, J., Clarkson, Q. D., Kuehnel, M., & Casciato, J. (1978). *A follow-up study of the Oregon Project.* Portland: Regional Research Institute for Human Services.

Landsman, M. J. (1998). Not another article about outcomes! *Prevention Report,* *1998* (1), 25–27.

Landsman, M. J., Nelson, K., Tyler, M., & Allen, M. (1990). *Interim evaluation report: The self-sufficiency project.* Oakdale, IA: National Resource Center on Family Based Services.

Lewis, R. E. (1991a). What are the characteristics of intensive family preservation services? In M. W. Fraser, P. J. Pecora, & D. A. Haapala, *Families in crisis: The impact of intensive family preservation services* (pp. 93–107). Hawthorne, NY: Aldine de Gruyter.

Lewis, R. E. (1991b). What elements of services relate to treatment goal achievements? In M. W. Fraser, P. J. Pecora, & D. A. Haapala, *Families in crisis: The impact of intensive family preservation services* (pp. 225–71). Hawthorne, NY: Aldine de Gruyter.

Littell, J. H. (1995). Evidence or assertions? The outcomes of family preservation services. *Social Service Review, 69,* 338–51.

Lindsey, D. (1994). *The welfare of children.* New York: Oxford University Press.

Lloyd, J. C., & Sallee, A. L. (1994). The challenge and potential of family preservation services in the public child welfare system. *Protecting Children, 10* (3), 3–6.

Magura, S., & Moses, B. S. (1986). *Outcome measures for child welfare services: Theory and applications.* Washington, DC: Child Welfare League of America.

Maluccio, A., Fein, D., & Davis, I. P. (1994). Family reunification: Research findings, issues, and directions. *Child Welfare, 73,* 489–504.

Maluccio, A. N., Pine, B. A., & Warsh, R. (1994). Protecting children by preserving their families. *Children and Youth Services Review, 16,* 295–307.

McCurdy, K., Hurvis, S., & Clark, J. (1996). Engaging and retaining families in child abuse prevention programs. *APSAC Advisor, 9* (3), 1, 3–9.

Meezan, W., & McCroskey, J. (1996, Winter). Improving family functioning through family preservation services: Results of the Los Angeles experiment. *Family Preservation Journal,* 9–29.

Nelson, K. E., Landsman, M. J., & Deutelbaum, W. (1990). Three models of family-centered placement prevention services. *Child Welfare, 69* (1), 3–21.

Pecora, P. J., Fraser, M. W., & Haapala, D. A. (1992). Intensive home-based family preservation services: An update from the FIT project. *Child Welfare, 71* (2), 177–88.

Pecora, P. J., Massinga, R., & Mauzerall, H. (1997). Measuring outcomes in the changing environment of child welfare services. *Behavioral Healthcare Tomorrow, 6* (2), 2–8.

Pecora, P. J., Nelson, K. E., Meezan, W., McCroskey, J., & Fraser, M. W. (1995). Evaluating family-based services. New York: Aldine de Gruyter.

Pelton, L. H. (1989). *For reasons of poverty: An evaluation of child welfare policy.* New York: Praeger.

Pelton, L. H. (1993). Enabling public child welfare agencies to promote family preservation. *Social Work, 38* (4), 491–93.

Raschick, M. (1997). A multifaceted, intensive family preservation program evaluation. *Family Preservation Journal, 2* (2), 33–52.

Ronnau, J. P., & Marlow, C. R. (1993). Family preservation, poverty, and the value of diversity. *Families in Society, 74* (11), 538–44.

Rossi, P. H. (1992). Assessing family preservation programs. *Children and Youth Services Review, 14,* 77–97.

Rubin, A. (1997). The family preservation evaluation from hell: Implications for program evaluation fidelity. *Children and Youth Services Review, 19,* 77–100.

Scannapieco, M. (1993). The importance of family functioning to prevention of placement: A study of family preservation services. *Child and Adolescent Social Work, 10,* 509–20.

Schorr, L. (1988). *Within our reach: Breaking the cycle of disadvantage.* New York: Doubleday.

Schuerman, J. R., Rzepnicki, T. L., & Littell, J. H. (1994). *Putting families first: An experiment in family preservation.* New York: Aldine De Gruyter.

Smith, M. K. (1995). Utilization-focused evaluation of a family preservation program. *Families in Society, 76* (1), 11–19.

Staff, I., & Fein, E. (1994). Inside the black box: An exploration of service delivery in a family reunification program. *Child Welfare, 73* (3), 195–214.

Stein, T. J., Gambrill, E. D., & Wiltse, K. T. (1978). *Children in foster homes: Achieving continuity of care.* New York: Praeger.

Thieman, A. A., & Dail, P. W. (1992). Family preservation services: Problems of measurement and assessment of risk. *Family Relations, 41,* 186–91.

Wald, M. (1988). Family preservation: Are we moving too fast? *Public Welfare, 46,* 33–38, 46.

Walton, E. (1991). *The reunification of children with their families following out-of-home placement: A test of intensive family treatment.* Unpublished doctoral dissertation, University of Utah, Salt Lake City, UT.

Warsh, R., Pine, B. A., & Maluccio, A. N. (1995). The meaning of family preservation: Shared mission, diverse methods. *Families in Society, 76,* 625–26.

Wells, K., & Whittington, D. (1993). Child and family functioning after intensive family preservation services. *Social Service Review, 67,* 55–83.

Yuan, Y-Y. T., & Struckman-Johnson, D. L. (1991). Placement outcomes for neglected children with prior placements in family preservation programs. In K. Wells & D. E. Biegel (Eds.), *Family preservation services: Research and evaluation* (pp. 92–118). Newbury Park, CA: Sage.

13 | Multisystemic Therapy

Theory, Research, and Practice

Colleen A. Halliday-Boykins
Scott W. Henggeler

Mental health services researchers and policymakers agree that children's mental health services are in great need of reform (Friesen & Koroloff, 1990; Washington State Institute for Public Policy, 1998).[1] More than three-quarters of the funds spent on mental health services for children and adolescents are directed toward out-of-home placements (Burns, 1991), which have little empirical support for being effective (Kiesler, 1993; Sondheimer, Schoenwald, & Rowland, 1994) and may even have iatrogenic effects (Weithorn, 1988). Identifying and disseminating effective community-based treatments, therefore, are greatly needed.

Multisystemic therapy (MST) (Henggeler & Borduin, 1990; Henggeler, Schoenwald, Borduin, Rowland, & Cunningham, 1998) has been identified as a highly promising treatment model by reviewers in the fields of substance abuse (e.g., McBride, VanderWaal, VanBuren, & Terry, 1997; National Institute on Drug Abuse, 1999; Stanton & Shandish, 1997), adolescent violence (e.g., Elliott, 1998; Farrington & Welsh, 1999; Tate, Reppucci, & Mulvey, 1995), and mental health (e.g., Fraser, Nelson, & Rivard, 1997; Kazdin & Weisz, 1998). MST is a family- and community-based intervention for children and adolescents with serious clinical problems that has been effective in reducing out-of-home placements and producing favorable long-term clinical outcomes (Henggeler, 1999). The most fundamental goal of MST is to decrease youth problem behavior by improving family functioning. Unlike treatment provided through office-based and institutional settings, MST treats youths within their social ecological contexts. This chapter is an overview of the theory, practice, and supporting evidence of MST.

THEORETICAL UNDERPINNINGS

MST is based on Bronfenbrenner's (1979) theory of social ecology, which assumes that behavior is determined by the interplay of individual characteristics and aspects of the multiple, interrelated systems within which the individual is embedded. For children and adolescents, these systems include the family, peers, school, neighborhood, and community. Social ecology theory also posits that the relationships between the child and social systems are dynamic and reciprocal in nature. Accordingly, not only do the family, peer group, school, and neighborhood influence the child, but the child also affects these systems in an ongoing, recursive fashion. Problematic transactions within a particular system, or between a combination of these systems, can lead to behavioral difficulties.

These theoretical assumptions give rise to a number of corollaries. First, behavior is best understood in the context of multiple systems. Thus it is important to determine the "fit" of problems to their systemic context, considering the role of individual child characteristics (e.g., social skills) as well as the possible roles of family (e.g., high conflict, low affection, poor monitoring of youth behavior, harsh or inconsistent discipline, parental psychopathology), peer (e.g., association with deviant peers), school (e.g., poor academic performance, poor caregiver-school relations), neighborhood (e.g., criminal subculture, disorganization), and community (e.g., support network) influences. Moreover, the more favorable treatment outcomes cannot be expected to come from merely changing the individual child. Rather, long-lasting effects can be expected only from interventions that modify risk factors within the child's social ecology, in addition to changing the child. Accordingly, effective interventions must be comprehensive and flexible enough to address the transactions among the multiple systems in the youth's ecology. Evidence to support the multidetermined nature of serious clinical problems is extensive (e.g., Loeber & Hay, 1997) and consistently shows that such problem behavior is directly or indirectly linked to individual, family, peer, school, and neighborhood factors.

CLINICAL FEATURES

The design and implementation of MST interventions are guided by a set of nine core principles (see table 13.1) and based on the fit of the identified

TABLE 13.1. MST Treatment Principles

1. The primary purpose of assessment is to understand the "fit" between the identified problems and their broader systematic context.
2. Therapeutic contacts should emphasize the positive and should use systemic strength as levers for change.
3. Interventions should be designed to promote responsible behavior and decrease irresponsible behavior among family members.
4. Interventions should be present focused and action oriented, targeting specific and well-defined problems.
5. Interventions should target sequences of behavior within or between multiple systems that maintain the identified problems.
6. Interventions should be developmentally appropriate and fit the developmental needs of the youth.
7. Interventions should be designed to require daily or weekly effort by family members.
8. Intervention efficacy is evaluated continuously from multiple perspectives with providers assuming accountability for overcoming barriers to successful outcomes.
9. Interventions should be designed to promote treatment generalization and long-term maintenance of therapeutic change by empowering caregivers to address family members' needs across multiple systemic contexts.

problems with the greater ecological context. Decisions about the specific intervention strategies to be used are informed by the evidence-based treatment literature. Treatment approaches include strategic family therapy (Haley, 1976), structural family therapy (Minuchin, 1974), behavioral parent training (Munger, 1993), and cognitive behavior therapies (Kendall & Braswell, 1993). Psychopharmacological treatment is also used when biological contributors to the identified problems are recognized. The empirically supported intervention techniques are integrated into a larger social ecological framework and target the relevant individual, family, peer, school, and community factors affecting the identified problems. Accordingly, interventions are tailored to meet the strengths and weaknesses of the particular family.

Although MST is individualized to the youth and family, several problems commonly occur in families with children and adolescents that present serious clinical problems. For example, such families are often characterized by high conflict and low warmth, and caregivers often employ harsh or ineffective discipline strategies or poorly monitor the youth (Haapasalo & Tremblay, 1994). Accordingly, MST family interventions typically identify and address barriers to competent parenting, promote effective communication among family members, and increase family structure and cohesion. For example, if a mother's substance abuse interferes with her ability to supervise and monitor her 15-year-old son effectively, an MST therapist would work directly with the mother to reduce her substance abuse.

Another common goal of MST interventions is to increase youth involvement with prosocial peers and decrease involvement with antisocial peers. This goal is accomplished by helping caregivers support and encourage their adolescents' association with prosocial peers and by providing sanctions for continued association with problem peers. School functioning problems are typically addressed by helping caregivers establish and maintain open communication with teachers and other school personnel and assisting these caregivers in supporting their youths' academic achievement. Although the focus of treatment is on the systems within which the child is nested, interventions addressing individual characteristics of the child are sometimes needed as well.

In general, interventions in extrafamilial systems are mediated by interventions with the caregiver. If, for example, a teacher does not respond appropriately to the needs of a learning disabled child, rather than communicating directly with the teacher, the MST therapist would teach the caregiver to communicate effectively with the school about the child's needs. When the caregivers are unable to perform the necessary tasks on their own, other people within the family's natural ecology (e.g., neighbor, church pastor) are sought to provide support for these functions. The youth's caregivers and other indigenous resources for support are key to treatment generalization and, consequently, long-term outcomes. A detailed presentation of the components of MST interventions is provided in the treatment manual (Henggeler, Schoenwald, et al., 1998). Detailed case examples are also published (Rowland et al., 2000).

Model of Service Delivery

MST is provided in the contexts in which the problem behaviors occur. Most interventions occur in the home, although many interventions also occur in the school and community. Providing home- and community-based services helps reduce barriers to treatment access as well as promote treatment generalization.

Therapists carry very low caseloads, typically treating four to six families at any point in time. This feature allows therapists to provide intensive treatment and thus obtain maximum results in a relatively short period of time. Therapists, available twenty-four hours a day, seven days per week, are thus able to meet at times convenient for the family, as well as to be present at key times during the day when a caregiver may need support or guidance (e.g., enforcing curfew). In most cases, therapists have daily contact with the family. The duration of each contact depends on the needs of the family, and therapists generally provide between three and fifteen hours per week of services. Treatment is time limited, typically lasting three to five months. The therapist is the primary service provider for the entire family, offering a comprehensive array of services. In instances when services are needed from other community agencies, therapists help caregivers coordinate such services.

OUTCOME STUDIES

Several studies support MST's favorable outcomes for children and their families. MST has demonstrated positive effects on adolescent behavior, family functioning, and out-of-home placement.

Early Studies

The effectiveness of MST was initially documented in three early studies. The first was a quasi-experimental study (Henggeler et al., 1986) that examined the effects of MST as compared to those of usual community services for inner-city juvenile offenders and their families. At posttreatment, youths who had participated in MST had fewer behavior problems, while youths who received usual community services showed no change. In addition, observational measures showed that family relations improved for MST families and deteriorated for those who received the usual community treatments. In the second of the early studies, families with at least one maltreating parent were randomly assigned to receive either behavioral parent training or MST (Brunk, Henggeler, & Whelan, 1987). MST proved more effective than parent training in restructuring parent-child relations. Although lacking long-term follow-up, these two studies demonstrated the promise of MST in treating serious clinical problems.

The third early study presented the first controlled intervention study with adolescent sexual offenders in the literature (Borduin, Henggeler, Blaske, & Stein, 1990). Participants included a small sample of adolescents arrested for sexual offenses (e.g., rape, molestation of young children, exhibitionism) who were randomly assigned to either MST or individual outpatient therapy. Analysis of three-year follow-up data showed that youths in the MST condition had significantly lower recidivism rates for both sexual and nonsexual crimes than did adolescents participating in individual outpatient therapy. Subsequently, several randomized clinical trials of MST have provided compelling evidence for long-term effectiveness.

Chronic and Violent Juvenile Offenders

MST has the strongest support for treating chronic and violent juvenile offenders. In the Simpsonville, South Carolina, study, Henggeler, Melton, and Smith (1992) studied eighty-four juvenile offenders who were at imminent risk for out-of-home placement because of criminal activity. These youths averaged 3.5 previous arrests, and over half (54 percent) had been arrested for violent crimes. Seventy-one percent had been incarcerated previously for at least three weeks. The youths and their families were randomly assigned to receive either MST or the usual services provided by the Department of Juvenile Justice (DJJ). At posttreatment, families who received MST reported significantly higher levels of cohesion and lower levels of adolescent aggression with peers than did counterparts who received the usual services. In addition, youths who participated in MST showed less criminal activity than did their counterparts in the usual services group. Analysis of follow-up arrest and incarceration data for 59 weeks after referral to the study also showed results favoring MST. During the study period, more than two-thirds (68 percent) of adolescents who received usual services were incarcerated, while only one-fifth (20 percent) of those who participated in MST experienced incarceration. In fact, usual services youths experienced an average of almost three times more weeks of incarceration ($M = 16.2$ weeks) and almost two times as many arrests ($M = 1.52$) as MST youths ($Ms = 5.8$ weeks and 0.87 arrests, respectively). Treatment gains were maintained at long-term follow-up (Henggeler, Melton, Smith, Schoenwald, & Hanley, 1993). At 2.4 years postreferral, twice as many MST youths had avoided arrest (39 percent) as had usual services youths (20 percent).

In the Columbia, Missouri, project (Borduin et al., 1995), participants were 200 chronic juvenile offenders and their families who were referred by the local Department of Juvenile Justice. These youths had an average of about four arrests, and all had been previously detained for at least four weeks. Twenty-four families who completed initial assessments refused to participate in treatment. The remaining families were randomly assigned to receive either MST ($n = 92$) or individual therapy (IT) ($n = 84$). Of these families, 140 completed treatment and the others dropped out prematurely ($ns = 15$ for MST and 21 for IT). At posttreatment, adolescents and families who participated in MST showed more improvements in functioning than did their counterparts who received IT. From pre- to posttreatment, MST youths had fewer behavior problems, while IT youths had more behavior problems. In addition, families who participated in MST showed more positive changes in their family interactions than did their IT counterparts, including increased cohesion and supportiveness, and decreased conflict (both through self-report and observational measures). Moreover, caregivers in the MST group showed greater reductions in psychiatric symptomatology. Four-year follow-up arrest data provide further support for the effectiveness of MST over IT. Not only were youths who received MST arrested less often than those who received IT, MST youths also avoided rearrest for longer periods than their IT counterparts. Moreover, while youths who completed a full course of MST had the lowest overall rearrest rate (22.1 percent), those who received MST but prematurely dropped out of treatment had better rates of rearrest (46.6 percent) than did IT completers (71.4 percent), IT dropouts (71.4 percent) and treatment refusers (87.5 percent).

In the Multisite South Carolina study, Henggeler, Melton, Brondino, Scherer, and Hanley (1997) examined the role of treatment fidelity in the successful dissemination of MST. MST services were provided by therapists at two community mental health centers. Unlike previous clinical trials in which the developers of MST provided ongoing clinical supervision and consultation, in the South Carolina study MST experts were not significantly involved in treatment implementation. This feature provided an opportunity to examine the degree to which therapists in real-world settings could provide treatment in a manner consistent with MST principles. To measure variability in therapist adherence to the MST protocol, adolescents, parents, and therapists responded to a standardized MST adherence questionnaire several times during treatment. The participants were 155 chronic or violent juvenile offenders who were at risk of out-of-home placement because of serious criminal involvement. They averaged 3.07 previous arrests, and 59 percent had been incarcerated at least once. Youths and their families were randomly assigned to receive either MST or the usual services offered by DJJ. Not surprisingly, MST treatment effects were weaker than in previous studies. Youths in the MST condition exhibited decreased psychiatric symptamotology, while youths in the usual services condition showed increases in psychiatric symptamotology. MST youths experienced significantly fewer days of incarceration than did usual services youths between pre- and posttreatment assessments, but these differences were not maintained between posttreatment and the 1.7-year follow-up. Significant treatment effects for self-reported or official (i.e., arrests) criminal activity were not observed

Examination of the manner in which MST therapists adhered to MST principles, however, showed that higher treatment fidelity predicted lower adolescent psychiatric symptamotology and fewer rearrests and incarcerations. Accordingly, the modest treatment effects in this study may be attributable to considerable variance in therapists' adherence to MST principles. These findings suggest that treatment fidelity is important in the effective dissemination of MST, and point to the importance of attending closely to treatment fidelity when disseminating complex treatments.

Substance Use and Abuse

Using data from two previously mentioned randomized clinical trials with violent and chronic juvenile offenders (Borduin et al., 1995; Henggeler et al., 1992), analyses were conducted to determine the effects of MST on substance use (Henggeler et al., 1991). Results from the Simpsonville, South Carolina, study (Henggeler et al., 1992) showed that MST significantly reduced self-reported alcohol and marijuana use posttreatment. Analysis of four-year follow-up data in the Columbia, Missouri, study (Borduin et al., 1995) demonstrated that youths in the control condition had four times as many substance-related arrests (16 percent) as did youths in the MST condition (4 percent).

In light of these encouraging findings, another clinical trial was designed to examine the degree to which MST treatment effects could be generalized to substance-abusing or dependent juvenile offenders (Henggeler, Pickerel, & Brondino, 1999). One hundred and eighteen adolescents who met *DSM-III-R* criteria for psychoactive substance abuse (56 percent) or dependence (44 percent) were recruited from the South Carolina DJJ and randomly assigned either to MST or to usual services treatment conditions. Seventy-two percent of participants also met criteria for at least one other diagnosis. Participants had an average of 2.9 previous arrests and 25 percent had previously received substance abuse treatment. Between the time of the initial referral and the six-month follow-up, MST decreased out-of-home placement by 50 percent (Schoenwald, Ward, Henggeler, Pickerel, & Patel, 1996) and significantly improved school attendance (Brown, Henggeler, Schoenwald, Brondino, & Pickerel, 1999). MST also reduced self-reported alcohol and marijuana use at posttreatment (Henggeler et al., 1999). However, the effects of MST on substance use were not supported by urine drug screens or maintained at the six-month follow-up. In addition, while MST decreased rearrests, the reductions were not as great as those of other trials of MST (e.g., Borduin et al., 1995). Thus, while MST had some impact on this challenging population, treatment effects appeared to be weaker in this trial than in other studies. Examination of treatment measures indicated that therapist adherence to the MST protocol was low, which may at least partly explain the modest outcomes in this study. Another possible explanation is that the current specification of MST requires enhancement to effectively address substance abuse and dependence among youths. As discussed subsequently, an investigation of the degree to which the effectiveness of MST with substance-abusing youths can be improved by integrating substance abuse–specific interventions is currently underway.

Adolescents in Psychiatric Crisis

Henggeler, Rowland, et al. (1999) evaluated MST as an alternative to psychiatric hospitalization for youths with psychiatric emergencies. Because most other randomized clinical trials of MST focused on juvenile justice populations, this study provided an opportunity to examine the transportability of MST to another serious clinical population. Participants were 113 youths who had been approved for admission at an inpatient psychiatric hospital because they were either suicidal, homicidal, psychotic, or otherwise at risk of harm to themselves or others. These youths had histories of serious clinical problems. At the time of admission, almost all (96 percent) met criteria for at least one *DSM-III-R* diagnosis. Most had received previous psychiatric treatment (87 percent), more than one-third had experienced previous psychiatric hospitalizations (38 percent), and more than one-third had previously been involved with juvenile justice (38 percent).

The youths and their families were randomly assigned to receive either MST ($n = 57$) or psychiatric hospitalization and aftercare ($n = 56$). Clinical outcomes suggest that MST was at least as effective as psychiatric hospitalizations for some outcomes, and was more effective at decreasing externalizing behavior both at home and at school and increasing school attendance. In addition, MST was more effective in improving family relations and providing consumer satisfaction than was psychiatric hospitalization (Henggeler, Rowland, et al., 1999). Placement data provide overwhelming support for MST. Four months after referral, MST youths spent 72 percent fewer days hospitalized than did their counterparts in the hospitalization condition (Ms 2.39 versus 8.82 days) (Schoenwald, Ward, Henggeler, & Rowland, 2000). The reductions in hospitalization for MST youths were not offset by increases in other out-of-home placements. When hospital days were excluded, youths in the hospitalization condition still spent almost twice as many days in placement settings (e.g., residential treatment, foster care) than did their MST counterparts. Moreover, when youths were put in out-of-home placements, MST adolescents were generally placed in less restrictive living environments than were youths in the hospitalization condition.

Cost Effectiveness of MST

The favorable clinical outcomes of MST paint a particularly compelling picture in light of cost-effectiveness analyses. The Washington State Institute for Public Policy (1998), reviewing sixteen programs for reducing juvenile crime, found MST to be the most cost-effective intervention. This study found that when program costs were weighed against victim costs, MST resulted in a net savings of $22,000 per youth. This finding is particularly noteworthy because boot camps actually resulted in a net loss of $8,000 per adolescent. Similarly, in the Simpsonville study, usual services were three times as costly as MST services, largely due to higher rates of incarceration for usual services youths (Henggeler et al., 1992). In the case of substance-abusing and dependent juvenile offenders, the incremental costs of MST were nearly offset by savings resulting from decreases in out-of-home placement (Schoenwald et al., 1996) by twelve months post-referral. Although these findings are impressive, they may underestimate the cost savings of MST resulting from long-term decreases in service utilization. In addition, although cost analyses have not yet been conducted for the aforementioned study of MST as an alternative to psychiatric hospitalization, the findings of reduced out-of-home placement are likely to have important cost-savings implications (Schoenwald et al., 2000).

CURRENT AND FUTURE DIRECTIONS

A number of clinical trials of MST are currently underway. These studies are examining alternate models of service delivery and the transportability of MST to community settings.

Neighborhood Solutions for Neighborhood Problems Project

Drs. Cynthia Swenson and Jeff Randall are directing a quasi-experimental neighborhood-level intervention project (Randall, Swenson, & Henggeler, 1999). This study examines the degree to which a neighborhood can be empowered through the provision of empirically based services implemented to address problems identified by neighborhood members. The neighborhood was selected on the basis of its rates of poverty, unemployment, child maltreatment, arrests, and school problems—having some of the highest rates of these factors in the state of South Carolina. Neighborhood residents and stakeholders identified adolescent drug dealing, adolescent drug abuse, child prostitution, and school expulsion and suspension as the most pressing child- and family-related problems in the neighborhood. With community collaboration, interventions were designed to address these issues. A comparison neighborhood with similar demographics is being used to evaluate cost savings and reductions in identified problems. This study can inform the ways in which evidence-based mental health services can be used to attenuate the deleterious effects of neighborhood disadvantage on child and family outcomes.

Healthy Children Through Healthy Schools

A second project, directed by Dr. Phillippe Cunningham, is a quasi-experimental study of evidence-based prevention and interventions at the school level. Two middle schools were selected that serve predominantly African American and economically disadvantaged children, and that have high rates of violence, drug use, and drop outs. A mental health team has implemented empirically based violence and drug abuse prevention programs for the entire student body and provides consultation to teachers. In addition, MST is provided to youths who have been expelled, have been found with drugs, or have perpetrated crimes in school. One school initially served as a comparison while the intervention was implemented at the other school. Subsequently, interventions are being conducted at both schools. Reductions in emotional and behavioral problems and cost savings are the key outcomes that will be examined. Findings will have implications for the development of school-based prevention programs and mental services.

Continuum of Care

A study funded by the Annie E. Casey Foundation and directed by Dr. Sonja Schoenwald examines the degree to which an MST-based continuum of care can provide improved clinical outcomes and cost savings relative to the usual community services provided to children and adolescents at risk for out-of-home placement. Rather than providing only intensive, home-based, time-limited MST, the continuum will also include MST outpatient as well as MST-oriented therapeutic foster care, MST-oriented respite, and MST-oriented psychiatric hospitalization. Youths from a northeastern city will be randomly assigned either to the MST continuum or to the usual community services. The continuum will assume responsibility for all the mental health needs of youths in the treatment condition throughout the duration of the study. This study will have implications for service delivery models and accountability of service providers for children's mental health.

Drug Court Study

Dr. Jeff Randall is the project coordinator on a randomized clinical trial of MST with substance-abusing and dependent juvenile offenders and their families. MST is provided in two treatment conditions. In one condition, MST is provided in its classic form. In the other, MST is enhanced with key aspects of the community reinforcement approach (CRA) (Budney & Higgens, 1998), an intervention that has strong empirical support for treating cocaine-abusing adults (Higgens et al., 1995). Participants are randomly assigned to one of four treatment conditions: community services without drug court, drug court with community services, drug court with MST, or drug court with MST and CRA. In addition to determining the degree to which the enhanced MST protocol has advantages over classical MST, the design of this study allows examination of the degree to which juvenile drug courts are clinically and cost effective.

Transportability Study

Dr. Sonja Schoenwald is the principal investigator of a study examining the effective transport of MST to community settings. MST has been identified by the National Institute of Mental Health (NIMH) and by the Office of Juvenile Justice and Delinquency Prevention as an effective treatment model that should be disseminated to community-based service providers. As is evident from the presentation of other studies, therapist adherence is key to obtaining favorable outcomes. Using consumers and service providers at twenty-six sites currently implementing MST in the United States and Canada, this study examines the manner in which therapist adherence is linked to intra- and extraorganizational factors as well as individual clinician variables. Participants will include 2,550 youths and families referred to MST programs, as well as the clinicians and administrators employed by these programs. Not only will this study help researchers understand the key elements of the effective dissemination of MST, it will also inform efforts to disseminate other types of community-based treatments.

Implications for Children's Mental Health Services

The success of MST has been attributed to several features that distinguish the model from prevailing mental health practices. First, it addresses the known determinants of clinical problems. Although extensive evidence suggests that serious clinical problems are influenced by individual, family, peer, school, neighborhood, and community factors (e.g., Loeber & Hay, 1997), prevailing mental health, juvenile justice, and drug abuse services address only a narrow range of these influences. Second, MST services are provided in the ecological contexts in which the problems occur. This model of service delivery reduces barriers to service access, helps to engage families in treatment, provides more ecologically valid assessment and outcome information, and improves treatment generalization. Third, considerable attention is devoted to MST quality assurance mechanisms, with intensive and ongoing supervision aimed at maintaining treatment fidelity. Adherence is assessed through caregiver ratings and audiotapes of treatment sessions, and MST experts provide weekly feedback through on-site group supervision or telephone consultation. Fourth, MST clinicians employ empirically based intervention models, such as the behavior therapies, cognitive behavior therapy, and pragmatic family therapies within a social ecological conceptual framework. Fifth, MST assumes that the caregiver is key to favorable long-term outcomes, regardless of the clinical challenges that he or she may present. Thus, treatment goals are largely defined by caregivers, and the vast majority of MST clinical resources are devoted to developing the capacity of the caregiver to achieve these goals (versus treating the child or adolescent individually). Finally, MST service providers are held accountable for engaging families in treatment and for achieving favorable youth and family outcomes.

These MST features differ considerably from the current state of mental health services and have major implications for policy change in at least three ways. First, financial resources should be redistributed from costly and ineffective residential and institutional services to ecologically valid family- and community-based services. Second, service providers should be held accountable for engaging families in treatment and obtaining outcomes, and incentives should be in place for accomplishing these tasks. Finally, mental health professionals should be trained in empirically based treatments, and should be provided with ongoing training and supervision to ensure treatment integrity (Henggeler, 1999; Henggeler et al., 1998).

This chapter began with a discussion of the need for change in children's mental health services. The research summarized demonstrates that the mental health technology needed to make reform currently exists. Because recent studies have demonstrated that MST not only provides more favorable clinical outcomes than usual services but does so in a more cost-efficient manner, the time seems particularly ripe for policymakers and service providers to strive for better mental health services.

NOTES

1. Preparation of this chapter was supported by grants MH51852 and MH59138 from the NIMH, AA122202 from the NIAAA, DA 10079 and DA-99-008 from the NIDA, and 96.2013 from the Annie E. Casey Foundation.

REFERENCES

Borduin, C. M., Henggeler, S. W., Blaske, D. M., & Stein, R. (1990). Multisystemic treatment of adolescent sexual offenders. *International Journal of Offender Therapy and Comparative Criminology, 34,* 105–13.

Borduin, C, M., Mann, B. J., Cone, L. T., Henggeler, S. W., Fucci, B. R., Blaske, D. M., & Williams, R. A. (1995). Multisystemic treatment of serious juvenile offenders: Long-term prevention of criminality and violence. *Journal of Consulting and Clinical Psychology, 63,* 569–78.

Bronfenbrenner, U. (1979). *The ecology of human development: Experiments by design and nature.* Cambridge: Harvard University Press.

Brown, T. L, Henggeler, S. W., Schoenwald, S. K., Brondino, M. J., & Pickerel, S. G. (1999). Multisystemic treatment of substance abusing and dependent juvenile delinquents: Effects on school attendance at posttreatment and 6-month follow-up. *Children's Services: Social Policy, Research, and Practice, 2,* 81–93.

Brunk, M., Henggeler, S. W., & Whelan, J. P. (1987). A comparison of multisystemic therapy and parent training in brief treatment of child abuse and neglect. *Journal of Consulting and Clinical Psychology, 55,* 311–18.

Budney, A. J, & Higgins, S. T. (1998). *A community reinforcement plus voucher approach: Treating cocaine addiction* (NIH Pub. No. 98-4309). Rockville, MD: National Institute on Drug Abuse.

Burns, B. J. (1991). Mental health service use by adolescents in the 1970s and 1980s. *Journal of the American Academy of Child and Adolescent Psychiatry, 30,* 144–50.

Elliott, D. S. (Series Ed.). (1998). *Blueprints for violence prevention.* University of Colorado, Center for the Study of Prevention of Violence. Boulder: Blueprints Publications.

Farrington, D. P., & Welsh, B.C. (1999). Delinquency prevention using family-based interventions. *Children and Society, 13,* 287–303.

Fraser, M. W., Nelson, K. E., & Rivard, J. C. (1997). The effectiveness of family preservation services. *Social Work Research, 21,* 138–53.

Friesen, B. J., & Koroloff, N. M. (1990). Family-centered services: Implications for mental health administration and research. *Journal of Mental Health Administration, 17,* 13–25.

Haapasalo, J., & Tremblay, R. E. (1994). Physically aggressive boys from age 6 to 12: Family background, parenting behavior, and prediction of delinquency. *Journal of Consulting and Clinical Psychology, 62,* 1044–52.

Haley, J. (1976). *Problem Solving Therapy.* San Francisco: Jossey-Bass.

Henggeler, S. W. (1991). Multidimensional causal models of delinquent behavior and their implications for treatment. In R. Cohen & A.W. Siegel (Eds.), *Context and Development* (pp. 211–31). Hillsdale, N J: Lawrence Erlbaum.

Henggeler, S. W. (1997). The development of effective drug abuse services for youth. In J. A. Egertson, D. M. Fox, & A. I. Leschner (Eds.), *Treating drug abusers effectively* (pp. 253–79). New York: Blackwell.

Henggeler, S. W. (1999). Multisystemic therapy: An overview of clinical procedures, outcomes, and policy implications. *Child Psychology and Psychiatry Review, 4,* 2–10.

Henggeler, S. W., & Borduin, C. M. (1990). *Family therapy and beyond: A multisystemic approach to treating the behavior problems of children and adolescents.* Pacific Grove, CA: Brooks/Cole.

Henggeler, S. W., & Borduin, C. M., Melton, G. B., Mann, B. J., Smith, L., Hall, J. A., Cone, L., & Fucci, B. R. (1991). Effects of multisystemic therapy on drug use and abuse in serious juvenile offenders: A progress report from two outcome studies. *Family Dynamics of Addiction Quarterly, 1,* 40–51.

Henggeler, S. W., Melton, G. B, Brondino, M. J., Scherer, D. G., & Hanley, J. H. (1997). Multisystemic therapy with violent and chronic juvenile offenders and their families: The role of treatment fidelity in successful dissemination. *Journal of Consulting and Clinical Psychology, 65,* 821–33.

Henggeler, S. W., Melton, G. B., & Smith, L. A. (1992). Family preservation using multisystemic therapy: An effective alternative to incarcerating serious juvenile offenders. *Journal of Consulting and Clinical Psychology, 60,* 953–61.

Henggeler, S. W., Melton, G. B., Smith, L. A., Schoenwald, S. K., & Hanley, J. H. (1993). Family preservation using multisystemic treatment: Long-term follow-up to a clinical trial with serious juvenile offenders. *Journal of Child and Family Studies, 2,* 283–93.

Henggeler, S. W., Pickerel, S. G., & Brondino, M. J. (1999). Multisystemic treatment of substance abusing and dependent delinquents: Outcomes, treatment fidelity and transportability. *Mental Health Services Research. 1,* 141–84.

Henggeler, S. W., Rodick, J. D., Borduin, C. M., Hanson, C. L., Watson, S. M., & Urey, J. R. (1986). Multisystemic treatment of juvenile offenders: Effects on adolescent behavior and family interactions. *Developmental Psychology, 22,* 132–41.

Henggeler, S. W., Rowland, M. D., Randall, J., Ward, D. M., Pickerel, S. G., Cunningham, P. B., Miller, S. L., Edwards, J., Zealberg, J. J., Hand, L. D., &

Santos, A. B. (1999). Home-based multisystemic therapy as an alternative to the hospitalization of youths in psychiatric crisis: Clinical outcomes. *Journal of the American Academy of Child and Adolescent Psychiatry, 38*, 1331–39.

Henggeler, S. W., Schoenwald, S. K., Borduin, C. M., Rowland, M. D., & Cunningham, P. B. (1998). *Multisystemic treatment of antisocial behavior in children and adolescents.* New York: Guilford Press.

Higgens, S. T., Budney, A. J., Bickel, W. K., Badger, G. J., Foerg, F. E., & Ogden, D. (1995). Outpatient behavioral treatment for cocaine dependence: One-year outcome. *Experimental Clinical Psychoparmacology, 3*, 205–12.

Kazdin, A. E., & Weisz, J. R. (1998). Identifying and developing empirically supported child and adolescent treatments. *Journal of Consulting and Clinical Psychology, 66*, 19–36.

Kendall, P. C., & Braswell, L. (1993). *Cognitive-behavioral therapy for impulsive children* (2nd ed.). New York: Guilford Press.

Kiesler, C. A. (1993). Mental health policy and the psychiatric inpatient care of children. *Applied and Preventive Psychology, 2*, 91–99.

Loeber, R., & Hay, D. (1997). Key issues in the development of aggression and violence from childhood to early adulthood. *Annual Review of Psychology, 48*, 371–410.

McBride, D., VanderWaal, C., VanBuren, H., & Terry, Y. (1997). *Breaking the cycle of drug use among juvenile offenders.* Washington, DC: National Institute of Justice.

Minuchin, S. (1974). *Families and family therapy.* Cambridge: Harvard University Press.

Munger, R. L. (1993). *Changing children's behavior quickly.* Lanham, MD: Madison Books.

National Institute on Drug Abuse. (1999). *Principles of drug addiction treatment: A research-based guide* (NIH Publication No. 99-4180). Rockville, MD: Author.

Randall, J., Swenson, C. C., & Henggeler, S. W. (1999). Neighborhood solutions for neighborhood problems: An empirically-based violence prevention collaboration. *Health, Education, and Behavior, 26*, 806–20.

Rowland, M. D., Henggeler, S. W., Gordon, A. M., Pickerel, S. G., Cunningham, P. B., & Edwards, J. E. (2000). Adapting multisystemic therapy to serve youth presenting psychiatric emergencies: Two case studies. *Clinical Psychology and Psychiatry Review, 5*, 30–43.

Schoenwald, S. K., Ward, D., Henggeler, S. W., Pickerel. S. G., & Patel, H. (1996). Multisystemic therapy treatment of substance abusing or dependent adolescent offenders: Costs of reducing incarceration, inpatient, and residential placement. *Journal of Child and Family Studies, 5*, 431–44.

Schoenwald, S. K., Ward, D., Henggeler, S. W., & Rowland, M. D. (2000). MST vs. hospitalization for crisis stabilization of youth: Placement outcomes 4 months post-referral. *Mental Health Services Research, 2*, 3–12.

Sondheimer, D. L., Schoenwald, S. K., & Rowland, M.D. (1994). Alternatives to the hospitalization of youth with a serious emotional disturbance. *Journal of Clinical Child Psychology, 23*, 7–12.

Stanton, M. D., & Shandish, W. R. (1997). Outcomes, attrition, and family-couples treatment for drug abuse: A meta-analysis and review of the controlled, comparative studies. *Psychological Bulletin, 122,* 170–91.

Tate, D. C., Reppucci, N. D., & Mulvey, E. P. (1995). Violent juvenile delinquents: Treatment effectiveness and implications for future action. *American Psychologist, 50,* 777–81.

Washington State Institute for Public Policy (1998). *Watching the bottom line: Cost-effective interventions for reducing crime in Washington.* Olympia, WA: Evergreen State College.

Weithorn, L. (1988). Mental hospitalization for troubled youth: An analysis of skyrocketing admission rates. *Stanford Law Review, 40,* 773–838.

Weisz, J. A., Weiss, B., & Donenberg, G. R. (1992). The lab versus the clinic: Effects of child and adolescent psychotherapy. *American Psychologist, 57,* 741–46.

14 Reclaiming a Family-Centered Services Reform Agenda

MARC MANNES

The professionally driven, family-centered services reform movement (Mannes, 1993), which has served as the stimulus for numerous policy and practice reforms in child and family services at the national, state, and local level since the mid-1970s (Early & Hawkins, 1994; Nelson, 1997), finds itself losing momentum. This occurs only a short time after the movement received an enormous national boost in prestige with the creation of a federal family-centered and prevention-oriented funding stream, entitled the Family Preservation and Support Services Program (Omnibus Budget Reconciliation Act, 1993). While some of the movement's waning can be attributed to the natural process of gradually losing energy and clout with the passage of time, progress has been handicapped by an apparent willingness on the part of many Americans to ignore and deny the social and economic reality of impoverished Americans (Johnson, 1994; Blendon, McCormick, & Young, 1997).

A booming economy appears to have become a detriment. Widespread economic prosperity has apparently generated a sense of contentment and general indifference to initiating national action on behalf of less fortunate Americans (Wolfe, 1998). A sense of entitlement has emerged for those who have amassed wealth and influence in the New Capitalism of the global market and information era at the same time as the entitlement for those who have been less fortunate has been eliminated (Schwarz, 1998; Sennett, 1998).

The family-centered services reform movement has been harmed politically by conservative Republicans' ability to effectively tap a segment of the electorate's fears and resentments in order to achieve electoral success (Balz & Brownstein, 1996) and then produce social legislation at odds with family-centered values. Finally, poor people's pervasive political apathy and disenfranchisement have robbed them of the ability to have any voice in the social policies that affect them (Galbraith, 1996), as well as preventing the movement from having a natural constituency.

The first portion of this chapter identifies major sociopolitical factors and events that have contributed to the family-centered reform movement's retreat. The second portion begins to sketch some of the core elements needed to reinstill a heightened sense of social trust and offers some initial thoughts on strategies that would help move family-centered service reform back to center stage in ongoing efforts to advance the cause of social justice and improve the lot of less-advantaged American children and families.

THE WANING OF THE FAMILY-CENTERED SERVICES REFORM MOVEMENT

Throughout the early portion of the 1990s, the federal budget deficit and the national social trust deficit were often identified as compelling evidence of the decline of contemporary American society. Public discourse on the two deficit topics often assumed a blustery tone as various special interest groups cavalierly spewed socially divisive rhetoric that attributed blame for the growth of the twin deficits, while simultaneously lobbying for public solutions to advance their private interests in a way that contributed to mounting fiscal red ink and an abdication of social responsibility (Lapham, 1995; Balz & Brownstein, 1996; Elshtain, 1996).

The Persistent Social Trust Deficit

Although the economic surge of the middle and latter 1990s and a measured dose of congressional and presidential penny-pinching during the Clinton administration years eventually combined to eliminate the budget deficit, produce a budget surplus, and buoy economic spirits for many Americans, the social trust deficit remains. Trust among Americans for their fellow Americans is at an all-time low. In 1960, when people were asked, "Do you believe most people can be trusted, or can't you be too careful?" nearly 60 percent of respondents agreed that people could be trusted. Since that time the social trust register has dropped markedly, and even with modest increases during the mid-1980s, the figure in 1996 reached an all-time low of 37.5 percent (Putnam, 1995). While the register appears to be rebounding somewhat since 1996, it remains far below its historic highs. In an atmosphere where social trust has plummeted, it is not surprising that one social commentator would describe contemporary American society as an "argument culture" wherein too many matters succumb to an oppositional orientation and are subjected to hotly contested debate (Tannen, 1998).

What is meant by the idea of trust? Trust comes from the German word *Trost*, which suggests comfort (Gibb, 1978). Defined as reciprocal faith in others' intentions and behavior, trust is grounded in a belief that those on whom we depend will meet our expectations of them (Kramer, Brewer, & Hanna, 1996). Trust serves as the basis for social cooperation (Earle & Cvetkovich, 1995). Johnson (1994), Dionne (1996), and Blendon et al. (1997) identify many of the major issues eating away at America's social fabric and undermining positive social relations: simmering racial antagonisms evident in affirmative action debates and ongoing acts of discrimination and racism that continue to manifest themselves in the banking and criminal justice systems; bitter outcries of cultural regression and an anguished sense of moral malaise awash in the land based on the content of products delivered by the purveyors of pop culture; vitriolic reactions to calls for tolerance and support for equal treatment of gays and lesbians; the fracturing of conventional political belief systems in ways that force people to reconstruct their political identities; and a lack of confidence in the ability of government to provide public health, social, and educational services.

Putnam (2000) shows how measures of participation in the structures that foster sociability, including church attendance, union membership, parent-teacher associations, and fraternal organizations, all show marked drops since the 1950s. The decline in the membership of voluntary organizations has been accompanied by the rapid expansion of lobbying organizations, professional associations, and trade organizations that, according to Fukuyama (1995), exist to "protect particular economic interests in the political marketplace" (p. 309). The proliferation of groups unwilling to subordinate their parochial interests to larger community goals mitigates against the production of social trust.

Americans' ability to effectively address issues that contribute to a more cohesive social order is compromised by these forces, and the financial costs are significant. According to Fukuyama (1995), the United States pays substantially more than other industrialized countries for police protection, picks up the exorbitant tab for keeping more than 1 percent of its population in prison, and shells out much more to lawyers for suits and countersuits than does either Europe or Japan. The enormous amount of public investment spurred by mistrust are resources diverted from more positive, productive, and purposeful ends and "amounts to a measurable percentage of gross domestic product and constitutes a direct tax imposed by the breakdown of trust in society" (Fukuyama, 1995, p. 311).

The Ascendancy of Domestic Fear Politics

In a speech given at Cape Elizabeth, Maine, on November 2, 1970, the late Senator Edmund Muskie (1970) differentiated between two distinct types of politics:

> There are only two kinds of politics. There are not radical and reactionary . . . or conservative and liberal. Or even Democratic and Republican. There are only the politics of fear and the politics of trust. . . . One says: You are encircled by monstrous dangers. Give us power over your freedom so we may protect you. . . . The other says: The world is a baffling and hazardous place, but it can be shaped to the will of men.

At the time of Senator Muskie's speech, a politics of fear was dominant, fueled in the international sphere by trepidation of the Russians, Chinese, and other communist regimes throughout the world, and driven on the national front by divisions over the war in Vietnam and the resurgence of a domestic politics practiced by President Nixon, which went for the "social issue jugular" (Dionne, 1991). While the politics of fear in the international arena currently dwells on the actions of terrorist groups and outlaw states, the domestic politics of fear is vigorously pursued as a bipartisan endeavor. Both political parties appear willing to use fear politics when they deem it useful to accomplishing their political ends. During difficult economic times, numerous Republicans played off job security anxieties by attacking affirmative action, while the Democrats perennially fan the fears of older Americans by intimating the "other side" is about to pull the rug out from under senior entitlements such as Social Security and Medicare (Balz & Brownstein, 1996). When politicians and political parties can choose between trust and fear, they appear inclined to pick fear because it seems much easier and more effective to employ. A good case can be made that people respond more readily to the anxiety and mongering that go hand in hand with playing the fear card. Furtive attempts to usher in a trust-oriented agenda have quickly fizzled. Clinton's 1992 campaign theme of a "new covenant" could have served as the basis for rebuilding social trust, but the concept quickly disappeared when victory was secured. According to Gibb (1978), trust and fear are vital to understanding people and social systems; when the level of trust exceeds the level of fear, people and social systems operate well, and when fear outweighs trust, they tend to break down.

The rise of fear politics most relevant to family-centered services dwells amid the bitter battle over family values (Stacey, 1996) and what many social observers have coined "the cultural war" (Hartman & Laird, 1998). The fearful perspective is captured in the radical right's traditionalist orientation to family values, championed primarily by conservative Republicans and fundamentalist Christian interest groups. Their thesis is that the problems with America's families are a direct result of bad government programs and bad values set loose on American society during the 1960s. The conclusion of their analysis is stark and foreboding: parents and children have much to fear from the permissive and immoral cultural norms.

Primary apostles of the traditionalist approach are James C. Dobson, head of the powerful Focus on the Family organization located in Colorado Springs, Colorado, and Gary Baur, who runs the Washington-based arm of the Colorado organization entitled the Family Research Council (Fisher, 1996). Dr. Dobson has a daily radio show with an audience equaling that of Paul Harvey and Rush Limbaugh and a mailing list bigger than that of Pat Robertson or Jerry Falwell. According to Fisher (1996), his ability to mobilize a political army is legendary. When Dr. Dobson encouraged listeners of his show to protest a congressional bill that would restrict home schooling, the congressional switchboard was paralyzed by nearly one million calls.

Fisher's (1996) investigation of Dobson's activities suggests that the turbulence of the 1960s drew Dobson from his professorship in pediatrics at the University of Southern California to his innovative mix of counseling, evangelism, and political activism and to the conclusion that America is caught up in a "civil war of values." Since his departure from higher education, his mission has been to counter the permissiveness and declining authority of the 1960s and to provide an alternative to the leader of that insurrection, Benjamin Spock, and the negative influence of his widely read and cited book *Baby and Child Care*. Dobson's counteroffering is entitled *Dare to Discipline*; the primer outsells Spock's work and advises parents to buy a switch and keep it in their child's dresser as a constant reminder of potential corporal punishment should the child fail to heed parental authority. Fear is the overarching commandment of the Dobson creed—not only should the young feel fear in the face of parental authority, but they should also fear the consequences of not fearing it. In Dobson's worldview, poor people's descent into crime, drugs, and illegitimacy are prime illustrations of the downward spiral of morality and authority in this country.

Even with the fairly routine attempts by political parties and special interest groups to demagogue issues for their electoral advantage, the concerted efforts of House Republicans to effectively transform fear into a politics of resentment leading to electoral and legislative accomplishments are striking (Balz & Brownstein, 1996). In the same way the cohort of Democratic representatives elected in 1974 viewed themselves as reformers determined to end the war in Vietnam (Kline, 1998), the group of Republicans arriving in 1994 saw themselves as reformers on a mission to dismantle the welfare state (Balz & Brownstein, 1996). They effectively tapped the anger of a sizable coalition of Americans who had come to revile centralized big government and fear its unwarranted intrusion in their daily lives. They exploited widespread disgruntlement with taxation levels by cunningly portraying federal taxes as the lifeblood of the welfare state instead of as the means by which Americans determine the extent of their obligations to each other. They harnessed currents of bitterness by characterizing redistributive policies as taking funds from the paychecks of hardworking Americans and turning the money over to federal bureaucrats, who then reallocated it to the "undeserving poor." Finally, they were able to delink the axiom of entitlement reflected in the Aid to Families with Dependent Children (AFDC) program from its historic expression of collective social responsibility for people suffering hardship as a result of their socioeconomic marginalization and effectively recast the idea as a prop for the lazy and indolent that promoted irresponsibility (Balz & Brownstein, 1996).

Republicans' eagerness to take advantage of a disdain for big government, a dislike for taxes, a distaste for services for the poor, along with their ability to stage polarizing political debates and frame issues in divisive terms, contributed to setting groups of Americans against other groups of Americans (Dionne, 1996). Moreover, their 1994 electoral success inhibited the federal government from exercising moral suasion on behalf of poor children and their families because they refused to appropriate a bank account to support such initiatives.

The interrelationship and consequences of the decline in social trust, the expression of a politics playing off of fears and resentments, and the manifestation of an argument culture are on continuous display in the institutions within which political discourse and social policymaking take place. While a certain degree of partisan wrangling and competition is essential—if not vital—to a healthy democratic process, many argue that we are caught in the maelstrom of a long and steady decline into a much more intense, conflictual politics (Elshtain, 1996). No doubt, divided government at the federal level, wherein different political parties control the legislative and executive branches, contributes to the contentiousness. But the decline in civility and an unprecedented degree of vituperation are especially evident in the legislative branch, where negative and polarized political arguments play out. According to Tannen (1998), as Congress—and even state legislatures—becomes more attack-oriented and less civil, the political airwaves are also filled with venomous rhetoric that undermines a more civil discourse and stymies trust building. Kline (1998) sees the rise of "tabloid politics" as the result of a fresh crop of abrasive, disrespectful, baby-boom representatives from the suburbs, a more partisan and ideological

Republican Party led by southerners, and the presence of television in the halls of Congress.

The rancorous political climate is evident in the different tone between the Nixon impeachment proceedings and the Clinton "affair." When confronted with clear abuses of public power in the mid-1970s, Congress worked hard to produce a bipartisan response, while two decades later the brouhaha over Clinton's peccadillo and his willingness to mislead and misrepresent is unmistakenly partisan. Certain members of the political class have labeled the more recent internecine warfare as "the criminalization of policy differences"; only in a mistrustful and angry environment where "political abuse" is on the rise could such a term come into vogue.

For many Americans, the heightened contentiousness only contributes to the continuing erosion of an already-reduced public faith in government and a skepticism toward policy solutions that emerge from such a poisoned political environment. For others, the politics of fear that capitalizes on mistrust to mobilize bitter and scornful voting blocks and employs strong-arm tactics leads to either political alienation and estrangement (Elshtain, 1996) or approval of selective benefits of the welfare state in lieu of general support.

The Intersecting Political Economy

For large numbers of Americans the economic successes of the mid-1990s have caused the short-lived "politics of the anxious middle" (Dionne, 1996) to give way to a much larger and disturbing "politics of contentment" (Galbraith, 1992). White-collar job insecurities and worries about losing health care benefits associated with the early 1990s recession were quickly swept away by restored employment opportunities and a soaring stock market—which made even the roughly 50 percent of Americans who don't own any equities feel better about their economic circumstances.

A sense of increased prosperity has caused many middle-class Americans to recalculate their social and economic interests, even if they've gone into deep debt to secure lifestyle changes (Wolff, 1999) and join the ever-growing ranks of what Galbraith (1992) labels the "constituency of contentment." This constituency is made up of those who feel financially secure and are interested in lower taxes, less governmental interference, and more opportunities to quickly secure short-term profits. They do, however, continue to support middle-class welfare state programs such as Medicare, Social Security, and the home interest tax deduction. Their contentment leads to complacency, and in their torpor they find themselves dismissive of or indifferent to government intervention on behalf of the less fortunate most likely because they cannot see any personal gain from greater public investment in the needs of the poor (Galbraith, 1992).

Schwarz (1998) cites the increasing power of a meritocracy mindset in America's thinking. Ascribers to the meritocracy doctrine believe that anyone who is willing can obtain the necessary academic credentials, find a job, and live decently, and that those without education, employment, or a decent wage have failed to demonstrate the acquisitiveness worthy of economic rewards (Lasch, 1991) and do not require alternative means of assistance.

For the "contented" and "meritocrats," any pretense of collective responsibility has evaporated in an atmosphere of materialistic self-gratification and a self-serving financial consciousness. Their human need for belonging is achieved through consumerism and their ability to purchase what others have bought (Golden, 1997). The contented constituency's interest in low taxes and small government and the meritocracy subscriber's unwillingness to help those who haven't "met the test" dovetail with the concerns of the resentful constituency courted by conservative Republicans to form a sizable voting coalition resistant to paying for social programs.

Elshtain (1996) points out how political withdrawal and disengagement—the hallmarks of the current era—undermine renewal of the public realm. Alienation and complacency lead to an abandonment of civic purpose and undermine the ability to forge social trust (Fukuyama, 1995).

The Expression of Social Policies Grounded in Mistrust and Indifference

If, according to Wolfe (1998), "in a democracy, good politics has to precede good policies," then the corollary may also be true. Given that the functions of the child welfare system are directly tied to social policy (Thomlinson, Maluccio, & Abramczyk, 1996), the deployment of fear-based social politics amid a social landscape consisting of resentful, alienated, and complacent citizen groups is not conducive to producing child and family policies grounded in trust. For Sennett (1998), "The attack on the welfare state . . . treats those who are dependent on the state with the suspicion they are social parasites, rather than truly helpless" (p. 139). Dreams and aspirations give way to suspicion and apprehension. Policy solutions favoring castigation and recrimination dominate at the expense of compassion. The threat of punishment—instead of the promise of improvement—is used as the basis for altering human behavior. Policy concepts emphasizing the "common good," "shared responsibility and sacrifice," "altruism," and "caring" give way to those demanding "self-sufficiency," "personal responsibility," and "retribution." Several examples highlight this phenomenon.

Income maintenance. Conservative politicians and organizations have worked diligently to crystallize in people's minds the existence of a "culture of poverty" and agitate existing public concern over the prospects of intergenerational welfare dependency (Balz & Brownstein, 1996). Even non-conservative critics as far back as Piven (1971) have argued that federal welfare policies and practices over the past several decades consistently punished the poor, denigrated their humanness, and kept them outside the mainstream of American life. The cumulative weight of rebuke and outrage with the status quo helped forge the political consensus that supported the version of welfare reform contained in the Personal Responsibility and Work Opportunity Reconciliation Act of 1996.

Concerns about the poor becoming dependent on financial assistance and ill will directed toward recipients of welfare are neither new nor surprising. Similar sentiments can be traced as far back as the English Poor Laws of the sixteenth century. They resurfaced in the late 1800s in this country by way of Charles Loring Brace's Children's Aid Society and the Charity Organization Society's philosophy of hard labor and individual enterprise as the solution to poverty (Bremmer, 1956). As welfare rolls grew during the 1960s, trepidation over children born out of wedlock and the resultant rise in the number of poor single-parent families served as sources of concern (Moynihan, 1965).

From the creation of the Aid to Dependent Children program in the 1930s to the unsuccessful welfare reforms initiated in the 1970s and 1980s, American income support policy shifted from keeping single mothers out of the paid labor force and at home caring for their children to having them become wage workers outside the home. The intersection of welfare dependency and job participation led policy analysts like David Ellwood and Mary Jo Bane to propose time-limited benefits for welfare recipients based on their research study findings (Balz & Brownstein, 1996). Ellwood and Bane's policy approach, however, retained the promise of other forms of assistance, such as public service jobs, should AFDC beneficiaries not be able—and the market not allow them—to make the transition to economic self-sufficiency. Their approach was consistent with the "end welfare as we know it" theme being enunciated by Bill Clinton in his presidential campaign, and the two eventually assumed high-level positions in the Clinton administration's welfare policy regime.

Ellwood and Bane's interest in time-limited support was advanced in dramatic fashion by conservative House Republicans such as Vin Weber and Clay Shaw, who also wanted time limits—but without the guarantee of public employment (Balz & Brownstein, 1996). Still another group of young House Republicans' passion for welfare reform was based on their aversion to out-of-wedlock births and their desire to produce legislation that would reduce that number (Horn, 1996).

Having attained majority status, House Republicans were finally positioned to alter fundamentally the federal entitlement to income maintenance (Balz & Brownstein, 1996). They forged an agreement with Republican governors to create the necessary momentum and get the fundamentals for the passage of welfare reform legislation in place. Governors' desire for block grants to expand their power and a willingness to accept less revenue to secure that power were easily melded with Republican congressional leaders' political themes of devolving power back to the states and balancing the federal budget. Conservative House Republicans could concoct legislation that was capable of punishing illegitimacy among the poor, cutting bureaucracy, reducing the federal budget, and affirming states' rights. Many Democrats in both chambers, some moderate Senate Republicans, and a wavering president who finally signed the legislation were able to demonstrate consistency with their previous rhetoric that pledged allegiance to self-sufficiency by supporting the welfare bill. The recipients themselves, and those who might advocate on their behalf, remained silent. The resentful coalition within the American electorate felt vindicated (Balz & Brownstein, 1996), the complacent constituency more than likely didn't care, and the meritocrats were preoccupied with their economic accomplishment bravado. Besides, with the economy sizzling and a historically tight labor market, there was finally a demand for the low-wage employment of many of those on welfare rolls. The passage of new income maintenance policy for disadvantaged Americans served as the punctuation point in an unfolding political narrative that revealed how personal culpability for individual moral problems is to take precedence over common political problems (Lapham, 1995).

Child welfare. A similar predisposition toward mistrust is evident in recent federal child welfare policy as embodied in the Adoption and Safe Families Act of 1997 (ASFA). Even though federal policy guidance would lead one to believe that the new law maintains relatively equal emphasis on the standard policy outcomes (Administration for Children and Families, 1998), greater scrutiny of the statute reveals how ASFA reaffirms safety as the primary objective of the child welfare system, highlights preferred means of attaining permanency for children, and virtually ignores the subject of well-being.

While a reasonable amount of agreement on the importance of safety, permanence, and well-being exists within professional policy program and practice communities, in the face of ever-changing political, economic, and social realities, consensus quickly breaks down regarding the relative value and importance of each in relation to the other two (McGowan, 1990). Agreement crumbles even more when the conversation shifts to determining the best "means" to accomplish those policy "ends." For example, the reasonable and straightforward concept of permanency becomes increasingly complicated and contentious because it can be attained at a number of different points and accomplished through a variety of means. Permanency can be accomplished by intervening to keep children with their biological parents, and it can be attained by terminating parental rights and securing an adoption. There are deep divisions within the professions and among advocates about which orientation ought to be emphasized, and in order for permanency to be secured in a particular situation, competing perspectives often need to be reconciled (Mannes, 1998).

The passage of ASFA was in part a response to the perception in certain quarters that previous federal child welfare legislation that created Title IV-B, subpart 2, of the Social Security Act, and was entitled the Family Preservation and Support Services Program, had compromised child safety at the expense of keeping children with their biological parents. Books in the policymaking and academic communities castigated leaders of the family preservation movement and their programs for sacrificing the lives of children as a consequence of blind adherence to a family preservation ideology that could not and should not be realistically applied in the day-to-day child welfare world (Costin, Karger, & Stoesz, 1996; Gelles, 1996).

Certainly, child safety needs to be of paramount concern and of utmost importance when data point out that nationally, approximately 9 percent of children served by public child welfare agencies are sexually abused, and almost 10 percent are physically abused (Sedlak & Broadhurst, 1996). But what is the appropriate and compassionate response to the more than one-half of the public caseload consisting of neglect cases in which harsh and severe poverty is very often the culprit and substance abuse is prevalent (Pelton, 1993; Wexler, 1990)?

The provisions of ASFA calling for expedited permanency and hastened termination of parental rights disregard these factors and smack of a punitive orientation. It also creates incentives somewhat at odds with the Adoption Assistance and Child Welfare Act of 1980, which established a preferred sequence of permanency options seen as being in the "best interests of the child." ASFA calls for public child welfare staff to strive simultaneously for the most preferred option of having children remain with their biological or extended family and the second option of adoption through an approach labeled "concurrent planning." Unfortunately, the complexities inherent in pursuing both options at the same time, and effective management by staff or understanding by parents, are conveniently sidestepped. The biggest potential danger of ASFA is that it will ignore what is considered to be good practice and generate undesirable unintended consequences as it creates an institutional bias that favors termination and adoption at the expense of placement prevention or reunification services.

ASFA embodies derisive social policy by viewing parents as unwilling to work on their problems, unable to be taught how to do better, and incapable of being trusted to do right by their children. The social learning approach, which undergirds much of family-centered services and ascribes to the proposition that parents can acquire the skills to do better in terms of raising and nurturing their children, gives way to a policy predicated upon reproachment.

The virtual absence of attention to well-being reveals just how callous and insensitive ASFA policy really is. One might argue that well-being is attended to as part of the focus on safety and adoption, and there is a degree of truth in that assertion. Yet, as a policy outcome well-being also needs independent attention. "Well-being" is typically defined more broadly than just the avoidance of harm; it encompasses having one's basic needs met, possessing good health, and enjoying proper functioning in a range of areas (Griffin, 1990). There is little mention in ASFA of the economic and psychosocial aspects of well-being, and no acknowledgment of how these dimensions have an impact on safety and influence permanency (Besharov & Laumann, 1997). Finally, no financing is made available to help families overcome the hardship and deprivation associated with poverty or the scourge of addiction that would demonstrate sensitivity to the issue of well-being. The policy is a betrayal of trust.

The moderating, but still prevalent, social trust deficit, the effective parlaying of a politics rooted in fear into punitive social policies, and a political economy in which social consciousness has succumbed to the hypnotic trance of personal financial gain and widespread disdain for those who can't make it breeds a social climate insensitive to those in need and is decidedly scornful of those who fail to conform and "play by the rules." These factors constrain family-centered advocates' ability to advance the cause of meaningful social reform through policies, programs, and practices. Most regrettably, the difficulties in achieving social progress are eventually felt by less-advantaged children and their families.

REVITALIZING THE FAMILY-CENTERED
SERVICES REFORM MOVEMENT

Reinvigorating the family-centered services reform movement is tied to the degree to which citizens demand that trust be reintroduced into American domestic politics and social policies, which is in turn linked to the presence of a supportive political orientation. Professionals committed to family-centered services can mitigate some of the egregious consequences of the current sociopolitical climate by responding to new and emerging political realities and remaining firmly grounded in professional principles and ethics.

Overriding the Sociopolitical Stalemate

In the same way that interpersonal trust is grounded in positive and supportive relationship (Deutsch, 1958), social trust depends on empathic and reliable social relationships. Not only is the social cohesion derived from such relationships essential to securing greater harmony in civil society, but the greater the degree of social harmony, the greater the likelihood of social policies rooted in trust. Many scholars have used the term "social capital" to describe the concept of cohesion. For Fukuyama (1995), social capital is simply "the ability of people to work together for common purpose in groups and organizations" (p. 10).

Building social capital necessitates reversing the downward trend of associational life in America and helping communities either develop shared norms and values or, more likely, be respectful of competing sets of norms and values. This task takes on a political edge because conservatives are predisposed to blame much of the decline of community on the rise of the welfare state. They see the expanding modern state replacing more informal and indigenous systems, usurping responsibility, and destroying individual initiative (Dionne, 1991). However, Fukuyama (1995) argues that the welfare state can only be a partial explanation, since many other nations with more extensive social welfare apparatus have much lower levels of social pathology and dysfunction.

Sennett (1998) places the blame for the breakdown in personal responsibility, trust, and community on the rise of New Capitalism and makes the argument that new organizational work norms demanded by the whipsaw global economy and a distinctive Anglo-American response to it fractures the sense of purpose, self, and commitment to family and community.

Still another alternative hypothesis, put forth by Fukuyama (1995), is that the rise of a unique American brand of "rights-based individualism"—a "rights entitlement" that Americans believe they have, and the ascendancy of a "rights culture"—are primarily responsible for the decline of community and impede greater social cohesion. Because these concepts of "individual rights" are so deeply inbred in American political theory and constitutional law, deferring individual interests to the benefit of the collective group poses a serious challenge.

Even the assertion of political rights in pursuit of social justice is likely to have a harmful impact on social cohesion. The drive to end racial discrimination undermined social relations as it sought social progress. Thwarted at the executive and legislative branches, civil rights movement leaders endeavored to accomplish their objectives through the courts. Their success in using the judiciary to end discrimination in public institutions and private institutions serving the public has resulted in increasingly broad interpretations of individual rights defined by the Constitution. Favorable court decisions motivated liberal activists to return to the courts in search of additional rights expansion, and their success inevitably led to their conservative counterparts also trying to use the courts to attain their social agenda.

This has resulted in what Wilson (1991) defines as the "juridical" model of politics. Turning to the courts to attain policy objectives has side-stepped the potential for compromise that characterizes legislative policy-making, reinforced oppositional approaches to issues, and placed a greater emphasis on winners and losers. As social activists of all ideological stripes increasingly turn to the courts to resolve social issues, the increasingly adversarial climate creates a more contentious citizenry less open to negotiation. Moreover, as government assumes responsibility for an expanded set of issues, including moral matters as a result of court decisions, political "wedge" issues, which polarize Americans, mushroom. Elshtain (1996) observes how using the courts avoids debate via deliberative processes, and instead deepens citizen frustration and helps expand the politics of resentment.

According to Fukuyama (1995), rekindling the spirit and sense of community can come about only by moderating the excesses of the "rights-based" culture that has dominated the nation and reawakening Americans to the need to subordinate some of their individual interests to those of a larger group.

Advancing a Politics of Social Cohesion

A politics that evokes greater cohesion would have to be a high-wire act capable of simultaneously maintaining multiple delicate and complicated balances such as (a) moderating the excesses of individualism and repudiating unsuccessful versions of communitarianism such as communism; (b) emphasizing shared rights and obligations and affirming group diversity while accepting a vital yet reduced sphere of individual rights; and (c) sustaining a measure of social continuity while retaining flexible and reflexive qualities capable of adjusting to changing social and economic conditions (Misztal, 1996).

It would encompass many of the tenets of traditional republicanism or civic humanism in the spirit of civic renewal (Lasch, 1991) in order to create a less adversarial and more deliberative civil society. It would entail reconstructing and sustaining systems of values and institutions that emphasize and reinforce cooperation by building into citizens' roles multiple levels of interdependence, thus making principles of reciprocity and fairness more normative. Then people have practice in exercising a common citizenship that recognizes their mutual relationships as it helps them acknowledge and attend to their role in collective duties. Greater numbers of Americans vigorously participating in public discussions and public life would indicate positive movement. Their willingness to participate, however, will be based on their comfort with the political climate, their faith in political institutions, and their ability to see political agreements as legitimate (Misztal, 1996).

The political doctrine must sidestep the altruistic expectation that people will cooperate because they have come to embrace common values and accept competing sets of norms and interests, and avert naive notions that a shared sense of belonging is attainable. The approach, however, also has to refute a cooperation driven by pure self-interest or the imposition of sanctions.

America's championing of acquisitiveness and effective "democratization of consumption" (Lasch, 1991) creates myopic socialization processes. Misztal (1996) argues that socializing institutions with the stated purpose of promoting human relationships and the building of bonds must move beyond educating people to define their interactions with others exclusively in terms of market transactions. People need to receive guidance and instruction in understanding human interactions as moral transactions and to accept and learn how to deal with the reality of moral conflicts.

A political orientation that endorses cohesion also faces the challenge of seeking strong interpersonal community ties and endeavors to "strengthen weak ties," but in a decidedly different way than the approach proposed by Granovetter (1973). As the personal, familial, and socially destructive consequences of weak ties become more apparent in the global/ information age economy, Granovetter's (1973) approach only serves to buttress social and economic conditions introduced by New Capitalism (Sennett, 1998). Enhancing social cohesion requires creative reconciliation between strong and weak ties. Establishing denser links in local communities brings about cooperation among groups within a circumscribed geographic setting; and developing weaker ties, which can cut across social fault lines, creates better prospects for broader cooperation.

Tact, restraint, civilized moderation, negotiation, compromise, and flexibility would need to be reestablished as operating norms in both the civic and political realms. Structures and processes in the social and political environment need to espouse openness and reciprocity as they demonstrate stability and predictability (Misztal, 1996). This entails operating within a pluralistic framework and involves reaching consensus on basic principles, finding agreement on the rules of the game, sparing individuals impossible choices as much as possible, and accepting competing allegiances that operate within a common framework. In this environment a politics of public interest can begin to make some inroads in the face of the dominant politics of private interest (Schlesinger, 1986).

It is hard to see the politics of public interest being met through the dominant governing philosophy of Bill Clinton and Tony Blair known as the "third way" and defined as a blending of economic conservatism and social liberalism (Kallick, 1999). The two are political siamese twins who ingeniously helped their discredited political parties recapture the top executive positions in their respective governments by fashioning an agenda catering to the socioeconomic interests of the rich and suburbanites and providing meager fare for rural and urban poor and working poor. Yet a closer inspection of the miracle economy of the 1990s for which Mr. Clinton takes enormous pride and credit reveals that it has been sustained by heightened personal borrowing and represents very narrow private gain. According to Wolff (1999), the lion's share of the wealth generated by the stock market's torrid rise has gone to the richest 5 percent of the nation's households, and while net worth has grown for the richest 10 percent of American households, the other 90 percent find themselves moving in the opposite direction primarily due to acquiring greater debt.

In the face of these circumstances, a domestic politics tethered to slogans such as "practical idealism" or "compassionate conservatism" has sound-bite appeal but ultimately comes up empty unless such slogans are tied to real actions distinct from the protracted—but doubtfully everlasting—exhilaration of the current economic joyride. A politics responsive to social cohesion involves moving beyond the common populist passions of envy and bitterness, breaking the feverish rise of resentment politics, and standing firm against patrician-inspired beneficence. It is more appropriately built on what Lasch (1991) characterizes as the positive features of "petty-bourgeois" culture: moral realism, an understanding that everything has its price, a sincere respect for limits, a capacity for forgiveness, and a healthy skepticism toward exhortations of progress.

Paying Heed to State Political Cultures

Devolution—often known as New Federalism—is experiencing a run as the preferred intergovernmental system philosophy. The rhetorical and ideological fervor over "states rights" and the reassertion of states as "laboratories of democracy" via policy authority transfers leads states to assume increasing responsibility for the design and delivery of child and family services. Advocates for family-centered reforms must now pay attention to and work in fifty state capitals and not just Washington, DC.

Zimmerman (1992) has studied how variability in state political culture plays a role in the formulation of family policies and how those policies contribute to family well-being. Building on the work of Elazar (1986), Zimmerman differentiates among three types of political cultures: (a) individualistic cultures, in which private concerns are emphasized over public ones and high value is placed on keeping public interventions minimal; (b) moralistic cultures, in which the good of the commonwealth is emphasized and there is greater commitment to the use of communal power and collective interventions to promote and protect the common good; (c) traditionalistic cultures, which, like the moralistic ones, maintain a positive view of government but choose to restrict governmental power to that of maintaining traditional patterns and arrangements.

According to Zimmerman (1992), states tend to be heterogeneous, containing aspects of two or all three cultures, one type typically dominating. The results of her survey of family professionals from twenty-three states demonstrates how attitudes toward the role of government and families vary with states' political cultures. Respondents from more individualistic states tended to attach greater importance to families than those from less individualistic states, who were more likely to see government as more important in meeting the needs of children and the elderly. Attitudes about the normative basis for making intergenerational distributive choices also varied. Professionals from more individualistic states tended to emphasize *fairness* whereas those from less individualistic states placed greater emphasis on *need*. Zimmerman (1992) was able to show that the effects of political culture persisted even when the effects of political preferences and variables typically related to policy attitudes in other studies were controlled for.

In addition to her survey research, a content analysis of legislative summaries of three states representing the three types of political cultures was conducted. The results highlighted the influence of political culture on legislative initiatives. Strongly moralistic Minnesota enacted more explicit family legislation, which focused on economic benefits and assistance of a distributive and redistributive nature. Strongly individualistic Nevada enacted regulatory legislation dealing with the relationship issues of marriage and divorce. Predominantly traditionalistic South Carolina tended to enact legislation that addressed both economic and relationship issues and was in part distributive, redistributive, and regulatory.

Finally, in order to ascertain whether states' policy approaches mattered in terms of individual and family well-being, Zimmerman (1992) assessed states' per-capita expenditures for public welfare for 1960, 1970, 1980, and 1984. States' divorce, poverty, suicide rates, and teen birthrates were used to gauge well-being. Political culture was measured by the percentages of persons in each of the fifty states who voted for a Republican presidential candidate in 1960, 1966, 1980, and 1984 based on the premise that Republicans in general prefer a smaller role for government. States seen as more individualistic appeared to do less to mediate connections among people and showed lower levels of individual and family well-being, while states characterized as less individualistic did more to mediate connections among people and accordingly possessed higher levels of individual and family well-being. Moreover, Zimmerman (1992) makes the case that political culture was more important in explaining interstate differences in social spending than was fiscal capacity, suggesting that actual spending on public welfare was driven more by traditional political culture than on the basis of taxes enacted to support the spending.

Working with State Legislators

In addition to accepting the current dominance of devolution and recognizing the influence of state political culture, family-centered revitalization efforts need to tap into critical leverage points within state government. While securing the understanding and support of governors and the executive branch of government is always important, building effective relationships with legislators cannot be overemphasized. And since state legislators' tenure typically exceeds those of governors, securing long-term allies and support with elected representatives is imperative. Policies that bolster a family-centered reform agenda can come about only when legislators are cognizant of the issues facing less-advantaged children and families and motivated to develop and help pass supportive legislation.

Even though the task will not be an easy one, some helpful guidelines for implementing a state legislature–based strategy emerged from a study of the perceptions of state legislative leaders regarding child and family issues (State Legislative Leaders, 1995). The State Legislative Leaders Foundation surveyed 177 state legislative leaders from all fifty states seeking information on issues such as how those leaders define child and family issues; their understanding of the status of children and families in their states; their perceptions of the role of state government in the lives of children and families; their perceptions of advocacy efforts and their impact on the state legislative process; their thoughts on how they can be engaged in campaigns to improve the well-being of children and families; and recommendations for moving an agenda for children and families in state legislatures.

Of particular relevance to this chapter are legislative leaders' thoughts on how those with an interest in improving the interests of children and families can be more influential. They suggest the following:

- Establish consistent visibility and ongoing relationships with legislative leaders, legislators, and legislative staff.
- Build consensus around a realistic and manageable agenda that recognizes the role of compromise in the legislative process.
- Develop grassroots support for child and family issues on a district by district basis.
- Involve new leaders and other voices from other sectors.
- Employ bipartisan strategies.
- Become active in the electoral campaign process.
- Provide legislative leaders with factual and compelling information in a usable form.
- Become actively involved in the state *budget* process; get involved early, identify the key legislators, and stay involved throughout the entire budget process.

Their recommendations are useful reminders for professionals and members of the general public who strive to get a family-centered reform agenda implemented at the state level.

Keeping Family-Centered Reforms Ameliorative

Child and family services professionals find themselves responding to wave after wave of reforms as they get caught up in the process of reforming reforms. Overwhelmed professionals need to be reminded that reforms are not all alike. Costin et al. (1996) cite the work of historian Joseph Gusfield, who distinguished between assimilative and coercive aspects of social and moral reform in his study of the temperance movement. For Gusfield, assimilative reform was sparked by benevolence and sought to ameliorate, while coercive change was fueled by hostility and intended to punish. Costin et al. (1996) point out how the two types of reform are evident in the history of child welfare; Hull House is seen as an example of assimilative and benevolent reform, whereas the work of Charles Loring Brace is viewed as coercive.

This chapter has put forth the argument that recent child and family reform policies, produced in a political and social climate of fear and contentment, are insensitive and vindictive. To make matters worse, public child and family agencies and their network of affiliated providers are easily and often forced to act in less-than-desirable ways because of the clash over competing orientations and belief systems within the profession itself (Maluccio, 1997). Child and family services professionals need to make sure that the work they do with young people and adults remains ameliorative and benevolent.

Family-centered service reforms have been based on a set of assumptions about human nature, a set of ethics about appropriate societal responses, a set of theoretical beliefs that guide practice, and a set of principles about how professional work is to be conducted (Nelson, 1997). There is trust that in many cases all family members' safety can be ensured. There is trust that many parents can learn how to create safe, stable, nurturing home environments that promote healthy child development. And there is trust that with assistance and services, many children and families can resolve their crises and issues. Although these assumptions are not always met, and despite the fact that a family or two might betray the trust, promoters of family-centered service reforms need to retain their positive and hopeful intent.

The excesses of the current mean-spirited and self-absorbed era will moderate over time. The opportunity to reintroduce trust into American domestic politics will emerge. Until then, even if professionals and portions of the general public who believe in a family-centered reform agenda don't have the power to fully reclaim ameliorative social policy and revitalize the reform movement, they can at least reassert trust and compassion in the professional politics, policies, and practices that guide family-centered services.

REFERENCES

Administration for Children and Families, U.S. Department of Health and Human Services (1998). *New Legislation—Public Law 105–89, The Adoption and Safe Families Act of 1997* (ACYF-PI-CB-98–02). Washington, DC: Author.

Adoption and Safe Families Act, Pub. L. No. 105-89 (1997).

Balz, D., & Brownstein, R. (1996). *Storming the gates: Protest politics and the Republican revival.* Boston: Little, Brown.

Besharov, D. J., & Laumann, L. A. (1997, Winter–Spring). Don't call it child abuse if it's really poverty. *Journal of Children and Poverty, 3* (1), 5–36.

Blendon, R. J., McCormick, M., & Young, J. (1997). *The Harvard University, Robert Wood Johnson Foundation/University of Maryland National Survey of American Views on Children's Health Care.* Princeton, NJ: Robert Wood Johnson Foundation.

Boyle, P. (1999). U.S. Anti-drug funds misfire, hit target. *Youth Today, 8* (1), 1, 37–39.

Bremmer, R. H. (1956). Scientific philanthropy, 1873–93. *Social Service Review, 30,* 168–73.

Brueggemann, W. G. (1996). *The practice of macro social work.* Chicago: Nelson-Hall.

Costin, L. B., Karger, H. J., & Stoesz, D. (1996). *The politics of child abuse in America.* New York: Oxford University Press.

Cuban, L. (1990, January–February). Reforming again, again, and again. *Educational Researcher, 19* (1), 3–13.

Deutsch, M. (1958). Trust and suspicion. *Journal of Conflict Resolution, 2,* 265–79.

Dionne, E. J. Jr. (1991). *Why Americans hate politics.* New York: Touchstone.

Dionne, E. J. Jr. (1996). They only look dead: Why progressives will dominate the next political era. New York: Simon and Schuster.

Earle, T. C., & Cvetkovich, G. T. (1995). *Social trust: Toward a cosmopolitan society.* Westport, CT: Praeger.

Early, B. P., & Hawkins, M. J. (1994). Opportunity and risks in emerging family policy: An analysis of family preservation legislation. *Child and Youth Services Review, 16* (5, 6), 309–18.

Elazer, D. (1986). Marketplace and the commonwealth and three political cultures. In M. Gittell (Ed.), *State politics and the new federalism* (pp. 172–78). New York: Longman.

Elshtain, J. B. (1996). Democracy at century's end. *Social Service Review, 70* (4), 507–15.

Fisher, M. (1996, July 2). The GOP facing a Dobson's choice. *Washington Post,* D1–D2.

Fukuyama, F. (1995). *Trust the social virtues and the creation of prosperity.* New York: Free Press.

Galbraith, J. K. (1992). *The culture of contentment.* Boston: Houghton Mifflin.

Galbraith, J. K. (1996). *The good society: The humane agenda.* Boston: Houghton Mifflin.

Gelles, R. J. (1996). *The book of David: How preserving families can cost children's lives.* New York: Basic Books.

Gibb, J. R. (1978). *Trust: A new view of personal and organizational development.* Los Angeles: Guild of Tutors Press.

Golden, R. (1997). *Disposable children: America's child welfare system.* Belmont, CA: Wadsworth.

Granovetter, M. (1973). The strength of weak ties. *American Journal of Sociology, 78,* 1360–80.

Griffin, J. (1990). *Well-being: Its meaning, measurement, and moral importance.* Oxford: Clarendon Press.

Gusfield, J. R. (1966). *Symbolic crusade: Status politics and the American temperance movement.* Urbana: University of Illinois Press.

Hartman, A., & Laird, J. (1998). Moral and ethical issues in working with lesbians and gay men. *Families in Society, 79* (3), 263–76.

Horn, W. (1996). Assessing the effects of the "Devolution Revolution" on children and families. *National Center for Children in Poverty: News and Issues, 6* (1), 1–2.

Johnson, H. (1994). *Divided we fall: Gambling with history in the nineties.* New York: Norton.

Kallick, D. (1999, March–April). The third way's a charm. *Utne Reader,* 27–29.

Kammerman, S., & Kahn, A. (1995). *Starting right: How America neglects its youngest children and what we can do about it.* New York: Oxford University Press.

Kline, J. (1998, November 23). The town that ate itself: The political scene. *New Yorker,* 79–87.

Kramer, R. Brewer, M., & Hanna, B. A. (1996). Collective trust and collective action: The decision to trust as a social decision. In R. M. Kramer & T. R. Tyler (Eds.), *Trust in organizations: Frontiers of theory and research* (pp. 357–89). Newbury Park, CA: Sage.

Lakis, S. G., & Blood, M. A. (1995). *State legislative leaders: Keys to effective legislation for children and families.* Centerville, MA: State Legislative Leaders Foundation.

Lapham, L. H. (1995, March). Reactionary chic: How the nineties right recycles the bombast of the sixties left. *Harpers,* 31–42.

Lasch, C. (1991). *The true and only heaven: Progress and its critics.* New York: Norton.

Leff, M. H. (1973). Consensus for reform: The mother's pension movement in the progressive era. *Social Service Review, 47,* 397–417.

Lindsey, D. (1994). *The welfare of children.* New York: Oxford University Press.

Maluccio, A. T. (1997). Time for an ideological shift in child welfare? *Social Service Review, 71* (1), 135–43.

Mannes, M. (1993). Family preservation: A professional reform movement. *Journal of Sociology and Social Welfare, 20* (3), 5–24.

Mannes, M. (1998). The new psychology and economics of permanency. *Prevention Report, 2,* 12–16.

McGowan, B. G. (1990). Family based services and public policy: Context and implications. In J. K. Whitaker, J. Kinney, E. M. Tracy, and C. Booth (Eds.). *Reaching high risk families: Intensive family preservation in human services* (pp. 65–88). New York: Aldine de Gruyter.

Misztal, B. A. (1996). *Trust in modern societies.* Cambridge: Polity Press.

Moynihan, D. P. (1965). *The Negro family: The case for national action.* Washington, DC: U.S. Department of Labor.

Muskie, E. S. (1970). *Remarks by Senator Edmund S. Muskie, Cape Elizabeth, Maine, November 2.* Edmund S. Muskie Archives, Box 3208, Folder No. 7, Bates College, Lewiston, Maine.

Nelson, K. E. (1997). Family preservation: What is it? *Child and Youth Services Review, 19* (1, 2), 101–18.

Omnibus Budget Reconciliation Act of 1993, Pub. L. No. 103-66, Title IV-B of the Social Security Act, Subpart 2, Family Preservation and Support Services, 45 CFR Part 92.

Pelton, L. (1993). The role of material factors in child abuse and neglect. In *Neighbors helping neighbors: A new national strategy for the protection of children.* Washington, DC: U.S. Advisory Board on Child Abuse and Neglect.

Piven, F. F. (1971). *Regulating the poor: The functions of public welfare.* London: Tavistock.

Putnam, R. (2000). *Bowling alone: The collapse and revival of American community.* New York: Simon and Schuster.

Sedlak, A. J., & Broadhurst, D. D. (1996). *Third national incidence study of child abuse and neglect: Final report.* Washington, DC: National Center on Child Abuse and Neglect.

Sennett, R. (1998). *The corrosion of character: The personal consequences of work in the New Capitalism.* New York: Norton.

Schlesinger, A. Jr. (1986). *The cycles of American history.* Boston: Houghton Mifflin.

Schwarz, J. (1998, October). The hidden side of the Clinton economy. *Atlantic Monthly, 282,* 4, 18–21.

Stacey, J. (1996). *In the name of the family: Rethinking family values in the postmodern age.* Boston: Beacon Press.

State Legislative Leaders. (1995). *Keys to effective legislation for children and families.* MA: State Legislative Leaders Foundation.

Tannen, D. (1998). *The argument culture: Moving from debate to dialogue.* New York: Random House.

Thomlinson, B., Maluccio, A. N., & Abramczyk, L. W. (1996). The theory, policy, and practice context of family reunification: An integrated research perspective. *Child and Youth Services Review, 18* (4, 5), 473–88.

Wexler, R. (1990). *Wounded innocents: The real victims of the war against child abuse.* Buffalo, NY: Prometheus Books.

Wilson, J. Q. (1991, June 3). The government gap. *New Republic*, 38.

Wolfe, A. (1998, March 15). Couch potato politics. *New York Times*, 17.

Wolff, E. N. (1999). Recent trends in wealth ownership. In T. M. Shapiro & E. N. Wolff (Eds.), *The benefits and mechanisms for spreading asset ownership*. Northampton, MA: Edward Elgar.

Zimmerman, S. L. (1992). *Family policies and family well being: The role of political culture*. Newbury Park, CA: Sage.

15 Shaping the Future of Family-Centered Services

Competition or Collaboration?

Kristine E. Nelson

It has been a quarter of a century since the prototypical family-centered programs were started and two decades since the Adoption Assistance and Child Welfare Act of 1980 (Public Law 96–272) required the child welfare system to make reasonable efforts to avoid placement and return children to their homes. Family-centered practice, one response to this mandate, has gone from being a controversial new idea to being a controversial part of the continuum of child welfare services (Pecora, Whittaker, & Maluccio, 1992). Family-centered practice has also taken hold in other systems, such as child mental health and juvenile justice, sometimes under different names (e.g., family-based services, wraparound services, multisystemic family therapy) (Dore, 1993; Henggeler, Melton, Smith, Schoenwald, & Hanley, 1993). Although many of the innovations originally pioneered by family-centered services have become incorporated into practice standards for child welfare and other human services, changes in the delivery of human services and a backlash fueled by misused research findings threaten to snuff out these innovations before their true potential can be realized.

Much of the political success of family-centered services was based on the promise that they could reduce foster care budgets (Adams, 1994). As with the movement to deinstitutionalize the mentally ill in the 1970s, some supporters in government agencies and private foundations were more concerned with reducing spiraling costs than with improving services. By the time family-centered practice was spreading, the outcome of the contradiction in motives behind deinstitutionalization was well known: state hospitals were closed, mental health budgets slashed, and persons with chronic mental illness left to the mercies of private board and care operators, revolving-door hospitalizations, and all too often, homelessness (Johnson, 1990). Do family-centered services face a similar fate? The future of family-centered practice, policy, and research in the face of massive changes in human service delivery systems is the subject of this chapter.

THREATS FROM WITHOUT:
PRIVATIZATION AND MANAGED CARE

Privatization

As part of the attack on the welfare state described by Mannes in this volume, conservative political forces have for some time encouraged the privatization of government functions. Although from the outset, family-centered services have involved partnerships between public and private child welfare agencies (Kramer, 1985; Smith, 1989; Pecora, Kinney, Mitchell, & Tolley, 1990), the cost cutting that often accompanies privatization has resulted in unstable and underfunded programs. Many private child welfare agencies now function as appendages of the state, dependent on the public sector for funding and referrals and held accountable for publically mandated outcomes (Smith, 1989; Withnow, 1995). This symbiotic relationship threatens to undermine the nonprofit sector's historic role in creating innovative services, limits workers' abilities to enter into true partnerships with families, and establishes a system of second-class professionals who receive lower pay and have less job security than civil service employees in the public sector (Nelson & Landsman, 1992). Although privatization of service delivery preceded the introduction of managed care, it relies on the same assumptions about the inefficiency of government programs and the advantages of competition in the private market (Wolfe, 1997), and it has the same effect of turning public responsibilities over to the private sector.

Managed Health Care

Although most family-centered services are not directly funded by managed health care organizations, the families they serve often have multiple needs, including treatment for health and mental health problems. Since managed care comes in as many shapes and sizes as do family-centered services, it is hard to describe exactly what it is (Bergman & Homer, 1998; Szilagyi, 1998). At its best, managed care holds out the promise of better-coordinated, more comprehensive services, with reduced reliance on expensive inpatient care and more effort directed at prevention, goals that are also shared by family-centered programs (Kimmich & Feild, 1999). Like family preservation services, however, managed care became a national policy without a sufficient research base to support its claims (Bergman & Homer, 1998). Originally introduced to control health care costs, managed care initially had the desired effect, but no one seems to know exactly why (Children and Managed Health Care, 1998).

Most research has tested the effects of managed health care on individual adult patients and on providers. The research describes a two-tier system with differing outcomes for patients with employment-based benefits and those dependent on the Medicaid program, which covers the same population of low-income families as do family-centered child welfare services (Szilagyi, 1998). Unlike private plans, Medicaid delivered through managed care organizations has resulted in fewer services and less access to services, especially for populations with special needs. Little research has been done on the effects of managed care on health care services for children; and a comprehensive set of outcome measures and clear performance standards for pediatric practice have yet to be developed (Bergman & Homer, 1998).

As managed health care has expanded, become more competitive, and spread to plans covering more vulnerable populations, initial cost savings have disappeared. Although initial savings were based on economies of scale and reduction of unnecessary procedures, further savings would come from reduced compensation to health care workers and poorer quality of care (Children and Managed Health Care, 1998), problems common to many privatization efforts.

Managed Mental Health Care

Managed care has also spread rapidly in mental health, or what is now known as behavioral health care, largely through carve-outs, which separate the delivery of mental and physical health care. In the area of children's mental health, where family-centered services have been developed to prevent hospitalization of children with serious emotional disorders, managed care is undermining a decade-long effort to establish comprehensive systems of care based on interagency collaboration, individualized and flexible treatment, and family involvement (Stroul, Pires, Armstrong, & Meyers, 1998). Because managed care has been implemented on the basis of ideology rather than evidence, the effect of managed care on children is largely unknown in mental health as it is in pediatrics.

The first major research project to track the effects of managed care on mental health and substance abuse services for children and adolescents provides qualitative data from ten states that were early implementers. The researchers found that in contrast to the system-of-care approach, the business philosophy of managed care stresses competition over collaboration, centralization over decentralization, and entrepreneurial implementation rather than participatory planning involving mental health experts and families. In areas where costs have been reduced, it is unclear whether this is due to budget cuts, reduced use of inpatient care, or shifting of costly cases to the juvenile justice, education, and child welfare systems (Jellinek & Little, 1998). While access to mental health services seems to have increased for the average child, children with serious disorders who are involved in multiple systems and who require services for an extended period of time have fared less well (Stroul et al., 1998).

Many barriers to providing mental health care for children remain. Managed care has done little to fill preexisting gaps in services or to improve interagency coordination. The lack of practice guidelines, outcome measures, and cost data frustrates the goal of improving service efficiency and effectiveness. Of the ten states studied, eight showed reduced hospital admissions or lengths of stay for psychiatric disorders, but three saw increased recidivism rates, and five reported increases in residential treatment. On the other hand, seven states reported increased use of home- and community-based services (Stroul et al., 1998).

Jellinek and Little (1998) are outspoken in their belief that the primary goal of many managed care organizations is to maximize profits for shareholders by reducing access to services and passing financial risk over to providers: "A part of every dollar saved leads to lower corporate benefit costs, profit for the managed care company, greater credibility on Wall Street, and better salaries or bonuses for all executives involved in the process" (p. 323). Far from encouraging interventions based on outcome research, Jellinek and Little (1998) characterize research as "unnecessary overhead" (p. 322), and see inpatient admissions and lengths of stay being cut without any research and valid outcome measures to document effects on children as "years away" (p. 324). Despite the lack of research and mixed effects of managed health and mental health care, the child welfare system seems to be headed down the same track (Child Welfare League of America, 1996; Kimmich & Feild, 1999; McClain, 1998).

Managed Care and Child Welfare

Many cost-cutting strategies have already been employed in child welfare services. Child protection has been restricted to the most serious cases, while preventive services and intervention for less obviously damaging maltreatment such as neglect have gone by the wayside (Kimmich & Feild,

1999). Unlike medical care, which requires elaborate physical facilities and access to technology, family-centered services are labor intensive, with most of their costs coming from employee compensation. As critics of public social service bureaucracies have argued, large-scale organizations with multiple levels of review are a costly and inefficient way to deliver personal social services. Yet national managed care organizations are spawning the same megabureaucracies. Privatization through contracting services has already reduced salaries in child welfare services and has made it easier to downsize or eliminate programs (Kimmich & Feild, 1999). The number of states operating their child welfare services under court orders or consent agreements indicates that there is little room or tolerance for further lowering of the quality of services.

While managed care has not yet had the impact on child welfare services that it has had on the provision of health and mental health services, experiments in contracting out-of-home placements to managed care organizations are occurring in several states. A 1998 report issued by the U.S. General Accounting Office describes early efforts to introduce managed care in child welfare services and identifies four approaches. In the most frequently implemented of these approaches, the lead agency model, contracts with private agencies provide all necessary services for a defined population. In the public model, the second most popular approach, public agencies incorporate managed care principles into existing practices and contracts. In the less frequent administrative services organization model, only management functions are privatized, while in the managed care organization model, a private organization manages child welfare services, which are delivered through a series of subcontracts.

Although a 1997 survey by the Child Welfare League of America's Managed Care Institute found that thirty states were involved in managed care initiatives (Hutchins, 1997), most of the experiments with managed care have involved only a small segment of the child welfare population, such as severely emotionally disturbed children, adolescents, or children in out-of-home care. One exception is the state of Kansas, which has established regional contracts with managed care organizations to serve foster care, adoption, and family preservation populations. No state has yet attempted to contract for child protective services investigations.

As the most comprehensive effort to date, Kansas' experience reveals some of the benefits and problems of using managed care principles in child welfare. While managed care's single point of entry and improved coordination of services have improved access to services, particularly in remote rural areas, and in the first ten months of operation surpassed performance standards in foster care, the managed care organizations were less successful in reuniting families and realizing cost savings (U.S. General Accounting Office [GAO], 1998, pp. 71–72). One study found that compared to a sample of children who were served before managed care, foster children changed homes almost twice as often under managed care, and fewer met the standard of three or fewer moves. The children in the managed care group were also less likely to be reunified with their families (Petr & Johnson, 1999). In a study almost three years after the implementation of managed care, Pheatt, Douglas, Wilson, Brook, and Berry (2000) found that family preservation services are being underutilized despite exceeding performance standards. Only 10 percent of families screened in for child abuse are referred to family preservation services, while 77 percent are referred for foster care. In addition, collaboration and cooperation among private providers has decreased.

After the first year of the program's operation, Kansas lowered performance standards for reunification, increased the case rate for foster care, and exempted 3 percent of the caseload when costs for some children were higher than anticipated (U.S. GAO, 1998, pp. 60, 65). In addition, court refusal to discharge children from foster care has led to greater costs (p. 61). Stroul et al. (1998) describe safety issues, court involvement, and the mobility of children in child welfare as problematic for managed care systems. Some of the other problems that have plagued managed care initiatives in children's mental health as well as in child welfare include inadequate data for setting performance standards and reimbursement rates, inadequate start-up funding that results in cash flow problems, downsizing or retraining of public agency staff who perform case-monitoring functions, lack of flexibility in funding streams, and inadequate management information systems for monitoring and evaluation (U.S. GAO, 1998, pp. 73–74). Desired outcomes, apart from system results such as placement or re-referral for child maltreatment, are not standardized, and there is no agreement on what constitutes a necessary or unnecessary placement.

As risky as the delegation of public responsibilities for child welfare to private nonprofit agencies is, the provision of health, mental health, welfare, and child welfare services to poor families by for-profit organizations is even more disturbing. From the specter of Lockheed Martin administering public welfare programs (Hartung & Washburn, 1998) to the constant merging and splitting of national health and mental health conglomerates, the purpose of publicly funded programs is being subverted. Rather than providing essential services to needy citizens, the primary goal of companies seeking control of the huge sums of money involved is to produce profits for private shareholders (Hartung & Washburn, 1998). As business principles replace humanitarian concerns, distant functionaries second-guess medical and mental health providers and the most vulnerable and costly to serve patients are dropped from the system. By looking at for-profit nursing home chains and franchised day care centers, professionals should know what making a profit on the care of dependent human beings means—low salaries, high turnover, and poor care (Davis, Freeman, & Kirby, 1998; Scarr & Eisenberg, 1993). Out-of-home care is often plagued with these difficulties already, and skimming profits from these underfunded services certainly isn't going to improve conditions.

Although family-centered services have flourished in the midst of these trends, the momentum toward privatization and managed care threatens to swamp the still tentative implantation of family-centered principles in the child welfare system. Just as efforts to provide family-friendly systems of care in children's mental health have foundered in the managed care tides, the principles embodied in family-centered practice will not fare well if profit-oriented managed care systems prevail.

THREATS FROM WITHIN

The dismantling of the federal safety net for the poor and the privatization of human services create an environment that is potentially toxic to the ideals of family-centered services: respect for and partnerships with families, a strengths-based and empowerment perspective, and collaboration with formal and informal sources of support in the community to provide comprehensive and preventive services. In this environment of the disappearing federal safety net and increasing privatization, family-centered services face two additional threats emanating from within: unrealistic standards regarding effectiveness and co-optation of their language.

Unrealistic Standards

The advent of family-centered services coincided with a new emphasis in human services on accountability for outcomes rather than process. Family preservation programs in particular have risen and fallen on the basis of evaluation data. Used successfully by Homebuilders and the Edna McConnell-Clark Foundation to sell family preservation programs to legislators and agencies (Adams, 1994), the initial data came from simple postintervention outcome studies that embodied none of the rigor imposed on later studies. As soon as placement prevention became part of national child welfare policy, however, critics abounded (Frankel, 1988; Magura, 1981; Rossi, 1991; Stein, 1985; Wald, 1988). Research went from descriptive and correlational studies (Fraser, Pecora, & Haapala, 1991; Nelson & Landsman, 1992) to large, complex experiments, without the intervening stages necessary to understand or replicate family preservation services with any fidelity to the original models (Nelson, Landsman, & Deutelbaum, 1990). Without small, controlled efficacy trials to determine what part of the complex intervention package that constitutes family-centered services worked with what kind of families, the research went to scale, overlaying experimental designs on statewide programs (Schuerman, Rzepnicki, &

Littell, 1994; Yuan, McDonald, Wheeler, Struckman-Johnson, & Rivest, 1990).

When these large studies showed no effect on the primary outcome measure, out-of-home placement, family preservation services were deemed a failure and sometimes terminated to the detriment of both families and children. After the Family First program in Illinois was canceled following negative evaluation findings, foster placements increased 30 percent, and the child fatality rate tripled (National Coalition for Child Protection Reform, n.d.). No other child welfare program has been held to such a stringent standard of effectiveness (Smokowski & Wodarski, 1996). For example, although federal funding for foster care outstrips spending on all other child welfare services by a margin of 10 to 1, it is impossible even to track children in foster care, let alone rigorously evaluate how they are doing. While this level of accountability for outcomes is consistent with current trends in human services, desired outcomes are seldom clear or measurable using current technologies, and effectiveness-based outcomes "may medicalize further the very home and community-based services systems in which social workers have for years advocated for social rather than medical models" (Kautz, Netting, Huber, Borders, & Davis, 1997).

The most thorough methodological critique of intensive family preservation programs reveals many of the faulty and unrealistic assumptions academic researchers have about field-based research. Heneghan, Horwitz, and Leventhal (1996) reviewed published and unpublished research on intensive family preservation programs from 1977 to 1993. Of the forty-six program evaluations, only ten met their criteria for review, and only two were rated as "acceptable," using the standards by which medical clinical trials are evaluated. Never mind that none of these studies were designed or funded as clinical trials of the efficacy of family preservation services. These studies were faulted for not having a standardized assessment of imminent risk of placement, for not describing criteria for excluding families from the study, for not demonstrating the similarity of comparison groups, for not describing the services that comparison group families received, and for not having the outcome measure, need for placement, determined by observers blinded to treatment group. Despite these shortcomings, these studies were able, to the authors' satisfaction, to "show no benefit in reducing rates of out-of-home placements of children at risk of abuse or neglect in 8 of 10 studies" (p. 535). Interestingly, in a review of intervention research in the much more broadly studied and better-funded area of children's mental health, Jensen, Hoagwood, and Petti, in the same year (1996), found only thirty-eight studies that met "minimal scientific criteria."

The standards of research promulgated by Heneghan et al. (1996) may be achievable in hospital- or clinic-based trials of the effectiveness of medications but are wildly unrealistic when applied to social programs in natural settings. Researchers have been meeting for more than ten years in attempts to develop standardized risk assessment tools for use in child protective services (CPS), and although there has been some success in predicting future reports of maltreatment, no tools have been developed that predict need for placement. The reality of decision making in CPS is that it is highly individualistic. Any researcher who has proposed random assignment or who has tried to enforce rigid eligibility or exclusionary criteria on referring workers knows the difficulty of convincing agencies to do research under these conditions and of policing ingenious workers intent on getting the best services for their families. Due to large caseloads and a crushing burden of paperwork, caseworkers cannot provide detailed descriptions of the services provided to comparison groups, whereas workers in the treatment groups with smaller caseloads are more willing to complete detailed research protocols. Nor have funding levels for research allowed the same level of measurement for comparison groups as for treatment groups.

Finally, the idea that workers, not to mention judges, making placement decisions could be "blinded" to the fact that family preservation services had been provided reveals a level of ignorance to the realities of child welfare practice exceeded only by those who call for untreated control groups of abused children. Heneghan et al. (1996) argue that "to advise public policy makers best, program evaluations must be held to the highest standards of scientific inquiry used in determining the effectiveness of any treatment regimen" (541), ignoring the lack of research on other child welfare programs and, indeed, on much more pervasive and expensive public policy initiatives, such as managed care.

The widespread publication of negative research findings and the equally widespread dissemination of child fatality horror stories have undermined family-centered services policy and practice. Many who oppose family-centered and family preservation services have used these negative findings to try to redirect the momentum of child welfare policy away from families and back toward placement and adoption. The Adoption and Safe Families Act of 1997 (PL 105–89) amended the Adoption Assistance and Child Welfare Act (PL 96–272) and shifted the goals of child welfare services from child protection and family preservation to safety, permanency, and child well-being, returning to the child rescue philosophy that family preservation had only recently replaced (Mannes, 1998). Although the act reaffirms the need for states to make "reasonable efforts" to preserve and reunify families (unless a child's safety is in jeopardy), strict time limits have been set on these efforts. Termination of parental rights must be initiated for any child who has been in placement fifteen of the prior twenty-two months. Although this is justified on the basis of children's developmental needs, it applies equally to infants and adolescents, disregarding their development stage and attachment to their birth parents.

The Adoption and Safe Families Act codifies an "unprecedented" change in the area of permanency planning, requiring, according to the Children's Bureau, changes in agency policy, practice, and procedures. The act refocuses family-centered practice on safety as the primary concern, while feebly adding, "without neglecting the needs of the family," as if they have not already and historically been neglected.

Co-optation and Misrepresentation

Perhaps more insidious than the frontal assault of the Adoption and Safe Families Act is the erosion of the integrity of the term "family preservation." In a recent book review, Tracy (1999) observed that "family preservation has come to mean everything and nothing at the same time" (p. 262). As early as 1993, Ann Hartman, in an editorial in *Social Work*, observed, "In fact, the term 'family preservation' has become so popular that anybody doing anything helpful in relation to a family could claim they were doing it. Multiple definitions make the term meaningless" (p. 511).

This erosion has been encouraged by such vocal and respected critics of the child welfare system as Leroy Pelton and Richard Gelles. When Pelton was asked at a federally sponsored symposium on chronic neglect to explain his use of "family preservation," he described the term as "the whole spectrum of services that we can deliver [to prevent maltreating families from having their children placed], some of which we provide now, some of which we have not imagined yet" (National Center on Child Abuse and Neglect, 1993, p. 77). Gelles criticizes these imaginary services in his widely publicized *Book of David: How Family Preservation Kills Children* (1996), which nowhere indicates that the composite family he describes received anything vaguely resembling intensive family preservation services. Instead he describes "open-ended" reunification services directed at another child a year before David's death. Although Gelles acknowledges that preventive family preservation services may have been helpful (pp. 123–24), he counters with another case example, this time the real-life experience of Eli Creekmore, who was killed a month after Homebuilders' services had been terminated and after subsequent placement and reunification. No matter that these decisions were made by the state department workers and the court, who ignored the recommendations of the Homebuilders therapist. Because Homebuilders had once been involved, family preservation was blamed for the tragedy.

The National Coalition for Child Protection Reform (n.d.), in reviewing Gelles's book, finds that he "ignores any data which contradict his thesis" and "offers no data whatsoever to support his view that family preservation has increased the danger to children" (p. 3). Gelles's argument that family preservation programs are applied by child protective services "to most families they serve" is belied by a glance at the number of families referred to CPS compared to the capacity of family preservation programs. And of course Gelles cites Heneghan et al. (1996) and the study of the Illinois Family First program to support his assertion that family preservation services do not work. Most infuriating is his claim that family preservation is the "best funded" approach in child welfare, a claim that ignores the vast amount of money still spent on foster care (Gelles, 1996, p. 128). In 1992 federal funding for foster care and adoption totaled $3 billion, compared to $442 million for all other child welfare services, including family preservation (Green & Waters, 1999). Most befuddling is Gelles's accusation that overburdened and untrained caseworkers, misled by the emphasis on family preservation, leave children in or return them to unsafe homes. If caseworkers are not competent to decide when children can be safely maintained in their own homes, how can they be competent to decide when placement is necessary? Indeed, in describing the need for better training for child protective services workers, Davidson (1999) argues that "we must begin to treat community child protection work as equal in importance to the public safety work of police officers and firefighters. That should mean equivalent compensation, supervision, and support services" (p. 22).

In the minds of critics, family preservation has come to indicate simply that the child has not been removed from the family. As the National Coalition for Child Protection Reform (n.d.) explains, "Gelles and other 'child savers' have given family preservation a new meaning: all purpose scapegoat. They have slapped the label onto any child abuse death anywhere under any circumstances" (p. 5). It is this default notion of family preservation services that underlies the charges that these services are responsible for child deaths when, in reality, true family preservation services have enviable records of child safety. There were only five deaths in five years during or after services among the 17,000 children served in the Illinois program (Schuerman, Rzepnicki, Littell, & Chak, 1993). In Michigan, only 2 of 40,000 children served by the statewide Families First program died as a result of child abuse or neglect, and these were in the program's early years (Nelson, 1997).

In addition to the appropriation of the term "family preservation" to mean any action (or inaction) of the child welfare system short of placement, other concepts have been equally decontextualized. From the outset, "empowerment" was operationalized in family-centered services by trying not to further disempower families rather than through any clear notion of how to empower them. Respect, collaboration, courtesy, and sharing information are all ways of reducing the social distance between families and workers. But empowerment implies a transfer of control that has not yet occurred in child welfare agencies. In terms of family-professional relationships, the National Peer Technical Assistance Network (1998) describes a "family-centered" approach as one in which professionals are "one down" to the family. In other words, the family is assumed to know best what its needs are, and the professional's role is to provide support and resources. In contrast, the National Peer Technical Assistance Network (1998) describes child welfare as having a "professional-centered" approach, which generates adversarial relationships between professionals, who are viewed as the experts, and parents, who are viewed as the problem. At best, some child welfare systems have moved to an intermediary "family-allied" approach, in which parents are seen as equals and work collaboratively with professionals to address mutually agreed on goals. Earlier in this volume, Apple et al. describe some of the changes that are needed in child welfare practice in order to institute a true family-centered approach.

However, even if a worker were willing to give up the driver's seat, without the resources needed to provide real choices to families about housing, employment, education, child care, and even safety, empowerment becomes a psychological process without a tangible outcome. In fact, neither workers nor families are empowered in bureaucratic child welfare systems that are driven by local headlines and federal mandates. A truly empowering approach to child welfare would involve massive rethinking and restructuring at all levels of government to establish policies and programs that are supportive of families and communities, as described earlier by Mannes. Without such policies and programs, "asking families to identify and prioritize their own treatment goals" is often an exercise in futility, and "encouraging families to assume greater responsibility and self-determination over their own lives" turns social problems into private responsibilities.

COUNTERVAILING FORCES

Although bleak, the future of family-centered services is not entirely without hope. That the language of child welfare has been transformed to include the notions of family strengths, collaboration, and empowerment is a major achievement. Turning around a century of emphasis on child rescue will, however, take more than two decades. The child welfare system has proven to be remarkably resistant to change, co-opting new programs and ideas into the old agenda. As Schorr (1997) discovered, many promising programs simply disappear after a brief life as demonstration projects. Or as Smale (1994) describes, agencies become "inoculated" against new ideas or adopt the language of a new approach without substantive change.

Most real change takes hold through a "contagion" of new ideas spread from worker to worker. Therein lies the promise of the family-centered approach: it truly works in engaging families and creating both the hope and, through collaboratively pooling resources, the potential for change. Success is self-reinforcing, and as workers and families experience even small successes they will be more likely to endorse and adopt a family-centered approach. Few human services workers want to be in an adversarial relationship with the people they are trying to help, and few families want workers dictating to them what to do. Any approach that lifts practice from this negatively reinforcing cycle has a real chance of surviving.

Further, collaboration is an alternative to competition in a resource-poor environment that enables few social service organizations to continue functioning in their accustomed ways. With increasing encouragement and mandates for collaborative approaches, professionals are beginning to break down boundaries and barriers that have fragmented human services in the past. This collaboration can produce more efficiency and effectiveness in service delivery, as well as bring potential allies together. For the first time, physicians, psychologists, social workers, and nurses have a common enemy in large, for-profit managed care corporations. If the professionals can engage in respectful and empowering relationships with each other, they may be able to forge alliances that will recapture the human services from business and bureaucratic control.

One example is the collaborative managed care model developed in Mesa County, Colorado. The initiative has engaged the Department of Human Services, the Colorado West Mental Health Center, and other community agencies in a partnership that provides a single point of entry; comprehensive services developed by multidisciplinary treatment teams within a single service plan; cross-agency training, policies, and procedures; and common utilization review and quality assurance procedures (Mitchell, 1999). The relationship formed with families by providing consistent contact with a minimum of service providers, the participation of families in setting goals and selecting services, and the families' key role in the utilization review meetings required every ninety days approximate the family-driven approach to managed care advocated by Kimmich and Feild (1990). With money saved by reducing expensive out-of-county and adolescent residential placements and by increasing the use of kinship care and volunteers, Mesa County has funded a visiting home nurse program for first-time mothers with high risk factors and developed a community education plan to address substance abuse. Mesa County's program is the only managed care child welfare system that has as yet successfully implemented the prevention services that are often promised but rarely seen in managed care systems.

As long as efficiency and the reduction of government expenditures remain the driving forces behind managed care, however, even collaborative projects such as Mesa County's are unlikely to benefit line workers, who bear the brunt of inadequate funding with high caseloads, low pay, and lack of resources. For many public social service employees, unionization has provided higher pay, better benefits, and better working conditions than are found in the private sector. Even historically exploitive services, such as residential care, are beginning to be unionized. While this is antithetical to the interests of management, unionization is the only proven way to increase wages, job security, and benefits in the service sector (Coelho, 1990).

In the 1930s, after a brief experiment with union organization, social work chose to pursue professional organization rather than unionization but has not been able through these means to secure the status and financial rewards accruing to other more prestigious professions. However, this brief experiment with unionization spawned practices that bear a remarkable similarity to the empowerment approaches advocated today. For example, workers and clients joined together to prevent families from being evicted and to demand more adequate social programs (Hunter, 1999). Indeed, quite unlike the image of selfishness projected onto unions by management, social service unions have included in their demands issues that directly improve services as well as working conditions, such as lower caseloads, more training, and increased resources. In work that is accomplished primarily through human relationships, empowerment must extend to workers as well as families in order to be successful.

Although professional alliances and unionization can provide powerful countervailing forces to the conservative trends engulfing human services, community-based practice offers a third, and perhaps less constrained, approach to challenging the status quo. As the short-lived successes of Community Action Agencies during the 1960s War on Poverty showed, partnerships between trained organizers and angry community members can create considerable pressure on local government for change. With the current devolution of authority for many social services from the federal to the state and local levels, traditional political approaches have less effect (Schneider & Netting, 1999). Collective action directed toward local government, politicians, and outlets of large managed care corporations can spark the community support and political will needed to reverse the conservatizing and reactionary approaches taken to human needs in the last two decades.

Collective efforts of social service unions and community-based organizations can not only empower the social workers and community residents involved in them but, with effective organization and action, can also change the terms of the debate away from cost cutting and competition and toward meeting the needs of children and families through cooperation and pooling resources in the community. This could also change the public perception of child welfare agencies from child snatchers to providers of essential preventive and supportive services to families (Speer & Hughey, 1995).

THE FUTURE OF FAMILY-CENTERED SERVICES

While the cup appears to be half empty and draining with regard to the future of family-centered practice, its revolutionary potential has not yet been lost. Significant reverses occurred only between the 1993 Omnibus Budget Reconciliation Act and the 1997 Adoption and Safe Families Act, ironically under a Democratic president. Although wounded, neither the welfare state nor family-centered practice is quite dead. A new understanding of the need for more effective techniques of collaboration not only with families but also with other professionals, coworkers, and communities can empower us to challenge current initiatives and redirect human services in this country.

Specific actions that can be undertaken to preserve family-centered services include the following:

☐ Continuing to document the successes and effective elements of family-centered services through field-based research and through disseminating both qualitative and quantitative findings in the popular press, as well as in professional newsletters, journals, and conferences

☐ Creating alliances with other professionals in order to oppose and subvert the constraints on human services imposed by managed care corporations

☐ Collaborating with community agencies, organizations, and residents to provide a community-based safety net for families in need

☐ Organizing professional and support staff into broad-based unions, such as Service Employees International Union and American Federation of State, County, and Municipal Employees, creating pressure on local agencies and governments in order to meet their needs as well as the needs of the families they serve

In a very real sense, the answer to the question of whether the future of family-centered services will be characterized by cooperation or competition is in our hands.

REFERENCES

Adams, P. L. (1994). Marketing social change: The case of family preservation. *Children and Youth Services Review, 16,* 417–31.

Bergman, D. A., & Homer. (1998). Managed care and the quality of children's health services. *Future of Children, 8* (2), 60–75.

Child Welfare League of America (1996). *Managed care and child welfare: Beyond the basics.* Washington, DC: Author.

Coelho, R. J. (1990). Job satisfaction of staff in unionized and non-unionized community residences for persons with developmental disabilities. *Journal of Rehabilitation, 56,* 57–63.

Davidson, H. A. (1999). Protecting America's children: A challenge. *Trial, 35* (11), 22.

Davis, M. A., Freeman, J. W., & Kirby, E. C. (1998). Nursing home performance under case-mix reimbursement: Responding to heavy-care incentives and market changes. *Health Services Research, 33,* 815–35.

Deal, L. W., Shiono, P. H., & Behrman, R. E. (1998). Children and managed health care: Analysis and recommendations. *Future of Children, 8* (2), 4–24.

Dore, M. M. (1993). Family-based services in children's mental health care. *Child and Adolescent Mental Health Care, 3,* 175–89.

Frankel, H. (1988). Family-centered, home-based services in child protection: A review of the research. *Social Services Review, 62,* 137–57.

Fraser, M. W., Pecora, P. J., & Haapala, D. A. (1991). *Families in crisis: The impact of family preservation services.* New York: Aldine de Gruyter.

Gelles, R. J. (1996). *The book of David: How preserving families can cost children's lives.* New York: Basic Books.

Green, R., & Waters, S. (1999). *The impact of welfare reform on child welfare financing.* Washington, DC: Urban Institute.

Hartman, A. (1993). Family preservation under attack. *Social Work, 38,* 509.

Hartung, W. D., & Washburn, J. (1998). Lockheed Martin: From warfare to welfare. *The Nation, 266,* 8, 11–16.

Henggeler, S. W., Melton, G. B., Smith, L. A., Schoenwald, M. A., & Hanley, J. H. (1993). Family preservation using multisystemic treatment: Long-term follow-up to a clinical trial with serious juvenile offenders. *Journal of Child and Family Studies, 2,* 283–93.

Heneghan, A. M., Horwitz, S. M., & Leventhal, J. M. (1996). Evaluating intensive family preservation programs: A methodological review. *Pediatrics, 97,* 535–42.

Hunter, R .W. (1999). *Voices of our past: The rank and file movement in social work, 1931–1950.* Unpublished doctoral dissertation, Portland State University, Portland, OR.

Hutchins, J. (1997). Managing managed care for families. *Children's Voice, 7* (1), 28–29.

Jellinek, M., & Little, M. (1998). Supporting child psychiatric services using current managed care approaches: You can't get there from here. *Archives of Pediatrics and Adolescent Medicine, 152,* 321–26.

Jensen, P. S., Hoagwood, K., & Petti, T. (1996). Outcomes of mental health care for children and adolescents II: Literature review and application of a comprehensive model. *Journal of the American Academy of Child and Adolescent Psychiatry, 35,* 1064–77.

Johnson, A. B. (1990). Out of bedlam: The truth about deinstitutionalization. New York: Basic Books.

Kautz, J. R. III, Netting, E., Huber, R., Borders, K., & Davis, T. (1997). The Government Performance and Results Act of 1993: Implications for social work practice. *Social Work, 42,* 364–73.

Kimmich, M. H., & Feild, M. A. (1999). *Partnering with families to reform services: Managed care in the child welfare system.* Englewood, CO: American Humane Association.

Kramer, R. M. (1985). *The future of the voluntary agency in a mixed economy.* Paper presented at the Annual Meeting of the Society for the Study of Social Problems, Washington, DC.

Magura, S. (1981). Are services to prevent foster care effective? *Children and Youth Services Review, 16,* 193–212.

Mannes, M. (1998). Promoting safe and stable families: Is it a renewed- or a new-Title IV-B, subpart 2? *Prevention Report, 1,* 2–4.

McClain, A. (1998). Lessons from managed behavioral health: Implications for managed child welfare. In *Third National Roundtable on Managed Care in Child Welfare Services: Keeping the focus on kids: From ethics to implementation* (pp. 93–98). Englewood, CO: American Humane Association.

Mitchell, R. L. (December 13, 1999). Personal communication.

National Center on Child Abuse and Neglect. (1993). *Chronic neglect symposium proceedings.* Washington, DC: Administration for Children and Families, U.S. Department of Health and Human Services.

National Coalition for Child Protection Reform (n.d.). *Putting child savers first hurts children: A rebuttal to "The Book of David."* Monaca, PA: Author.

National Peer Technical Assistance Network (1998). Family-professional relationships: Moving forward together: A summary of the National Peer Technical Assistance Network's 1998 publication. *Focal Point: A National Bulletin on Family Support and Children's Mental Health, 12* (1), 23–26, 28.

Nelson, K. E. (1997). Family preservation—what is it? *Children and Youth Services Review, 1 & 2,* 101–18.

Nelson, K. E., & Landsman, M. J. (1992). *Alternative models of family preservation: Family-based services in context.* Springfield, IL: Charles C Thomas.

Nelson, K. E., Landsman, M. J., & Deutelbaum, W. (1990). Three models of family-centered placement prevention services. *Child Welfare, 69,* 3–21.

Pecora, P. J., Kinney, J. M., Mitchell, L., & Tolley, G. (1990). Selecting an agency auspice for family preservation services. *Social Service Review, 64,* 288–307.

Pecora, P. J., Whittaker, J. K., & Maluccio, A. N. (1992). *The child welfare challenge: Policy, practice, and research.* Hawthorne, NY: Aldine de Gruyter.

Petr, C. G., & Johnson, I. C. (1999). Privatization of foster care in Kansas: A cautionary tale. *Social Work, 44,* 263–67.

Pheatt, M., Douglas, B., Wilson, L., Brook, J., & Berry, M. (2000). Family preservation services under managed care: Current practices and future directions. *Family Preservation Journal, 5,* 21–39.

Rossi, P. (1991). *Evaluating family preservation programs: A report to the Edna McConnell Clark Foundation.* Amherst, MA: Social and Demographics Research Institute.

Scarr, S., & Eisenberg, M. (1993). Child care research: Issues, perspectives, and results. *Annual Review of Psychology, 44,* 613–45.

Schneider, R. L., & Netting, F. E. (1999). Influencing social policy in a time of devolution: Upholding social work's great tradition. *Social Work, 44,* 349–57.

Schorr, L. B. (1997). *Common purpose: Strengthening families and neighborhoods to rebuild America.* New York: Doubleday.

Schuerman, J. R., Rzepnicki, T. L., & Littell, J. H. (1994). *Putting families first: An experiment in family preservation.* New York: Aldine de Gruyter.

Schuerman, J. R., Rzepnicki, T. L., Littell, J. H., & Chak, A. (1993). *Evaluation of the Illinois Family First placement prevention program: Final report.* Chicago: University of Chicago, Chapin Hall Center for Children.

Smale, G. (1994, Fall). Innovations transfer and community-centered practice. *Prevention Report,* pp. 6–12.

Smith, S. R. (1989). The changing politics of child welfare services: New roles for the government and the nonprofit sectors. *Child Welfare, 68,* 289–99.

Smokowski, P. R., & Wodarski, J. S. (1996). The effectiveness of child welfare services for poor, neglected children: A review of the empirical evidence. *Research on Social Work Practice, 6,* 504–23.

Speer, P. W., & Hughey, J. (1995). Community organizing: An ecological route to empowerment and power. *American Journal of Community Psychology, 23,* 729–49.

Stein, T. J. (1985). Projects to prevent out-of-home placement. *Children and Youth Services Review, 7,* 109–22.

Stroul, B. A., Pires, S. A., Armstrong, M. I., & Meyers, J. C. (1998). The impact of managed care on mental health services for children and their families. *Future of Children, 8* (2), 119–33.

Szilagyi, P. G. (1998). Managed care for children: Effect on access to care and utilization of health services. *Future of Children, 8* (2), 39–59.

Tracy, E. (1999). Review of The Family at Risk: Issues and trends in family preservation services. *Social Service Review, 73,* 262–63.

U.S. General Accounting Office. (1998). *Child welfare: Early experiences implementing a managed care approach.* Washington, DC: Author.

Wald, M. S. (1988). Family preservation: Are we moving too fast? *Public Welfare, 46* (3), 33–38, 46.

Withnow, R. (1995). Between the state and market: Voluntarism and the difference it makes. In A. Etzioni (Ed.), *Rights and the common good: The communitarian perspective* (pp. 209–21). New York: St. Martin's Press.

Wolfe, P. J. (1997). Why must we reinvent the federal government? Putting historical developmental claims to the test. *Journal of Public Administration Research and Theory, 7,* 353–89.

Yuan, Y. T., McDonald, W. R., Wheeler, C. E., Struckman-Johnson, D., & Rivest, M. (1990). *Evaluation of AB1562 in-home care demonstration projects* (Vol. 1: Final report). Sacramento, CA: Walter R. McDonald and Associates.